D1606321

SPEECH ACT THEORY AND PRAGMATICS

SYNTHESE LANGUAGE LIBRARY

TEXTS AND STUDIES IN
LINTUISTICS AND PHILOSOPHY

VOLUME 10

SPEECH ACT THEORY AND PRAGMATICS

Edited by

JOHN R. SEARLE
University of California, Berkeley, U.S.A.

FERENC KIEFER
Hungarian Academy of Sciences, Budapest, and La Sorbonne Nouvelle, Paris

and

MANFRED BIERWISCH
Academy of Sciences of the G.D.R., Berlin

D. REIDEL PUBLISHING COMPANY

DORDRECHT : HOLLAND / BOSTON : U.S.A.
LONDON : ENGLAND

Library of Congress Cataloging in Publication Data

Main entry under title:

Speech act theory and pragmatics.

(Synthese language library ; v. 10)
Includes bibliographies and indexes.
1.   Speech acts (Linguistics)—Addresses, essays, lectures.   2.
Semiotics—Addresses, essays, lectures.   I.   Searle, John R.   II.   Kiefer,
Ferenc.   III.   Bierwisch, Manfred.   IV.   Series.
P95.55.S63   412   79—26973
ISBN 90—277—1043—0
ISBN 90—277—1045—7 pbk.

Published by D. Reidel Publishing Company,
P.O. Box 17, 3300 AA Dordrecht, Holland.

Sold and distributed in the U.S.A. and Canada
by Kluwer Boston Inc., Lincoln Building,
160 Old Derby Street, Hingham, MA 02043, U.S.A.

In all other countries, sold and distributed
by Kluwer Academic Publishers Group,
P.O. Box 322, 3300 AH Dordrecht, Holland.

D. Reidel Publishing Company is a member of the Kluwer Group.

Printed in The Netherlands

TABLE OF CONTENTS

INTRODUCTION

In the study of language, as in any other systematic study, there is no neutral terminology. Every technical term is an expression of the assumptions and theoretical presuppositions of its users; and in this introduction, we want to clarify some of the issues that have surrounded the assumptions behind the use of the two terms "speech acts" and "pragmatics".

The notion of a speech act is fairly well understood. The theory of speech acts starts with the assumption that the minimal unit of human communication is not a sentence or other expression, but rather the performance of certain kinds of acts, such as making statements, asking questions, giving orders, describing, explaining, apologizing, thanking, congratulating, etc. Characteristically, a speaker performs one or more of these acts by uttering a sentence or sentences; but the act itself is not to be confused with a sentence or other expression uttered in its performance. Such types of acts as those exemplified above are called, following Austin, *illocutionary acts*, and they are standardly contrasted in the literature with certain other types of acts such as *perlocutionary acts* and *propositional acts*. Perlocutionary acts have to do with those effects which our utterances have on hearers which go beyond the hearer's understanding of the utterance. Such acts as convincing, persuading, annoying, amusing, and frightening are all cases of perlocutionary acts. Illocutionary acts such as stating are often directed at or done for the purpose of achieving perlocutionary effects such as convincing or persuading, but it has seemed crucial to the theorists of speech acts, unlike earlier behavioristic theorists of language, to distinguish the illocutionary act, which is a speech act proper, from the achievement of the perlocutionary effect, which may or may not be achieved by specifically linguistic means. Furthermore, within the illocutionary act there are certain subsidiary propositional acts such as referring to an object, or expressing the proposition that such and such. It has seemed necessary to speech act theorists to make the distinction between propositional and illocutionary acts because the same reference or the same expression of a proposition can occur in different illocutionary acts. Thus, for example, in a statement about President Carter or in a question about President Carter, the same act of reference to President Carter is made even though the total illocutionary acts are different. Also, in the sequence of utterances, "Please

vii

J. R. Searle, F. Kiefer, and M. Bierwisch (eds.), *Speech Act Theory and Pragmatics*, vii–xii.
Copyright © 1980 *by D. Reidel Publishing Company.*

leave the room", "You will leave the room", and "Will you leave the room?" the same proposition, that you will leave the room, is expressed in the performance of three different illocutionary acts, one a request, one a prediction, and one a question. This last distinction between the illocutionary act and the propositional act has suggested to most theorists who write about speech acts that there is a typical logical form of the illocutionary act whereby it has a propositional content (p) and that propositional content is presented with a certain illocutionary force F, giving the total act the structure F(p). Finally, in the theory of speech acts there is a customary distinction between direct speech acts, where the speaker says what he means, and indirect speech acts where he means something more than what he says. For example in a standard dinner table situation when a speaker says "Can you pass the salt?" he performs the *direct* speech act of asking whether the hearer can pass the salt but normally also the *indirect* speech act of requesting the hearer to pass the salt.

Most of the standard authors on the subject of speech acts would accept something like the above distinctions, but when it comes to the notion of pragmatics, the situation is much more confused. "Pragmatics" is one of those words ("societal" and "cognitive" are others) that give the impression that something quite specific and technical is being talked about, when often in fact it has no clear meaning. The motivation for introducing this term, which was done by Charles Morris and later Rudolf Carnap, was to distinguish pragmatics from syntax [or "syntactics"] and semantics. According to Morris's earliest formulation of this distinction (1938), syntactics studies "the formal relations of signs to one another". Semantics studies "the relations of signs to the objects to which the signs are applicable." And pragmatics studies "the relations of signs to interpreters". But this distinction between pragmatics and semantics is very unsatisfactory. For example, taken strictly, the above definitions would have the consequence that pragmatics is a branch of semantics, since signs are clearly "applicable" to interpreters. Morris later modified this definition, and redefined pragmatics as "that branch of semiotics which studies the origins, the uses, and the effects of signs" (1946). Carnap (1942), following Morris's earlier position, gave the following definition, which has proved influential to subsequent authors:

If, in an investigation, explicit reference is made to the speaker, or to put it in more general terms, to the user of the language, then we assign it to the field of pragmatics ... If we abstract from the user of the language and analyze only the expressions and their designata, we are in the field of semantics. And if, finally, we abstract from the designata also and analyze only the relations between the expressions, we are in [logical] syntax. The whole science of language, consisting of the three parts mentioned, is called "semiotics".

With the background of these early statements (or confusions) in Morris and Carnap, it is now possible to distinguish at least three different more or less traditional attitudes to "pragmatics". They are related to the development of formal philosophy, linguistic semantics, and ordinary language philosophy. The differences among these attitudes, growing out of their respective traditions and orientations, are mainly determined by different conceptions of the nature of meaning, yielding different views about the relation between semantics and pragmatics. The key notions in these different accounts of meaning are the denotation, sense, and use of linguistic expressions.

The first tradition, the direct descendant of Carnap's work, is that of formal philosophy and logic, as exemplified by such authors as Montague, Lewis, and Cresswell. According to this view, language is an interpreted formal system, where the interpretation in question assigns a denotation to each expression belonging to the system. On this account, the meaning of an expression is explained in terms of the things it denotes. Thus a sentence like "It is raining" denotes the class of all situations where it is raining, or in sum, the proposition that it is raining. Pragmatics, then, is concerned with the way in which the interpretation of syntactically defined expressions depends on the particular conditions of their use in context. A recent formulation of this view is to be found in Stalnaker [1972]:

Syntax studies sentences, semantics studies propositions. Pragmatics is the study of linguistic acts and the contexts in which they are performed. There are two major types of problems to be solved within pragmatics: first to define interesting types of speech acts and speech products; second, to characterize the features of the speech context which help determine which proposition is expressed by a given sentence. The analysis of illocutionary acts is an example of the problem of the first kind; the study of indexical expressions is an example of the second.

According to this use, speech act theory, together with the study of indexical expressions, make up most, or perhaps all, of the domain of pragmatics.

Contrasting with these views, the second tradition assumes sense rather than denotation to be the core notion of semantics. According to this conception, the meaning of an expression is determined by the sense relations (such as synonymy, antonymy, entailment, etc.) that it bears to other expressions within the system. On this account, the sense of an expression can be distinguished as its context-free, literal meaning from the context-dependent, actual meaning of an utterance of that expression. The utterance meaning, although determined by the sense of the sentence uttered, differs from it in various ways, just as the acoustic realization of an utterance differs from the phonological structure of the sentence uttered. Thus, semantics, according to this tradition, studies all aspects of the literal meaning of sentences and other expressions, while pragmatics is concerned with the conditions according to which speakers and hearers determine the context- and use-dependent utterance meanings. A typical expression of this view is in Katz (1977): "Pragmatics is performance theory at the semantic level." According to this position, the analysis of both indexical expressions and speech acts belongs in part to semantics, in part to pragmatics. As to indexical expressions, semantics is basically concerned with conditions of coreference, leaving the determination of actual reference to pragmatics. Thus the rules — according to which "he" and "his" in "He hurt his hand" may or may not be coreferential, while "he" and "her" in "He hurt her hand" cannot have the same referent — are part of semantics, whereas the determination of the actual referents of "he", "his", and "her" in a given context follows from rules of pragmatics. A similar partition applies to speech acts. Insofar as the illocutionary potential of a sentence is determined by its context-free, literal meaning, then it is part of its semantic structure, and its study is in the domain of semantics. Insofar as its illocutionary potential depends on the context of utterance, including the intentions of the speaker, its study belongs to the domain of pragmatics. A typical example of the distinction would arise in the study of indirect speech acts. In an indirect speech act, the speaker says one thing, means what he says, but he also means something more. A speaker might, for example, say to a hearer, "You are standing on my foot." And he might mean "You are standing on my foot", but in most contexts, he would likely mean something more, such as "Please get off my foot." In such an utterance, the direct speech act expressed by the literal meaning of the sentence lies in the domain of semantics. The indirect speech act, expressed in the speaker's utterance meaning insofar as it differs from the literal meaning of the sentence, lies within the domain of pragmatics.

It is perhaps an ironic feature of the use of the expression "pragmatics" in the current philosophical and linguistic literature that many of the authors who are most commonly described as working within the area of pragmatics do not use this expression at all, for example, Austin, Grice, and Searle. In this third tradition, which derives in part from the late Wittgenstein, the core notion in the explanation of meaning is the use of the expressions of a given language. This is in turn explained in terms of the intentions speakers conventionally have in using these expressions. Although there is a fairly clear distinction between the speaker's (actual) meaning and the conventionalized sentence meaning, there is on this account no way of sorting out the context-free meaning of a linguistic expression, since even the strictly conventionalized usage is always related to a background of unstated assumptions and practices. From this it follows that, contrary to the assumption made in the second approach, literal meaning cannot be identified with context-free meaning. It can now be seen, why the authors working in this tradition hardly ever use the term "pragmatics": taking the conventionalized, context-dependent use of linguistic expressions to be the essence of meaning, they find no clear distinction between semantics and pragmatics, except that semantics might be considered a branch of pragmatics, viz. that branch which deals with how literal meanings of sentences determine their truth-conditions, other conditions of satisfaction, and general semantic relations, such as entailment, against a background of practices and assumptions. From this point of view, indexical expressions and speech acts have no particularly "pragmatic" status. Indexicals, just like any other referring expressions, are means of performing the act of referring, under the appropriate conditions. And the illocutionary force of an utterance is as much a part of its meaning — i.e., of the rules of its use — as any other semantic component.

It has not been our aim in this discussion to attempt to adjudicate between these three traditions, or even to insist that the three traditions represent well-defined philosophical-linguistic theses rather than tendencies or attitudes. In all three traditions something like a notion of literal meaning is essential, and some contrast between literal meaning and speaker's utterance meaning seems essential to any account of language. Speaker's utterance meaning may differ from literal meaning in a variety of ways. Speaker's meaning may include literal meaning but go beyond it, as in the case of indirect speech acts, or it may depart from it, as in the case of metaphor, or it may be the opposite of it, as in the case of irony. The distinction, in short, between speaker's meaning and sentence meaning is common to all theories of speech acts; the question is whether *that* distinction is the same as the distinction between context-free meanings (semantics) and context-dependent meanings (pragmatics).

THE EDITORS

BIBLIOGRAPHY

Carnap, R.: 1942, *Introduction to Semantics*, Cambridge, Harvard University Press.
Katz, J.: 1977, *Propositional Structure and Illocutionary Force*, New York, Crowell and Co.
Morris, Charles: 1938, *Foundations of the Theory of Signs*, International Encyclopedia of Unified Science, Vol. 1, No. 2, Chicago, University of Chicago Press.

Morris, Charles: 1946, *Signs, Language and Behavior*, New York, Prentice Hall.
Stalnaker, R. C.: 1972, 'Pragmatics,' in Davidson and Harman (eds.), *Semantics of Natural Language*, Dordrecht, D. Reidel.

MANFRED BIERWISCH

SEMANTIC STRUCTURE AND ILLOCUTIONARY FORCE*

1. It is by now commonplace that an utterance of (1) can be taken under appropriate conditions e.g., as a promise, a prediction, a warning, or a remark on the speaker's and the addressee's dispositions.

(1) I'll be there before you.

According to current terminology, in each of these cases a different speech act has been performed. What these speech acts have in common is called their propositional content, what they differ in is called their illocutionary force. The present paper is primarily concerned with the question how these two components or aspects of a speech act are related to the linguistic, or more specifically to the semantic structure of the linguistic utterance used to perform it. In cases like (1) the answer to this question seems to be quite straightforward: the propositional content of the various speech acts is more or less directly determined by the complete linguistic structure of (1), while their different illocutionary forces have practically no connection with it. I will argue that this answer is essentially right in cases like (1), albeit with necessary qualifications even for simple cases like this; yet it cannot simply be extended to speech acts in general.

The major counterexamples, apparent or true, are utterances containing so called illocutionary force indicating devices (IFIDs for short), that is elements which more or less directly determine the illocutionary force of the speech act in which they are used. IFIDs are of two main types, which I will show to require principally different analyses. The first type consists of explicit performative formulas like "I promise you to" or "I request that" in appropriate utterances of (2), the second type is represented primarily by grammatical moods, i.e., means characterizing sentence types like imperatives or interrogatives as in (3).

(2)　　(a)　I promise you to be there before you.
　　　　(b)　I request that you come in the evening.
(3)　　(a)　Could you come in the evening?
　　　　(b)　Come in the evening!

Although practically the same speech act can be performed by uttering either

1

J. R. Searle, F. Kiefer, and M. Bierwisch (eds.), Speech Act Theory and Pragmatics,
1–35.
Copyright © 1980 *by D. Reidel Publishing Company.*

(2) (b) or (3) (b), these sentences have different semantic structures (in a sense to be made precise below) and hence a different relation between semantic structure and illocutionary force. Notice incidentally that (3) (a) cannot only be used as a question but also as a request with roughly the same illocutionary force as (3) (b). Hence IFIDs determine by no means uniquely the illocutionary force of a speech act.

Different types of problems are connected with the propositional content of a speech act and its relation to the semantic structure of the utterance involved in cases where things are less simple than in (1)–(3). Consider e.g., an utterance of (4), which under appropriate circumstances can be used to make the same promise as an utterance of (1) or (2) (a), although this time the content of the promise is not determined by the linguistic structure:

(4)   You can rely on me.

What I have illustrated here is but a small number of the problems dealt with in the large body of literature concerned with the analysis of speech acts. The reason for taking them up once more is the fact in spite of interesting results and insights gained so far there are certain crucial problems which are still in need of clarification. More specifically, it seems to me that almost all of the competing accounts of the relation between illocutionary force and semantic structure suffer in one way or the other from an original sin inherited by the speech act theory from its very beginnings. In fact, the consequences of this sin have intruded in all central topics of the speech act theory.

2. What I have called the original sin of speech act theory is expressed by Wunderlich (1977) in the following way: 'I consider speech act theory to be an extension of the theory of meaning in natural language' (p. 243). In a similar vein, Searle (1969) calls his analysis of speech acts 'An essay in the philosophy of language'. The problem with these and many other programs is that they obscure the basic distinction between language and communication. To be sure, natural language is the most important means of human communication, and communication is the primary objective of language use. They must nevertheless clearly be distinguished for at least three reasons.

First, there is a wide variety of cases where language is used outside of any communicative interaction. Clarifying one's thought by monologues or using language as an external memory by making notes are just two examples, which cannot be explained in terms of communication in any serious way, but are still fully-fledged instances of language use.

Second, even if there were no language use outside of communication, one would nevertheless have to admit that there is a large amount of communication which is not based on language at all. Moreover, there are many nonverbal acts having the same illocutionary force and propositional content, as it were, as certain corresponding speech acts. (A hand-shake might, e.g., have the same force and content as an utterance of (1) or (4) under particular circumstances.)

Third, the linguistic and the communicative aspect are determined by different and largely independent principles and rules even in clearcut cases of verbal communication, i.e., in speech acts. In other words, language and communication (or more generally: social interaction) are based on different systems of knowledge. Under certain conditions you may therefore understand very well what someone wants to communicate without understanding what he says, and you may in other cases understand what someone says without understanding what he wants to communicate.

Given a domain of language use based on the rules and structure of language, and a domain of communication based on its own principles, rules, and structures belonging to the more inclusive area of social interaction, speech acts must be construed as instances interconnecting the two domains in a particular way. To put it in simple terms: A speech act makes a linguistic utterance, mainly by virtue of its meaning, the bearer of what would best be called a communicative sense. Notice that a communicative sense belongs to the domain of social interaction and can in general be implemented in various ways, among which the use of verbal utterances is the most elaborate and often the most effective one.

Seen in this way, the speech act theory turns out to be an extension of the theory of meaning in a similar way as, say, a putative theory of forest economy would be an extension of the biology of trees. To say it in a less metaphorical way: Speech act theory is a branch of the theory of communication, viz. that involving linguistic utterances, rather than a part of the theory of language. Although this sounds very much like a terminological quarrel, it will be shown to have serious consequences for central problems of speech act theory.

One might object that, terminological issues aside, Austin (1962), Searle (1969) and others have taken pains to make even more careful distinctions than I have just indicated. In fact, the phonetic act, the phatic act, and the rhetic act distinguished by Austin (1962, p. 94 ff.) are closely related to the phonetic, morpho-syntactic, and semantic aspect of a linguistic utterance, whereas the illocutionary and the perlocutionary act correspond to the communicative sense of a speech act and its eventual consequences, respectively.[1]

4 MANFRED BIERWISCH

These careful distinctions do not detain, however, the sin of mixing language and communication. The various acts are rather construed as interlocked layers within the domain of language use. The reason behind this view seems to be first the lack of a systematic theory of language explaining the coherent principles underlying the phonetic, syntactic and semantic organization of linguistic utterances, and second the lack of any systematic notion of communication as based on genuine principles of social interaction. One of the consequences is the tendency to consider the relation between illocutionary acts and linguistic structures as a matter of interesting detail, not of systematic explanation.

As I have claimed above, the consequences of the failure to distinguish language and communication have affected practically all central topics of speech act theory, including primarily:

(a)   the distinction between constative and performative utterances and the role of truth conditions;
(b)   the classification of illocutionary force or types of illocutionary acts;
(c)   the status of performative formulas and the role of speech act verbs (verbs describing illocutionary acts);
(d)   the nature of illocutionary force indicators.

Before turning to these topics in some detail I will make the alternative view on which the discussion will be based a little bit more precise.

3. Adapting a proposal of Kasher (1971), I will consider a linguistic utterance u to be an inscription *ins* related by a person p at a time t to a linguistic structure ls:

(D 1) $u = \langle ins, p, t, ls \rangle$.

The inscription is the acoustic or visual stimulus produced or perceived by p. Thus (D 1) encompasses both speech production and perception. It merely says that *ins* is an utterance if and only if a person maps on it a linguistic structure ls. The highly complex actual processes involved in this mapping do not concern us here. The linguistic structure ls is a triple

(D 2) $ls = \langle pt, syn, sem \rangle$

of a phonetic (or graphic) structure pt, a morpho-syntactic structure syn, and a semantic structure sem, where syn determines a fairly complicated compositional correlation between parts of pt and components of sem. ls is based on the linguistic knowledge that p has acquired, i.e., on the rules, schemes, and principles forming his internal grammar G. The set of all ls determined by G constitutes the language L that p knows. It is the central concern of theoretical linguistics to specify the general schemes and principles on which possible grammars are based. I take the theory of grammar developed in Chomsky (1965, 1977) to be the most adequate approximation proposed so far, although I need not make any specific assumptions in this respect, except that any grammar G and its language L are subject to the following condition:

(C 1)   For any ls there is nothing in *sem* that is not related by *syn* to some part or configuration in *pt*.

If we assume that *syn* is to be described in terms of transformational derivations, (C 1) is something like a generalized version of the constraint blocking unrecoverable deletion. Anyway, it seems to me a natural principle which prevents one from postulating arbitrary semantic specifications.[2]

An ls can quite naturally be construed as a highly organized complex rule according to which meaningful utterances are to be produced and interpreted: *pt* is a complex rule determining the production or perceptual identification of inscriptions, *syn* is a complex rule according to which the results of the application of *pt* are related to *sem*, and *sem* is a complex rule according to which an utterance meaning is specified.[3] Hence *sem* determines an utterance meaning m, roughly like *pt* determines the inscription *ins*. The determination of m by a person p at time t depends on a context ct with respect to which u is interpreted. Let me call a triple consisting of an utterance u, its utterance meaning m, and the context ct to which it is related a meaningful utterance $mu = \langle u, ct, m \rangle$. On the background of (D 1) and (D 2) this expands in the following more complete definition:

(D 3) $mu = \langle ins, p, t, \langle pt, syn, sem \rangle, ct, m \rangle.$

Again, (D 3) is neutral with respect to production and perception and does not account for the actual processes relating *ins* on the basis of ct to an utterance meaning m. (Notice that (D 3) by and large specifies what Austin and Searle call a locutionary act and a propositional act, respectively.) From what has been said so far it follows that *sem* is a rule that p applies (at time t) to ct in order to specify m. Hence *sem* is a function mapping contexts into utterance meanings. This is precisely the notion of semantic structure developed in intensional logic: *sem* is the intension determining m as the extension of mu in the context ct. In other words, the formal apparatus of possible worlds semantics proposed by Lewis (1972), Cresswell (1973), and others provides the formal framework to deal with *sem, ct*, and *m*. In Bierwisch (in press) I have argued that this framework is to be reconciled with the linguistic tradition of componential analysis such that, roughly speaking, any semantic structure can be construed as a configuration of basic components drawn from a universal set *B* of semantic primes, just as any *pt* is construed as a configuration of basic phonetic features. Anyway, *sem* can be taken as specifying the truth conditions associated with an utterance *u*, and *m* as the specification of a state of affairs that meets these conditions, i.e., makes the utterance true. (Certain amendments are to be discussed below.)

So far I have specified the domain of language, or to be more precise: a narrower domain of linguistic structures as defined in (D 2), and a wider domain of language use characterized by (D 1) and (D 3). We may now say that a person *p* (linguistically) understands a meaningful utterance *mu* with respect to a given context *ct*, if he assigns an utterance meaning *m* to the inscription *ins*.

According to possible worlds semantics, the context *ct* and the utterance meaning *m* would have to be specified in terms of possible worlds and objects, which are characterized by means of certain set theoretical structures. In Bierwisch (in press) I have argued that these are to be interpreted as the formal structure of mental states, i.e., of internal representations of worlds, objects, states of affairs, etc. Instead of being just arbitrary set theoretical structures, possible worlds are then generated by th system *PC* of perceptual and conceptual rules, schemes, and operations of a person *p*, analogous to the way in thich the *ls* are generated by *G*. Without pursuing the far-reaching consequences of this assumption, I will simply point out that on this view any serious account of language use becomes a joint venture of linguistics and cognitive psychology — a fairly natural consequence, it seems to me, if language use is taken to be the expression of thought.

Turning finally to the domain of communication, I will first define a communicative act *ca* as a meaningful activity *ma* to which a communicative sense *cs* is assigned with respect to a given interactional setting *ias*:

(D 4) $ca = \langle ma, ias, cs \rangle$.

A meaningful activity must be thought of as any piece of external behavior or product of behavior that a person *p* at time *t* produces or perceives as the manifestation of a certain scheme or structure. Hence *ma* might be a gesture, a particular type of dressing, a specifically placed stone, or what not. *ma* thus corresponds to *u*, except that in general it is not related to a codified semantic structure. In fact, linguistic utterances turn out to be highly specialised meaningful activities.

The crucial point is that p must have available a system of rules, principles, and schemes of social interaction according to which the interactional setting *ias* of *ma* is construed and its communicative sense is determined. Let us tentatively call this system *SI*.[4] A theory of this sort of system would have to specify what types of structures are possible interactional settings and communicative senses, and what types of rules are involved in generating them and relating them to meaningful activities. I don't have to say any more about these issues than what is commonplace: there are on the one hand certain general principles like those of rational cooperation, obeying obligations, acknowledging motivations, needs, and interests, etc.[5] On the other hand, there are various forms of conventional, more or less institutionalized rules and structures. Lacking any systematic framework, I will discuss *ias* and *cs* in purely intuitive terms.

Summarizing this highly oversimplified outline, we can characterize a speech act by combining (D 1) through (D 4) in the following way:

(5) 　　《*ins, p, t,* 《*pt, syn, sem*》, *ct, m*》, *ias, cs*》.

Our initial question can now be rendered as: How and to what extent is *cs* determined by *sem*?

4. Let me briefly illustrate the above framework by considering a simple assertion, i.e., what Austin calls a constative utterance.

(6) 　　You have to pay for it.

Insofar as (6) is taken as an utterance u, a person p assigns to it a semantic structure which is determined by the semantic structure of the words and the syntactic structure of (6). In an informal way, it can be characterized roughly by (7):

(7) 　　At the time x of producing *ins* it is necessary for the addressee y to pay for some identified z.

Taking (6) as a meaningful utterance *mu, p* relates it to a context and identifies the structure of a particular state of affairs satisfying the truth condition (7). Of course, many different states of affairs are compatible with (7). Specifications are required not only for the referential variables y, x, z, but also for predicates like *pay*, which might be satisfied by an appropriate exchange

of coins or notes, by signing a check, etc. Let (8) describe a state of affairs
that p selects on the basis of (7) with respect to a particular context ct:

(8)   John is obliged at time t to give one dollar to the bar keeper as
         the equivalent for a drink.

The internal representation of this state of affairs in p would then be the
utterance meaning m that p assigns to (6) in context ct. So far, I have described what it would mean for p — according to Austin — to interpret a token
of (6) as a constative utterance. (p might be the utterer, the addressee, or
some other party.) Notice, that according to my proposal, we have not described a speech act at all. In order to take it as a speech act, p must interpret
(6) furthermore with respect to a certain interactional setting, assigning to it
a communicative sense cs. Let us assume that (9) would be a rough-and-ready
description of one such cs:

(9)   The speaker of (6) wants John to know that (8) is a fact and that
         the speaker has reasonable evidence for (8).

It is only with respect to the cs indicated in (9) that justifications, objections,
doubts, etc. become relevant. Let us assume that (9) indicates the cs assigned
to (6) in a speech act of asserting. In spite of the awful incompleteness of this
account, the crucial point should be obvious: Although (9) is closely related
to the utterance meaning (8) and the truth condition (7) on which (8) is
based, the cs of an assertion is not to be confused with its truth condition. It
is one of the consequences of Austin's original sin to identify these two
aspects.[6]

It is now easy to see, at least in principle, how changes in the interactional
setting may yield changes in the communicative sense. Thus on the basis of
the same utterance meaning, but with respect to a different ias, an utterance
of (6) might become a kind of request with a cs roughly indicated by (10):

(10)   The speaker requests that John gives a dollar to the bar keeper at
         time t'.

In fact, variations within ias (or in meaningful activities accompanying u, like
gestures or tone of voice) can turn (10) into the cs of a polite request or a
strict order. And probably somewhere between (9) and (10) lies the cs of a
speech act in which (6) is used for an admonition.

The remarks made above with respect to (1) are to be construed in a similar way. It is of course an intricate task to replace intuitive comments like
those I have just made by systematic explanations. I don't take this to be a

manageable task for the time being. One should keep in mind, however, that any serious attempt to this effect must be concerned with conditions and rules belonging to the system *SI*.

5. The above discussion brings us immediately to the constative/performative distinction, which was created when Austin observed that normal utterances of sentences like (11) cannot appropriately be analysed in terms of truth conditions.

(11)   I bet you sixpence it will rain tomorrow.

In order to cope with the peculiarities of so called performative utterances like (11), Austin introduced the notion of felicity conditions. They are supposed to determine what makes e.g., an utterance of (11) a bet, just as truth conditions determine what makes a constative utterance true. Within the framework outlined above, the important observation that there is something more to (11) than just truth will be accounted for by the communicative sense. In fact, the felicity conditions Austin has in mind are just a particular aspect of the rules and structures of social interaction. The dilemma with Austin's analysis is that he deprives the performative utterances of their truth conditions, just as he deprives the constative utterances of their communicative sense (or felicity conditions, for that matter). That truth conditions and felicity conditions are not mutually exclusive (and hence do not lead to the bipartition of utterances into constatives and performatives) is rather obvious in cases like "I will come" or (1) uttered as a promise, where the two aspects can easily be identified within one and the same speech act. What has fascinated speech act theoreticians since Austin is the fact that the two aspects seem to exclude each other in cases like (11), which are called explicit performatives (as opposed to implicit performatives like (1)). The natural, and by no means new answer to that supposition is that speech acts based on an explicit performative utterance may have both truth- and felicity conditions. I will return to this problem below.

The most careful attempt to explicate Austin's position within an explicit semantic theory has been made by Katz (1977). He assumes that constative and performative utterances (and moreover different types of performative utterances) are distinguished by their respective illocutionary force, which he takes to be determined by the propositional type of the sentence involved. The propositional type is a designated part of the semantic structure. In other words, Katz assumes *sem* (in the case of sentences) to be of the form ⟨*type*, (*pc*)⟩, where *type* is a specific configuration of semantic markers, and *pc* the propositional content. The latter specifies an 'unconverted condition', that is then turned by *type* into a converted condition, viz. a truth condition, if *type* is specified as assertive, and various other conditions (like answerhood, compliance, fulfillment, etc.) if *type* is specified as one of the various performative types. Katz thus traces the constative/performative contrast, and hence the mutual exclusion of truth- and felicity-conditions, to the semantic structure of sentences. This position implies a direct answer to the question how the communicative sense is determined by the semantic structure of an utterance: *sem* directly determines *cs*.[7] In fact, Katz makes in a sense the contamination of language and communication a part of the theory of semantics. That is particularly astonishing in view of his otherwise rather strong inclination to separate semantics strictly from extrasemantic aspects, like encyclopaedic knowledge, effects of performance, etc. Certain more specific problems emerging from Katz' position are dealt with below.

Opposed to the view that the constative/performative distinction is a basic one, there are two attempts to get rid of it. The respective claims are:

(A)   All sentences are performative, and
(B)   All speech acts can be explained in terms of truth conditions.

Position (A) assumes that an explicit performative formula like "I tell you . . ." is part of the underlying structure of any sentence, but may possibly be deleted in its surface form. Thus (12) and (13) are assumed to be essentially synonymous:

(12)   I tell you that the earth is flat.
(13)   The earth is flat.

This analysis, originally motivated by syntactic arguments, has been shown to be inadequate for a large number of reasons, which I need not repeat here.[8] Let me point out, however, that Austin too tried to assimilate sentences like (12) and (13), albeit for a different reason: Observing that both sentences can be used to perform the speech act of asserting that the earth is flat, he took sentences like (12) to undermine the constative/performative distinction, since it constitutes at the same time a constative and an explicit performative utterance. Ironically, Austin feels himself to be forced to give up the distinction for the same reason he introduced it: the conflation of language and communication. The trouble vanishes if we observe that (12) and (13) have different semantic structures, different utterance meanings, but may acquire closely related communicative senses.[9] Notice that in any case, a slight but clear difference remains between the *cs* of (12) and (13): Only with respect to (12) would an utterance of (14) be an interpretable reply:

(14)   You had better not!

Position (B) has a strong and a weak version:

(B 1)   All speech acts are to be explained in terms of nothing but truth conditions.

(B 2)   All speech acts can and must be explained in terms of truth conditions plus something else.

I take (B 1) to be obviously false and will not consider it any further.[10] Although (B 2) is also wrong in its unrestricted form, it accounts for a large range of cases, including the explicit performative utterances.

6. Before turning to (B 2) more closely, it is useful to consider the status of illocutionary or speech act verbs like "promise", "order", "ask", "claim", "name" etc. The central position they have occupied in speech act theory since Austin derives from the fact that they are considered as the most explicit link between linguistic structures and illocutionary acts. In fact they are taken as a plausible means to turn the analysis of speech acts into a genuine linguistic task, viz., that of analysing the meaning of particular lexical elements. Although the more scrutinized versions distinguish between the analysis of speech acts and the analysis of illocutionary verbs, there is a persisting tendency to confuse them.[11] The reason should by now be obvious: The occurrence of illocutionary verbs in explicit performative formulas seem to obviate the distinction between language and communication, thus providing a way to analyse the latter in terms of the former.[12]

I will therefore be absolutely explicit: Illocutionary verbs form a class of lexical items very much like other classes, e.g., verbs of motion, of emotional states, of exchange of possession, or what not. Like any other class, they are not clearly delimited, i.e., the class overlaps with other clasces. Consider e.g., a borderline case like "give up":

(15)   After his second fall he gave up jumping.
(16)   I give up.

Although an utterance of (15) need not describe a speech act at all, (16) qualifies for a performative utterance according to all criteria. Hence "give up" (among a number of other verbs) is only occasionally an illocutionary verb, just as "money" may be a concrete noun (as in "the money on the table") or an abstract noun (as in "the money he lost during the slump").[13]

The existence of illocutionary verbs is, of course, due to the fact that natural languages, being 'complete' in the sense of e.g., Searle's principle of expressibility, provide the means to talk, among others, about communication and verbal interaction, i.e., about phenomena to be analysed theoretically in terms of *SI*. Thus a verb like "order" specifies certain conditions of a class of (essentially verbal) interactions, just as "sell" specifies certain conditions of a class of commercial events, or "tiger" species certain conditions of a class of animals. They are thus to be analysed semantically just as any other lexical items.[14] So far, there is nothing peculiar with illocutionary verbs. Let us consider now what happens when they enter the critical performative formulas, that is, when they take present tense and a subject identifying the producer of the inscription such as "I", "the present speaker", or, in a given utterance context, "John", "the host", etc. We will see that the underlying principle of this possibility is less unique then speech act theoreticians made it appear.

7. The crucial point is that under certain conditions a sentence having an explicit performative formula as its topmost clause specifies a truth condition that can be satisfied by the speech acts in which the sentence is used. In other words, the sentence describes (has as utterance meaning a specification of) the speech act that can be performed in producing a token of the sentence. (16), (17), and (18) are examples of this type.

(17)   The present author claims to have solved the problem.

(18)   All of us ask you to stay.

In simple terms: Utterances of explicit performatives like (16)–(18) describe what they are used to do. More explicitly:

(i)   Whether an utterance of (16) constitutes the speech act (i.e., has the communicative sense *cs*) of giving up, depends on its interactional setting *ias*.

(ii)   If it has the *cs* in question, then its inscription *ins* must be the inscription of a meaningful utterance *mu* whose utterance meaning *m* is true in virtue of (i), i.e., *m* specifies the state of affairs consisting in the speakers giving up.

(iii)   The utterance meaning *m* is determined by the semantic structure *sem* assigned to *ins*, where *sem* is applied to the utterance context *ct*, which includes, for obvious reasons, specifications of the interactional setting *ias*.

This account immediately extends to explicit performatives in general. The crucial point is that an explicit performative utterance has the communicative sense *cs* specified by its utterance meaning *m* if and only if the meaningful utterance on which it is based is true.

Let me add a few clarifying remarks. First, it is an inherent feature of the framework outlined in section 3 that truth is connected to the utterance meaning *m* (viz., the state of affairs satisfying *sem*), while interactional appropriateness would be connected to *cs*. (In Austin's terms: truth belongs to *m*, felicity to *cs*.) This holds for speech acts in general. The peculiarity of explicit performatives is merely that *m* and *cs* are related to each other in virtue of the performative formula, i.e., the illocutionary verb, its tense, and subject. In a well defined sense we can now say that an explicit performative utterance is true just because it performs a certain speech act. That in general we are primarily or even exclusively interested in the fact that the speaker of "I give up" actually gives up, rather than in the fact that he produces a true meaningful utterances must not obscure the fact that he really produces a true utterance.[15] In a similar vein someone putting a coin in a music box is not very much interested in its size, although the coin actually must have the required size.

Notice, secondly, that the contraposition of (ii) correctly holds: If someone utters "I give up" without e.g., having the appropriate intentions (if he is violating the pertinent sincerity condition, in Searle's terms), or without being in the position to give up, then by the same token the utterance is false: he is not really giving up.

Third, *pace* Austin, explicit performatives (*qua* utterances) describe what they perform (*qua* speech acts) just in virtue of the illocutionary verb they contain. This follows automatically from the semantic structure of illocutionary verbs. The potential duplicity of 'saying' and 'performing' is in fact a crucial feature of illocutionary verbs. This type of duplicity is not restricted to performative formulas, however. Lewis (1972) has invented sentences like "In trochaic hexameter I am talking", which describe what happens when they are correctly pronounced.[16] A printed instruction such as

(19)   Use CAPITALS if . . .
       Use *italics* if . . .
       Use **bold face** if . . .

is another instance of the same type of duplicity. Perhaps the most striking case is "Me" uttered in reply to the question "Who is outdoors?" where it is actually the voice that identifies the speaker. (The duplicity in question can

even be found outside of language: A teacher showing how to fill a pen shows
how to fill a pen and by the same token fills a pan.) In a sense, the peculiarity
of performative formulas is but a special case of the general problem of token
reflexivity, as born out by the optional indicator "hereby".

Finally, it should be observed that condition (i) is crucial also for explicit
performatives. It is not the mere utterance that determines whether a speech
act is performed and which. Notice that fairly special conditions within the
ias of (16) must obtain in order to make it the speaker's act of giving up. The
situation described by (20) might be a concrete example.

> (20)   An utterance of (16) occurs during a chess game when the speaker
>   finds himself in a bad position.

Notice that within a situation like (20), laying down the king would be a
communicative act with exactly the same *cs*. On the other hand, in a situation
like (21) the speaker only expresses (states) his intention or decision, but
does not perform the act of giving up:

> (21)   An utterance of (16) occurs during a discussion between the
>   speaker and his adviser concerning a chess game in which the
>   speaker is involved at the time of the discussion.

In this case, the speaker of (16) might afterwards go to the chess board and
perform the act of giving up in one of the ways indicated above. Notice that
only with respect to (20) is the truth of the utterance meaning of (16) due
to the fact that it describes what the speaker does, i.e., only with respect to
(20) are the conditions (ii) and (iii) met. In the case of (21) the utterance
meaning is true if and only if the speaker just decides to give up, i.e., if it
truthfully specifies a certain mental act. This analysis also explains why the
possibility of using certain explicit performatives either as a statement, as in
(21), or as a 'true' performative, as in (20), does not turn on an ambiguity in
their semantic structure. It is just their interactional setting that induces the
distinction. This distinction is of exactly the same type as that between an
utterance of (22) referring to the utterance itself, and an utterance of (22)
referring to some other utterance occurring in the context:

> (22)   This utterance is stressed.

One would not say that "this" is semantically ambiguous because of the
different references. This parallel brings out the token reflexivity of explicit
performatives quite clearly. In fact, only within the setting of (20) can the
utterance be expanded into

(23)   I hereby give up.

where "hereby" refers to the speech act, not to the sentence. This reference to the act as a whole is even more obvious in complex interactions involving a meaningful utterance and some other activity; an appropriate utterance of (24) would be a case in point:

(24)   I hereby return the book you gave me last week.

To sum up, what is needed for a full analysis of explicit performatives is nothing but a truth theoretical account of their ordinary semantic structure, and a theory of social interaction providing interactional settings and communicative senses. We can formulate this as a specification of (B 2):

(B 2′)   All explicit performative utterances must be explained in terms of truth conditions plus conditions of social interaction.

This is both less and more than what the Austinian tradition assumes. It is less, because there is no need for a particular theory of felicity conditions. It is more, because we need a theory of the system *SI* of rules and structures of social interaction, of which we have vague fragments, at best. But it is a rational task to construct such a theory, albeit not a task that linguists or philosophers of language are competent to accomplish in any serious way.

8. By way of example, let me mention a few of the more complicated cases that come out quite neatly on the basis developed so far. First consider modified explicit performatives like (25):

(25)   I gladly promise to help you move.

We need neither a particular speech act of gladly promising besides simple promising, nor a decomposition into a speech act of promising and a (simultaneous) comment on the speakers attitude toward this first act. Given the usually determined compositional utterance meaning, it is related to the communicative sense of the speech act in question in the way described in (i)–(iii) above.

Compare next utterances of the following sentences:

(26)   I remind you especially of John's paper.
(27)   I should remind you especially of John's paper.
(28)   Bill asked me to remind you especially of John's paper.

The first might be an ordinary act of reminding. But what about the others?

Consider first (28), which Austin, Katz and others would have to treat as a statement about Bill's request. The peculiarity of (28) is that it would be pointless to reply with something like "OK, remind me of it!" or "and, will you?", for the simple and obvious reason that (28) cannot be uttered without reminding the addressee of John's paper: To understand the utterance meaning of (28) has the effect of being reminded. Hence in a sense, (28) is an act of reminding very much like (26), which does not prevent it, however, from being a statement about Bill's request, as it can naturally be answered e.g., by (29):

(29)   But you would probably have preferred not to mention it.

In other words, (28) is an act of stating and inherently also an act of reminding. In a similar way, it follows from the utterance meaning of (27) plus an appropriate interactional setting that an act of reminding is actually made, rather than merely deliberated. By the same token, (30) has the form of a statement about the wishes of the speaker's wife and the communicative sense of transferring greetings:

(30)   My wife wants me to give you her kind regards.

The 'interlocked' speech acts result automatically from the utterance meaning in much the same way as the pertinent communicative sense in cases of simple explicit performatives.[17]

Consider finally cases like (31) or (32) which might be uttered with the intention to inform the audience about the rejection of his application:

(31)   I am definitely asked not to tell you that your application has been rejected.

(32)   I don't inform you that your application has been rejected.

Given appropriate conditions, an utterance of (32) is a kind of self defeating speech act: in spite of the explicit disclaimer it cannot fail to proliferate information, just as — inversely — an utterance of "I insult you" inspite of the explicit performative formula cannot succeed in insulting. The logic is that of the paradox of the liar, as Katz (1977, p. 187) has pointed out, i.e., (32) resembles in a crucial respect sentences like "this sentence is false", including the apparent ambiguity discussed above with respect to (16) and (22). Without spelling out the details, I take the communicative sense of (31) and (32) to be fully accounted for by the truth of the utterance meaning and the interactional setting.

It should by now be obvious that the principle inherent in the position

(B 2′) can be extended to all speech acts based on truth bearing sentences. In other words, that our initial example

(33)   I'll be there before you.

can be uttered as a prediction, a promise, etc. follows from its utterance meaning together with its respective interactional setting, the difference between (33) and (34) being only the fact that what makes (33) true is a future state of affairs, while what makes (34) true is the act of promising.

(34)   I promise to be there before you.

We are thus left with sentences that cannot be reduced to truth conditions.[18]

9. What we have to consider are sentences like

(35)   Be careful!
(36)   Have you seen the Chagall exhibition?
(37)   Who wants to be with us in the evening?

Let me say right from the beginning that the *cs* of these sentences again depends on the *ias* of the utterances. Thus (37) might be a real question if the speaker e.g., compiles a list of potential guests; it might be an invitation; and it might fail to be a speech act at all if uttered in a pondering monologue. The point at issue is that imperatives and interrogatives cannot naturally be said to determine truth conditions.

There are essentially three ways that have been proposed for the analysis of these sentences.

The first is that of e.g., Lewis (1972) who proposes to assimilate (35)–(37) semantically to their corresponding explicit performative versions (35′)–(37′) thus reducing them to the pertinent truth conditions:

(35′)   I order you to be careful.
(36′)   I ask you whether you have seen the Chagall exhibition.
(37′)   I ask you who wants to be with us in the evening.

The second way, proposed by Katz (1977), is identical to the first one with respect to the assumption that (35) and (35′) etc. have practically identical semantic structures, this time leading to identical 'converted conditions' rather than truth conditions. Katz simply assumes the imperative morpheme and the question morpheme to have the semantic structure of an explicit performative formula.[19]

This assimilation is empirically incorrect. Curiously enough, both Katz and

Lewis point out that (12) and (13) must be semantically different. But by the same token, (35) and (35′) cannot have the same semantic structure. Thus e.g., (35′), but not (35) can naturally be objected to by (38):

(38)   You are in no position to do so.

Of course, (38) states a disagreement with respect to the *ias* required to make an utterance of (35′) an order.[20] Hence grammatical moods, i.e., imperative and interrogative, must be kept separate from explicit performatives.

This condition is observed on the third way, which is now faced with the problem of distinguishing between (35) and (36) as opposed to (39) and (40):

(39)   You are careful.
(40)   You have seen the Chagall exhibition.

An explicit proposal to this effect has been made by Hausser (this volume, p. 71–95). The idea is to assign different semantic types to indicative, imperative, and interrogative sentences such that imperatives and interrogatives do not determine a (true or false) state of affairs as their respective utterance meaning, but rather a property of the addressee and the set of possible non-redundant answers, respectively. (I need not go through Hausser's more sophisticated specification of these notions.) Whether an utterance of (35), having the addressee's property of being careful as its utterance meaning m, actually performs an order or request, is determined by what Hausser calls 'use conditions', just as it depends on use conditions whether (35′) constitutes an act of ordering. Similarly (37) has as its utterance meaning the specification of the set of people who, given a certain utterance context ct, possibly want to be with the speaker in the evening. Again, use conditions are supposed to determine whether an utterance of (37) constitutes an act of questioning (or inviting, or what not).

Let us assume that the use conditions are actually a part of the system SI, and that semantic structures specify not merely truth conditions — what they actually do in the case of declarative sentences, including explicit performatives — but more generally denotation conditions. Then the following general principle emerges:

(B 2″)   The communicative sense of all speech acts must be explained in terms of denotation conditions plus the conditions of SI.

This then is the corrected version of (B 2) which does justice also to non-declaratives.

There are three reasons that make me reluctant with respect to Hausser's particular way of extending truth conditions to denotation conditions.

First, the completely general and elegant system of semantic types developed in possible worlds semantics provides appropriate denotation conditions for practically every category of linguistic expression. Adopting this system directly as an account of the way imperatives and interrogatives acquire their utterance meaning misses their particular status as opposed to other semantic types. In other words, without any additional restriction, one would have to countenance the possibility of languages with arbitrarily differing sentence types. (It is not even clear why declaratives are basic in the sense they obviously are.)

Second, there are, it seems to me, fairly strong intuitions that the utterance meaning of imperatives and interrogatives is not merely the denotation Hausser assumes. Rather an imperative specifies some attitude or intention toward the realization of the denoted property, just as an interrogative has the attitude of wanting a specification within the denoted range.

Third, there is a number of subtle, but important (albeit poorly understood) phenomena of semantic scope and compatibility which seem to require a kind of operator status for the semantic conditions that distinguish the sentence types in question. To take but one example:

(41)   I probably order you to leave at night.
(42)   I probably ask you whether you will leave at night.

These are quite correct sentences which cannot be used, however, to order or to ask. (In fact they can get a communicative sense only in rather peculiar circumstances.) Now a somehow related restriction seems to exclude sentences like:

(43)   Leave probably at night!
(44)   Will you probably leave at night?

(Of course, (44) must not be confused with the different sentence "Is it probable that you will leave at night?" or even "You will probably leave at night?") Although (43) would be excluded also on Hausser's account, since the sentence adverbial "probably" does not combine semantically with a property, (44) is not excluded in a similar way.

I will therefore sketch an alternative proposal to interpret the principle (B 2″), or more precisely a slightly different notion of denotation. I should emphasize, however, that this is the most tentative part of my considerations.

10. Let me begin with Frege's distinction between 'thought', 'judgement' and 'assertion': "Denken ist Gedankenfassen. Nachdem man einen Gedanken gefaßt hat, kann man ihn als wahr anerkennen (*urteilen*) und dieses Anerkennen äußern (*behaupten*)" (Frege, 1973, p. 76) What Frege calls a thought has been reconstructed in modern logic as a proposition, or as I have put it: the structure of a state of affairs that makes the proposition true. Hence Frege's 'thought' is roughly what I have called until now the utterance meaning *m* of a sentence. Pursuing Frege's consideration we might now say that an utterance does not merely express the thought, but rather the judgement that the thought is true, i.e., that the state of affairs obtains.[21]

"Doch fehlt es in den Sprachen an einem Worte oder Zeichen, das allein die Aufgabe hätte zu behaupten" as Frege observes. In his 'Begriffsschrift' he introduced the prefix '⊢' to indicate the status of a judgement. It should be clear that it is a kind of attitude or evaluation that turns a proposition into a judgement. The simplest case is to take the proposition to be true (or false).[22] It is in fact this type of evaluation whose heritage has been the primary concern of logical analysis.

It is a natural step to construe Frege's third entity, the 'assertion', as the communicative sense of a judgement uttered in a communicative setting. Hence it is the assertion that eventually requires justification, is open to objections, etc.

If one accepts this view, the utterance meaning of a sentence is a judgement, i.e., an evaluated specification of a state of affairs, which, in the simplest case, determines — on the level of communication — an assertion concerning this state of affairs. On this view, the 'judgement-operator' is not the illocutionary force of a speech act, but rather an attitude belonging to the level of utterance meaning.

My proposal is now to take the attitude determining a judgement as an element of a well defined system of alternative cognitive attitudes. I would like to consider such cognitive attitudes as pre-reflexive ways of appreciating actual or possible states of affairs. Thus exploring whether a state of affairs obtains (wanting to know), hypothesizing that it obtains (assigning subjective probability), wanting that it obtains (wishing) are tentative candidates. I take them to be pre-reflexive in three respects: First, any thought (in the sense of a specified possible state of affairs) must be conceived in the light of a basic cognitive attitude. Second, this attitude cannot be backed by or reduced to some underlying, more basic attitude. Third, it can itself become the object or content of a thought reflecting it (which is then conceived, however, in the light of its own basic attitude). It would be a joint venture of epistemology, cognitive psychology, and logic to give empirical substance to these considerations.

Let us assume that ATT is the system of cognitive attitudes in the sense discussed. We may then define the utterance meaning m of a sentence to have the following general form:

(D 5) $m = \langle att, m' \rangle$ where $att \in ATT$

Here m' is the 'content' of the utterance meaning, i.e., simply m minus the attitude. (D 5) is, of course, reminiscent of Searle's distinction between illocutionary force and propositional content, as well as Katz' distinction between illocutionary type and propositional content. Notice, however, that att is neither the specification of an illocutionary force, nor an element of the semantic structure.

Let D, I, and Q designate the attitude of the utterance meaning of an ordinary declarative, imperative, and interrogative sentence, respectively. It is obvious from the foregoing that the impact of these attitudes cannot be adequately paraphrased by explicitly designating expressions. If one bears this in mind, the following approximations can be given as a hint:

(45)　(a)　D: the utterer takes it that . . .
　　　(b)　I: the utterer intends that . . .
　　　(c)　Q: the utterer intends to know . . .

The form of something like an explicit cognitive formula used in (45) is completely misleading as it involves explicit designation of the utterer and the cognitive attitude, which is in open conflict with the pre-reflexive character of the attitudes.

Since I have argued above that explicit performatives are just declarative sentences, the attitudes in utterance meanings are essentially reduced to D, I, and Q.[23] How these utterance meanings are converted into the respective communicative sense, is fairly obvious for simple interactional settings:

(46)　By uttering mu with the utterance meaning m the speaker wants the audience to recognize that he has the attitude att towards m'.

The consequences resulting from this act of expressing one's mental state both for the speaker and his audience are determined by the rules of SI, which determine also the consequences of e.g., someone's knocking at the door or looking demonstratively for a chair, or what not. For indirect and more complicated consequences see section 12.

11. If one accepts the notion of attitudes as developed so far, the conclusions for the semantic structure of imperative and interrogative sentences are fairly obvious. Imperative sentences have a semantic structure *sem* = $\langle Imp, pc \rangle$ where *pc* is the propositional content that determines a (future) act of the addressee with respect to the context *ct*, and *Imp* determines the attitude *I*. Similarly, interrogative sentences have a semantic structure *sem* = $\langle Qu, pc \rangle$ where *pc* determines the field of search with respect to *ct* (i.e., the state of affairs to be decided on or to be satisfied by certain individuals), and *Qu* determines the attitude *Q*.[24]

One might now be tempted to analyse the semantic structure of declarative sentences as $\langle Decl, pc \rangle$ with *Decl* determining the 'judgment' attitude *D*. It seems to me more adequate, however, to assume that declarative sentences normally have no attitude specifier at all, or perhaps an empty or 'unmarked' attitude specifier. (Remember Frege's observation that in general natural languages do not have expressions representing the judgement operator.) Hence the semantic structure of a declarative sentence is normally of the form *pc* only.[25] We might adopt then a universal principle to the effect that the neutral or unmarked utterance meaning of a declarative sentence is the attitude *D* with respect to the state of affairs determined by *pc* on the basis of *ct*:

(47)   Let *pc* be the full semantic structure of a declarative utterance *u*. Then the unmarked (or normal) utterance meaning *m* of *u* with respect to *ct* is $\langle D, m' \rangle$, where *pc* applied to *ct* determines *m'*.

Hence the unmarked interpretation of a sentence like "You opened the door" would be the specification of a state of affairs which is taken to be true with respect to the context *ct*. There are two remarks to be made with respect to (47).

First, there may be non-neutral interpretations specifying a different attitude in the utterance meaning of a declarative sentence. Depending on the pertinent *m'*, they may even be prevailing. Thus (48), though specifying a simple 'judgement' in its unmarked interpretation, might more often be assigned the attitude *I*:

(48)   You leave at night.

(It is, of course, still a different issue what communicative sense results from the utterance meaning together with the interactional setting. In this respect, (48) might even be a harsh order.)

Second I take (47) to determine the attitude D, if nothing else changes it to a more 'marked' attitude. It does preclude, however, the total lack of an attitude. In fact, an utterance meaning without an attitude assigned to it turns out to be impossible. One might take (49) to be a way of expressing the mere m' of (48), but an utterance of (49) would not normally be a complete utterance.

(49)   That you leave at night.

In a sense, then, (47) accounts for the fact that declarative sentences are basic or neutral as opposed to other sentence types and that their assertive interpretation is the neutral or unmarked case. Notice that (47) is to be taken as a universal, but empirical principle governing the semantic structure of natural languages. Its presumed universality is not at variance with the possibility that in spite of Frege's observation a language might have a judgement operator.[26] The principle merely claims that pure declaratives always determine the neutral attitude D, if there is nothing particular in the utterance context that induces another, more marked attitude. And it claims that it is a marked property for a language to have a particular D-specifier alongside with specifiers of I, Q, and possibly other marked attitudes.

Let us assume for the sake of argument that, e.g., "want" describes in an explicit way the attitude I that I have assumed to characterize the utterance meaning of imperatives. Then (50) and (51) would be closely connected in the sense that (50) indicates a pre-reflexive attitude which (51) explicitly describes (with D as its own pre-reflexive attitude).

(50)   Come in!
(51)   I want you to come in.

It is now easy to see that and how these sentences differ in their semantic structure. In a semi-formal, self-explaining way they can be represented as follows:

(50') $\langle Imp, \langle Come\ in, you \rangle \rangle$.
(51') $\langle Want, I, \langle Come\ in, you \rangle \rangle$.

Here (51') has no (or perhaps rather an empty) attitude specifier.[27] Similar considerations apply to pairs like (52) and possibly also (53):

(52)   (a) Who comes first?
              (b) I want to know who comes first.

(53)   (a) He probably knows it.
       (b) It is probable that he knows it.

It is an interesting and by no means trivial task to incorporate attitude specifiers into the formal apparatus of possible worlds semantics, both with respect to their semantic type and their denotation. Although I see no difficulties in principle, I will not go into these problems here.

Returning to our initial question how the communicative sense and especially the illocutionary force of speech acts is related to semantic structures, the following fairly traditional picture emerges:

(a) The illocutionary force of a speech act is a more or less complex condition belonging to its communicative sense, and hence to the level of social interaction. It is, strictly speaking, not part of the semantic structure (nor even of the utterance meaning). Thus in the strict sense, there are no IFIDs at all. In a looser sense, one might consider as IFIDs those elements of an utterance that more or less directly influence its *cs* with respect to a particular *ias*. These elements are largely of two types: explicit performative formulas, and sentence types, possibly alongside certain sentence adverbials.

(b) Explicit performative formulas are semantically just ordinary declarative sentences with the only peculiarity that they are in a sense token reflexive, viz., that the state of affairs they describe (i.e., make known to obtain) is just the speech act in which they are used.

(c) Sentence types distinguish different types of utterance meaning, which are normally (but not uniquely) related to certain types of illocutionary forces.

(d) The semantic components that distinguish different sentence types are attitude specifiers in the sense that they determine the basic cognitive attitude in which a certain state of affairs is conceived. Principle (46) characterizes the way in which attitudes determine the communicative sense in simple (or direct) cases.

In a sense, then, the task of characterizing semantic structures remains what it has been before the appearance of the speech act theory, although the speech act theory has clarified a great deal of what this task should be and how it relates to problems of language use in communication.

Notice, incidentally, that even if one does not accept the theory of attitudes considered here, (a) through (c) are still to be maintained. As noted above, Hausser (this volume) makes an explicit proposal to this effect.

I should finally point out that the semantically determined attitudes provide a fairly natural basis to develop a general theory of evaluation with truth values being a particularly basic mode. See Iwin (1975) for a general program of this type from a logical point of view. Adapting the proposals of Katz (1977, chapter 6) one might define truth conditions, compliance conditions, and answerhood conditions with respect to D, I, and Q, respectively and investigate the heritage of these conditions in various types of inferences. In this respect, examples like (54), which constitute a valid inference on the basis of Katz' analysis of questions and imperatives, but not on the one proposed here, seem to argue that my more traditional account of sentence types is the more adequate one.

(54) (a) Is John having a nightmare?
      (b) I ask you whether John is having a dream.

It is not difficult to show that with respect to a natural notion of inference the (b)-sentences should be derivable from the (a)-sentences in (55), but not in (54):

(55) (a) Is John having a nightmare?
      (b) Is John having a dream?

I have dealt now with all main topics of speech act theory mentioned in section 2, except the classification of illocutionary forces. It should be clear however that I don't take this to be a problem within the range of language, but rather within the range of communication. Lacking any serious theory of social interaction, one can only speculate what parameters are available and relevant for such a classification. I can easily imagine a large number of them (just as, say, sentences can be classified in a large number of dimensions such as complexity, number of terms, type of word order, and what not). What comes closest to the issues raised in this connection e.g., by Searle (1975) is the problem of finding a systematic account of the system ATT of basic attitudes. But that is a problem of utterance meaning, rather than communicative sense. Hence, if one accepts the conclusions (a)–(d) above (or even (a)–(c)), the classification of illocutionary forces is no longer a problem of linguistic analysis.

12. After all I have said so far I ought to refrain from writing this final section, as it is definitely outside the scope of language. I will nevertheless dare to sketch some of the lines along which a more complex communicative sense is to be analysed. In other words, I will mark some points of a putative theory of *SI*.[28]

The basic idea is rather simple: A meaningful activity *ma* as introduced in section 3 may have a series of layers in the communicative sense assigned to it, according to more and more inclusive interactional settings. Consider the following simple example:

(56) (a) ma: John raises his hand.
      (b) ias_1: A class room discussion.
          cs_1: John wants it to be recognized that he intends to say something.
      (c) ias_2: John's participation in the ongoing course and his relation to the teacher.
          cs_2: By indicating that he wants to say something John wants it to be known that he is carefully following the subject matter.
      (d) ias_3: John's participation in the course with respect to his future career.
          cs_3: By making the teacher aware that he is carefully following the subject matter, he intends to propose himself as a candidate for the next exam.
          etc.

We may consider (56) (b)–(d) as three interlocked communicative acts ca_1, ca_2, ca_3 with each being based on the success of its 'predecessor'. I do not claim that the characterization given in (56) is clear, complete, and adequate in any serious sense. In fact, I have no idea about how the structure of the pertinent ias_i and cs_i is to be specified. I just take (56) to be sufficiently suggestive to base on it the following general observations:

First, in a hierarchy of interlocked communicative acts an act ca_{i+1} is based on the success of ca_i. Second, the acts are based on each other in terms of their ias: ca_i is based on ca_{i-1} if ias_{i-1} is contained in ias_i. Hence a theory of social interaction has to specify what it means for the structure of an ias to be contained in the structure of some ias'. For the time being I can only rely on an intuitive understanding of this relation. Anyway, the difference ias' minus ias will be some interactional 'superstructure' in which ias is embedded. Third, any hierarchy of communicative acts must be based on a meaningful activity ma and a primary setting ias_1 which together determine the cs_1 of the ca_1. We can summarize these conditions in the following recursive definition of a generalized communicative act:

(D 6) $ca' = \langle ca, ias', cs' \rangle$ iff ias' contains the ias of ca

It is a matter of the underlying system SI of interactional schemes and rules to determine cs' on the basis of ias' and (the success of) ca, just as it has to determine the cs on the basis of ias and ma of the primary or basic act in the hierarchy. Let us assume that SI somehow defines a function F such that $F(ca, ias') = cs'$ holds for those pairs of interlocked acts ca and ca' which satisfy (D 6) with respect to a given system SI.

Turning now to speech acts, we only have to insert a meaningful utterance mu instead of the meaningful activity ma of the primary communicative act ca_1. The following observations are immediately forthfoming:

First, it is the principle (46) above that determines the cs of a speech act based on the meaningful utterance mu (with utterance meaning m) with respect to the primary setting ias_1.

Second, it is the primary speech act ca_1 with respect to which the particulat token reflexivity of explicit performatives holds: "I hereby ask you to come in." may have the (remote) cs that the speaker wants to talk to the addressee. The token reflexive "hereby" refers, however, to the act of asking to come in, not the act of indicating that the speaker wants to talk to the addressee.

Third, a completely natural account of what Searle (1975a) calls 'indirect speech acts' emerges: An indirect speech act is a complex ca, where the cs_i with $i > 1$ is focussed for one reason or another. As Searle observes, the primary cs_1 is not eliminated in such cases, but it is not paid separate attention. One might turn back to it if some higher ca_i fails to succeed: The indirect request "Can you pass the salt?" might appropriately be answered as a question by saying "Sorry, I can't". All of this immediately follows from the considerations implemented in (D 6).

For the sake of illustration, consider the following abbreviated verbal analogue to the non-verbal act described in (56):

(57)   (a) mu: The door is open.
       (b) cs_1: The speaker wants it to be recognized by the addressee that the door is open.
       (c) cs_2: The speaker wants the addressee (on the basis of succeeding with ca_1) to come in.
       (d) cs_3: The speaker wants the addressee to recognize (on the basis of succeeding with ca_2) that he proposes to have a talk.

. . .

I omit the indication of the pertinent ias_i since they would be vague and provisional anyway. The example makes clear, however, how utterances of our initial example can become a statement, a prediction, or a promise, and utterances of (57) (a) a statement, a request, and/or a proposal. Whether or not the various cs_i are to be related by the kind of implicit reasoning that Searle proposes (see note 17 above for a similar type of inference), might be left open. If so, it must be accounted for by the function F mentioned above, that has much wider application than just speech acts: One can easily write inference chains describing the conditions according to which a door keeper in a football game determines his behavior.

Notice, furthermore, that it is only with respect to the primary act ca_1 that — according to our initial approximation — the propositional content pc of the meaningful utterance determines something like the propositional content of cs_1. Whatever one might sort out as the propositional content of (57) (c) and (d), it is no longer determined by sem of (57) (a).

This treatment of indirect speech acts also brings out the fact that there are two completely different ways of 'not meaning literally what one says': One way is the creation of indirect speech acts by relying on different ias as just discussed. The other is the creation of metaphoric or figurative meaning, which is based on assigning non-literal utterance meanings m on the basis of the utterance context ct. See Bierwisch 1979 for some discussion of this distinction.

I will add one final feature to the framework outlined so far, in order to account for the fact that two or more communicative acts may jointly serve to establish one more complex act. This kind of combination (which is completely general anyway) is needed in order to deal with complex acts like uttering (58) and simultaneously handing over a book:

(58)   I hereby return you the *Principia Mathematica*.

The combination in question would be accounted for by the following definition:

(D 7) $ca' = \langle\langle ca_1, \ldots, ca_n\rangle, ias', cs'\rangle$ iff ias' contains ias_i of ca_i for $1 \leqslant i \leqslant n$ and $n \geqslant 1$.

The framework we have arrived at by now is at least as much in need of elaboration as of restriction; it is both too unspecific and too narrow. It is meant only to indicate what kind of problems have to be faced if the embedding of language into social interaction is to be taken seriously. One of the most intricate extensions required in this respect is the incorporation of the structure of a communicative act into that of an interaction involving two or more participants mutually determining the interactional setting they are operating in.

The hierarchical structure of communicative acts which I have sketched can be schematized in a straightforward way to bring out quite clearly the analogy with the plans of complex behavior developed by Miller, Galanter, Pribram (1960) on the basis of elementary building blocks called TOTE-units.

Let a simple box represent the *ias* of a certain *ca*. We may then represent a meaningful activity by a box that is placed within the *ias* thereby popping up a particular *cs* on the basis of the underlying rules of *SI*. The resulting figure (59) can now be taken to represent the complete communicative act *ca*:

(59)

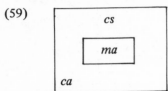

According to (D 6) this *ca* can now be placed within an encompassing *ias'*, and so on. We thus get complex structures like (60):

(60)

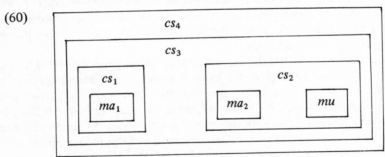

The same type of schematization can be used to represent the different way in which the utterance meaning *m* of a meaningful utterance *mu* is determined with respect to its context *ct*:

(61)

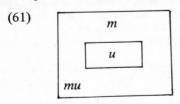

If we expand the *mu* in a communicative act *ca* in the way indicated in (60), we have to consider the following problem: The *ct* of *mu* and the *ias* of the embedding *ca* may actually overlap, i.e., a part of the communicative setting can be a part of the utterance context and vice versa. (The notion 'part of' must be understood in the sense of 'belonging to' suggested above.) For a simple case this can still be represented in a two dimensional diagram:

(62)

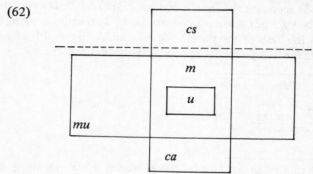

The limits of this type of representation are obvious. But it indicates to some extent how the component parts of a simple speech act may be interrelated. The dotted line marks, in a somewhat artifical way, the borderline between language and communication.

I do not want to give the impression that the proposals presented here can in any serious sense replace the insights gained in the development of the speech act theory. They simply rearrange them in a way which seems to me somewhat more perspicuous with respect to the place they should have in a sufficiently broad framework that allows one to pursue the relevant problems in accord with their genuine nature. The results of this rearrangement should have consequences, however, for both linguistics and philosophy of language.

NOTES

* The ideas presented here have profited, among others, from discussions with Monika Doherty, Roland Hausser, Karl-Erich Heidolph, Jerry Katz, Ferenc Kiefer, Ewald Lang, Wolfgang Motsch, John Searle, Anna Szabolcsi, and Dieter Wunderlich. The different views are too obvious from the text to require the usual comment on the author's responsibility.
[1] For revisions of these distinctions like those proposed in Searle (1969), slightly different correspondences can be established; such modifications do not change the point at issue, though.

[2] Notice that (C 1) is dependent on the particular assumptions about syntactic structures that have to be justified empirically. Hence (C 1) is not meant to exclude e.g., the well motivated assumption that imperatives like "come in!" have semantically a second person subject. I need not go into details here.

[3] Notice that G is a system of rules according to which the elements of L are to be built up, which are themselves complex rules. Hence the usual assumption that language behavior is a rule governed activity veils two crucially different, though interrelated aspects: application of the rules of G in order to determine an ls, and application of the complex rule ls in performing an utterance. Grammarians are primarily concerned with the first aspect, philosophers like e.g., Wittgenstein, construing the meaning of a word as a rule to use it, concentrate on the second aspect.

[4] I don't bother about the question whether a particular subsystem of communication is to be sorted out within SI. Although there are certainly rules and conditions that are specifically designed for communicative interaction, it is also obvious that there are rules and principles that determine all kinds of social interaction. A case in point is what Grice (1975) has expressed as the cooperative principle and the maxims derived from it. A fairly different example is the structure of social institutions, like school, factory, restaurant, etc. which determine the communicative sense e.g., of certain gestures or utterances, but by the same token also a large range of practical interaction.

[5] The proposals of Motsch (this volume) can be viewed as an attempt to specify just one aspect of the involved rules and structures. Also an important part of the speech act rules as discussed e.g., in Searle (1969) would have to be incorporated here.

[6] This reduction of assertive (i.e., constative) speech acts to their truth condition has been taken over in one way or the other by almost all later treatments. Lewis (1972) and Katz (1977) are otherwise rather different examples.

[7] Actually, sem is identified with cs in the case of what Katz calls the null context. Besides the problematic character of this notion, there are two further problems with Katz' position. First he does not distinguish between what I have called the context ct of an utterance and the interactional setting ias of a speech act. He thus lumps together ct and ias in one global notion, thereby participating in the conflation of language and communication. Second, Katz assumes the utterance meaning m to be identical to the semantic structure sem if ct is null, thereby ignoring the principal distinction between sentence meaning and utterance meaning. What is required here is the notion of a neutral context ct_0 instead of the null context, where ct_0 specifies all and only that information that would be necessary for sem to determine an utterance meaning. ct_0 would by and large be determined by the semantic presupposition of a sentence. I will not pursue this suggestion here any further. For some discussion of the problems involved see Bierwisch (1979), and also Searle (this volume, pp. 221–232) for a similar line of argument.

[8] See e.g., Heal (1977), Katz (1977), Lewis (1972), Stampe (1975) for pertinent discussion. Notice, incidentally, that position (A) is blocked by condition (C 1) above, if it is to be taken as an account of the illocutionary aspect at all: Either the underlying performative frame that (A) requires for a sentence like "I'll come" is in accord with (C 1). Then it must be some constant formula, say "I tell you that . . ." But this is empirically inadequate, as it would wrongly interpret assertions, promises, warnings etc. as being performatively identical. Or·else there are various different frames in the underlying structure of "I'll come", but that would violate any reasonable interpretation of (C 1).

[9] That is, by the way, the gist of the treatment that Katz (1977, p. 177 ff.) proposes

32

MANFRED BIERWISCH

in order to "save Austin from Austin": having different semantic structures, (12) and (13) are said to be pragmatically equivalent under certain conditions. The flaw with this proposal is that it construes the use of (12) which makes it similar to the normal use of (13) as a kind of non-literal meaning, since 'literally' (12) determines an assertion about the speaker saying that the earth is flat, not an assertion about the flatness of the earth. Although the latter point is in a sense correct, I would still not consider the use of (12) as an assertion that the earth is flat to be 'non-literal'. It is just one of the normal communicative senses that can be assigned to an utterance of (12).

[10] In fact, (B 1) is a formulation of what Austin (1962) calls the 'descriptive fallacy'. It is Austin's fallacy that he never considered the possibility of (B 2).

[11] Searle (1975) clearly distinguishes between the task of classifying illocutionary acts and illocutionary verbs. But in Searle (1969) he explicitly invoked the 'principle of expressibility' as a methodological means to reduce the analysis of speech acts to that of illocutionary verbs. A large number of papers have been trapped precisely by this spurious bridge.

[12] This view seems to be almost irresistible. Thus Wunderlich (1976, p. 64 ff.) develops a framework resembling that proposed in section 3 above in many respects. He nevertheless states in Wunderlich (1977, p. 244): "Each speech act concept of L, i.e., generic speech act of L, will be identified with the meaning of certain sentences of L." Thus speech acts are supposed to belong to language, rather than to communication.

[13] Notice that the different interpretation of "give up" in (15) and (16) as well as the different concreteness of "money" does not turn on a semantic ambiguity. It is rather a difference on the level of utterance meaning. Hence being an illocutionary verb is a property that is determined on the semantic level in cases like "tell", "name", "ask", but only on the level of utterance meaning in cases like "give up", "give" (cf. "he gave check", "he gave the permission", etc.) and others. Actually, the classification is even more complicated: while "ask" is strictly illocutionary, "warn" is strictly communicative, but not necessarily bound to verbal communication; verbs like "donate" are strictly interactional, involving (verbal) communication only optionally. These remarks by no means exhaust the relevant distinctions.

[14] In this sense, Katz (1977) and especially Miller and Johnson-Laird (1976, p. 619–664) give a fairly detailed and systematic exemplification of a componential analysis of verbs of communication. In Bierwisch (in press) I have argued that this type of analysis can profitably be reconstructed in terms of possible worlds semantics mentioned earlier.

[15] Notice that this analysis does not fall under the 'descriptive fallacy' which would ascribe truth instead of felicity, rather than truth together with felicity. Hence my analysis differs from a proposal made by Bach (1975) who argues that explicit performatives are statements whose additional illocutionary force is derived by applying an inferential procedure based on Gricean principles of cooperation.

[16] The phenomenon appearing in Lewis' example can actually be used for highly interesting purposes in poetry. Thus I found the following lines in *Die Zeit der Wunder* by the German poet Stephan Hermlin:

Die Zeit der Wunder ist vorbei. Hinter den Ecken
Versanken Bogenlampensonnen. Ungenau
Gehen die Uhren, die mit ihrem Schlag uns schrecken,
Und in der Dämmrung sind die Katzen wieder grau.
Die Abendstunde schlägt für Händler und für Helden.

Wie dieser Vers stockt das Herz, und es erstickt der Schrei.
Die Mauerzeichen und die Vogelflüge melden:
Die Jugend ging. Die Zeit der Wunder ist vorbei.
These are fairly regular jambic hexameters, except for the half verse italicized by the author, which is intentionally irregular, thereby performing what the words say.

[17] I refrain from giving semi-formal accounts in terms of implicit reasons like

In uttering (30) the speaker states that his wife wants him to greet me.
I assume that he is stating sincerely.
Hence his wife wants him to greet me.
Making someone aware of the intention to greet him is an act of greeting.
Now the speaker makes me aware of his wife's intention to this effect by uttering (30).
Hence his uttering (30) counts as an act of (i.e. has the communicative sense of) transferring his wife's greetings.

Such deductions, which are fairly widespread in the literature, are but an intuitive anticipation of parts of the required theory of social interaction, insofar as they are to the point at all. Though they might be revealing as a preliminary characterization of the problems at hand, their status as an account of the actual rules and structures involved is fairly dubious.

[18] I am ignoring here speech acts not based on sentences at all, although I claim that they also follow the principle developed here, namely determination of cs by m and ias. Consider e.g., vocatives like "Alexander!" whose cs is to make a particular person aware of being addressed. Now, the utterance meaning m of "Alexander" is to identify (or to refer to) a particular person, and the ias of the meaningful utterance determines the pertinent interactional effect. A non-verbal communicative act such as touching someone's shoulder combines precisely these two components: the person to be addressed is identified and made aware of the intention in question.

[19] In fact, the whole approach of Katz is much less different from that of Lewis than their respective comments and formalisms make it appear. Katz' formal apparatus somewhat obscures the fact that the converted condition is nothing but a kind of truth condition that is satisfied if and only if the sentence is used to perform the speech act it describes. As he assumes this to be guaranteed in what he calls the null context (cf. Note 7 above in this respect), the communicative sense becomes, moreover, a matter of semantic structure.

[20] As Fodor (1977, p. 52 f.) points out it would also be queer to reject an inappropriate use of (35') by saying "that is false" which should be possible on Lewis' account (or rather on one way to interpret it), but is excluded on Katz' account, as Katz does not claim a normal utterance of (35') to be based on truth conditions. As I have said earlier, objectons, replies, comments, etc. are (primarily) directed towards the communicative sense, not the utterance meaning of a speech act: hence a normal, though infelicitous use of (35') should naturally be objected to on the level of its cs by uttering something like (38), rather than on the level of utterance meaning by uttering "that is false", which it (irrelevantly) is, if the speaker does not succeed in ordering.

[21] The two steps of forming a thought (Gedankenfassen) and judging (Urteilen) must not be construed as a temporal sequence, but rather as an inherent dependency. In fact, to contemplate a thought without evaluating its truth is rather a derived than a primary psychological situation.

[22] In a sense, then, a judgement is a proposition plus the truth value assigned to it. Wittgenstein (1922), who identified 'Satz' and 'Gedanke' from a logical point of view, therefore remarked correctly: "Frege's 'Urteilsstrich' ist logisch ganz bedeutungslos; er zeigt bei Frege (und Russell) nur an, daß diese Autoren die so bezeichneten Sätze für wahr halten. '⊢' gehört daher ebensowenig zum Satzgefüge, wie die Nummer eines Satzes. Ein Satz kann unmöglich von sich selbst aussagen, daß er wahr ist" (Tractatus 4.442). An utterance, however, is interpreted by a person p, and hence it is subject to an attitude toward the state of affairs it identifies.

[23] Actually, this is an oversimplification, as it ignores attitudes not determined by sentence types, like hypothesizing, expecting, etc. As Doherty (personal communication) observes, various German modal particles like "wohl", "doch", "ja" and also various sentence adverbials are indicators of such attitudes. This seems to be born out, among others, by their co-occurrence restrictions with respect to particular sentence types.

[24] There are plenty of problems, of course, with respect to the determination of scope in WH-questions. But these have to be solved anyway, they are not created by the analysis proposed here. They are, moreover, part of the structure of pc, i.e., within the scope of Qu, technically speaking. This follows from what I have called the basic or pre-reflexive character of the attitudes. Syntactically, both Imp and Qu might be bound to the COMP-constituent (the 'complementizer' in the sense of Chomsky (1977)) of the topmost clause of a sentence.

[25] I say 'normally' in order to leave open the possibility to have structures like ⟨Hyp, pc⟩ for declarative sentences, where Hyp determines an attitude of hypothesizing, this being the semantic effect of modal particles, or sentence adverbials like "probably".

[26] At first glance, the indicative mood seems to be a candidate for this type of operator. Notice, however, that it can appear as the unmarked mood in practically all subordinate clauses having no attitude specifier at all. On the other hand, there seem to be empirical data apt to relativize Frege's observation. Ewald Lang has pointed out to me that e.g., the sentence final particle yè in Classical Chinese displays distributional properties and communicative functions which make it a rather direct judgement operator. (See also the revealing characterization this particle is given in von der Gabelentz (1883, p. 316): "Satzschließendes yè ist constatierend, aber unübersetzbar.") On closer inspection, similar conclusions might turn out to hold with respect to the nature of Θe, ti in Modern Burmese, and possibly other particles in various languages.

[27] Although I take "I want" to be a closer parallel to the semantic impact of the imperative, nothing depends particularly on this assumption. If you consider "I request" or "I order" to be closer to the imperative, much the same argument applies to those paraphrases.

[28] As will be seen immediately, the aspect I am concerned with is even more general than social interaction. It concerns in fact the structure of all purposive behavior. And my proposals will be nothing but an adaptation of certain general notions as developed e.g., in Miller, Galanter, Pribram (1960).

REFERENCES

Austin, J. L.: 1962, *How to do Things with Words*, Oxford.
Bach, K.: 1975, 'Performatives are Statements Too', *Philosophical Studies* 28, 229–236.

Bierwisch, M.: 1979, 'Wörtliche Bedeutung: Eine pragmatische Gretchenfrage', *Linguistische Studien* 60, hrsg. ZISW der AdW der DDR, Berlin, pp. 48–80, also in G. Grewendorf (ed.), *Sprechakttheorie und Semantik*, Frankfurt, M., pp. 119–148.

Bierwisch, M.: (in press), 'Utterance Meaning and Mental States', F. Klix (ed.) *Memory and Cognition, Proceedings of the 1978 Symposium*, Berlin.

Chomsky, N.: 1965, *Aspects of the Theory of Syntax*, Cambridge, Mass.

Chomsky, N.: 1977, *Essays on Form and Interpretation*, New York, Amsterdam, Oxford.

Cole P. and J. L. Morgan (eds.): 1975, *Syntax and Semantics Vol. 3 Speech Acts*, New York, San Francisco, London.

Cresswell, M. J.: 1973, *Logics and Languages*, London.

Fodor, J. D.: 1977, *Semantics: Theories of Meaning in Generative Grammar*, New York.

Frege, G.: 1973, 'Einleitung in die Logik', *Schriften zur Logik* Berlin, pp. 75–92.

von der Gabelentz, G.: 1883, *Chinesische Grammatik*, Leipzig.

Grice, P.: 1975, 'Logic and Conversation', in *Cole and Morgan*, pp. 41–58.

Hausser, R.: 1980, 'Surface Compositionality and the Semantics of Mood', this volume, pp. 71–96.

Heal, J.: 1977, 'Ross and Lakoff on Declarative Sentences', *Studies in Language, Vol. 3*, pp. 337–362.

Iwin, A. A.: 1975, *Grundlagen der Logik von Wertungen*, Berlin.

Kasher, Asa: 1971, 'A Step toward a Theory of Linguistic Performance', in: Bar-Hillel (ed.), *Pragmatics of Natural Languages*, Dordrecht, Holland, pp. 84–93.

Katz, J. J.: 1977, *Propositional Structure and Illocutionary Force*, New York.

Lewis, D.: 1972, 'General Semantics', in Davidson and Harman (eds.), *Semantics of Natural Language*, Dordrecht, Holland, pp. 169–218.

Miller, G. A., E. Galanter, and K. H. Pribram: 1960, *Plans and the Structure of Behavior*, New York.

Miller, G. A., and P. N. Johnson-Laird: 1976, *Language and Perception*, Cambridge, London, Melbourne.

Motsch, W.: 1980, 'Situational Context and Illocutionary Force,' this volume, pp. 155–168.

Searle, J. R.: 1969, *Speech Acts*, Cambridge.

Searle, J. R.: 1975, 'A Taxonomy of Illocutionary Acts,' in Gunderson (ed.), *Language, Mind, and Knowledge*, Minnesota Studies in the Philosophy of Science, Vol. VII, Minneapolis, pp. 344–369.

Searle, J. R.: 1975a, 'Indirect Speech Acts,' in Cole and Morgan, pp. 59–82.

Searle, J. R.: 1980, 'The Background of Meaning', this volume, 221–232.

Stampe, D. W.: 1975, 'Meaning and Truth in the Theory of Speech Acts,' in Cole and Morgan, pp. 1–40.

Wittgenstein, L.: 1922, *Tractatus logico-philosophicus*, London.

Wunderlich, D.: 1976, *Studien zur Sprechakttheorie*, Frankfurt.

Wunderlich, D.: 1977, 'On Problems of Speech Act Theory,' in Butts and Hintikka (eds.), *Basic Problems in Methodology and Linguistics*, Dordrecht, Holland, pp. 243–258.

STEVEN DAVIS

PERLOCUTIONS*

Suppose that in normal circumstances in a loud and forceful tone of voice I say to you 'There's a spider on your lap' and that because of what I say you become frightened. In saying what I have said I have told you that there is a spider on your lap, and by saying what I have said I have frightened you. I have, it would seem, performed several different acts. I have said something; I have told you something; and I have frightened you. In J.L. Austin's nomenclature I have performed, respectively, a locutionary act, an illocutionary act, and a perlocutionary act. These do not exhaust the acts I have performed. Within the locutionary act Austin further distinguishes three other acts, two of which, the phonetic act and the phatic act, I will describe here.[1] A phonetic act is the act of uttering certain noises and the phatic act is the act of uttering certain sounds which belong to a language and uttering them as belonging to that language. In this case uttering 'There's a spider on your lap' is the performance of a phonetic act and uttering it with the recognition that it is a sentence of English is a phatic act.

John Searle has persuasively argued that there is no real distinction to be drawn between locutionary and illocutionary acts and that the former is a species of the latter.[2] According to Austin, 'I said to you that there's a spider on your lap', reports a locutionary act. But as Searle shows, saying that something is the case meets all the tests for an illocutionary act. This still leaves us, however, with a distinction among phonetic, phatic, illocutionary, and perlocutionary acts.[3] But Austin's main concern in *How to Do Things with Words* is with the illocutionary act and he uses these other acts to contrast with it.[4] Despite this, I would like to focus attention on perlocutions. I have two reasons for doing so. First, they are especially interesting for certain issues arising in current action theory. There are those, like Donald Davidson, who argue that in the example above I have performed one action which can be described in different ways and there are others, like Alvin Goldman, who claim that I have performed different actions of the sort which Austin discriminates.[5] The distinction between illocutionary and perlocutionary

*A version of this paper was delivered at a conference on speech acts and pragmatics at Dobogoko, Hungary. I would like to thank Annette Baier, Charles E. Caton, David Copp and the referee of *Linguistics and Philosophy* for many valuable suggestions for improving this paper.

J. R. Searle, F. Kiefer, and M. Bierwisch (eds.), Speech Act Theory and Pragmatics, 37–55.
Copyright © 1979 by D. Reidel Publishing Company.

acts provides, I believe, a particularly clear test case for adjudicating
between these different positions. Second, I think that a proper understanding of perlocutionary acts will throw some light on the complex
phenomena involved in communication. In this paper I shall have little
to say about the former issue, but I hope to be able to say a bit more
about the latter problem.

I shall begin by presenting what Austin takes perlocutions to be. He
tells us that

> Saying something will often, or even normally, produce certain consequential effects upon
> the feelings, thoughts or actions of the audience, or of the speaker, or of other persons:
> and it may be done with the design, intention, or purpose of producing them; and we may
> then say, thinking of this, that the speaker has performed an act in the nomenclature of
> which reference is made either. . ., only obliquely, or even. . ., not at all, to the performance
> of the locutionary or illocutionary act. We shall call the performance of an act of this kind
> the performance of a 'perlocutionary' act, and the act performed. . . a 'perlocution'.[6]

It might seem from this quotation that a necessary condition for a
perlocutionary act to be performed is that it be done intentionally. But
Austin makes it clear, elsewhere, that there is no such requirement.

> Since our acts are actions, we must always remember the distinction between producing
> effects or consequences which are intended or unintended;. . . and when [The speaker]
> does not intend to produce it or intends not to produce it it may nevertheless occur. To
> cope with [this] complication. . . we involve the normal linguistic devices of disclaiming
> (adverbs like 'unintentionally' and so on) which we hold ready for general use in all cases
> of doing actions.[7]

And, Austin claims "it is in connexion with perlocution that it is most
prominent. . . .".[8] However, there is a necessary condition for the performance of perlocutionary acts which can be drawn from this quotation.
A speaker performs a perlocutionary act only if

(1)   The speaker's saying something produces an effect on the
         feelings, thoughts, or actions of his audience, other persons, or
         himself.

To have a clearer understanding of (1), I shall reformulate it as containing
three features:

(2)   (i) The speaker's saying something,
         (ii) The occurrence of an effect on the feelings, thoughts or
         actions of the speaker's audience, of the speaker or of other
         persons,

(iii) A causal connection between (2)(i) and (ii).

To have a suitable nomenclature for the issues that arise here I shall introduce the following terms:

(3)   (i) 'S's saying something' designates a *perlocutionary cause*.
          (ii) 'H's X-ing' designates a *perlocutionary effect*.
          (iii) 'S's causing H to X' designates a *perlocutionary act*.

S and H designate speaker and hearer respectively and x is a variable ranging over linguistic expressions which, when substituted for x, preserve grammaticality. (3)(i) and (3)(ii) correspond to Austin's (2)(i) and (2)(ii). The terminology in (3) might mislead one into thinking that perlocutionary causes produce perlocutionary acts. This would be mistaken, for my telling you that there is a spider on your lap does not cause my frightening you, rather it causes you to be frightened. That is, perlocutionary causes bring about perlocutionary effects, not perlocutionary acts.

What are perlocutionary causes? It would appear from Austin's nomenclature that Austin intends them to be locutionary acts which produce *per*locutionary effects. Moreover, Austin tells us that

To use the 'by saying' formula as a test of an act being perlocutionary, we must first be sure... that 'saying' is being used... in the full sense of a locutionary act.[9]

Austin takes it, then, that 'S's saying something' designates a locutionary act. However, there is evidence that Austin, also, holds that illocutionary acts may be perlocutionary causes. In giving examples of perlocutionary acts Austin claims that

You may, for example, deter me... from doing something by informing me.. what the consequences of doing it would be... [Or] you may convince me... that she is an adultress by asking her whether it was her handkerchief which was in X's bedroom...[10]

Your deterring me from doing something and your convincing me that she is an adultress are perlocutionary acts. In turn these acts are achieved by, respectively, your informing me and your asking her a question, both of which Austin takes to be illocutionary acts. It appears, then, that Austin regards both locutionary and illocutionary acts to perlocutionary causes. But, since Searle has shown conclusively that locutionary acts are a species of illocutionary acts, what remains of Austin's position is that perlocutionary causes are illocutionary acts.

However, I believe that there is more to the story than this. There are many other things, including other acts, which may in the appropriate circumstances bring about the same perlocutionary effects as would an illocutionary act. And it might, then, be appropriate in such a case to attribute to the speaker an act which would appear to be a perlocutionary act. Let us consider some examples. Suppose you are frightened by anyone's uttering a sound and I say 'There's a spider on your lap'. Then,

(4)   By uttering the sound 'There's a spider on your lap', I frightened you.

Or suppose you are frightened by anyone's uttering an English sentence and I say 'There's a spider on your lap', uttering it as an English sentence. Then,

(5)   By uttering the English sentence 'There's a spider on your lap', I frighten you.

Or suppose you are frightened by my mentioning spiders or referring to your lap and I say ' There's a spider on your lap'. Then,

(6)   By saying that there's a spider on your lap and in so doing mentioning spiders or referring to your lap, I frighten you.

And finally suppose that what frightens you is my telling you that there's a spider on your lap and I do so. Then,

(7)   By telling you that there's a spider on your lap I frighten you.

In (4) I frighten you by performing a phonetic act, in (5) by performing a phatic act, in (6) by performing what Searle calls propositional acts and in (7) by performing an illocutionary act.[11] These do not exhaust the ways in which I can frighten you by saying something. You might correctly take me, when I say 'There's a spider on your lap', to be suggesting that you should leave and this, in turn, frightens you. There are even more farfetched cases. Suppose you are blind and deaf and I say 'There's a spider on your lap' causing a stream of air to hit your face which frightens you. In all these cases and in (4)–(7), I frighten you by saying something and hence, they all appear to be perlocutionary acts.

Should a perlocutionary act, then, be any act which involves an effect on the speaker's audience which can be brought about by any feature of the speech situation, including such things as sounds, noises and puffs of air? I believe that it is Austin's intention to rule these out and to restrict perlocutionary acts to only some of those mentioned above. Evidence for this is found in his claim that in the performance of a perlocutionary act it is the feelings, thoughts and actions of *persons* which are changed by the speaker's saying something. There does not appear on the surface to be a good reason for this restriction, for I can frighten or startle a dog, a cat, or even a goldfish by saying something. And it would seem that these acts of mine should be classified as perlocutionary acts.

Austin's reason for restricting perlocutionary effects to persons is contained in his views about the relationship between the speaker's saying something and the effect it has on his audience.

... The sense in which saying something produces effects on other persons, or *causes* things, is a fundamentally different sense of cause from that used in physical causation by pressure, etc. It has to operate through the conventions of language and is a matter of influence exerted by one person on another: this is probably the original sense of 'cause'.[12]

In the above quotation, Austin claims that there are two senses of 'cause', a physical and a non-physical sense, and it is the latter which is relevant to his discussion of the relationship between illocutions and perlocutions. Moreover, he holds that the way in which our saying something non-physically causes effects on hearers is by operating through the conventions of language. However, it is not very clear what Austin means by 'the conventions of language'. Rather than attempt to give an interpretation of what Austin means, I will reformulate his claim. When a speaker/hearer knows how to speak and understand his language there are various kinds of knowledge he posesses by virtue of which he is competent in that language. Borrowing a term from Chomsky, let us call this knowledge the speaker's linguistic competence. For Chomsky, this includes tacit knowledge of the phonological, semantical, and syntactical rules of the language which constitute a grammar of that language. I shall broaden 'linguistic competence' to include knowledge of the rules which govern the use of language. That is, in addition to a grammar, a speaker konws the rules which govern the performance of illocutionary and propositional acts. To reformulate Austin's point we can replace 'conventions of language' with 'linguistic competence'. Hence, Austin's thesis is that for a perlocutionary act to be performed a speaker's saying something must produce an effect on the hearer through linguistic competence.

There are two respects in which linguistic competence plays a role in the production of a perlocutionary act. Firstly, the speaker uses his competence to say what he does and secondly, the hearer's use of his competence is involved in the production of an effect on him. To illustrate this let us reconsider our example. Suppose that in saying to you 'There's a spider on your lap' I use my knowledge of the grammar of English, of the maxims governing conversation, and of the rules for telling someone something and for referring to something. If I do this success-fully, I have, thereby, told you that there's a spider on your lap. Let us suppose further that you understand that I have told you that there's a spider on your lap by using your linguistic competence. And consequently, because of what you understand you become frightened. In such a case by telling you that there's a spider on your lap, I have frightened you and in so doing, I have performed a perlocutionary act. Let us add, then, as a necessary condition for a speaker's performing a perlocutionary act that both the speaker's and hearer's linguistic competence is involved in the performance of the act. That is,

(8) S's causing H to A by saying something is the performance of a perlocutionary act only if
        (i) for S to say what he does must use his linguistic competence
        (ii) for H to A he must use his linguistic competence.

(8), of course, excludes a speaker's frightening a goldfish by saying something from the class of perlocutionary acts, since fish do not have linguistic competence.

Corresponding to (8), we can provide a necessary condition for an act of saying something's being a perlocutionary cause.

(9) S's saying something is a perlocutionary cause only if S must use his linguistic competence to say what he does.

(9) does not exclude illocutionary acts from the class of perlocutionary causes, since a speaker must use his linguistic competence to perform such acts. But does it exclude phonetic and phatic acts from being perlocutionary causes? This depends on the theory of act individuation we accept. On Goldman's view it does, but on Davidson's it does not. For Goldman when a speaker performs an illocutionary act, and in doing so performs a phonetic and a phatic act, he has performed three distinct acts. And all that is required for the successful performance of a phonetic act is that the speaker utters a sound, which can be ac-

complished without the use of his linguistic competence. A bit more is
necessary for the performance of a phatic act. The speaker must utter a
grammatical construction belonging to a certain language and as belonging to that language. But, this can be done by mimicking what someone
said and by knowing that what he said belongs to a particular language,
neither of which requires any competence in that language. Consequently,
according to Goldman's theory of act individuation, since phonetic and
phatic acts can be performed without the speaker's utilizing his linguistic
competence, these acts cannot be perlocutionary causes. On Davidson's
theory of act individuation, when a speaker performs an illocutionary
act which has a perlocutionary effect, he has performed one act which
can be described as a phonetic or phatic act. Since an act correctly
described as an illocutionary act requires for its performance a speaker's
using his linguistic competence, so, too, does the act described as a
phonetic or phatic act. For there is only one act and whatever is so
required for its performance is required no matter how we describe it.
Consequently, on Davidson's theory of act individuation phonetic and
phatic acts can be perlocutionary causes. In addition on either theory of
act individuation there are other acts which can be perlocutionary
causes. For example, propositional acts, such as referring and acts like
joking, hinting, and telling a story require for their performance and
understanding the use of linguistic competence.

I think we are now in a position to understand Austin's remark that
the way in which perlocutionary effects are produced is a matter of the
influence of one person on another. One of the ways people influence or
try to influence one another is through saying something. And when this
influence is achieved it is most commonly acheived because the person
influenced uses his linguistic competence to understand what is said. Of
course 'influence' is not quite the right word here. Suppose I tell you that
it is raining and because of this, you come to believe that it is raining.
Now, I would, thereby have brought it about that you believe that it is
raining, which is, I think, a perfectly good example of a perlocutionary
act. But in bringing this about I have not exerted any influence on you.
However, Austin's central point remains, for commonly in such a case
you would come to believe that it is raining in part because you understood what I said. And you understood what I said in part because of
your linguistic competence.

Austin introduces perlocutionary acts to contrast them with illocutionary acts. I would now like to consider some of the differences
between these two speech acts. It might be thought that one difference is
that perlocutionary acts, but not illocutionary acts involve effects.

However, Austin argues that illocutionary acts are also connected to effects, although not in the same way in which perlocutionary acts are. According to Austin, illocutionary acts are connected to effects in three ways. They must secure uptake; they take effect; and they invite a response or sequel.[13]

Austin claims that for an illocutionary act to be happily or successfully performed it must secure what he calls *uptake*. This is achieved when the speaker's audience hears what he says and takes it in a certain sense, that is, when the speaker gets his audience to understand the meaning and the force of what he says.[14] To be more precise S performs illocutionary act A in uttering p, only if uptake is achieved. And uptake is achieved if and only if

(10)　　　(i) H hears p
　　　　　(ii) H understands what S means by p
　　　　　(iii) H understands what illocutionary act, namely A, which S means to perform in uttering p.

For example, a witness at a trial has not correctly been sworn in unless his oath is heard and it is taken as an oath. Nor will the chair have vetoed a motion at a meeting, assuming that he is in a position to do so, unless the others at the metting hear what he says and take it as a veto. However, not all illocutionary acts require hearer uptake for their performance. I can ask a question without anyone understanding that I have done so. Perhaps what is required is that the speaker intends that uptake be secured. But even this does not seem to be necessary, since as Austin points out, illocutionary acts can be performed unintentionally. For example, a witness might blurt out a state secret, unintentionally, when questioned at a hearing. And certainly the witness does not intend that his audience understands what he means by what he says.[15]

Uptake, or at least something like it, is required for the successful performance of a perlocutionary act. I have not frightened you in the requisite way by telling you that there's a spider on your lap, unless you hear my words and your being frightened is caused by what you understand by my words. However, you need not understand what I mean by my words. Suppose you take it that I have asked you whether it is a snake on your lap and this frightens you.[16] In such a case it would still be true that I have frightened you by telling you that there's a spider on your lap. Hence perlocutionary acts require for their performance hearer 'uptake' of what the speaker says. And perlocutionary 'uptake' of a speaker's A-ing that p is achieved if and only if

(11)   (i) H understands something by p
          (ii) H understands S to perform some illocutionary act in
          uttering p.

According to Austin, the second way that illocutionary acts differ
from perlocutionary acts is that the former 'take effect'. For example,
my saying

'I name this ship the *Queen Elizabeth*' has the effect of naming or christening the ship;
then certain subsequent acts such as referring to it as the *Generalissimo Stalin* will be out
of order.[17]

In this quotation there are two features that Austin attributes to illocutionary acts which must be distinguished. First, as a result of my naming
the ship the *Queen Elizabeth*, the ship has that name. That is, my act of
naming makes it a fact that the ship has the name that it does. Second,
once the ship has a name, then it is incorrect to call it by another name.
There are other illocutionary acts of this sort such as appointing someone to a position, vetoing a motion, and finding someone guilty or
innocent. In each of these cases the performance of an illocutionary act
brings about certain institutional facts, a ship having a name, someone's
having a position, etc.[18] However, not every illocutionary act brings
about such institutional facts and makes other acts 'out of order', for
example, asking a question or telling someone something.

Finally, Austin claims that illocutionary acts in contrast to perlocutionary acts "... invite by convention a response or sequel".[19] The
response or sequel can be on the part of the speaker or hearer. For
example, if I order you to do something, then I seek your obedience,
while if I promise you something, then you expect me to carry out my
promise. The way in which ordering and obeying and promising and
fulfilling a promise are related by convention is complicated. But it is
unnecessary to discuss the issue here, since not all illocutionary acts
"invite by convention a response". No response need be forthcoming if
I tell you that it is raining or deny what you said. Consequently, this
does not provide a criterion for distinguishing illocutionary from perlocutionary acts.

To summarize these points, Austin claims that illocutionary acts are
connected to effects in three ways: securing uptake, taking effect, and
inviting a response which distinguishes them from perlocutionary acts. I
have argued against this that these three features do not apply to all
illocutionary acts and so cannot be used to mark off illocutionary from
perlocutionary acts.

Austin maintains that another feature distinguishing illocutionary and
perlocutionary acts is that the former are conventional, but the latter are
not. Further, he holds that an illocutionary act "...may... be said to be
conventional, in the the sense that at least it could be made explicit by
the performative formula; but [a perlocutionary act] could not".[20] There
are two theses about perlocutions that must be kept separate. The first
is that perlocutionary acts are not conventional and the second is that
they cannot be made explicit by the use of the explicit performative
fórmula. I believe the second, but not the first of these theses to be
correct. There is a sense, I shall argue, in which some perlocutionary
acts are conventional.

Explicit performative verb formulas are in the first person, present
tense, indicative, active. Examples of such phrases are:

> (12)   (i) *I promise* that I'll be there.
>   (ii) *I tell* you that there's a spider on your lap.
>   (iii) *I request* that you tell me the time.

There are two views, due to Strawson and Searle, about how these
phrases function in the successful performance of an illocutionary act.
On Strawson's theory their purpose is to make explicit a complex
Gricean intention of the speaker, while on Searle's view they invoke a
set of rules constituting part of the meaning of these phrases. Exactly
how use of these phrases enters into the successful performance of an
illocutionary act is complicated, a complication which we need not
consider here. However, what is important for our purposes is that on
either theory the connection between these phrases and on the one hand
Gricean intentions and on the other linguistic rules is a matter of
linguistic convention.[21] Moreover, the sense in which promising,
requesting and telling are conventional is that the means of performing
these acts by using explicit performative verb formulas involves linguistic conventions. In contrast perlocutionary acts do not have connected
with them verb phrases which can be used to perform either of the
functions adduced by Strawson or Searle. There are no linguistic conventions connecting my utterance of,

> (13)   I persuade you to fly the kite.

with a complex intention or a set of rules the making explicit or invoking
of which are means to persuade you to fly the kite.

However, there is a sense in which some perlocutionary acts are conventional. Let us consider an example. Eliciting an answer is one of the purposes of asking a question. Now eliciting an answer is a perlocutionary act. Moreover, there are conventional devices for asking a question, such as the explicit performative 'I ask you', interrogative sentence type and intonation. Furthermore, if A is a conventional means of ϕ-ing and ϕ-ing has as one of its purposes ψ-ing, then A is a conventional means for ψ-ing. Consequently, a conventional means for asking a question , for example saying, 'I ask you', is a conventional means for eliciting an answer. Hence, eliciting an answer, a perlocutionary act, is conventional in the sense that there are conventional means for its performance. Contary to Austin, then, there are some perlocutionary acts which are conventional, namely those perlocutionary acts which are a purpose of some illocutionary act.

I would like to forestall a misunderstanding and a criticism. First, I am not maintaining that every illocutionary act has a perlocutionary purpose. Neither promising, thanking, nor christening has such purposes. However, there are illocutionary acts, central to the use of language, which do have such purposes. For example, one of the purposes of telling someone something is to inform them and one of the purposes of asking someone to do something is to get them to do it. Second, an obvious counterexample to my argument above is that although saying 'I ask you' is a conventional means for asking a question and one of my purposes in asking you a question might be to amuse you, it does not follow that saying 'I ask you' is a conventional means for amusing you. This criticism can be avoided by a qualification. When I say that a purpose of asking a question is to elicit an answer, I do not mean that a purpose of every question is to elicit an answer. As the counterexample shows, someone can certainly ask a question with other purposes. Rather, the sort of purpose involved here is generic. The connection between asking a question and eliciting an answer is similar to the connection between being a tiger and being striped. Although a tiger is a striped carnivore, there might be a tiger who has had its stripes removed and eats only vegetables. This would not show that tiger is not a striped carnivore. What we would have would be a non-standard or deviant tiger. Similarly, a question asked the purpose of which is not one of those standardly connected with asking a question is still a question, although a non-standard one. That this is so can be seen by the fact that speakers who ask non-rhetorical questions, but do not want the answer are open to criticism.

Austin considers three linguistic tests for distinguishing illocutionary from perlocutionary act verbs. One test which we have already consi-

dered is that an illocutionary act verb occurring as the main verb of a
phrase in the first person, present tense, active indicative can be used to
make explicit what act the speaker is performing. However, there are
difficulties with the criterion, for there seems to be performative verb
phrases which do not occur in the required form. Consider for example,

(14)   You are fired.

In saying (14) I would be firing my hearer, but I cannot do so by saying,

(15)   I fire you.[22]

In addition the criterion does not mark off the class of perlocutionary act
verbs from other verbs. Any verb which is not an illocutionary act verb
fails the criterion.

Austin's second test is, also, designed to pick out illocutionary act
verbs. Any verb phrase substituted for y in (16) with appropriate
substitution for x which yields truth contains as its main verb an
illocutionary act verb.

(16)   To say x was to y.[23]

Austin, himself, provides a counterexample to this test.

(17)   To say that she spent the night at Sam's is to convince him
         that she is an adultress.[24]

However, 'convince' is a perlocutionary act verb. Again, this criterion,
even if there were no counterexamples, would not provide a test for
perlocutionary act verbs, for all non-illocutionary act verbs, including
non-perlocutionary act verbs, fail the test.

The third test turns on the difference between the following schemata:

$$(18) \quad \text{(i) In saying } X \text{ I} \left\{ \begin{matrix} y \\ \text{was } y \end{matrix} \right\}^{25}$$

$$\qquad \text{(ii) By saying } X \text{ I} \left\{ \begin{matrix} y \\ \text{was } y \end{matrix} \right\}$$

(18) (i) is supposed to pick out illocutionary act verbs, while (18) (ii) is
supposed to discriminate perlocutionary act verbs. For example,

(19)   (i) In saying 'I promise' I was promising.
       (ii) By saying 'There's a spider on your lap' I frightened Jones.

'Promise' and 'frighten' are, then, respectively, illocutionary and perlocutionary act verbs, the gerundives of which pick out the corresponding acts. However, as Austin points out, the schemata in (18) do not pick out all and only illocutionary and perlocutionary act verbs. Since our interest here is perlocutions, I shall concentrate on (18) (ii). Substituting in this formula, we obtain

(20)   By saying 'It was late' I was suggesting that he go home.

However, 'suggest' is not a perlocutionary act verb.

I would like to propose a linguistic test which, I believe, does distinguish perlocutionary act verbs from other verbs and avoids the above counterexample.

(21)   (i) By ϕ-ing X S ψ-s H Y
       (ii) S's ϕ-ing X ψ-s H Y
       (iii) H was ψ-ed Y by S's ϕ-ing X.

S is a variable for a designation for a speaker and H is a variable for a designation for a hearer. ϕ ranges over illocutionary and propositional act verbs. And we can substitute for X and Y any linguistic expressions or nothing as long as grammaticality is preserved. A verb substituted for ψ is a perlocutionary act verb just in case there are substitution instances for the other variables which render (21) (i)–(iii) grammatical. To illustrate the criterion consider the following example.

(22)   (i) By objecting to her criticism Abel amused Mabel.
       (ii) Abel's objecting to her criticism amused Mabel.
       (iii) Mabel was amused by Abel's objecting to her criticism.

Hence, 'amuse' is a perlocutionary act verb. The criterion excludes 'suggest' from being a perlocutionary act verb.

(23)   (i) By telling Mabel it was late Abel suggested to her that she leave.
       (ii) Abel's telling Mabel it was late suggested to Mabel that she leave.

(iii) Mabel was suggested that she leave by Abel's telling her it
      was late.

Although (23) (i) and (ii) are grammatical, (23) (iii) is not.

The criterion for perlocutionary act verbs can be used in determining
the class of act types tokens of which under certain conditions are
perlocutionary acts. I shall call these act types 'perlocutionary types'.
But it should be understood that not all tokens of them are perlocutionary acts. Given the class of perlocutionary act verbs, we can use the
following schemata to form gerunds which designate perlocutionary act
types.

(24) ϕ-ing some X.

Where ϕ is a variable for a perlocutionary act verb and X ranges over
any linguistic expression or nothing, provided grammaticality is preserved. On this criterion amusing someone, persuading someone to believe
it is raining, and causing someone to become frightened are perlocutionary act types.

Some gerunds for perlocutionary act types contain the verb 'cause', an
obvious mark of the causative characteristic of such act types, but other
gerunds, such as 'amusing someone' and 'frightening someone' do not.
To distinguish these two sorts of perlocutionary act types, I shall call the
former 'explicit causatives' and the latter, 'implicit causatives'. I shall
use these terms, as well, to refer to the corresponding gerunds and to
any phrase which contains a grammatically related from of such
gerunds. Let us consider two sentences containing implicit and explicit
causative phrases.

(25)   (i) Abel frightened Mabel.
          (ii) Abel caused Mabel to become frightened.

Some linguists see a close grammatical relationship between sentence
pairs of this sort.[26] George Lakoff, for example, has proposed that a
structure similar to (25) (ii) is the underlying semantic representation of
(25) (i) from which this latter sentence is derived. A consequence of this
proposal is that (25) (i) and (25) (ii) are marked as being synonymous.
However, it is possible for (25) (ii) to be true and (25) (i) to be false.
Suppose Abel tells Sam to frighten Mabel which he does. Then it would
be true that Abel caused Mabel to become frightened, but false that he
frightened her.[27] There are a number of other criticisms of Lakoff's

proposal and in turn several attempts to meet these criticisms.[28] However, I believe that the criticisms either show that a sentence containing an explicit causative might be true while the sentence containing the corresponding implicit causative is false or that the particular proposal of Lakoff, deriving sentences containing implicit causatives from underlying semantic representations related to explicit causatives, is false. What they do not show is that implicit causative constructions do not have as part of their meaning explicit causative constructions. That is, (25) (ii) is part of the meaning of (25) (i). In what follows this will play a role in my analysis of a perlocutionary act.

I would now like to propose necessary and sufficient conditions for the performance of a perlocutionary act.

(26) S's ϕ-ing H (to ψ) by uttering p is the performance of a perlocutionary act if and only if
  (i) S performs an illocutionary act or propositional acts in uttering p
  (ii) S means by p what p means in the language of which it is a part
  (iii) H understands S to mean to perform some illocutionary act or propositional acts by uttering p
  (iv) H understands S to mean something by p
  (v) What H understands S to mean causes H to ψ or be ϕ-ed.

S and H are variables for designations for speaker and hearer, respectively. The hearer can be the person addressed, the speaker, or someone else. ϕ is a variable for a perlocutionary act verb. ψ is a variable for any verb phrase which preserves grammaticality. Parentheses indicate that the 'to' phrase is optional. I assume that the illocutionary or propositional acts in (26) (i) are performed in the standard ways. That is, p is a sentence or a sentence fragment of a language S speaks. Moreover, in uttering p S uses his linguistic competence; S utters p seriously; S has the requisite intentions and follows correctly the appropriate rules for performing the illocutionary and propositional acts which he intends to perform; S successfully refers to whatever he intends to refer to in uttering p; and S employs the appropriate Gricean maxims. Lastly, what S means by p is what p means. Similarly, I take it that (26) (iii) and (iv) are, also, achieved in the standard way. H uses his linguistic competence to understand something by what S utters, although H need not understand what S means. For, as I have pointed out, H could

understand *S* to mean something other than what *S* means. And this
could cause some effect on *H*.

In (26) (v) 'what *H* understands *S* to mean' is left vague. What *H*
understands *S* to mean which causes the effect on *H* could be

(27)   (i) the illocutionary act *H* understands *S* to perform
         (ii) the propositional acts *H* understands *S* to perform
        (iii) the thought *H* understands that *S* means to express by *p*.

Anyone of these or a combination of them might be the cause of the
effect on *H*. Lastly, what *H* understands *S* to mean might not be the
immediate cause of the effect in question, but only the proximate cause.
Because of what *H* understands, he might form some belief, thought,
want, desire, etc. which in turn causes the particular effect.

Ordinarily when a speaker achieves some effect on his hearer, it is
brought about because his hearer understands rather than misunder-
stands him. To take account of what I believe to be the standard case,
the following should replace (26)(iii) and (iv):

(28)   (i) *H* understands what illocutionary act and perlocutionary
             acts *S* means to perform
         (ii) *H* understands what *S* means by *p*.

Moreover, quite often speakers intend to perform perlocutionary acts.
They intend that their illocutionary and/or propositional acts produce a
particular effect on their hearers. To capture this I propose the following
criterion:

(29)   *S*'s *φ*-ing *H* (to *ψ*) by uttering *p* is the intentional performance
          of a perlocutionary act if and only if
          (i) *S* performs an illocutionary act or propositional acts in
              uttering *p*
         (ii) *S* means by *p* what *p* means in the language of which it is a
              part.
        (iii) *H* understands *S* to mean to perform some illocutionary
              act or propositional acts by uttering *p*.
         (iv) *H* understand *S* to mean something by *p*.
          (v) What *H* understands *S* to mean causes *H* to *ψ* or be *φ*-ed.
         (vi) By uttering *p* *S* intends *H* to *ψ* or be *φ*-ed.

Not only do speakers intend to produce effects on their hearers by saying something, but they intend, also, that these effects be brought about because their hearers understand what they mean by what they say. This I take to be the standard case of the intentional performance of a perlocutionary act.

(30)   Standardly, S's ϕ-ing H (to ψ) by uttering p is the intentional performance of a perlocutionary act if and only if
   (i) S performs an illocutionary act or propositional acts by uttering p.
   (ii) S means by p what p means in the language of which it is a part.
   (iii) H understands what illocutionary act or propositional acts S means to perform by uttering p.
   (iv) H understands what S means by p.
   (v)   What H understands S to mean causes H to ψ or be ϕ-ed.
   (vi) S intends H to ψ or be ϕ-ed because H understands what he means.

To illustrate (30), let us return to the example considered at the beginning of the paper, my frightening you by telling you that there's a spider on your lap. I intentionally perform this act in the standard way by uttering 'There's a spider on your lap' if and only if

(31)   (i)   I tell you that there's a spider on your lap by uttering 'There's a spider on your lap'.
   (ii) I mean by 'There's a spider on your lap' what it means in English.
   (iii) You understand that I have told you something by uttering, 'There's a spider on your lap'.
   (iv) You understand what I mean by 'There's a spider on your lap'.
   (v)   What you understand me to mean causes you to become frightened.
   (vi) I intend that you become frightened because you understand what I mean.

There are an infinite number of different sorts of acts which speakers can perform in and by saying something, many of which are of no theoretical interest. For example, there is the class of acts speakers perform by uttering sentences beginning with 'the'. What theoretical

interest is there, then, in the class of perlocutionary acts? I believe that
part of the answer to this question can be provided by turning to an
issue that I promised to say something about at the beginning of this
paper, namely the relationship between communication and the performance of perlocutionary acts. Let me close, then, by making a few
comments on a very complicated topic. When we talk to one another,
one thing we normally seek is to be understood. That is, we want our
hearer to understand what we mean in saying and by saying what we do
and what our thoughts are which we intend to express by the words we
utter. If these are achieved, then we can be said to have communicated
to our hearer. But often, and in some cases standardly, we want more
than this. We ask questions to elicit answers; we tell others something to
inform them;[29] and we make requests to get others to do our bidding.[30] It
is not enough in these cases to be understood, but what we want to bring
about are certain effects, on the thoughts, actions, or feeling of our
hearers, for our purpose in bringing these about is the point or purpose
of our communicating and the achieving of our purpose is the performance of a perlocutionary act.

Simon ᷉raser University,
British Columbia,
Canada

NOTES AND REFERENCES

[1] Austin, J. L.: 1975, *How To Do Things With Words*, Eds. J. O. Urmson and Marina
Sbisa, 2nd edition, Harvard University Press, Cambridge. p. 92.
[2] Searle, J. R.: 1971, 'Austin on Locutionary and Illocutionary Acts', In *Readings in the
Philosophy of Language*, Eds. J. Rosenberg and C. Travis, Prentice-Hall, Englewood Cliffs,
pp. 262–275.
[3] There are other acts which can be distinguished here which Searle calls propositional
acts, but these are unnecessary for our present purposes. *Cf.* Searle, J. R.: *Speech Acts*,
1969 Cambridge University Press, Cambridge, p. 24.
[4] Austin, *Ibid.*, p. 103.
[5] Davidson, Donald: 1975 'The Logical Form of Action Sentences'. In *The Logic of
Grammar*, D. Davidson and G. Harman, (Eds.) Dickenson publishing Company, Encino,
pp. 235–246.
Goldman, Alvin: 1970, *A Theory of Human Action*, Prentice-Hall, Inc., Englewood Cliffs.
[6] Austin, *Ibid.*, p. 101.
[7] Austin, *Ibid.*, p.106.
[8] Austin, *Ibid.*, p. 106.
[9] Austin, *Ibid.*, pp. 130–131.
[10] Austin, *Ibid.*, pp. 110–111.
[11] Searle, *Ibid.*, pp. 24–29. A propositional act is an act which is performed in the course of
performing an illocutionary act. Searle includes only referring and predicating in this class
of acts.

[12] Austin, *Ibid.*, p. 113.

[13] Austin, *Ibid.*, p. 118.

[14] Austin, *Ibid.*, p. 116.

[15] Strawson, P. F., 'Intention, Convention, and Speech Acts'. In *Readings in the Philosophy of Language*, p. 606.

[16] This was pointed out to me by A. Baier.

[17] Austin, *Ibid.*, p. 117.

[18] Anscombe, G.E.M.: 1958, 'On Brute Facts', *Analysis*, Vol. XVIII.

[19] Austin, *Ibid.*, p. 117.

[20] Austin, *Ibid.*, p. 103.

[21] Searle, J. R., *Speech Acts*, pp. 62–64.
Strawson, P. F., *Ibid.*, pp. 608–612.

[22] The examples in (14), (15), and (20) are from Austin, p. 130. See, also, Sadock J. 1977. 'Aspects of Linguistic Pragmatics'. In Rogers, Wall, and Murphy, (Eds.), *Proceedings of the Texas Conference on Performatives, Presuppositions, and Implicatives*, Center for Applied Linguistics, Arlington, Virginia p. 68 and p. 75.

[23] Austin, *Ibid.*, p. 131. This is not the schema Austin proposes. His is 'To say x was to do y. But substitution does not preserve grammaticality.

[24] Austin, *Ibid.*, p. 131.

[25] Austin, *Ibid.*, p. 122. Again these are not the schemata Austin proposes. I have made changes for the same reason as in Note 23.

[26] Lakoff, G: 1970, *Irregularity in Syntax*, Holt, Rinehart, and Winston, New York.
McCawley, J: 1968,'Lexical Insertion in a Transformational Grammar without Deep Structure'. In *Papers of the Chicago Linguistic Society*, Chicago Linguistic Society, Chicago.

[27] Katz, J. J: 1970, 'Interpretive Semantics vs Generative Semantics', *Foundations of Language*, Vol. VI, p. 253.

[28] Chomsky, N: 1970, 'Remarks on Nominalizations', In *Readings in English Transformational Grammar*, R. Jacobs and P. Rosenbaum (Eds.), Ginn and Co., Waltham.
Fodor, J: 1970, 'Three Reasons for Not Deriving "Kill" from "Cause to Die" ', *Linguistic Inquiry*, Vol. XIII,
Wierzbicka, A: 1975, 'Why "Kill" Does Not Mean "Cause to Die": The Semantics of Action Sentences', *Foundations of Language*, Vol. XIII,

[29] I take it that to inform someone is to make them aware of certain facts. All that might be required to achieve this is that the hearer understands what the speaker says.

[30] *Cf.* Cohen, T: 1973, 'Illocutions and Perlocutions', *Foundations of Language*, Vol. II, pp. 492–503, who makes a similar proposal about the point or purpose of some illocutionary acts.

GILLES FAUCONNIER

PRAGMATIC ENTAILMENT AND QUESTIONS

I. ENTAILMENT-REVERSING ENVIRONMENTS

Sentential structures may contain positions that can be filled by other sentential structures:

(1)   Although _____ , we arrived late.
(2)   Galileo believes that _____ .
(3)   It is too early for _____ .
(4)   If _____ , then Monaco will attack.

I will call such structures environments and symbolize their semantic content,
with a corresponding empty slot, as U ___ V, U' ___V' etc. If the sentential
structure S that fills the empty slot has propositional content P, then the
propositional content of the entire construction (environment filled in by S)
will be UPV.

For example, in the case of (1), U would represent the semantic content of
although, V the semantic content of *we arrived late*; if the slot was filled by
S: *we left early*, expressing the proposition that we left early, UPV would
represent the proposition associated with:

(5)   Although *we left early*, we arrived late.

An interesting property of some environments is their ability to reverse
entailment relations as follows:

U ___ V reverses entailment if whenever P entails Q (P → Q), then UQV
entails UPV:

$$UQV \rightarrow UPV.$$

For example, negative environments such as

    "It is not the case that _____ ".

reverse entailment: if P entails Q, "it is not the case that Q" will entail "it is
not the case that P."[1] This is formalized by the famous contraposition law of
propositional logic.[2]

Conditional environments "if _____ then A" also have this property.

57

J. R. Searle, F. Kiefer, and M. Bierwisch (eds.), *Speech Act Theory and Pragmatics*,
57–69.
Copyright © 1980 by D. Reidel Publishing Company.

Suppose, by way of illustration, that we have the following (pragmatic) entailment: for Harry to live in California entails that he would get plenty of sunshine:

Harry lives in California → *Harry gets plenty of sunshine.*
P   →   Q

Now consider the environment:

If _____ then Harry will regain his health.
U _____ V.

If we take UQV as a premise

UQV = "if Harry gets plenty of sunshine, then Harry will regain his health."

along with the entailment above (P → Q), we can deduce:

"If Harry lives in California, then Harry will regain his health."

i.e., UPV.

The result is valid in general because of the transitivity and entailment properties of the *if____ then* relation: From $P \rightarrow Q$, and *if Q then A* (=UQV) we get:

$$
\begin{array}{l}
\text{if P then Q} \\
\underline{\text{if Q then A}} \\
\text{transitivity:} \quad \underline{\text{if P then A}} \quad (= \text{UPV})
\end{array}
$$

I have described elsewhere[3] a number of linguistic contexts which have this property, and pointed out how it accounts for the distribution of *even*-phrases, polarity items, and other elements which stand for the extremity of an implicational scale.[4] For example, take a quantity scale such as (6):

(6)

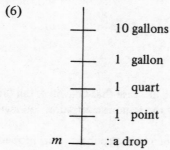

       10 gallons

       1   gallon

       1   quart

       1   point

m   : a drop

The minimum quantity m is indicated by the expression *a drop*. Now take a propositional schema like (7):

(7)   Albert drinks x.

in which x could be replaced by a specified quantity. With respect to (7), scale (6) is implicational: if Albert drinks a gallon, then he also drinks all the quantities which are lower on the scale, 1/2 gallon, 1 quart, . . . , 1 drop. Letting $R(x)$ stand for (7) and $>$ for the ordering relation on the scale, we have:

$$\text{if } x_2 > x_1,$$
$$\text{then } R(x_2) \rightarrow R(x_1).$$

In particular, of course, for any x on the scale, we have

$$R(x) \rightarrow R(m).$$

Now if $R(x)$ is embedded in one of the entailment-reversing environments mentioned above, we get another propositional schema:

$$U\ R(x)\ V.$$

But given the entailment $R(x) \rightarrow R(m)$ and the entailment-reversing property of $U\_\_\_V$, it follows that:

(8) $U\ R(m)\ V \rightarrow U\ R(x)\ V.$

This is easily verified in the case of negative environments,[5] e.g.,

$$U\_\_V = \text{not}\_\_\emptyset.$$
(9)   Albert drank a gallon $\rightarrow$ Albert drank a quart $\rightarrow$ Albert drank a drop.[6]
(10)   Albert did not drink a drop $\rightarrow$ Albert did not drink a quart $\rightarrow$ Albert did not drink a gallon.

Crucially, implication (8) is valid for any x on the scale, so the assertion of a sentence corresponding to $U\ R(m)\ V$ will yield entailments for all elements of the scale; essentially:

$$U\ R(m)\ V \rightarrow \forall x\ U\ R(x)\ V.$$

To say that Albert did not drink a drop is to say that he did not drink any quantity on scale (6). This accounts for why such end-points of scales are commonly used to express the equivalent of universal quantification.

The following are other examples where the entailment-reversing environment is "not ___ $\emptyset$":

(11)   This knife cannot cut the most tender meat. (= cannot cut any meat)

(12)   Harry did not lift a finger to help us. (= didn't do anything to help us; *lift a finger* is a minimum on a scale of possible actions)

The relevant superficial property in all these cases is that R(m) by itself does not have any universal entailments, but embedded in the entailment-reversing environment U ____ V, it does. The other entailment-reversing environment mentioned above, "if ___ (then) A" produces the same effect, as predicted: from (13) one can infer (14), (15) etc. which amount to (16):[7]

(13)   If Albert drinks a drop, he will die.
(14)   If Albert drinks a pint, he will die.
(15)   If Albert drinks 10 gallons, he will die.

⋮

(16)   If Albert drinks anything, he will die.[8]

U ____ V is "if ___ , he will die"[9] (13) is U R(m) V, (14) is U R(x) V for x = 1 pint.

The "modifier" *even* will explicitly signal reference to a scale and its end-point:

(17)   This knife cannot cut even the most tender meat.
(18)   If Albert drinks even a drop, he will die.

Notice that *even* in (17) and (18) eliminates the "literal" reading possible in (11) or (13), and imposed by later discourse in (19) and (20):

(19)   This knife cannot cut the most tender meat: it is only appropriate for tough meat.
(20)   If Albert drinks a drop, he will die; but if he drinks more he will survive.

In (19) and (20), there are no scalar implications.[10]

It should also be noted that end-points of scales need not have any reference or even any possible reference:[11] their function is to produce induced universal quantification; it is not referential.

(21)   Gertrude would turn down even the most handsome man.
(22)   With this telescope you can see even the most distant stars.

These sentences readily express that Gertrude would turn down any man and that the telescope enables one to see any stars, without entailing the existence of a man who is the most handsome or of stars which are the most distant: the end-points are formal closures of sets with the sole purpose of allowing the scalar implications to function and yield induced quantification over the sets.

II. QUESTION-CLAUSES

Entailment-reversal accounts for contrasts between isolated sentences like those of (23) and their embedded counterparts in (24):

(23)   a. *You ever come to Paris.
        b. +Albert drank even a drop.[12]
        c. +This knife can cut even the most tender meat.
           (+ indicates anomaly of semantic or pragmatic nature)
(24)   a. If you ever come to Paris, don't miss the Plateau Beaubourg.
        b. If Albert drank even a drop, he is certainly dead.
        c. If this knife can cut even the most tender meat, I will buy it.

Sentences like (23) correspond to $R(m)$ in the preceding section: since the entailments go in the x to m direction ($R(x) \rightarrow R(m)$), such sentences cannot produce entailments for the rest of the scale, and they are anomalous.[13] In sentences like (24) on the other hand, $R(m)$ is embedded in an entailment-reversing environment U____V: U $R(m)$ V entails U $R(x)$ V for any x; the sentences produce entailments for the rest of the scale; they are not anomalous.

Now consider the following examples:

(25)   I wonder if you *ever* come to Paris.
(26)   I wonder if Albert drank *even a drop*.
(27)   I wonder if this knife can cut *even the most tender meat*.

Here too sentential structures corresponding to those in (23) are embedded in a linguistic environment:

(28)   I wonder if ____ $\emptyset$.

And as in (24) the resulting complex sentences are not anomalous. This suggests that (28), like "not ____ $\emptyset$", "If ____ then A", and the others mentioned in Note 4 is an entailment-reversing environment, in which scalar elements like *ever, even a drop* etc. will play the same role as in (24). But in fact, such is not the case. If P entails Q, it does not follow that

>"I wonder if Q"

entails

>"I wonder if P".

We can illustrate this directly by means of our earlier example,

>"Harry lives in California" entails "Harry gets plenty of sunshine"
>P   →   Q

Assuming this entailment, it would not follow from

>(UQV) "I wonder if Harry gets plenty of sunshine"

that

>(UPV) "I wonder if Harry lives in California"

because I could be quite sure that Harry does *not* live in California, and still not know whether he gets plenty of sunshine or not.

This correlates with another superficial difference between polarity items[14] in ordinary entailment-reversing environments and in question clauses:

(29)   If you go anywhere, take along some cash.
(30)   Harry did not go anywhere.
(31)   I wonder if Harry went anywhere.

In (29) and (30), the meaning produced by scalar implications and entailment-reversal has the force of a universal quantification:

(29') $\forall x$ (if you go to x, take along some cash).
(30') $\forall x$ (not (Harry go to x)).

But in (31) it doesn't: (31) does not amount to anything like:

(31') $\forall x$ (I wonder if Harry went to x),

because I may well know of a lot of places where Harry most certainly did not go and still wonder "if he went anywhere."

These observations indicate that environments may interact with implicational scales in a more interesting way than mere entailment-reversal. The case of question-clauses is in fact easy to analyze from this point of view, and I will sketch the analysis in a semi-abstract way, using again the example of *wonder*.

Suppose a linguistic context[15] includes propositions $P_0, P_1, P_2 \ldots P_i,$ $P_{i+1}, \ldots P_n$ on an implicational scale.[16]

(32)

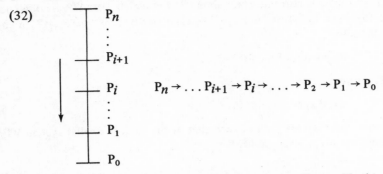

$$P_n \to \ldots P_{i+1} \to P_i \to \ldots \to P_2 \to P_1 \to P_0$$

With respect to any entailment-reversing environment U___V, this scale will be reversed: For any P_i, P_{i+1} on the scale, such that $P_{i+1} \to P_i$, $UP_iV \to UP_{i+1}V$.

$$UP_0V \to UP_1V \to \ldots \to UP_iV \to UP_{i+1}V \to \ldots$$

But such a scale is not reversed with respect to environments like "I wonder if ..." (W___) because it is possible for (33) and (34) to be true simultaneously.[17]

(33)   I wonder if P_i (= WP_i).
(34)   I know that *not* P_{i+1}.

And (34) entails:

(35)   *not* (I wonder if P_{i+1})   (= $\sim WP_{i+1}$).

It would be a mistake however to conclude that the set of WP_i's is accordingly without structure: if the speaker of (33) wonders about P_i he cannot believe P_{i+j}, because since P_{i+j} entails P_i, he would also believe P_i. His attitude with regard to P_{i+j} can only be of two kinds: either, as in (34) he believes "*not* P_{i+j}" or he is also uncertain about P_{i+j} in which cases WP_{i+j} holds. But in the first case, belief of "not P_{i+j}" he must also believe "*not* $P_{i+j'}$" for any $j' > j$, because

$$P_{i+j'} \text{ entails } P_{i+j} \text{ if } j' > j$$

and therefore

$$not \; P_{i+j} \text{ entails } not \; P_{i+j'}.$$

It follows that there exists a k, such that in the subject's belief system WP_k holds and for any j, $\sim P_{k+j}$ holds.[18]

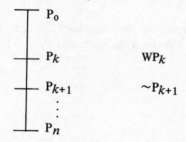

k is the cutoff point between the propositions that the subject either believes or is uncertain about $(i \leqslant k)$ and the ones he does not believe $(i > k)$. As noted before, the entire scale is not reversed with respect to "W___", but the subscale $< P_0, \ldots P_k >$, is reversed: WP_i, for $i < k$, entails WP_{i+1}. In particular, the proposition WP_0, corresponding to the scale minimum P_0, *will* have implications with respect to every P_i on the scale, since:

(36) $WP_0 \rightarrow WP_i \text{ or } \sim P_i.$

and more precisely:

$$WP_0 \rightarrow \exists k \; (\forall i \leqslant k \; WP_i \text{ and } \forall j > k \; \sim P_j).$$

In other words, with respect to the original scale $< P_0, \ldots P_n >$ the effect of the environment W___ is to produce two reversed subscales:

$$< WP_k, \ldots WP_0 > \quad : \quad WP_i \rightarrow WP_{i+1}.$$

and

$$< \sim P_n, \ldots \sim P_{k+1} > \quad : \quad \sim P_j \rightarrow \sim P_{j+1}.$$

But of course, while WP_0 entails the existence of these two scales (the second one possibly empty if $k = n$), it does not specify the cutoff point k.

Returning now to concrete examples like (25), (26), (27), we see how this dual reversal operates.

(27)   I wonder if this knife can cut even the most tender meat.

P_0 in this case would be: "this knife can cut the most tender meat." By questioning P_0, the subject indicates either ignorance or disbelief regarding all propositions higher than P_0 on the scale: $P_i = R(x) =$ "this knife can cut meat x" as expressed schematically in formula (36). And we see that, as in the regular cases of entailment-reversal, the implication for all propositions on the scale operates on $R(m)$ ($m = $ *the most tender meat*) without entailing the actual existence of a referent for m. Furthermore, the propsoitions which the subject is ignorant about and the ones he disbelieves cannot be interspersed on the scale; they are on two separate continuous segments:

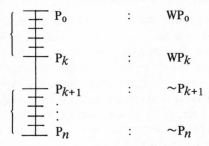

P_0	:	WP_0
P_k	:	WP_k
P_{k+1}	:	$\sim P_{k+1}$
P_n	:	$\sim P_n$

To put it in yet another way, there is no proposition on the scale such that the subject of *wonder* believes that proposition: for instance, (27) entails that the subject knows of no meat which the particular knife can cut. This aspect of the entailment over the set of propositions interacts, to yield negative implicatures, with the conversational maxim that "no evidence for P" is "evidence against P" illustrated in the following:

(37)   I have no reason to believe you. ($\Longrightarrow$ I don't believe you.)
(38)   I have never heard of anybody who could do a quadruple flip. ($\Longrightarrow$ Nobody can do a quadruple flip.)
(39)   I have yet to see an elephant that can fly. ($\Longrightarrow$ No elephant can fly.)

Accordingly, a sentence like (27) will easily implicate that the knife cannot cut any meat, (26) that Alfred did not drink at all, and (25) that *you* never come to Paris: to question the extreme proposition on an implicational scale is to express that no proposition on that scale is believed, according to formula (36).

Clearly, the same entailments and possible implicatures hold for direct questions such as:

(40)   Do you ever come to Paris?
(41)   Did Alfred drink even a drop?
(42)   Can this knife cut even the most tender meat?

These aspects of the interaction of questions with implicational scales clarify some empirical observations regarding polarity items in interrogative structures. It has been observed[19] that so-called "negative polarity items" could appear in questions and give rise to an expected negative answer or even carry declarative negative force (rhetorical questions):

(43)   Did you *lift a finger* when I needed it?

It has been shown that such polarity items are only special (idomatic) cases of expressions denoting end-points on scales: thus (43) is not different from (25), (26), (27); in particular the negative force does not come from the polarity item per se: rather, as shown above, scale minimums are admissible if they produce entailments over the entire scale: this is the case for many environments including questions; furthermore questioning at scale extremities favors negative implicatures; (43), taken literally, entails: "I have no evidence that you did even the slightest thing when I needed it" and consequently has the same negative implicatures.[20]

The interaction studied here also accounts for why *anywhere* looks superficially like a universal quantifier in (29) and (30) but not in (31). In the case of entailment-reversing environments, we have:

$$U\ R(m)\ V \rightarrow \forall x\ U\ R(x)\ V.$$

So it is not unnatural to take the effect for the cause and to assume like Quine, and Reichenbach before him, that m (i.e., *any, anywhere*, etc.) *is* the universal quantifier. In fact m only triggers universal quantification through scalar implication. But in the case of questions (like (31)) the entailment is (cf. (36)):

$$W\ R(m) \rightarrow \forall x\ (W\ R(x)\ _{\text{V}} \sim R(x)).$$

Again, this follows from the scalar implications and the semantics of W——— but it shatters the idea that m itself could be the universal quantifier, since

W R(m) is no longer semantically equivalent to $\forall x$ W R(x). The scalar account which emerges in the study of all these phenomena provides the only uniform explanation for examples like (30), (31), (24), (26) and (27).

Another respect in which implicatures influence the logic of questions may be mentioned in the present context. With ordinary entailment-reversing environments we have, for any propositions P and Q:

$$P \rightarrow P \text{ or } Q$$
$$Q \rightarrow P \text{ or } Q$$

therefore, by entailment-reversal:

$$U \, P \, or \, Q \, V \rightarrow UPV$$
$$U \, P \, or \, Q \, V \rightarrow UQV$$

or, equivalently:

$$U \, P \, or \, Q \, V \rightarrow UPV \text{ and } UQV.^{21}$$

This property accounts for the apparent conjunction value of *or* in entailment-reversing environments:

> If they find our hideout *or* James is caught, the game will be up.

entails:

> If they find our hideout, the game will be up *and* if James is caught the game will be up.

But again *or* has this value also in question-clauses even though they do not reverse entailment in the simple sense:

(44)   I wonder if Harriet *or* Gertrude will be at the party.
   $\Longrightarrow$ I wonder if Harriet will be at the party *and* I wonder if Gertrude will be at the party.

From W (P or Q) it does not follow that "WP and WQ" but rather (cf. (36)):

$$(WP \text{ or } \sim P) \text{ and } (WQ \text{ or } \sim Q).$$

So W (P or Q) is compatible with any of the following:

(a)   WP and WQ
(b)   WP and $\sim$Q
(c) $\sim$P and WQ

$\sim$P and $\sim$Q is excluded, since it is equivalent to $\sim$(P or Q). But (b) and (c) in turn can be naturally eliminated by appealing to the Gricean Maxim of quantity. Just as "P or Q" is *true* but inappropriate if Q is known to be false, "John wonders if P or Q" can be true, but inappropriate if John is known to believe ~Q. Similarly the speaker of (44) may be considered guilty of under-informing if in fact he knows (or strongly believes) that Gertrude will not be at the party.

Questions such as (43), used to express negative statements can be viewed as indirect speech acts. The linguistic distribution of polarity items might suggest superficially that such questions actually contain negative elements at some underlying structural level. I hope to have shown that this is not the case: previously established characteristics of questions, scales and implicature interact to yield the observed surface distributions.

L.A.D.L., Centre National de la Recherche Scientifique,
and University of California at San Diego

NOTES

[1] To simplify the exposition, I use the same symbols (P, Q . . .) to represent propositions and the corresponding sentences. I also use the natural language expressions (e.g., "it is not the case that . . .") to represent their own semantic content.

[2] If $P \rightarrow Q$, $\sim Q \rightarrow \sim P$.

[3] 'Etude de certains aspects logiques et grammaticaux de la quantification et de l'ana-phore en français et en anglais', Thèse, U. de Paris VII. 'Implication reversal in a natural language', *Formal Semantics*, eds. Guenthner and Schmidt, D. Reidel.

[4] Some such linguistic environments are *comparatives, degree clauses* (too . . . for to . . .), *before clauses, predicates expressing doubt, surprise, universal relatives* (anyone who . . .). The number of such environments is in fact infinite because they can combine among themselves, or with *entailment-preserving* environments to yield new ones: an even number of *entailment-reversing* environments yields an *entailment-preserving* one.

[5] This environment is best formulated with respect to underlying syntactic structure, with *not* appearing initially.

[6] This entailment is valid before possible application of Grice's Maxim of Quantity, which allows for "Albert drank a quart" the interpretation "Albert drank exactly a quart". Cf. L. Horn *On the Semantic Properties of Logical Operators in English*, UCLA Dissertation.

[7] As noted in Note 6, another interpretation is possible with *a drop* = *exactly a drop*, for which (13) would not entail (14). The presence of *even*, as in (18), removes this interpretation, by explicitly pointing to the relevant scale.

[8] *anything* itself is best viewed as a scalar end-point. Cf. my 'Pragmatic scales and logical structure', *Linguistic Inquiry* 6, 3.

[9] *he* is given the unambiguous denotation "Albert" in all these examples and schemata.

[10] Cf. Note 7.

[11] This aspect of induced quantification, and its importance were pointed out to me by A. Lentin and independently by B. de Cornulier.

[12] Marking the anomaly as semantic rather than syntactic seems largely arbitrary for (b) and is in fact irrelevant, since the same explanation is offered for (a), (b), (c).

[13] Note that (21c) can be perfectly good with other pragmatic assumptions, but (21a) and (21b) cannot be saved: the corresponding scales (temporal and quantity) are semantically rigid.

[14] And other scale minimums.

[15] The implicational scales we consider are in the belief-system of the speaker, and he assumes they are also in the belief system of the hearer and others, such as the subject of *wonder*.

[16] n may be ∞: the number of propositions on the scale does not have to be finite.

[17] Cf. Note 1.

[18] Of course k may be equal to n, in which case the subject is uncertain about all the propositions.

[19] A. Borkin, 'Polarity Items in Questions' CLS, A. Borillo 'Questions Rhétoriques', Colloque de Vincennes, 1977.

[20] This is reflected in the lexical meaning of the verb "to question" as in "I question your honesty".

[21] Cf. "Implication reversal . . ." (Note 3).

ROLAND R. HAUSSER

SURFACE COMPOSITIONALITY AND THE
SEMANTICS OF MOOD

0. INTRODUCTORY REMARKS

The goal of the present paper is to extend the principles of truth-conditional semantics to non-declarative sentence moods.[1] My basic hypothesis is that the different syntactic moods should be characterized semantically in terms of their characteristic kind of possible denotation. In the same way as the declarative mood is characterized semantically by the fact that declaratives denote propositions (i.e., functions from points of reference into truth values), I want to characterize the imperative and the interrogative mood by assigning suitable and natural kinds of possible denotations, which are a strictly compositional result of the characteristic syntax defining each mood.

In order to motivate my hypothesis I will outline a syntactico-semantic analysis of the English declarative, imperative, and various kinds of interrogatives in the style of a canonical extension of the grammar defined in Montague's PTQ (Montague 1974, chapter 8). This mode of presentation makes it possible to formulate the specifics of my analysis in brief, yet formally precise terms.

I will rely in particular on the intensional logic of PTQ, which is a type system with λ-calculus, and on the categorial surface syntax of PTQ, which characterizes the meaning of English surface expressions indirectly by systematic translation into formulas of intensional logic. These semantic representations are interpretable in explicit model-theoretic terms according to the truth-conditions of intensional logic as stated in PTQ. In order to handle certain phenomena of context-dependency arising with the imperative and with the interpretation of 'non-redundant answers', I will also refer to the system of a context-dependent intensional logic based on context-variables presented in Hausser (1979).

Unfortunately, in PTQ a declarative sentence is defined as denoting a truth-value rather than a proposition (i.e., a function from points of reference to truth-values). I agree with Tichy (1971) and Maderna (1974), who have criticized such "relics of extensionalism" in Montague's semantics. Rather than redefining PTQ in this respect (which would be space consuming, but

J. R. Searle, F. Kiefer, and M. Bierwisch (eds.), Speech Act Theory and Pragmatics,
71–95.

technically routine), I will gratuitously intensionalize translation-formulas where it is semantically relevant.[2]

1. SYNTACTIC MOOD VERSUS SPEECH ACTS

When we talk about syntactic moods we are talking about formal properties of linguistic surface expressions. These are to be kept clearly distinct from (the properties of) the speech acts in which a linguistic expression may function. For example,

(1)   Could you pass the salt?

is by virtue of its form an expression of the interrogative mood. If we use (1) at the dinner table we are normally performing a speech act of a request. But we may use (1) also as a question, for example when we use (1) to ask a disabled person about his physical abilities. The difference between these two types of speech acts may be characterized in terms of different appropriate responses: if (1) is used as a request, the appropriate response would be passing the salt; if (1) is used as a question about the hearers state of recovery, on the other hand, a simple 'yes' or 'no' would be an appropriate response. The crucial point is, however, that the literal meaning of (1) is exactly the same in the two different speech-acts indicated.

In the same sense as a linguistic expression like (1) may be used in different types of speech-acts, different linguistic expressions may be used to perform the same type of speech act. Consider for example (2) and (3):

(2)   You know were the can opener is.   (declarative)
(3)   Get the can opener!   (imperative)

I take it that the locutionary acts indicated in (4) and (5)

(4)   John says to Mary at 10.45: "You know where the can-opener is."
(5)   John says to Mary at 10.45: "Get the can-opener!"

may constitute the same illocutionary act, namely (6):

(6)   John requests from Mary at 10.45 to give him the can opener.

In other words, (2) and (3) may be used in locutionary acts which are *equivalent on the illocutionary level*, despite the fact that (2) and (3) are syntactically of different mood and denote semantically different things: while (2) denotes a proposition, (3) does not.

There is a certain feeling that declarative sentences are used primarily or predominantly as statements, while imperatives and interrogative sentences are used mostly as requests or questions, respectively. The above examples demonstrate clearly, however, that the syntactic mood does not determine the speech act. Rather, syntactic mood *participates* with all the other linguistic properties of a given surface expression ϕ in delimiting the set of use-conditions of ϕ. Since there is no one to one relation between syntactic moods and speech acts, it would be a mistake to implement speech act properties in the semantic characterization of syntactic mood.

This conclusion stands in contrast to the practice of Austin (1959), Lewis (1972), and many others, who proceed in their analyses on the assumption that examples like (7) and (8) are *semantically equivalent*.

(7)   I order you to leave.   (declarative)
(8)   Leave!   (imperative)

Before we scrutinize this assumption, let us note that (7) and (8) are of quite different syntactic structures. Comparison of (7) and (9), furthermore,

(9)   You ordered me to leave.

shows clearly that (7) and (9) are in the same syntactic paradigm.

It is curious that Austin and Lewis draw quite contrary conclusions from the presumed equivalence. Lewis recognizes that (7) is a declarative sentence and therefore wants to treat it semantically as a proposition. The presumption of semantic equivalence between (7) and (8), however, leads him to the counterintuitive consequence that (8) likewise denotes a proposition. Austin, on the other hand, notes correctly that (8) does not denote a proposition. The presumption of semantic equivalence between (7) and (8), however, leads Austin to the counterintuitive conclusion (and contrary to Lewis) that (7) does *not* denote a proposition, which means breaking the linguistic paradigm (according to Austin, (9) denotes a proposition while (7) does not).

Austin and Lewis agree that (7) and (8) are semantically equivalent and disagree about whether (7) (the explicit performative sentence) should denote a truth value or not. I take the position that (7) is a normal declarative sentence and denotes a proposition, while (8) is an imperative and does not denote a proposition. Consequently, (7) and (8) cannot be semantically equivalent in the sense that they have the same denotation at any given point

of reference: if (7) and (8) have different types of possible denotations they
cannot be semantically equivalent.

The assumption of semantic equivalence between, e.g., (7) and (8) must
go. Instead the relation between (7) and (8) is one of overlapping use conditions, just as in the case of (2) and (3) above. Furthermore, it is easy to show
that an explicit performative sentence like (7) denotes a proposition (pace
Austin). Imagine a run-down Hobo who walks by the docked Q.E.II, throws
an empty champange bottle at her hulk and says:

(10)   I hereby christen this ship the Q.E.II.

If we were to report this incident by saying (11),

(11)   The Hobo christened this ship the Q.E.II.

(11) would be *false* under the indicated circumstances. Thus the so-called
happiness conditions for an act of christening must be part of the truth conditions of the performative verb *christen*. (11) is false *because* the happiness
conditions for christening are not satisfied in the 'ceremony' refered to. And
(10) would be as false as (11). This truth value assignment reflects that in the
indicated circumstances no christening has taken place in the moment of
pronouncing (10).

The alleged semantic equivalence between, e.g., (12a) and (12b)

(12a)   I order you to leave.
(12b)   leave!

has served as the corner stone of the so-called performative analysis of non-
declaratives. Lewis, for example, treats (13b), and (14b) as *paraphrases* of
(13a), and (14a), respectively, and proposes to derive the latter from the
former via meaning-preserving transformations.

(13a)   I command that you are late.   (13b)   Be late!
(14a)   I ask whether you are late.   (14b)   Are you late?

Lewis says:

I propose that these non-declaratives (i.e., (13b) and (14b), R.H.) ought to be treated as
paraphrases of the corresponding performatives, having the same base structure, meaning,
intension, and truthvalue at an index or an occasion. And I propose that there is no

difference in kind between the meanings of these performatives and non-declaratives and the meanings of the ordinary declarative sentences considered previously.

Lewis 1972, p. 208.

It seems to me however, that by deriving (13b) and (14b) from the indicated declaratives, Lewis relies not only on the unsubstantiated semantic equivalence discussed above, but also fails to respect the distinction between syntactic mood and speech acts. The problems resulting are easy to see: if the surface syntactic form of imperatives, and interrogatives is systematically related to the 'underlying' performative clauses 'I command', and 'I ask', respectively, then also examples like (15a, b) or (16a, b) are rendered as paraphrases:

(15a)   I command that you feel yourself at home.
(15b)   Feel yourself at home!
(16a)   I hereby ask you whether you could pass the salt.
(16b)   Could you pass the salt?

The desire to reduce different syntactic moods to the same kind of meaning is also apparent in the analysis of Stenius (1967), according to which examples like (12b), (13b) and (14b)

(12b)   You are late.
(13b)   Be late!
(14b)   Are you late?

share the same sentence radical (propositional content) and differ only in their underlying mood operators. However, as Lewis points out correctly, "it is hard to see how it (i.e., the method of sentence radicals, R.H.) could be applied to other sorts of questions . . ." (op. cit., p. 207). Compare for example (17) and (18):

(17)   Who came?
(18)   John came.

There is no complete propositional content which could serve as the basis of (17).

The only reason for the popularity of the performative approach and the sentence radical method I can see is that it derives different moods from the same kind of structure. This way one can continue to practice logic in the ways one has long been accustomed to and evades the task to provide the syntactic structure of each mood with its own characteristic semantics. While I believe that the principles of referential semantics should be rigorously

maintained, there is no reason why we shouldn't use these principles crea-
tively. The performative approach and the sentence radical approach proceed
as if *propositions* were the only interpretable expressions of logic, which is a
completely unwarranted assumption.

Consider for example (19) and (20):

(19)   stop to kiss Mary
(19')   ˆstop' (kiss'$_*$ (*m*))
(20)   John stops to kiss Mary
(20')   ˆstop' (ˆ*ĵ*, *ŷ* kiss' (*y*, p̂p {ˆ*m*}))

The denotation of a complex IV-phrase like (19) can be interpreted in exactly
the same compositional manner (relative to a model and a point of reference)
as a complete declarative sentence like (20). The only difference is that (19)
denotes a function from points of reference into functions from individuals
into truthvalues, such as indicated in (a):

(a)   I×J → (A → {0,1}).

while (20) denotes a function from points of reference into truth values, such
as indicated in (b):

(b)   I×J → {0,1}.

The meaning of (19)/(19') is characterized in terms of the same kind of truth-
conditions as the meaning of (20)/(20'). (It would perhaps be more appropriate to speak of denotation-conditions rather than truth-conditions, since
the rules in question characterize the meaning of expressions of *any* semantic
type in general model theoretic terms.)

Propositions are like other possible denotations in that they occur as the
denotation of subordinate clauses. So why shouldn't other types of possible
denotation be like propositions in that they may serve as the denotation of
complete linguistic expressions? I will present a treatment of interrogatives
(section 5), according to which (21) translates into (21'):

(21)   Who talks?
(21')   ˆλ*P*[*P* ˆtalks'] ϵ ME$_{\langle s,f(t/\mathrm{T})\rangle}$

(where *P* is a variable of type $\langle s,f(\mathrm{T})\rangle$)

(21') is treated as a complete expression of intensional logic, denoting a
function from points of reference into sets of term-denotations (*John'*, *Bill'*,
the man you saw yesterday', etc.). According to my view, this type of possible

denotation is as characteristic of the type of interrogative involved as propositions are the characteristic type of possible denotations for declaratives. As far as I can see, the indicated semantic characterization of the meaning of (21) does in no way exceed the basic principles of intensional logic.

The point I want to make here is that it is logically *conceivable* that possible denotations other than propositions may serve as denotation of *complete* linguistic expressions, such as, for example, interrogatives, or imperatives. Note in this connection that a type system (such as the one employed the intensional logic defined in PTQ) provides *infinitely many* different types of possible denotations (compare the recursive definition of types, p. 256, and the recursive definition of possible denotations, p. 258, in PTQ). Later (section 4, 5) I will discuss the further question of which types of possible denotations should be defined as characteristic of which kinds of syntactic mood. This decision will be motivated in linguistic terms, since we proceed on the hypothesis that different syntactic moods are different kinds of syntactico-semantic composition occurring in natural language.

2. LINGUISTIC STANDARDS OF ANALYSIS (SURFACE COMPOSITIONALITY)

One reason why I have chosen to present my analysis of syntactic mood in form of an extension of PTQ is that PTQ is a *complete* grammar in the sense that the *generation and interpretation* of a fragment of English is *coordinated* in a rigorously formal generative system. Lewis (1972), on the other hand, is incomplete because the transformations which supposedly make an explicit performative categorial structure into a (non)-declarative surface structure are not spelled out. I take it however, that it would be a rather nasty job to explicitly define these transformations and give a 'reasonable' linguistic motivation for them.

As long as we don't coordinate the surface syntactic analysis with the semantic characterization of an expression in terms of a *complete, formal generative grammar* generating a fragment of a natural language, we can postulate any kind of logic for the characterization of syntactic mood — as witnessed also by Hintikka's (1976) analysis of questions. According to Hintikka, a direct interrogative such as (17)

(17)   Who came?

is derived by means of the 'usual two-step transformation' (op. cit., p. 22) from the following 'semantic representation':[3]

(17′)

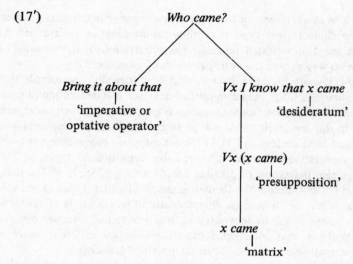

Far from being complete (in the indicated technical sense), Hintikka's analysis is nevertheless much more detailed than Lewis (1972). It also contains a number of claims which are theoretical artefacts. Hintikka claims for example that interrogatives such as analyzed in (17′) are systematically ambiguous between an 'existential' (e.g., (17′)) and a 'universal' (e.g., (17″)) reading.

(17″)   Bring it about that Λx I know that x came.

Or take the distinction between 'standard' and 'non-standard' questions. A standard question according to Hintikka is one in which the desideratum of the utterer can be truly stated in terms of *I know that*. . . . It follows that an examination question does not count as a 'standard' question because the interrogator presumably knows the answer to his question before he asks. In order to account for this 'observation', Hintikka proposes "that in examination questions we have a different imperative operator. Moreover, they obviously involve the second (grammatical) person instead of the first one" (op. cit., p. 45). In other words, if (17) is used as an examination question it would have to be derived from something like (22):

(22)   *Tell me whether* $\left\{ \begin{matrix} V \\ \Lambda \end{matrix} \right\}$ x such that *you* know that x came.
         | |
         (different impera-   (second
         tive operator)   person)

It seems to me that the four 'readings' of (17) (i.e., (17′), (17″) and (22)) are a straightforward result of confusing putative speech-act properties with semantic properties of linguistic expressions. In the treatment of interrogatives outlined in section 5, (17) is treated as a syntactically unambiguous expression.

I have discussed the analyses of non-declaratives by Lewis (1972) and Hintikka (1976) because they demonstrate the need for a rigorously *formal* and syntactico-semantically *complete* analysis of mood. The confusion of semantic properties and speech act features shows, furthermore, that in addition to the *methodological standard* of completeness we need some kind of *linguistic standard* to guide our use of mathematical power to linguistically well-motivated analyses. But which standard of linguistic analysis should we adhere to?

The assumption that the semantics of natural languages works like the semantics of formal languages in that the meaning of complex expressions is the systematic result of the meaning of the basic parts (and the mode of syntactic combination) suggests a principle which I would like to call the principle of *surface compositionality*. According to this principle, the semantic representation of a linguistic expression should contain nothing that does not have concrete surface syntactic motivation. Furthermore, a surface compositional analysis must characterize explicitly how the meaning of a *complex surface* expression is composed from the meaning of its *basic surface* constituents. For example, an analysis which derives *passive* via transformation from the corresponding *active* violates the principle of surface compositionality though it might still be complete in the sense that the linguistic expressions investigated are systematically characterized in model-theoretic terms by means of formal translation into intensional logic (compare Partee (1975), Cooper (1975)).

Thanks to the presence of λ-calculus, the principle of surface compositionality[4] can be easily accommodated in a PTQ-style grammar. Consider for example (23):

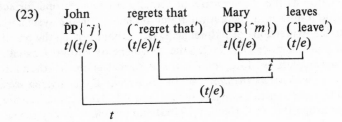

(23)   John   regrets that   Mary   leaves
        $\hat{P}P\{\check{}j\}$ (ˆregret that′)   (PP{ˆm})   (ˆleave′)
        $t/(t/e)$ $(t/e)/t$ $t/(t/e)$ (t/e)

The semantic representation in (23) assigns standard logical translations to every surface constituent — apart from the unresolved analysis of *regret that*, which would require further attention. Since the surface syntax and the logical syntax are completely parallel in their respective function-argument structures, the composition of the meaning in the surface expressions is explicitly characterized. Yet our surface compositional analysis remains strictly within the realm of standard semantics. The formula in (23) reduces 'automatically' via λ-conversion into the equivalent formula (24):

(24)   ˆregret that$'$ (ˇj, ˆleave$'$ (ˆm)).

Neither Lewis (1972) nor Hintikka (1976) follow the principle of surface compositionality because their semantic representations contain a lot more than can be surface-syntactically motivated, and because the structure of the surface syntax is completely disregarded in their respective semantic analyses. The movement, deletion, and insertion transformations of transformational grammar in general run counter to the principle.

The linguistic literature of recent years has been quite concerned with 'evaluation measures', designed to help finding the 'right' grammar for a natural language (c.f. Chomsky (1965), Partee (1978)). It seems to me that the combination of

(a)   the principle of formal completeness (regarding the coordination of syntax and semantics), and
(b)   the principle of surface compositionality

would result in a restriction on linguistic analysis of natural language which would induce the following desirable properties: an approach conforming to (a) and (b) would have to be such that (i) different 'local' analyses in the system must really be shown to be *compatible* with each other, and (ii) all aspects of linguistic analysis would have to be motivated over concrete surface properties (rather than putative speech act and/or paraphrase properties).

The combination of the requirements of formal completeness and surface compositionality results in a theoretical frame designed for the systematic analysis of surface expressions of natural language without leaving the principles of referential semantics. The larger the 'fragment of natural language' generated by a complete, surface compositional formal grammar, the more instances of *independent motivation* can be expected. By analyzing each surface constant according to category, type of possible denotation, subcategory, P-inducer properties, (c.f. Hausser 1976a), context-dependency aspects (c.f. Hausser (1979)), etc., complex syntactic and semantic patterns may be explained as the systematic result of the formal nature of the basic words and the structure of their combination in the linguistic surface (e.g., the treatment of 'negation-any' versus 'intensional-any' in Hausser (1976b)).

3. DENOTATION CONDITIONS VERSUS USE-MARKERS

There is no question that the syntactic mood of an expression ϕ is relevant for the use-conditions of ϕ. However, since *all* properties of ϕ are relevant for the use-conditions of ϕ, this statement does not say anything about the nature of syntactic mood. The real question is whether syntactic mood is a syntactico-semantic phenomenon to be characterized in terms of the classical denotation-conditions (truth conditions) or whether syntactic mood should be treated as a use-marker. The interrelation between denotation-conditions, use-markers and use-conditions of an expression of natural language may be indicated as follows:

(25)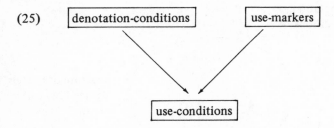

Since the question of whether syntactic mood should be treated semantically in terms of the general denotation conditions or pragmatically as a use-marker touches on some very basic issues concerning the relation between semantics and pragmatics, it might be appropriate to briefly elaborate the notions in question.

The denotation-conditions of an expression capture its literal meaning in general model theoretic terms. Take for example (26):

(26)   John walks.

The logic characterizes the meaning of (26) as a function from the meaning of its parts by saying roughly that 'John walks' is true if the denotation of John is an element of the set of walkers. We may illustrate this basic idea in form of the following diagram (which represents an indirectly interpreting system such as PTQ):

(27)

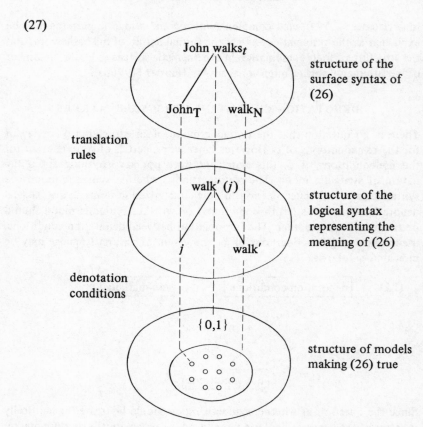

What kinds of meaning may be characterized in a given system depends on the kind of logic employed. (27) represents an *extensional* characterization which is well suited for demonstrating the basic idea of referential semantics, but not sufficient for a general semantics of natural language. I don't want to go here into the many reasons showing that a typed higher order logic is over-whelmingly better qualified to account for the kinds of meaning found in natural language than first order predicate calculus.[5] Let us just remember that the semantic characterization of meaning in model theoretic terms is a completely general theory which, based on a system of syntactic categories and corresponding types of possible denotations, characterizes the meaning of a complex expression as a systematic result of the structure of the expression and the meaning (denotation) of its basic parts.

We turn now to the *use-markers* in natural language. The expressions of a language like English may be divided into two classes:

(28a)   Expressions like *walk, kiss Mary, believe that the man left,* etc., the meaning of which is defined in terms of denotation conditions.

(28b)   Expressions like *ah, oh, hurray, phew, yak, boo,* etc. which don't have a syntactic category and don't denote. Instead, these words are what I call use-markers: they directly influence the use-conditions of the expressions containing them (if they are contained).

The distinction between denotation-conditional features and usemarkers applies to all levels of the linguistic surface. For example, in phonology we have denotation-relevant intonation (syntactic intonation) as illustrated by the comparison of (29a) and (29):

(29a)   John came.
(29b)   John came?

(29a) denotes a proposition, while (29b) does not. On the other hand, we also find intonation features which are relevant solely in terms of use, as exemplified by different ways to pronounce, e.g., (30):

(30)   It's nice to see you. (warmly, politely, routinely, etc.)

(See also example (46) in section 5 below).
   In syntax, furthermore, the structural difference between (31a) and (31b)

(31a)   The man who arrived yesterday kissed every girl at the party.
(31b)   The man at the party kissed every girl who arrived yesterday.

is obviously denotation relevant (different truth-conditions), while the difference between (32a) and (32b)

(32a)   It is amazing that Mary left.
(32b)   That Mary left is amazing.

is relevant solely in terms of use.[6]
   Let us return now to our question of whether syntactic mood should be treated in surface-compositional syntactico-semantic terms or as a use-marker. The latter position is quite clearly expressed in the following quotation from Lewis (1972):

Fundamentally, however, the entire apparatus of referential semantics (whether done on a categorial base, as I propose, or otherwise) pertains to sentence radicals and constituents thereof. The semantics of mood is something entirely different. It consists of rules of language use. .... In abstract semantics, as distinct from the theory of language use, a meaning for a sentence should simply be a *pair* of a mood and an S-meaning (mood being identified with some arbitrarily chosen entities).

Lewis (1972), p. 207.

Yet, there is no one to one relation between mood and use/speech-act (compare section 1). Furthermore, to identify mood with arbitrarily chosen entities violates the principle of surface compositionality (c.f. section 2). Finally, why should referential semantics be limited to sentence radicals? As Lewis points out himself, sentence radicals are a theoretical construct and do not normally appear on the linguistic surface.

4. A COMPOSITIONAL ANALYSIS OF IMPERATIVES

The crucial question for a surface compositional analysis of non-declarative sentence moods is: What do complete but non-declarative expressions denote? I take it that an *imperative* denotes a property (roughly that property which the speaker wants the hearer to aquire). This concept is formally captured in the semantic representation $(33')$ of (33):

(33)   Leave! $\epsilon \, P_{IV}$
$(33')$ $^\wedge\lambda x \, [\Gamma_2 \{x\} \backsim \text{leave}'(x)]$ $\epsilon \, ME_{\langle s, f(IV) \rangle}$

$(33')$ denotes the property of being the hearer (Γ_2) and to be leaving. Γ_2 is a *context-variable* representing the property of being the hearer. For detailed definitions of the presumed treatment of context-dependency see Hausser (1979), where Γ_2 appears in the translation of second person pronouns such as *you* $(\epsilon \, B_T)$, *your* $(\epsilon \, B_T/CN)$, *yours* $(\epsilon \, B_T)$, *our* $(\epsilon \, B_T/CN)$, etc. Γ_2 is of type $\langle s, f(CN) \rangle$.

The indicated treatment of imperatives may be implemented into the PTQ-system by adding the following two rules:

S20.   If $\alpha \, \epsilon \, P_{IV}$, then $F_{20}(\alpha) \, \epsilon \, P_{IV}$ and $F_{20}(\alpha)$ is $\alpha!$.

T20.   If $\alpha \, \epsilon \, P_{IV}$ and α translates into α', then $F_{20}(\alpha)$ translates into $\hat{x} [\Gamma_2 \{x\} \backsim \Gamma'(x)]$.

Thus, (33) and $(33')$ are derived in our extension as follows:

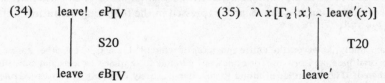

(34)   leave! ϵP_{IV} (35) $^\wedge\lambda x \, [\Gamma_2 \{x\} \backsim \text{leave}'(x)]$

                 S20   T20

         leave ϵB_{IV} leave'

Our analysis may be motivated linguistically as follows:

It is a fact that imperatives in English do not have subjects. Therefore, it seemed best to avoid the postulation of an 'underlying' subject. Since the syntactic structure of English imperatives is identical to the structure of un-inflected IV-phrases, it suggests itself to take such IV-phrases as the point of departure for the derivation of imperatives. The presence of the context-variable Γ_2 in the semantic representation of imperatives is motivated over the universal fact that second person personal T-pronouns serving as the direct or indirect object of the main verb in an imperative must be *reflexive pronouns*. With regard to this important detail, our treatment of imperatives plugs in directly to the surface compositional treatment of pronouns presented in Hausser (1979) (for the analysis of reflexives see section 8). The context-variable Γ_2 is crucial, furthermore, for distinguishing imperatives semantically from the corresponding IV-phrases (which are not considered to be complete linguistic expressions). The 'propositional content' of imperatives, finally is captured in the semantic representation without the counterintuitive assumption that imperatives denote propositions and without invoking putative speech-act properties.

The *fulfillment-conditions* for imperatives used as requests may be roughly characterized as in (36):

(36)   If the speaker s utters $f_{20}(\alpha)$ (where $\alpha \in P_{IV}$) towards a hearer h at time j in order to make a request, then this utterance is a *fulfilled* request if and only if there is a time j', $j' > j$, such that $[h=x \frown \alpha(x)]$ is true at j'.

Whether a certain imperative expression is used as a request or an order, etc. depends on pragmatic criteria concerning the status of the speaker (authority), his wishes (sincerity), etc. But assuming that an utterance of an imperative constitutes a request, (36) specifies the conditions under which this request would be fulfilled.

Our semantic representation of the imperative (33) may seem rather parsimonious. Is (33') sufficient as the semantic representation of the literal meaning of (33)? And what is the literal meaning? In order to clarify my position regarding the relation of meaning and use, semantics and pragmatics, it might be helpful to consider a metaphor.

Imagine A and B sitting at the dinner table, B looks quietly at A and flashes the little card indicated in (37).

(37)

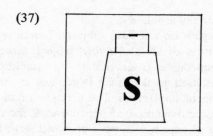

Wouldn't A quite normally understand the flashing of this card under the indicated circumstances as a request to pass the salt? No illocutionary force indicator is necessary to use the card in (37) for making a request. Furthermore, we could use the same card also in a descriptive function if the circumstances are of an appropriate nature. For example, (37) could serve as a label on a box containing little bags with salt (in distinction to another box containing little bags with pepper).

Now, does (37) have two or more meanings depending on how many different uses we can find for it? Or is (37) one sign with one meaning? Though (37) has an extremely rudimentary 'surface-syntax' and there is no special syntactic mood to speak of we may extend the performative approach to this example by postulating 'underlying' meanings.

> If (37) is used as a request then it means 'I request from you that you pass the salt.'. But if (37) is used as a label then it means 'This container contains salt.'.

I would like to argue, on the other hand, that (37) has only one simple meaning, as represented in the picture of a salt-shaker. We may say that this picture denotes like the English word *salt-shaker* denotes.

It seems to me that the study of speech-acts makes sense only if we operate with concrete linguistic signs in their literal meaning. Only if we stick to the meaning concretely given in the sign can we study the use-conditions of this sign. By making explicit assumptions about the beliefs, intentions, emotions, and preferences of the speaker and other relevant features of the utterance situation, we can systematically deduce the intended use of the sign. The theory of pragmatics should be able to account for different uses of cards like (37) in the same way as it should account for the use of natural language signs.

In order to further motivate my surface compositional approach (with its consequences for syntax, semantics, and pragmatics), I will present below an analysis of the interrogative mood which illustrates how 'literal' the translation of linguistic surface structures into the standard notation of intensional logic can be (though much could be improved in a more thorough and detailed analysis).

5. THE SYNTAX AND SEMANTICS OF INTERROGATIVES[5]

While the imperative mood in English is characterized by one basic type of surface syntactic construction, the interrogative mood exhibits a systematic variety which creates a whole spectrum of different surface syntactic constructions. For reasons which will become apparent shortly, we may distinguish between the following two basic types of interrogatives: *non-restricted* interrogatives and *restricted* interrogatives.

Examples of non-restricted interrogatives are (38—42):

(38)	Who came?	(John.)
(39)	Why did John come?	(Because he admires Mary.)
(40)	When did John arrive?	(Early.)
(41)	How often did John kiss Mary?	(A 103 times.)

Examples of restricted interrogatives, on the other hand, are (43) and (44):

(43)	Did John kiss Mary?	(Yes./No.)
(44)	Does Mary love John or Bill?	(Yes./No.)
		(John./Bill.)

The expressions in brackets in the above examples are *compatible answer expressions*. In the same sense as we have to distinguish between an interrogative X and a speech act of asking which contains X as a token, we have to distinguish between 'answer-expressions' and the speech act of answering.[8] Which kind of expressions may serve as answers to which kind of interrogatives? Consider the following example:

(45)	John asks Bill: "Who came?"	
	Bill answers:	
(a)	"Peter."	(non-redundant answer)
(b)	"Peter did."	(pseudo-redundant answer)
(c)	"Peter came."	(redundant answer)
(d)	"Peter, on Mary's bicycle."	(explicatory non-red.an.)
(e)	"Peter did, on Mary's bicycle."	(explicatory pseudo-red.an.)
(f)	"Peter came, on Mary's bicycle."	(explicatory red. answer)

The non-redundant and pseudo-redundant answers (i.e., (45a), (45b), (45d), and (45e)) are special surface expressions which (i) are *not* a complete declarative expression, (ii) denote a truthvalue (proposition) if interpreted relative to a suitable interrogative, and (iii) exhibit highly specific structural properties which delimit the class of interrogatives they may function to answer. The redundant answers (i.e., (45c) and (45f), on the other hand, are complete and regular declarative expressions. Whether these declaratives are used as answers or not is solely a matter of the speech-act they are used in.

The answers indicated in (38–44) are all non-redundant answers. They demonstrate that a *non-redundant* answer-expression may be related only to two kinds of interrogative because it is structurally incompatible with all other kinds. The expression "John.", for example, is a possible answer only to (38) and (44), on the 'disjunctive reading' of (44). The declarative sentence (46),

(46)   John came early because he admires Mary.

on the other hand, may serve as an explicatory *redundant* answer to (38), (39), and (40). Which interrogative (46) is used to answer is indicated only in the intonation. Note that this specific intonation is a *use marker*: it has no influence on the denotation of the sentence.

How can the structural properties of interrogatives, answer-expressions, and the important property of compatibility observed in the above examples be formally characterized in a complete and surface compositional analysis? In the analysis presented in Hausser & Zaefferer (1977) and Hausser (1977, chapter 5), an interrogative is analyzed syntactico-semantically in such a way that it fits together with a compatible non-redundant answer and vice versa. Their combination results in a proposition which is semantically equivalent to the translation of the corresponding redundant answer:

(48)   interrogative expression   non-redundant answer

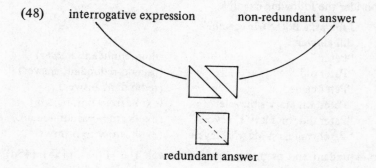

redundant answer

Note that the interrogative elements *who, why, when,* and *how* in the non-restricted interrogatives (38–41) have the *same* syntactic category as the *constituents* of their respective non-redundant answers. This fact is taken into account in the analysis of the following example:

(49)   Who came? $(\epsilon\, P_t/\mathrm{T})$ John. $(\epsilon\, P_t)$

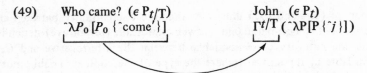

where P_0 is a variable of type $\langle s, f(\mathrm{T})\rangle$ ranging over term-denotations, while $\Gamma t/\mathrm{T}$ is a context-variable of type $\langle s, f(t/\mathrm{T})\rangle$ ranging over translations of t/T-interrogatives provided by the context.

The non-redundant answer (49b) is interpreted with respect to the interrogative (49a) by replacing the context-variable by the translation of (49a). The result is (50a), which reduces via λ-conversion to (50b).

(50a) $\hat{}\lambda P_0 [P_0 \{\hat{}\mathrm{come}'\}](\hat{}\lambda P[P\{\check{}j\}])$.
(50b) $\hat{}\mathrm{come}'(\check{}j)$.

(50b) is the translation of the corresponding redundant answer 'John came.', as desired. For the details of *contextual reconstruction* (i.e., replacement of a context-variable as indicated in (49)) see Hausser (1979).

According to the indicated treatment, an interrogative denotes a function from points of reference into *sets of corresponding non-redundant answer constituent denotations*. The category variation (type-variation) of different interrogatives (i.e., interrogatives with interrogative elements of different category) is crucial for the characterization of compatibility between an interrogative and its non-redundant answers. As an example of a t/IAV-interrogative consider (51):

(51)   When did John arrive? $(\epsilon\, P_t/\mathrm{IAV})$ Early. $(\epsilon\, P_t)$

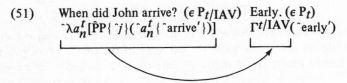

The result of contextual reconstruction is:

$$\hat{P}P\ \check{}j\ (\hat{}\mathrm{early}'(\hat{}\mathrm{arrive}')).$$

(The variable a_n^t is of type $\langle s, f(\text{IAV}) \rangle$, where IAV=IV/IV, ranging over the denotation of time-adverbs. In order to differentiate between different kinds of adverbs, I assume that the variables representing IAV-interrogative elements are sorted with respect to time, place, manner, etc.)

Comparison of (50) and (51) illustrates that the compatibility between an interrogative and a non-redundant answer expression (responsive) depends largely on the category correspondence between the interrogative and the context-variable in the answer (where the type of the context-variable must always be such that the answer denotes a proposition). Further restrictions are induced by sub-categories such as different kinds of adverbs:

(52)   *Where did John go?   Yesterday.

Where corresponds to an IAV-variable sorted with respect to places. Though the constituent in the answer-expression in (52) is of category IAV, it is not of the right subcategory.

Our semantic treatment covers also the multiple interrogatives (which are likewise non-restricted interrogatives). Consider (53):

(53)   Who kissed whom where? $(\epsilon\ P_{(((t/\text{T})/\text{T})/\text{IAV})})$
$\lambda a_2^p \lambda P_1 \lambda P_0 [P_0({}^\smallfrown a_1^p({}^\smallfrown \text{see}'(P_1)))$

John Mary in the kitchen. $(\epsilon\ P_t)$
$\Gamma t/\text{T}/\text{T}/\text{IAV}({}^\smallfrown \text{in the kitchen}')(\hat{\text{P}}\text{P}\{{}^\smallfrown m\})(\hat{\text{P}}\text{P}\{{}^\smallfrown j\})$
$= \Gamma t/\text{T}/\text{T}/\text{IAV}(\hat{\text{P}}\text{P}\{{}^\smallfrown j\}, \hat{\text{P}}\text{P}\{{}^\smallfrown m\}, {}^\smallfrown \text{in the kitchen}');$

where a_2^p is a variable of type $\langle s, f(\text{IAV}) \rangle$ sorted with respect to places. P_0 and P_1 are variables of type $\langle s, f(\text{T}) \rangle$.

Contextual reconstruction renders again a formula which is equivalent to the translation of the corresponding redundant answer:

John kissed Mary in the kitchen.
$\hat{\text{P}}\text{P}\{{}^\smallfrown j\}({}^\smallfrown \text{in the kitchen}'({}^\smallfrown \text{kiss}(\hat{\text{P}}\text{P}\{{}^\smallfrown m\})))$.

(53) demonstrates that the category of interrogative elements as well as their number and relative order determine the category of the whole interrogative expression. Furthermore, the number of interrogative elements in a non-restricted interrogative is theoretically indefinitely large and restricted only by limitations of perception (a parallel case is the stacking of relative clauses). This means that there are indefinitely many kinds of non-restricted interrogatives, having different types of possible denotations and different types of

compatible non-redundant and pseudo-redundant answers. Semantically, we may motivate the postulated syntactico-semantic structure of interrogatives by saying that interrogatives denote *sets of* their non-redundant *answer constituent-denotations*.

We have thus captured the intuition underlying the hypothesis in Hamblin (1973) that interrogatives denotes *sets of possible answers*, though in a manner quite different from Hamblin's. Hamblin proceeds on the assumption that an answer must be a declarative sentence, which leads him to define interrogatives as uniformly denoting *sets of propositions*. He motivates this move by proposing to treat declaratives as denoting unit-sets of propositions. Thus imperatives and declaratives denote the same kind of function — though imperatives are apparently not included in this 'generalization'. Needless to say, the question of compatibility between interrogatives and suitable answer-expressions is not raised in his paper.

The basic principles of my approach to non-restricted interrogatives are suited also for a logically standard treatment of restricted interrogatives. Consider (54):

(54)   Did John leave?
$$\char94\lambda r_n[r_n(\char94 leave'(\char94 j)) \char92 [(r_n=\hat{p}[\char92 p]) \vee (r_n=\hat{p}[\char92 \sim p])]]$$

No.
$$\ulcorner t/(t//t)(\hat{p}[\char92 \sim p])$$

(r_n is a variable of type $ME_{f(t//t)}$. I assume that *yes* and *no* ($\epsilon\ B_{t//t}$) translate into $\hat{p}[\char92 p]$ and $\hat{p}[\char92 \sim p]$, respectively. Contextual reconstruction renders an expression which is equivalent to the translation of the corresponding redundant answer 'John didn't leave', i.e., $\char94\sim leave'(\char94 j)$.)

Yes/no-interrogatives like (54) are morphologically and semantically related to the socalled alternative interrogatives, such as (55),

(55)   Did John kiss Mary or Suzy?

which is ambiguous between the following two meanings:

(55a) $\hat{r}_n[r_n(\text{kiss}'(\char94 j, \hat{P}[P\{\char94 m\}\vee P\{\char94 s\}])]]$ (yes/no-reading)
(55b) $\hat{P}_n[\text{kiss}'(\char94 j, P_n)\ [(P_n=\hat{P}P\{\char94 m\}) \vee (P_n=\hat{P}P\{\char94 s\})]]$ (term-reading)

Expressions like (54) or (55) are called restricted interrogatives because the possible values of the variables in their translation is restricted via explicit enumeration. Note that there are again indefinitely many kinds of restricted interrogatives, as shown by example (56):

(56)   Did John kiss Mary or Bill Suzy?   ($\epsilon\ P_{t/T/T}$)   John Mary.

The different readings (55a) and (55b) are marked on the surface in terms of different intonation. These intonation patterns constitute an instance of 'syntactic intonation' (are not a use-marker). The rules implementing the indicated syntactico-semantic treatment of restricted and non-restricted interrogatives, redundant and non-redundant answer-expressions as well as the so-called 'indirect questions' into a complete and canonical extension of PTQ are given in Hausser (1976c), and need not be repeated here.

6. CONCLUSIONS

Let us return now to our basic hypothesis according to which different moods should be characterized semantically in terms of their characteristic kind of possible denotation (induced by their characteristic syntax). We have seen that different moods arise in form of very clearly defined different kinds of surface structures. We argued that

(a)   declaratives denote propositions, i.e., they are expressions of type $\langle s,e \rangle$,

(b)   imperatives denote properties of individual concepts (restricted in the indicated way), i.e. they are expressions of type $\langle s, f(t/e) \rangle$,

(c)   interrogatives denote functions from s into sets of non-redundant answer constituent denotations, i.e., they are expressions of type $\langle s, \langle\langle s,\alpha \rangle, t \rangle\rangle$, where α is the type of the constituent of the respective compatible non-redundant answer expressions.

Thus there is no type-overlap between different syntactic moods. It seems to me that the kinds of possible denotations assigned to different moods are completely natural. To say that an imperative denotes properties of individual concepts (restricted to the hearer) is no less motivated than saying that an declarative denote propositions.

While the presented treatment of non-declaratives logically completely standard, it is linguistically close to the surface and maintains the original categories of the constituents. In line with the principle of surface compositionality, our semantic representations of different moods contain nothing that is not concretely reflected in the linguistic surface.

But don't we need at least some 'underlying' interrogative or imperative *operators* for the semantic characterization of *non-declarative* moods? The answer is *no* for the reasons given in sections 1, 2, and 3, which may be summarized as follows:

(i)   there are no features in the linguistic surface which could be constitently interpreted as mood-operators or mood-markers;

(ii)   there is no necessity for postulating operators or markers since different moods are sufficiently differentiated in terms of their surface syntax and the corresponding types of possible denotations.

(iii)   the use of such operators amounts to introducing speech act properties and would lead to the same problems in connection with 'indirect speech-acts' as Hintikka (1976) and Lewis (1972) encounter.

Our analysis of mood has shown that the principle of surface-compositionality leads not only to a highly restricted syntactico-semantic analysis of expressions of natural language, but is also of greatest consequence for the analysis of the use-conditions of these expressions. The systematic study of speech-acts cannot be successful as long as we don't proceed on the basis of concrete linguistic signs in their literal meaning.

ACKNOWLEDGEMENTS

This paper was first presented at the Dobogokö-Conference, Hungary, July 1977. I would like to thank Ferenc Kiefer and John Searle for the opportunity to participate at this stimulating conference. I benefited especially from discussions with Manfred Bierwisch, Harry Bunt, Anna Szabolsci, and Dieter Wunderlich. In January 1978, this paper was read at the Second Amsterdam Colloquium on Montague Grammar and Related Topics. In the summer of 1978, a preliminary version appeared in the proceedings of the Amsterdam Conference.

NOTES

[1] The term 'mood' can be used either in connection with *verbal mood*, such as indicative, subjunctive, optative, etc., or in connection with *syntactic mood*, such as declarative, imperative, or interrogative. The specifics of a certain mood may vary from language to language, and different languages may have different moods, as a comparison of the verbal moods of Greek vs. English demonstrates. The present paper will be concerned with syntactic mood only.

[2] Strictly intensional logics have been explicitly defined in Hausser 1978 and 1980.

[3] As far as I can reconstruct.

[4] For a more extensive discussion of the principle of surface compositionality see Hausser (1978).

[5] For example, Hintikka (1976), who uses a semiformal first order predicate calculus as his semantic representation, cannot distinguish between *terms* (*John, the man who*

arrived yesterday, etc.) and *adverbs* (*there, in the kitchen*, etc.) in terms of category and type of possible denotation (op. cit., p. 29).

[6] I treat topicalization as a syntactic use-marker. Pragmatically based alternations such as in (32) are in my opinion the only occasion in which the mechanism of a meaning preserving transformation could be appropriate. Furthermore, it could be argued that a pragmatically based movement transformation does not violate the syntactico-semantic principle of surface compositionality.

[7] The discussion of interrogatives in the present section summarizes the main points of Hausser (1976c).

[8] We use the terms 'statement', 'question' and 'request' to refer to *speech acts*, in contrast to the terms 'declarative', 'interrogative', and 'imperative', which refer to structural properties of surface *expressions*. In order to carry this terminological practice over to the class of answer expressions in (38–44) consider the distinction between the terms 'answer' (referring to a speech act) and 'responsive' (referring to surface expressions of a certain kind, such as 'John.', 'In the garden', etc., which are of category t). Thus 'Mary is in the garden.' and 'In the garden.' could both be *used* as an answer to the question using the interrogative 'Where is Mary?', but the former must be classified as a *declarative* and the latter as a *respondative*.

REFERENCES

Austin, J. L.: 1962, *How to do Things with Words*, Cambridge, Mass., Harvard University Press.

Chomsky, N.: 1965, *Aspects of a Theory of Syntax*, Cambridge, Mass., MIT-press.

Cooper, R.: 1975, *Montague's Semantic Theory and Transformational Syntax*, unpublished Ph.D. dissertation, Univ. of

Hamblin, C. L.: 1973, 'Questions in Montague English', *Foundations of Language* 10, 1973, pp. 41–54.

Hausser, R.: 1974, *Quantification in an Extended Montague Grammar*, unpublished Ph.D. dissertation, Univ. of Texas at Austin.

Hausser, R.: 1976a, 'Presuppositions in Montague Grammar', in *Theoretical Linguistics*, Vol. 3.3.

Hausser, R.: 1976b, 'Scope Ambiguity and Scope Restriction in Montague Grammar', in *Amsterdam Papers in Formal Philosophy*, eds. R. Bartsch, J. Groeneddijk, and M. Stokhof, Dept. of Philosophy, The University of Amsterdam.

Hausser, R.: 1976c, 'The Logic of Questions and Answers', unpublished manuscript.

Hausser, R. and D. Zaefferer: 1978, 'Questions and Answers in a Context-dependent Montague Grammar', in *Formal Semantics and Pragmatics* of Natural Language, eds. F. Guenthner and S. J. Schmidt, Synthese Language Library, D. Reidel, Dordrecht.

Hausser, R.: 1978, 'Surface Compositional Semantics, chapter I', unpublished manuscript.

Hausser, R.: 1979, 'How do Pronouns Denote?', in *Syntax and Semantics*, Vol. 10, eds. F. Heny and H. Schnelle, Academic Press, New York.

Hausser, R.: 1980, 'A Constructive Approach to Intensional Contexts, remarks on the Metaphysics of Model Theory', in *Ambiguities in Intensional Contexts*, ed. F. Heny, Synthese Language Library, D. Reidel, Dordrecht.

Hausser, to appear: *Studies in Montague Grammar*, Academic Press, New York.

Hintikka, J.: 1976, *The Semantics of Questions and the Questions of Semantics*, Acta Philosophical Fennica, Vol. 28, No. 4, North-Holland Publishing Company, Amsterdam.

Lewis, D. K.: 1972, 'General Semantics', in *Semantics of Natural Language*, eds. Davidson and Harman, D. Reidel, Dordrecht.

Maderna, P.: 1974, 'Some Remarks on Montague's Language L_0 in comparison with Tichy's language L_μ', in *Linguistische Berichte* 34/74.

Montague, R.: 1974, *Formal Philosophy*, The Papers of Richard Montague, edited and with an introduction by Richmond Thomason, Yale University Press, New Haven.

Partee, B.: 1975, 'Montague Grammar and Transformational Grammar', *Linguistic Inquiry* 4, 2.

Partee, B.: 1979, 'Montague Grammar and the Well-Formedness Constraint', in *Syntax and Semantics* Vol. 10, eds. F. Heny and H. Schnelle, Academic Press, New York.

Stenius, E.: 1967, 'Mood and Language-Game', Synthese 17, pp. 254–274.

Tichy, P.: 1971, 'An Approach to Intensional Analysis', Noûs 5, 273–297.

FERENC KIEFER

YES-NO QUESTIONS AS WH-QUESTIONS*

1

In this paper I am going to discuss some types of yes-no questions which —
under normal circumstances — cannot be answered equally well by a plain
'yes' or a plain 'no'. My account of these questions will principally be based
on the theory of indirect speech acts and the theory of conversation.

Before embarking on the discussion of the types of yes-no questions which
I have in mind let me briefly mention some other types of yes-no questions
which, too, behave idiosyncratically with respect to yes-no answers but which
will not be my concern in this paper.

1.1. Indirect speech acts

Although I am going to claim that the yes-no questions to be discussed in the
present paper, too, are interpretable as indirect speech acts, the yes-no questions that people usually treat under the heading of indirect speech acts are of
the following type:[1]

(1)   (a) Can you pass the salt?
        (b) Have you got change for a dollar?
        (c) Would you kindly get off my foot?
        (d) Would you mind not making so much noise?

Such questions are indirect requests: the speaker wants the hearer to do
something. That is, (1) (a)–(d) are requests for actions, consequently no
verbal response is required. Under normal circumstances it would even be
inappropriate to answer questions such as (1) (a)–(d) by 'yes' or 'no'.

There are also cases where yes-no questions are requests for information.
Consider

(2)   (a) Can you give me some kind of idea of that conversation?
        (b) Can you describe him to us?
        (c) Will you give me the date when you last saw your wife?
        (d) Can you tell me when the next train leaves?

Once again, a plain 'yes' as an answer to (2) (a)–(d) would be utterly inadequate and a plain 'no' may sound impolite in certain speech situations.

97

J. R. Searle, F. Kiefer, and M. Bierwisch (eds.), Speech Act Theory and Pragmatics,
97–119.

In what follows I am not going to discuss indirect speech acts of types (1) and (2) though some of the problems to be touched upon will be related to indirect speech acts of type (2).

1.2. Rhetorical questions

Most of the things which have traditionally been called rhetorical questions would now come under the heading of indirect speech acts. There are, however, 'genuine' rhetorical questions which, I think, should not be treated as indirect speech acts. Genuine rhetorical questions are, for example, (i) questions used in soliloquy and (ii) questions used for asking ourselves (e.g., in contexts of argumentation).[2] Consider

(3)   (a) Am I that stupid?
        (b) Is this really a problem?

(3) (a) is rhetorical if uttered in soliloquy and (3) (b) is rhetorical if the speaker doesn't want the addressee to answer this question: he knows the answer perfectly well, in fact, he answers the question himself.

In general: rhetorical questions do not require an answer (and they do not require a non-verbal response either) because they are uttered in soliloquy or because the answer is given by the speaker himself.

1.3. Conducive questions

Quite a few yes-no questions are conducive to a particular type of answer. From the point of view of conduciveness the following three question types deserve special attention: (i) negative inverted yes-no questions, (ii) assertive yes-no questions and (iii) tag questions.

In contrast to positive yes-no Qs, which normally may be considered neutral as to the expected reply, each of these special Q-type reflects the speaker's beliefs, expectations, or emotional reactions to the previous discourse. (Wikberg 1975:124)

The three types of questions are exemplified in (4)–(6).

(4)   (a) Weren't you at the scene of the crime at 10:00 on the night
             of the murder?
        (b) Were you at the scene of the crime at 10:00 on the night of
             the murder?

                                                      (Pope 1976:68)

(5)   (a) The guests have had $\left\{\begin{array}{l}\text{nothing}\\\text{something}\end{array}\right\}$ to eat?

         (b)+The guests have had anything to eat?

                                                    (Wikberg 1975:130)

(6)   (a) You are going now, aren't you?
         (b) You aren't going now, are you?

Whereas (4) (b) is a neutral question, (4) (a) is conducive to a positive answer. (5) (a), too, is conducive to a positive answer. (6) (a) and (b) exhibit opposite conduciveness: in the case of (6) (a) the expected answer is in the affirmative and in the case of (6) (b) in the negative.

Notice, however, that conduciveness or bias does not make one of the logically possible answers inadequate. (4) (a) and (b) can equally well be answered by 'yes' and 'no'. The same holds for (6) (a) and (b). Thus, I do not subscribe to E. Pope's view who thinks that only the expected answer is 'grammatical' (Pope 1976:37). In support of her view she adduces the following examples (my numbering, FK).

(7)   (a) Don't you want to grow up big and strong?
         (b) Yes, of course I do.
(8)   (a) Do you want people to think we live in a pigsty?
         (b) No, of course I don't.
(9)   (a) Don't I work my fingers to the bone for you?
         (b) Yes, of course you do.
(10)   (a) Is it necessary to shout like that?
         (b) No, of course it isn't.

I admit that in certain speech situations the (b)-answers are the expected answers to the (a)-questions. However, it is quite easy to imagine other situations in which they are not or in which some of the (a)-questions are neutral rather than biased. Furthermore, it is also easy to think of situations in which only the non-expected answers are adequate. This shows clearly that what is at stake here has nothing to do with grammar.

Since biased or conducive questions may appropriately be answered by either a blunt 'yes' or a blunt 'no', they do not belong to the problems to be discussed in this paper.[3]

2. FOCUSSED YES-NO QUESTIONS: A CASE STUDY

Compare the following questions:

(11)   (a) Is John leaving for Stockholm tomorrow?
        (b) Is John leaving for Stockholm *tomorrow*?
(12)   Is John leaving for *Stockholm* tomorrow?
(13)   Is *John* leaving for Stockholm tomorrow?

where underlining indicates the focussed part of the sentence. Consider first
(11) (a)–(b). Though both of these questions carry some kind of assumptions
with respect to John's eventual journey, these assumptions are only made
explicit in (11) (b). In (11) (b) it is taken for granted that John is going to
Stockholm, this is not part of the question. On the other hand, it is the
speaker's assumption about John's eventual journey that prompts the question
(11) (a): the speaker asks this question because he is not quite sure whether
his assumptions are right. His assumptions are thus part of what is questioned.
Consequently, what the speaker wants to know in the case of (11) (a) is this:
Is John leaving?, Is John leaving for Stockholm?, and, Is John leaving tomorrow? A positive answer to (11) (a) means that the proposition 'John is
going to leave for Stockholm tomorrow' is true and a negative answer to
(11) (a) means that this proposition is false. On the other hand, when asking
(11) (b) the speaker, in general, may wish to know *when* John is leaving for
Stockholm. Of course, a positive answer to (11) (b) will mean the same as
in the case of (11) (a), i.e., that the proposition 'John is going to leave for
Stockholm tomorrow' is true. A negative answer to (11) (b), however, may
mean that the hearer admits that John is leaving for Stockholm, what he
denies is that John is leaving tomorrow. In other words, the propositions
'John is leaving' and 'John is leaving for Stockholm' are accepted as being
true and the proposition 'John is leaving tomorrow' is denied.

By comparing (11) (a) and (12) we find that in the case of (12) – in contradistinction to (11) (a) – the speaker takes for granted that John is leaving
tomorrow and what he wants to know is *where* John is going to leave. A positive answer to (12) (b) means that the hearer accepts the proposition 'John
is going to leave for Stockholm tomorrow' as being true. On the other hand,
a negative answer to (12) means that the addressee – while accepting the
proposition 'John is going to leave tomorrow' as being true – denies the
proposition 'John is going to leave for Stockholm'.

As to the pair (11) (a)–(13), once again, the speaker's assumptions play
different roles in these sentences. Notice that positive answers to these questions lead to identical results. In the case of negative answers, however, essential differences emerge. Thus, a negative answer to (11) (a) may mean that the
addressee thinks that the proposition 'John is going to leave for Stockholm

tomorrow' is false and a negative answer to (13) may mean that the hearer accepts the proposition 'somebody is going to leave for Stockholm tomorrow' as being true and denies the proposition 'the person who is going to leave for Stockholm tomorrow is John'. He thus denies what the speaker may wish to know by asking the question (13).

Before proceeding let us define the notion of 'background assumption of a yes-no question'. Let p be a proposition, ? the question operator (which forms yes-no questions out of p's) and F that part of p that is focussed. *By background assumption of ?p* we shall understand the proposition p' which we get by replacing F in p by the corresponding Pro-element. By 'corresponding Pro-element' I mean 'somebody' or 'someone' for persons, 'something' for objects, 'some time' for time, 'somewhere' for place, etc. From the definition of background assumption it follows that questions of type (11) (a) cannot have background assumptions since they do not contain focussed constituents. The background assumptions of (11) (b), (12) and (13) are given below.

(14)   (a) John is going to leave for Stockholm some time.
        (b) John is going to leave somewhere tomorrow.
        (c) Somebody is going to leave for Stockholm tomorrow.

Notice that the background assumptions of wh-questions are different from the background assumptions of yes-no questions in at least one important aspect. Consider the following wh-questions and their background assumptions.

(15)   (a) Who is leaving tomorrow?
        (b) Somebody is leaving tomorrow.
(16)   (a) When is the doctor coming?
        (b) The doctor is coming at some time.
(17)   (a) Where is my book?
        (b) My book is at some place.

To be sure, when asking questions such as (15) (a), (16) (a) or (17) (a) the speaker normally assumes that the respective propositions (15) (b), (16) (b) and (17) (b) are true. It need not be the case, however, that these assumptions be shared by the speaker and the hearer. These assumptions are typically speaker assumptions. On the other hand, the background assumptions of yes-no questions are typically assumptions shared by the speaker and the hearer. This is an immediate consequence of the topic (or thematic) character of these assumptions. Of course, focus is not a privilege of yes-no questions: wh-questions, too, may contain focussed constituents. Consider, for example,

(18)　(a)　Who is leaving *tomorrow*?
　　　(b)　When is the *doctor* coming?
　　　(c)　Where is *my* book?

Notice, however, that (18) (a)–(c), too, have the background assumptions (15) (b), (16) (b) and (17) (b), respectively but in addition they are associated with further assumptions. Thus, (18) (a), for example, may suggest that there are people who are leaving today or the day after tomorrow or on some other day. Similarly, (18) (b) may suggest that apart from the doctor somebody else is expected to come. A question such as (18) (c) may be uttered, for example, in the following situation. I am looking for my book and I have found yours but not mine. Now, in general, these secondary assumptions are shared by the speaker and the hearer but the status of the original background assumptions (15) (b), (16) (b) and (17) (b) is left unchanged.

Let us return to the examples (11)–(13), however. One may get the impression that the speaker who asks questions like (11) (b), (12) or (13), may have wished to ask the following wh-questions:

(19)　(a)　When is John leaving for Stockholm?
　　　(b)　Where is John leaving tomorrow?
　　　(c)　Who is leaving for Stockholm tomorrow?

Let us now inquire into this question somewhat more thoroughly. For simplicity's sake we shall say that in the cases under discussion yes-no questions are interpreted as wh-questions. Notice, however, that, since it is the hearer that has to answer the question, when we speak of the wh-interpretation of yes-no questions, we always mean that it is the hearer who provides this interpretation.

It would seem that the wh-interpretation of yes-no questions is only possible if the yes-no question is associated with a background assumption of type (14). Yes-no questions such as (11) (a) can never be interpreted in such a way.

Another important point is this: the wh-interpretation of yes-no questions is a pragmatic rather than a semantic matter. It is quite conceivable that by asking (11) (b) one is only interested in knowing whether John is going to leave tomorrow or not, and by asking (12) one only wants to inquire whether John is going to leave for Stockholm or not and, finally, by asking (13) the speaker is only interested in John's travel plans. Take, for example, the following situation. The speaker has some ideas as to when or where John is going to leave or as to who is going to leave. He, then, starts the relevant piece of conversation with one of the following sentences:

(20)   (a) Let me guess which day John is leaving.
         (b) Let me guess where John is leaving.
         (c) Let me guess who is going to leave tomorrow for Stockholm.

It is quite clear that in this case — given the contexts (20) (a)–(c), respectively, — the questions (11) (b), (12) and (13) will be taken as plain yes-no
questions. Another context in which the yes-no interpretation of these
questions would prevail would be a game in which the only answers allowed
are 'yes' or 'no'. And, to mention yet another situation, imagine, for example,
that the speaker would not like that John leaves tomorrow and the addressee
is aware of this. In such a situation, once again, a blunt 'no' to the question
(11) (b) would be perfectly allright. And I am quite sure that it would not
be too difficult to find many other contexts which would exclude the wh-
interpretation of yes-no questions. If, however, no such contexts are given,
sentences such as (11) (b), (12) and (13) suggest quite strongly this interpretation.

Let us call questions of type (11) (b), (12) and (13) *focus questions*. We
may thus say that if not indicated otherwise in the context, a yes-no focus
question may be interpreted as a wh-question. The question word of the
wh-question is uniquely determined by the focussed constituent of the yes-
no question.

Let S be the set of situations which do not exclude the wh-interpretation
of yes-no questions. Given S the hearer H may interpret a focus question Q as
a wh-question. Is there any indication that H does this interpretation? And on
what grounds does he do it?

It would seem that yes-no questions which do not contain focussed constituents and where the context does not indicate a strong obligation to do or
not to do something, can equally well be answered by 'yes' or 'no'.[4] Also
uses mentioned in Sections 1.1. and 1.2. should be excluded here. In the case
of yes-no focus questions, however, the situation is different. The typical
answers to (11) (b), (12) and (13) would be something like (21).

(21)   (a) Yes.
         (b) No, John is going to leave *the day after tomorrow*.
             No, John is going to leave for *Paris*.
             No, *Bill*.

A blunt 'no' is felt to be inappropriate in this case. If (11) (b), (12) and (13)
were 'pure' yes-no questions, it should be possible to answer them by 'no'.
Of course, it *is* possible to do so but a blunt 'no' would be taken to mean

that the hearer is not willing to cooperate. It goes without saying that in all question-answer games one of the main requirements which must be fulfilled by the answer is the following maxim (Grice 1975:45):

"Make your contribution as informative as required (for the current purposes of the exchange)."

This maxim alone would not explain (21) (b), however. What is the information required? It makes only sense to invoke the Maxim of Quantity if we can answer this question. Notice, however, that the hypothesis about the wh-interpretation of yes-no focus questions provides us with an answer. We have stipulated that on the basis of what he knows about his language and by the aid of certain extralinguistic assumptions the hearer is able to figure out that (11) (b), (12) and (13) may mean (19) (a), (b) and (c), respectively. Incidentally, (19) (a)–(c) require *semantically* the second part of the answer in (21) (b). One might thus say that (21) (b) answers both the superficial yes-no question (by 'no') and the hidden wh-question (by 'the day after tomorrow', 'Paris' and 'Bill', respectively).

In sum, the assumption that (11) (b), (12) and (13) may mean (19) (a), (b) and (c), respectively, and that the hearer observes the Maxim of Quantity account for the answers in (21) (b).[5]

What reasons may the speaker have to formulate a yes-no question instead of a wh-question? Notice first that the semantic structure of yes-no questions is simpler than that of wh-questions.[6] The answer set of the former consists of two elements whereas the answer set of the latter is much richer. Let us denote the answer set of a wh-question Q by $A = (a_1, a_2, \ldots, a_n)$. It is easy to see that Q can be split up into n yes-no questions. Let $Q^\S$ be the question operator which forms yes-no questions. Then, any Q is equivalent with the following conjunction of yes-no questions:

$$(22) \qquad Q^\S(a_1) \,\&\, Q^\S(a_2) \,\&\ldots\&\, Q^\S(a_n)$$

Any yes-no question can be viewed as a member of the conjunction (22). On the other hand, no yes-no question can be split up into a conjunction of wh-questions (or any other type of questions, for that matter). Hence yes-no questions are simpler than wh-questions. This in itself does not motivate the choice of a yes-no question instead of a wh-question, however.

Notice next that when one asks a question such as (23) (a) one knows in a way more than when one asks a question such as (23) (b).

(23)   (a) Is John coming tomorrow afternoon?
         (b) When is John coming?

One asks (23) (b) when one has no idea whatsoever about the possible time of John's arrival. On the other hand, one asks (23) (a) if one has some reason to think that John will come tomorrow afternoon. (23) (a) is clearly one of the elements of (22), the factorization of (23) (b). But there are preferences among these elements. The speaker will choose that yes-no question out of (22) to which he would most likely get a positive answer. I think, it is reasonable to assume that the choice between (23) (a) and (b) is again based on the Maxim of Quantity. As already pointed out, (23) (a) is more informative than (23) (b). The hearer may react to (23) (a), but not to (23) (b), by saying:

(24)   What makes you think so?

To which the speaker of (23) (a) may answer with a sentence such as:

(25)   It just occurred to me.

What has been said above is generally valid for any pair of a yes-no focus question and the corresponding wh-question. The more informative question is at the same time the simpler question. For our purpose we may now reformulate the Maxim of Quantity in the following fashion: Don't ask a wh-question if you can ask a yes-no question! Since yes-no questions are simpler to answer, the job required by the hearer, too, will be simpler than in the case of a wh-question. This means that the choice of a yes-no question is mainly motivated by the Maxim of Quantity. In some cases, simplicity may be sufficient for choosing a yes-no question. Imagine the following situation. The speaker has the choice between a wh-question Q_{wh} and a yes-no question Q_{yes-no}. Both Q_{wh} and Q_{yes-no} are equally informative. In this case the Maxim of Quantity cannot determine the choice between them. Q_{yes-no} is, however, simpler than Q_{wh} for both the speaker and the hearer. Therefore, the speaker may prefer asking Q_{yes-no} instead of Q_{wh}.

We saw that yes-no focus questions are normally not answered by a blunt 'no'. In discussing this problem we have found out several things about the relationship between yes-no and wh-questions, about the interpretation of focus questions, about the role of conversational maxims in asking and answering questions. One might, however, get the impression that focus questions play a rather marginal role among questions and that therefore one should not pay that much attention to them. In what follows I want to show that focus questions are not marginal, and that they are not at all restricted to the types of questions exemplified in (11) (b), (12) and (13).

3. SOME FURTHER TYPES OF YES-NO FOCUS QUESTIONS

3.1. Cleft questions

Clefting is just another way to express focus: the clefted constituent is always the focussed constituent. Consequently, it does not come as a surprise that cleft questions behave in the same way as the focus questions of type (11) (b), (12), (13) do. Consider

(26)   Was it *yesterday* that you met John?
(27)   Was it in *Stockholm* that you met John?
(28)   Was it *you* that met John in Stockholm?

(26)–(28) can be answered by 'yes' but in the case of a negative answer in addition to 'no' something else must be said, quite similarly to (11) (b), (12) and (13). Everything which was said in connection with these latter sentences carries over to cleft questions.

3.2. Negative focus questions

Negation does not change the interpretation of focus questions given above, though it may change their interpretation in others aspects. Consider, for example, the negative counterparts of (26)–(28).

(29)   Wasn't it *yesterday* that you met John?
(30)   Wasn't it in *Stockholm* that you met John?
(31)   Wasn't it *you* that met John is Stockholm?

(29)–(31) are biased toward the positive answer in contrast to (26)–(28), which are indifferent in this respect. In all other aspects that are relevant here (29)–(31) are identical to (26)–(28).

In English some negative questions, more precisely, negative questions with positive polarity, do not admit a simple 'yes' answer. Consider, for example,

(32)   (a) Hasn't he left already?
        (b) Yes, of course.
        (c) Of course, he has.
        (d) Yes.
        (e) Yes, he has.

(cf. König 1977:79). (32) (b) and (c) are possible answers to (32) (a) whereas (32) (c) and (d) cannot be used to answer this question. That is, one cannot agree with the positive bias of the speaker by answering with a plain 'yes'.

This might suggest that we have to do here with a case where a simple positive answer is not appropriate, i.e., that the problem exemplified by (32) is something which has some bearing on the topic of this paper. Notice also that the same phenomenon can be observed in the case of focus questions as well.

(33)   Isn't John going to Stockholm *tomorrow*?
(34)   Isn't John going to *Stockholm* tomorrow?
(35)   Isn't *John* going to Stockholm tomorrow?

It is easy to see, however, that this problem has nothing to do with the wh-interpretation of yes-no questions and with the conversational maxims. There are many languages which have a special morpheme to express agreement with positive bias: cf. German 'doch', French 'si', Swedish 'jo', Hungarian 'de'. For example,

(36)   (a) Arbeitest du heute nicht?
             'Don't you work today?'
        (b) Doch.
        (c) Ja.

Only (36) (b) is possible, (36) (c) would not only be inappropriate it would simply be ungrammatical. English does not have such a morpheme: its function must be expressed by the means exemplified by (32) (b) or (c). This shows quite clearly that what is at stake here lies outside of the scope of the present paper.

3.3. Manner adverbials

In the examples (11) (b), (12) and (13) focus is optional. Furthermore, these sentences are in a way more marked than the corresponding sentences which do not contain any focus (cf. (11) (a)).

There are cases, however, where the focussed sentence is more natural, less marked than the unfocussed one. Questions containing manner adverbials is a case in point. Consider

(37)   (a) ??Are you going to Stockholm by train?
        (b) Are you going to Stockholm by *train*?

It would seem that it is almost impossible to ask questions such as (37) (a) (with no focus at all). Compare next (37) (b) with (38):

(38)   Are you going to *Stockholm* by train?

(37) (b) sounds clearly more natural than (38) which may have to do with the

different degrees to which place adverbials and manner adverbials are accessible to focus position.[7] The examples (37) (b) and (38) might suggest that in case a sentence contains both a place and a manner adverbial, the manner adverbial is easier accessible to focus position than the place adverbial.

Notice that (37) (b) cannot appropriately be answered by 'no'. The same holds true, however, for (37) (a) as well which may be taken as an evidence for the claim that (37) (a) and (b) are not really different, i.e., if a manner adverbial occurs in a sentence then either it must be focussed (unmarked case) or some other constituent in the same sentence must bear focus (marked case).

The behavior exemplified on manner adverbials is also exhibited by some other types of adverbials.

(i) Adverbial modifier of state

(39)   (a) Did you buy the car in *pieces*?
        (b) Have you got the car as a *present*?

(ii) Adverbs of degree

(40)   (a) Have you forgotten Hungarian *completely*?
        (b) Was he *fatally* wounded?

(iii) Instrumental adverbs

(41)   (a) Did you slice the salami with your *knife*?
        (b) Did you slice the salami with *your* knife?

It would seem that the sentences (39) (a)–(b) – (41) (a)–(b) (i) must contain a focus and that (ii) it is more natural to have the focus on the corresponding adverbial than on any other constituent of the sentence. What has been said with respect to the felicitous responses to sentences containing manner adverbials holds with equal force here: the sentences (39) (a)–(b) – (41) (a)–(b) cannot be appropriately answered by a blunt 'no'.

3.4. Quantifiers and quantifier-like expressions

Consider the following sentences

(42)   (a) Have you been staying in Stockholm *long*?
        (b) Do you have *several* children?
        (c) Do you have *many* bedrooms?

As Wikberg correctly remarks (Wikberg 1975:109):

When a yes-no Q contains an unspecified quantifier, the R (= response, FK) tends to yield this information in much the same way as if Q were a WH-Q. In such circumstances, yes-no-ness is implied, but may sometimes be open to different interpretations.

Once again, the focus position of the quantifiers in (42) (a)–(c) is quite natural. It seems to be impossible to have such questions with no background assumption at all. Consequently, they must contain a focussed constituent. From among all the other possible focus positions, the focus on the quantifier seems to be the most natural or the least marked. Compare (42) (a)–(c), for example, with (43) (a)–(c).

(43) (a) Have you been staying in *Stockholm* long?
      (b) Do you have several *children*?
      (c) Do you have many *bedrooms*?

We may thus conclude that questions containing quantifiers are, in general, focus questions. (44) seems to indicate that quantifiers are more accessible to focus position than manner adverbials.

(44) Will you be going *several* times to Stockholm by car?

(43) (a)–(c), on the other hand, shows that quantifiers are more accessible to focus position than place adverbials or head nouns. In other words, quantifiers seem to occupy a rather high position in the hierarchy defined by the accessibility relation. Unfortunately, we cannot pursue this topic any further here.

Since the quantifiers in (42) (a)–(c) are unspecified, a positive answer to these questions does not identify any specific member of the answer set (in contrast to the questions considered thus far where this has always been the case). Therefore, neither a positive nor a negative answer to (42) (a)–(c) is felicitous. One need not be quite explicit in one's answers, of course. Thus, (42) (a) may also be answered by something like 'quite long' but this, too, is more than just a positive answer.[8]

If the questions contain specific quantifiers, then a simple 'yes' is adequate but a simple 'no' remains inappropriate.

(45) (a) Do you have *two* children?
      (b) Do you have *three* homes?

In contrast to unspecified quantifiers, however, specified quantifiers need not be focussed. (Think of questions of a questionnaire: Do you have two, three, four, etc. children?)

3.5. Complex questions

Questions which contain relational adverbs (adverbial constructions which express the 'cause-consequence' or the 'means-purpose' relation) seem always to be focussed. Consider

(46)   (a) Did you go to Stockholm in order *to see your wife*?
           (b) Did you go to Stockholm because *your wife was there*?

In a way in these cases the whole complement clause may belong to the focus the corresponding background assumption being 'You went to Stockholm for some reason'. It is thus quite clear that the speaker of (46) (a)–(b) wants to know what the reason of the addressee's going to Stockholm was. Consequently, an answer which does not provide a reason is not appropriate.

Adverbial clauses of place or time may, but need not, be focussed:

(47)   (a) Did you *leave* when John arrived?
           (b) Did you leave when *John arrived*?
(48)   (a) Have you *seen* the place where Mary was born?
           (b) Have you seen the place where *Mary was born*?

In some languages this distinction is expressed by different constructions. Consider, for example, the Hungarian equivalents of (47)–(48).

(49)   (a) *Elmentél*, amikor János megérkezett?
           (b) *Akkor* mentél el, amikor János megérkezett?
(50)   (a) *Láttad* azt a helyet, ahol Mária született?
           (b) *Azt* a helyet láttad, ahol Mária született?

Questions (47) (a)–(50) (a), but not questions (47) (b)–(50) (b), can felicitously be answered by either 'yes' or 'no'. Questions (47) (b)–(50) (b) do not admit a simple negative answer. (47) (b), but not (47) (a), is associated with the background assumption 'The addressee left at some time'. Similarly, (48) (b), but not (48) (a), has the background assumption 'The addressee has seen some place' (relevant for the present piece of conversation). Thus, questions where main stress lies on the main verb of the main clause do not seem to be focus questions.

What has been said with respect to adverbial clauses of place or time holds also for *that*-clauses and relative clauses: these clauses may, but need not, be focussed. Consider

(51)   (a) Have you *forgotten* that John will come to see us tonight?
           (b) Have you forgotten that *John will come to see us* tonight?
(52)   (a) Did you *see* the man who was running in that direction?
           (b) Did you see *the man who was running in that direction*?

Once again, the situation is clearer in languages where this difference is marked syntactically. The Hungarian equivalents of the main clauses of (51)–(52) are given in (53).

(53)   (a) *Elfelejtetted*, hogy . . .
         (b) *Azt* felejtetted el, hogy . . .
         (c) *Láttad* azt az embert, aki . . .
         (d) *Azt* az embert láttad, aki . . .

Under normal circumstances, questions such as (53) (b) and (d) cannot be answered by a blunt 'no'.

It goes without saying that my discussion of focus is extremely sketchy and very often unprecise. The examples I have discussed thus far may, however, suffice to show that focus questions occur rather frequently and that they are often more normal (less marked) than the corresponding questions with no focus. In some cases (if the question contains certain types of constituents) focus is unavoidable. We also saw that all focus questions can naturally be interpreted as wh-questions.

Before considering some types of yes-no questions which are not focus-questions, let me conclude this section by a special type of focus question which I shall call identification questions.

3.6. Identification questions

Our next example concerns questions in which the speaker asks the hearer to identify somebody or something for him. Consider

(54)   (a) Is this your *sister*?
         (b) Is this the *post office*?
(55)   (a) Is *this* your sister?
         (b) Is *this* the post office?

By uttering (54) (a) the speaker wants the hearer to identify the woman or girl he is looking at and by uttering (54) (b) he wants to have identified the building in front of him. On the other hand, the speaker of (55) (a) is not so much interested in the woman or girl he is looking at but rather in the hearer's sister. Similarly, the speaker of (55) (b) wants to know where the post office is. (Cf. also Wikberg 1975:146) Consequently, (54) (a)–(b) may be associated with the wh-questions (56) (a)–(b) and (55) (a)–(b) with the wh-questions (57) (a)–(b).

(56)   (a) Who is this?
         (b) What is this?

(57)   (a) Which one is your sister?
        (b) Which building is the post office?

(54) (a)–(b) and (55) (a)–(b) have evidently different background assumptions. These background assumptions, however, cannot be defined so easily as in the case of our previous examples. No doubt, this has to do with the deictic character of these questions. Notice that the same difficulty arises in the case of the wh-questions (56)–(57) as well. One thing seems to be clear: the noun phrase 'your sister' need not be associated with an existential presupposition in the case of (54) (a) whereas such a presupposition must be present in the case of (55) (a). Similarly, the city in which a question such as (54) (b) is uttered need not have a post office, (55) (b), on the other hand, presupposes the existence of a post office.

All the questions in (54) (a)–(b), (55) (a)–(b) can appropriately be answered by 'yes' since an affirmative answer, in fact, does identify the person or thing requested. On the other hand, a negative answer to these questions fails to identify. If the hearer is unable to make the identification, he must say so. If, on the other hand, he is in the position to carry out the identification, the Maxim of Quantity requires him to do so.

Next, we shall consider some cases which do not have to do with focus. Consequently, the questions to be considered will not have specifiable background assumptions, i.e., background assumptions automatically derivable from the structure of the questions. Nevertheless these questions, too, seem to require more than just a straightforward simple answer. In contrast to the (majority of) questions discussed thus far, what these questions have in common is that they often cannot appropriately be answered by 'yes' only.

4. SOME YES-NO QUESTIONS WHICH CANNOT APPROPRIATELY BE ANSWERED BY 'YES'

4.1. Existential questions

Existential questions containing an indefinite pronoun may be interpreted as wh-questions under certain circumstances. Consider

(58)   (a) Has anybody seen John?
        (b) Does anyone have an idea of how to solve this problem?

In both cases a blunt 'no' may be appropriate, but a positive answer which does not say anything about the person (or persons) who has seen John or who has an idea of how to solve the problem may be felt to be inadequate.

If the context makes it clear that what the speaker of (53) (a)–(b) wants to know is mere existence then, of course, a 'yes' answer, too, is felicitous. The interpretation of questions such as (58) (a)–(b) depends not only on the context but also on the semantic structure of these questions. In some cases the non-existential reading seems to be less likely. Consider, for example,

(59)　　(a) Is anybody there?
　　　　(b) Has anyone ever climbed the top of this mountain?

In other cases, the non-existential reading seems to be even more likely than in the case of (58) (a)–(b). Consider

(60)　　(a) Does anyone know this person?
　　　　(b) Has anything happened?

In the case of the non-existential reading (58) (a)–(b) and (60) (a)–(b) are interpretable as wh-questions:

(61)　　(a) Where is John? (coupled with 'Who knows him?')
　　　　(b) How can this problem be solved? (coupled with 'Who knows it?')
　　　　(c) Who is this person? (coupled with 'Who knows her?')
　　　　(d) What has happened?

Now we understand why a blunt 'no' is appropriate and a blunt 'yes' is not. If we answer (58) (a) by 'no', we have also answered (61) (a) ('nobody') but if the answer to (58) (a) is 'yes' we have only answered the 'superficial' yes-no question but not the wh-question (61) (a) which is associated with this question. Thus, once again, the interpretation of (58) (a)–(b) and (60) (a)–(b) as hidden wh-questions explains why one of the answers is appropriate whereas the other is not.

4.2. Questions containing the verb 'know'

In many cases yes-no questions whose topmost verb is 'know' are readily interpretable as hidden wh-questions. This often happens when 'know' is used for identification. Consider

(62)　　(a) Do you know this person?
　　　　(b) Do you know this?

Assuming that the speaker does not know the person or the object in question, i.e., that (62) (a)–(b) are genuine identification questions, it is evident that (62) (a)–(b) should be taken to mean (63) (a)–(b).

(63)   (a) Who is this person?
         (b) What is this?

Once again, a blunt 'no' is quite appropriate since it answers not only (62) (a)–(b) but also (63) (a)–(b). On the other hand, a plain 'yes' is clearly inadequate since it would only answer (62) (a)–(b) but not (63) (a)–(b): 'yes' fails to identify.

The phenomenon just mentioned is not restricted to identification questions. The verb 'know' is used widely in many other cases as well. Consider

(64)   (a) Do you know if there is another train to Stockholm?
         (b) Do you know by chance what John did yesterday?

Evidently, the speaker does not put more information into (62) (a)–(b) than into (63) (a)–(b), consequently the Maxim of Quantity does not enter into play here. No doubt, one may still argue that (62) (a)–(b) are simpler than (63) (a)–(b). Nevertheless, the decisive factor that seems to determine the choice between (62) (a)–(b) and (63) (a)–(b) is politeness. The former are clearly more polite than the latter. In general, as Wikberg correctly points out, (Wikberg 1975:169) "it is more polite to ask whether somebody knows something than what somebody knows." Politeness has also been mentioned by Searle as being the chief motivation for using indirect speech acts (Searle 1975:74).

We may conclude that in certain cases it is the Maxim of Politeness that determines the choice of a yes-no queston instead of the corresponding wh-question. This is particularly so in cases involving the verb *know*. For the case of existential questions I do not have any explanation to offer at present.

In all the cases discussed thus far we have had to do with indirect forms: by asking a yes-no question the speaker has in some sense indirectly asked a wh-question.[9] The question which has to be answered now is whether this phenomenon could be accounted for by the theory of indirect speech acts. What is exactly the relation between the indirect questions we were considering here and indirect speech acts?

Indirect speech acts are speech acts in which one illocutionary act is performed indirectly by way of performing another. (Cf. Searle 1975:59–60) What kind of speech act is performed by sentences such as (62) (a)–(b)? Searle thinks that questions belong to the class of directives (Searle 1976). They differ from other types of directives in that they require a verbal response and not a non-verbal action. One may argue, however, that questions should rather constitute a separate class of speech acts, the class of interrogatives (König 1977) or the class of erothetic acts (Wunderlich 1976: 167). Notice, for example, that most languages have a formally distinguishable category 'interrogative' which can be divided into subclasses in a similar fashion as one divides into subclasses representatives, directives, commissives, etc. (cf. König 1977:25). There are many things which distinguish interrogatives from other directives. Thus, for example, directives have mainly to do with the addressee's actions. It is sufficient if the addressee knows the speaker's language and if he knows how to accomplish the actions requested. On the other hand, in the case of interrogatives the addressee does not play an essential role. In order to respond to a question it is not sufficient if the addressee knows the speaker's language and if he is able to accomplish certain actions. He must also have some knowledge about the world and he must be able to process this knowledge (he must be able to judge what is relevant and what is not relevant in the given situation). Interrogatives are thus connected with certain cognitive processes which was not the case with other directives. (Cf. Wunderlich 1976:167−8).

For the present discussion, however, it is immaterial whether we consider questions as a speech act type different from directives or as belonging to directives. What is important for our present purpose is the fact that questions, as any other speech act type, can be classified according to what kind of sub-type of speech act they are characteristically used to perform.

There are many ways of classifying questions. Whatever classification one adopts, however, there will be a class of questions which may be called information questions. Information questions can in turn be classified into yes-no and wh-information questions. Within the speech act type of interrogatives one may thus have several subtypes. By asking a question such as (62) (a) we may say that the speaker performs the speech act of asking for information. The information which the speaker wants to have may refer either to the answer set (yes, no) or to an answer set containing terms and/or propositions (T_i, P_j). One may think of (62) (a) as directly performing the speech act of asking for a binary information and at the same time performing indirectly the speech act of asking for information to be taken from (T_i, P_j). If this is correct, we have a general theoretical framework at our disposal which enables us to account for the aspects of questions and answers discussed in this paper on a principled basis.

For simplicity's sake let us denote the speech act of asking for a binary information by I_1 and the speech act of asking for a more complex informations by I_2. In order to answer the question in which cases one (or both) of the binary answers is excluded one may make use of the following principle:

(65)   *One of the binary answers (or both of them) is inappropriate just in case the speaker performs the speech act I_2 indirectly by performing the speech act I_1 directly.*

Which one of the answers will be considered to be inappropriate will depend on the formal properties of the question underlying I_1.[10]

In view of the fact that yes-no questions which are indirect speech acts of request, order, etc., too, require in general more than just a blunt 'yes' or 'no' we may generalize our principle in the following way:

(66)   One (or both) of the binary answers is inappropriate just in case the speaker performs a speech act A indirectly by performing the speech act I_1 directly $(A \neq I_1)$.

It is evident that this principle covers not only all the indirect requests expressed by yes-no questions but also the rhetorical questions mentioned in Section 1.2. Furthermore, it automatically accounts for all cases discussed in the present paper.

Which one of the answers will be considered to be inappropriate will depend on (i) the illocutionary force of A, (ii) the background assumptions of the speaker, (iii) the rules of conversation and (iv) certain formal properties of the sentences underlying I_1.

Since it is the addressee that is supposed to answer the question it might be the case that (66) expresses the addressee's views only. (66) could thus be weakened in the following way:

(67)   One (or both) of the binary answers is inappropriate (infelicitous, inadequate) just in case the addressee has good reason to believe that the speaker may wish to perform a speech act A indirectly by performing the speech act I_1 directly. $(A \neq I_1)$

The principle (67) will undoubtedly account for the hearer's behavior in figuring out what kind of answer is expected of him, i.e., which answer (or answers) is appropriate in the given situation.

NOTES

* The work reported here was carried out within the framework of the cooperation between the Institute for Information Sciences (KVAL), Stockholm and the Institute of Linguistics, Hungarian Academy of Sciences, Budapest.
[1] I have taken these examples from Searle 1975:65. Alice Davison discusses similar examples (Davison 1975).
[2] Wikberg quotes Quintilian in connection with rhetorical questions. (Wikberg 1975: 43–44) Among the chief figurative uses of questions mentioned by Quintilian we find

many things which we would consider to be indirect speech acts. This can be seen quite clearly from Wikberg's comments on Quintilian's figures: He says: "Since none of Quintilian's figures concerns 'asking for knowledge', several of the interrogative figures are such as require no reply at all. This is true of those which express the speaker's feelings or attitude (. . .), and also of (. . . questions, FK), which is what logicians would refer to as 'metaphisical questions'. The *primary function* (my italics, FK) of these questions, then, is to assert, exclaim or command, and therefore also to influence the listener's conduct." (Wikberg 1975:44).

3 I would also like to exclude questions containing meta-tags (cf. Moravcsik 1971:178) as, for example, in (i)–(ii):

(i)   You are going now, right?
(ii)   You aren't going now, right?

In these questions first a statement is made and then the speaker asks for consensus by using the meta-tag 'right'. Of course, it is quite possible to disagree with the speaker in these cases as well despite of the strong bias expressed in (i)–(ii).

4 There are cases where one of the answers is excluded on the basis of factors determined by the speech situation only. The linguistic structure of the question does not contribute anything to the choice of the answer in such cases. Consider, for example, the following question:

(i)   Have you read the book?

Let us imagine the following two situations.

Situation 1. The hearer knows that he should have read the book and he also knows that the speaker has the right to require from him the fulfillment of this obligation.

Situation 2. The hearer knows that he should not have read the book and he also knows that the speaker has the right to blame him for not having observed this prohibition.

    Now in Situation 1. the hearer may very well answer with a plain 'yes' but hardly with a blunt 'no'. He has to add some excuse or the like.
    In situation 2. it is the other way around. The hearer may answer with a blunt 'no' but a positive answer requires an excuse or the like.
    In what follows I will only be interested in yes-no questions where the asymmetry of the possible answers can – at least partly – be explained on linguistic grounds.

5 One could also think of paraphrasing (11) (b), (12) and (13) as a conjunction of two questions:

(i)   Are you going to Stockholm *tomorrow*? If not, when?
(ii)   Are you going to *Stockholm* tomorrow? If not, where?
(iii)   Are *you* going to Stockholm tomorrow? If not, who?

Notice that the wh-interpretation of (11) (b), (12) and (13) takes effect only in the case of a negative answer.

6 The possibility of accounting for the choice of yes-no questions instead of wh-questions on the basis of the simplicity of the structure of yes-no questions has been pointed out to me by Ewald Lang.

7 The accessibility of various constituents for focus position is an interesting and intriguing question which, however, cannot be discussed in detail here. Let me, however, point out

that — as we saw above — place and time adverbials may be optionally focussed whereas manner adverbials seem to lead — almost always — to focussed structures. Therefore, what has been said here with respect to the accessibility difference between place adverbials and manner adverbials holds with equal force with respect to the accessibility difference between time adverbials and manner adverbials as well. Moreover, as we shall see presently, there are some further classes of adverbials which behave exactly like manner adverbials in this respect. For a revealing discussion of the accessibility relation cf. E. Kiss 1977.

[8] One could say that unspecified answers to questions such as (42) (a)—(c) are appropriate just in case such answers are appropriate to answer the following wh-questions:

(i)   How long have you been staying in Stockholm?
(ii)   How many children do you have?
(iii)   How many bedrooms do you have?

Notice also that very often the answer will depend on what the hearer thinks that the speaker thinks that the hearer normally knows. Consider, for example, the following two questions.

(iv)   Do you have many children?
(v)   Do you have many books?

In general, (iv) must be answered by the number of children, (v), however, may be answered by 'quite many' or the like.

[9] The list of yes-no questions which are not really yes-no questions is quite large. I could therefore mention here a few of them only, though, I think, the most characteristic ones. There are cases such as

(i)   Have you seen my pencil?

which may mean

(ii)   Where is my pencil?

or

(iii)   Have you talked to your father?

which, under certain circumstances, may mean

(iv)   What did your father say?

etc. Then there are cases where we have an embedded wh-question and the only function of the matrix sentence (which makes the whole sentence a yes-no question) is to put the question in a more polite form. For example,

(v)   Do you know who this person is?
(vi)   Do you know where I could get a cup of coffee?

The examples which I have discussed in this paper were intended to make the principles clear that contribute to the interpretation of yes-no questions. My aim was thus not to give a full taxonomy of yes-no questions that may ellicit a wh-question under certain circumstances.

[10] As far as I can see there is no purely formal principle which would account for the phenomena at hand. One thing which might come to one's mind is the following:

'yes' or 'no' (or both) are inappropriate answers just in case the yes-no question cannot be paraphrased by 'either p or -p'.

Though such a principle would certainly be very attractive, unfortunately it does not work. Notice that the majority of tag-questions are not paraphrasable as 'either p or -p' and yet they allow for both 'yes' and 'no' as their answers.

REFERENCES

Davison, A.: 1975, 'Indirect Speech Acts and What to Do with Them,' *Syntax and Semantics* 3, pp. 143–186.

Grice, H. P.: 1975, 'Logic and Conversation,' *Syntax and Semantics* 3, pp. 43–58.

Kiss, E.: 1977, 'Topic and Focus in Hungarian Syntax,' *Montreal Working Papers in Linguistics*, Vol. 8, pp. 1–43.

König, P.: 1977, 'Form und Funktion. Eine funktionale Betrachtung ausgewählter Bereiche des Englischen,' Niemeyer: Tübingen.

Moravcsik, P.: 1971, 'Some Cross-linguistic Generalizations about Yes-no Questions and their Answers,' *Working Papers on Language Universals* 7, pp. 45–193, Stanford, California.

Pope, P. N.: 1976, 'Questions and Answers,' Mouton: The Hague.

Searle, J. R.: 1975, 'Indirect Speech Acts,' *Syntax and Semantics* 3, pp. 59–82.

Searle, J. R.: 1976, 'A Classification of Illocutionary Acts,' *Language in Society* 5, pp. 1–23.

Wikberg, K.: 'Yes-no Questions and Answers in Shakespeare's Plays,' A Study in Text Linguistics, Acta Academiae Aboensis, Ser. A, Vol. 51, No. 1, Åbo Akademi.

Wunderlich, D.: 1976, 'Studien zur Sprechakttheorie,' Suhrkamp: Frankfurt am Main.

HANS-HEINRICH LIEB

SYNTACTIC MEANINGS

1. THE PROBLEM OF SYNTACTIC MEANINGS

1.1 Introduction

The problem of distinguishing 'semantic' and 'pragmatic' aspects of sentences has not yet been solved. One of the most suggestive lines of attack is based on the following idea: 'semantic' aspects are those which can be related to truth conditions, 'pragmatic' aspects are the ones that concern 'conditions of use'.

In the present paper I shall propose a 'meaning-as-use' conception for syntactic meanings, that is, for meanings of syntactic units (in particular, sentences) and their constituents. Adopting the criterion for distinguishing 'semantic' and 'pragmatic' aspects, syntactic meanings would all be 'pragmatic'. Semantics would thus become a part of pragmatics to the extent that it studies syntactic meanings. Alternatively, we might decide to reject the criterion. And indeed, it should be rejected. On a truly functional conception, which I would advocate, all systematic aspects of sentences should ultimately determine conditions of use. Thus, the notion of a 'pragmatic' study of sentences would become all-embracing, and therefore useless. (Surprisingly, the main problem with the 'semantics-pragmatics' criterion is not its frequently attacked reliance on truth conditions for semantics but its reliance on conditions of use for pragmatics.) I adopt the position that the 'syntactical' ('formal') aspects of sentences, their 'semantic' aspects, and their 'pragmatic' ones should be characterized by three independent criteria so that syntactics, semantics, and pragmatics can be established as separate though interrelated disciplines.

In the present paper I shall be concerned with a *semantic* problem. My discussion of syntactic meanings will lead to a criterion by which a 'meaning-as-use' conception of syntactic meanings can be considered as truly semantic. I will not, in this paper, propose a criterion for identifying 'pragmatic' aspects. Even so, it will be possible to demonstrate why speech act theory, contrary to the intentions of one of its originators (Searle 1969), cannot in its entirety be assigned to semantics.

The conception outlined in this paper further develops the proposals made in Lieb 1976: Section 4, and Lieb forthcoming: Section 3, for the construal

J. R. Searle, F. Kiefer, and M. Bierwisch (eds.), Speech Act Theory and Pragmatics,
121–153.

of sentence meanings. It presupposes the conception of lexical meanings proposed in Lieb forthcoming: Section 2, and Lieb 1977a.

There is a vast literature relevant to the topics that will be discussed. I shall assume sufficient familiarity with this literature, in particular, with the more important proposals for explicating the concept of meaning; with the literature on definite descriptions, or referring noun phrases in general; and with the philosophical and linguistic work in speech act theory. It is for lack of space that I refrain from explicitly discussing previous work in the field. I trust that the readers of this paper will need few pointers to place it in its proper research context.

I shall outline my conception of syntactic meanings by means of an extended analysis of a single example. The example is strictly this, an example. The conception itself is based on rather extensive investigations into the semantic aspects of German and English sentences.

In Sections 1.2 to 1.4, the problem of how to construe syntactic meanings is formulated, and the basic ideas for its solution are outlined by discussing a specific meaning of a particular sentence. This meaning is characterized in an informal way. In Section 2, the theoretical notions are introduced that are needed for a formal reconstruction of the informal example. This reconstruction is undertaken in Section 3. Finally, the general conception of sentence meanings is presented and discussed in Section 4.

1.2 Formulating the problem

We shall be concerned with *syntactic meanings*, i.e. meanings of constituents of syntactic units, and of units themselves. We will mainly consider units that are sentences. The concept of sentence and similar concepts (syntactic unit, word, meaning) are relativized not to an entire language such as English ('sentence of English') but to systems S of 'idiolects' that belong to a language ('sentence of S'). Such a system determines an individual 'means of communication', or 'idiolect'. This is not a person's entire share of a language but only a certain 'homogeneous' part of his share of the language, a part belonging to a specific dialect, sociolect, style of speech etc. The conception of 'idiolect system', developed in detail in Lieb 1970 and defended in Lieb 1977b, will here be used without further explanation.

We shall consider only systems of 'spoken' idiolects. A sentence of an idiolect system S may then be identified with a sequence of forms that as a rule are 'phonological word forms'. Thus, the following sequence f would be a sentence of an appropriate English idiolect system (system of an idiolect that belongs to English):

(1) $f =_{df} \{\langle 1, the\rangle, \langle 2, thief\rangle, \langle 3, has\rangle, \langle 4, died\rangle\}$
          (= *the thief has died*).

The phonological word forms are denoted orthographically in (1), and a *sequence* is construed as a binary relation (actually, a function) between the integers 1, . . . , n and certain objects (phonological word forms, in this case). A binary relation is identified with a set of ordered pairs. In (1), an abbreviated name for the sequence f has been added in parentheses.

Any *constituent* of sentence f is a part of f, i.e. a (proper or improper) subset of the set specified in (1). Among the constituents we may assume the following sets of pairs:

(2)   a. $\{\langle 1, the\rangle, \langle 2, thief\rangle\}$ (= *the thief*).
         b. $\{\langle 3, has\rangle, \langle 4, died\rangle\}$.
         c.   f.

(Note that (2a) but not (2b) specifies a sequence; hence, only (2a) can be abbreviated: *the thief*.)

Strictly speaking, constituents are relative to a syntactic structure. Assuming the syntactic theory of Lieb 1976: Section 2.1, Lieb 1977b, a *syntactic structure* of a syntactic unit is identified with a triple consisting of a 'constitutent structure', a 'marking structure', and an 'intonation structure'. I shall not comment on this conception any further. Obviously, a part of a sentence is a *constituent of* the sentence *relative to* a syntactic structure of the sentence in a sense that has to be made precise by reference to the constituent structure part of the syntactic structure.

The concept of syntactic meaning is relativized to a syntactic unit, a syntactic structure, and an idiolect system: something is a *meaning* of a constituent of a syntactic unit of an idiolect system *relative to* the unit, a syntactic structure of the unit, and the system. It should be intuitively obvious that without this relativization the concept of syntactic meaning — for meanings of *constituents* — would be rather pointless. The relativization is brought out more clearly by using appropriate variables:

(3)   a.   "*S*" for arbitrary idiolect systems.
         b.   "*f*", "f_1", "f_2", etc. for arbitrary relations between positive integers and 'phonological forms' of idiolect systems, in particular, phonological word forms.
         c.   "*s*", "s_1", etc. for arbitrary syntactic structures of syntactic units of idiolect systems.

(Generally, *variables* are in italics, e.g. "*S*"; the same letters are used as *constants* if they are in bold face, e.g. "**S**".) *In speaking of a sentence (or other syntactic unit) and of its constituents, we will use "f" with respect to the unit and "f_1", "f_2" etc. with respect to its constituents whenever possible.* This has mnemotechnic reasons and does not alter the interpretation of "*f*", "f_1", etc. given in (3).

We now introduce *the syntactic meaning function csm* as a function that takes triples $\langle f, s, S \rangle$ as arguments and relations between 'meanings . . .' and entities f_1 (i.e. sets of pairs $\langle \ldots, f_1 \rangle$) as its values:

(4)   a.   csm $(f, s, S) \ldots f_1$ (or $\langle \ldots, f_1 \rangle \in$ csm (f, s, S)).
       b.   . . . is a complete syntactic meaning of f_1 relative to f, s, and S.

(4b) is a reading of (4a). The qualification "complete" has been introduced to allow for syntactic constituent meanings of other types. These are so-called *basic* and *intermediate* syntactic meanings, which will be briefly exemplified later on in this paper (Section 3.2.2) but will not be discussed any further. Whenever we speak simply of 'syntactic meanings', it is *complete* syntactic meanings that are under discussion.

For the syntactic meaning function csm it will be assumed that

(5)   For all f, S, f_1, and . . . , if $\langle \ldots, f_1 \rangle \in$ csm (f, s, S), then f is a syntactic unit of S, s is a syntactic structure of f in S, and f_1 is a constituent of f relative to s.

(Note, in passing, the relativization of "syntactic structure", which may be taken as denoting a three-place relation among entities s, f, and S.)

The key questions of this paper can now be formulated as follows:

(6)   How exactly are we to construe complete syntactic meanings, in particular, sentence meanings:
       a.   what are the entities referred to by the three dots in (4) and (5)?
       b.   what are the specific properties of sentence meanings, in particular, is a sentence meaning structured in a specific way?

In the two following subsections I shall characterize my basic ideas for construing complete syntactic meanings in general (1.3) and sentence meanings in particular (1.4). Question (6a) will already be answered in Section 1.3. The rest of the paper will be devoted to answering question (6b). My answer provides typical examples for complete syntactic meanings not only of sentences but also of proper constituents of sentences.

1.3 Basic ideas for complete syntactic meanings

Very vaguely, a syntactic meaning of a sentence constituent is to represent part of a necessary condition for normal utterances of the sentence. This idea will now be explained.

To begin with, the following point should be emphasized: sentences, and syntactic units in general, are *abstract* entities, and so are their constituents. A speech event, whether identified with the movements of the speech organs during a certain time or, preferably, with the acoustic result of such movements, is an entity in space-time. A sentence, understood as a sequence of phonological word forms, is not (the word forms themselves will hardly be understood as entities in space-time either). In this sense, then, a speech event is *concrete*, while a sentence is *abstract*.

A sentence may be 'realized' by a speech event, and a speech event that is to be a 'normal utterance' of a given sentence must satisfy specific conditions. Some of these conditions may be considered as 'semantic' ones, as in the following example.

Consider

(1) f = *the thief has died*

as a sentence of an appropriate English idiolect system. Then, in any normal *non-reportive* utterance of f (non-reportive: any utterance in which f is not used to represent, either directly or indirectly, the form or content of a speech act or of a mental act or state), speech event and speaker must satisfy at least one of the following conditions: (α_1) in realizing *the thief* in the speech event, the speaker is referring to exactly one person and presupposes that whomever he is referring to is a thief; (α_2) in realizing *the thief* in the speech event, the speaker is referring to thieves in general and presupposes that there is at least one thief; ... (α_n) ... Put differently, it is a necessary condition for normal non-reportive utterances of f (condition (α)) that speech event and speaker satisfy (α_1) or (α_2) or ... or (α_n).

Each of the formulations (α_1) to (α_n) characterizes a relation that may hold between arbitrary speech events and speakers; e.g.,

(7) $R(\alpha_1)$ = the relation between arbitrary speech events and speakers such that: in realizing *the thief* in the speech event the speaker is

referring to exactly one person and presupposes that whomever he is referring to is a thief.

Similarly, for $R(\alpha_2)$, . . . , $R(\alpha_n)$. It would be unrealistic to treat these relations as specifiable by enumeration of any kind; we shall consider them as 'relations-in-intension'. (Relations-in-extension are sets of ordered n-tuples. Relations-in-intension are related to relations-in-extension as are properties to 'simple' sets. We shall leave it undecided how exactly relations-in-intension and properties are to be construed, whether in the way proposed by Richard Montague or in some other way.)

It is a necessary condition on normal non-reportive utterances of **f** that speech event and speaker be related by at least one of the relations $R(\alpha_1)$ to $R(\alpha_n)$. In this sense, then, *the relations jointly, – i.e. disjunctively, not conjunctively – represent a necessary condition on speech event and speaker in any normal non-reportive utterance of* **f**.

We shall adopt a conception of syntactic meanings by which *the relations* $R(\alpha_1)$ *to* $R(\alpha_n)$ *are the (complete) syntactic meanings of the constituent* $\{\langle 1, the \rangle, \langle 2, thief \rangle\}$ *in* **f**. We may thus say that the meanings of *the thief* in **f** jointly represent a necessary condition on speech event and speaker in any normal non-reportive utterance of **f**. On our conception of complete syntactic meanings this example generalizes to the constituents of arbitrary syntactic units (hence, to the units themselves): the complete syntactic meanings of a constituent of a syntactic unit, in particular, a sentence, are relations between speech events and speakers that each consist in the speaker having certain intentional or doxastic attitudes with respect to the speech event, and that jointly represent a necessary condition on speech event and speaker in any normal non-reportive utterance of the unit.

For a more precise formulation of this idea, we introduce the following variables:

(8)   "V", "V_1", "V_2" etc. for any object or event in spacetime, and any part of such.

Speakers, speech events and their spatio-temporal parts are all covered by these variables. *When speaking about utterances we will use "V_1" with respect to the speaker and "V" with respect to the speech event whenever possible.* This has mnemotechnic reasons only and does not alter the interpretation of the variables as given in (8). Our basic idea for construing complete syntactic meanings may now be formulated as follows:

(9)   *Basic idea for complete syntactic meanings.*

    a. *Status of meanings.* For all f_1, f, s, and S: any complete syntactic meaning of f_1 relative to f, s, and S is a relation-in-intension between objects or events V and persons V_1 that consist in V_1 having certain intentional or doxastic attitudes relative to V such as: V_1 tries to direct the intention of any addressee of V to certain objects (V_1 is making certain references by means of V); V_1 has certain beliefs connected with V; V_1 wants any addressee of V to acquire certain beliefs; and the like.

    b. *Meanings as representing utterance conditions.* For all V, V_1, f_1, f, s, and S: if there is a complete syntactic meaning of f_1 relative to f, s, and S, and V is a normal non-reportive utterance by V_1 of f and s in S, then V and V_1 are related by at least one of the complete syntactic meanings of f_1.

(9b) embodies a meaning-as-use conception for complete syntactic meanings: the meanings of a constituent of a unit jointly represent a necessary condition for the normal use of the unit. This idea is further pursued in Lieb forth., Section 3, and will not be elaborated in the present paper. (9a) answers question (6a) in such a way that a meaning-as-use conception makes sense. Adopting (9a), we may refer to arbitrary meanings by means of the following variables:

(10)   "u", "u_1", etc. for any relation-in-intension between entities V and V_1.

(9a) gives a first indication of the *kind* of relations u that are complete syntactic meanings. The idea embodied in (9a) remains to be explicated. This will be done by answering question (6b) concerning the nature of sentence meanings. For orientation, I shall now outline the conception of sentence meanings that will be developed in the main body of this paper.

1.4 Basic ideas for sentence meanings

Consider once more **f** = *the thief has died*, assuming

(11)   a. **S**: a certain English idiolect system.

    b. **s**: a certain syntactic structure of **f** in **S** whose intonational component represents statement intonations of a specific type.

We are going to propose a conception of sentence meanings by which one of the meanings of **f** (i.e. one of the complete syntactic meanings of **f** relative to **f, s,** and **S**) is a relation **u** that may be characterized roughly as follows:

(12)   **u** = df the relation between any V and V_1 such that:

    a. V_1 is referring to exactly one person in realizing *the thief* in V and presupposes that whomever he is referring to is a thief.

    b. V_1 wants any addressee of V to assume, at least provisionally, that, if (12a) is true, then whomever V_1 is referring to in realizing *the thief* in V died before V_1's realizing of $\{\langle 3, has \rangle, \langle 4, died \rangle\}$ in V.

Formulation (12a) characterizes what may be called *the thematic part of* **u**, and (12b) its *rhematic part*. The concepts of 'thematic part' and 'rhematic part' will eventually be defined, cf. Section 4.1, below. As these definitions belong to the results of the present paper, the two terms have to be used informally to begin with. They will be used in the discussion of examples that motivate their later definition. Use of the two terms, though necessarily somewhat vague, is in agreement with the definitions that will be formulated. The same remarks apply to the terms "content", "rhema", and "directive part", to be introduced immediately.

The thematic part, which corresponds to $R(\alpha_1)$ in (7) (one of the complete syntactic meanings of *the thief*), determines a possible way of making references in normal utterances of **f**, and of introducing presuppositions concerning the objects of reference.

The rhematic part has two components, which may be called *the content of* **u** and *the directive part of* **u**. The content of **u** is formulated in (12b) by "if (12a) is true, then whomever V_1 is referring to in realizing *the thief* in V has died before V_1's realizing of $\{\langle 3, has \rangle, \langle 4, died \rangle\}$ in V". The directive part is formulated by "V_1 wants any addressee of V to assume, at least provisionally, that". The directive part determines a possible 'communicative intention' of the speaker in a normal utterance that concerns the content of **u**. This intention is 'directive' by aiming at a reaction of the (any) addressee of the speech event; it is 'communicative' by aiming at a reaction of the addressee ("assume, at least provisionally, that ... ") which involves the content of **u** ("if (12a) is true, then ... ").

In (12b) the content of **u** was formulated by means of an implication ("if (12a) is true, then ... ") whose consequent again is an implication ("whomever V_1 is referring to ... died before ... "). This second implication formulates what will be called *the rhema of* **u**.

A conception of sentence meanings developed along these lines has a number of desirable features provided the following comments on **u** can be generalized.

Comment 1. The content of **u** obviously is a function of the thematic part of **u** and of the rhema of **u**: given the rhema as formulated by "whomever ... " and the thematic part as formulated by (12a), the content is characterized by the implication "if (12a) is true, then, whomever ... ". This agrees well with an intuition underlying many traditional semantic analyses of sentences: for knowing the 'meaning' of a sentence we must know both what the sentence says and what entities it is about.

Comment 2. The thematic part of **u** essentially represents reference conditions that may be satisfied in normal utterances of the sentence. The content of **u** is conditionalized to the thematic part, hence, involves the reference conditions. On the other hand, the content is independent of whether the reference conditions are actually met in an utterance. Thus, the content of **u** may be 'understood' in an utterance even if there is failure of reference. Similarly, the directive part, which determines a possible 'communicative intention' of the speaker, concerns the content of **u** independently of whether the reference conditions of the thematic part are met. Thus, the 'communicative intention' of the speaker may be 'understood' even if there is failure of reference.

Comment 3. A sentence meaning may differ from **u** in its thematic part, its directive part, or its content. If it differs in its thematic part, it automatically differs in content. If it differs in content, it may still have the same rhema as **u**. If it has a different directive part, it may have the same thematic part and the same content as **u**.

For instance, let **f** be *the thief has died* as before; let s_1 be a syntactic structure that differs from **s** only in its intonational component, which is to represent question intonations of a specific type. As a complete syntactic meaning of **f** relative to **f**, s_1 and **S**, we might have

(13) $u^* = {}_{df}$ the relation between any V and V_1 such that:
   a.   [= (12a)]
   b. V_1 wants any addressee of V to let V_1 know whether, if (12a) is true, then, whomever V_1 is referring to in realizing *the thief* in V died before V_1's realizing of $\{\langle 3, has \rangle, \langle 4, died \rangle\}$ in V.

While the directive parts of **u** and u^* are different, the two meanings are identical in content: they have the same rhema and identical thematic parts.

Comment 4. The rhematic part of **u**, more specifically, the directive part and the rhema of **u** determine the type of (direct) speech act that can be performed by a normal nonreportive utterance of sentence **f** given the structure **s** as in (11b). The directive part of **u** allows speech acts such as asserting or formulating a hypothesis because of the intended hearer attitude ("assume, at least provisionally, that"); it excludes speech acts like asking a question. Speech acts like making a prediction are excluded by the rhema of **u** (" ... died before ... "), and speech acts like giving a command are excluded both by the directive part and the rhema of **u**.

Comment 5. There is a systematic way of determining the different parts and components of **u** by relating them to various syntactic relations that hold on **f** given the structure **s**.

First, consider the *rhema* of **u** (as formulated in (12b) by "whomever V_1 is referring to in realizing *the thief* in V died before V_1's realizing of $\{\langle 3, has \rangle, \langle 4, died \rangle\}$ in V"). The rhema may be determined mainly on the basis of the *subject relation* that may be assumed to hold between *the thief* and $\{\langle 3, has \rangle, \langle 4, died \rangle\}$ (the temporal part of the rhema as formulated by "before ... " has to be determined differently, cf. below, Section 3.2.2).

Next, take the *thematic part* of **u**. The thematic part is identical with a complete syntactic meaning of a constituent (*the thief*) that is identifiable on the basis of the subject relation. The meanings of this constituent are obtained on the basis of a syntactic *determiner relation* that holds between $\{\langle 1, the \rangle\}$ and $\{\langle 2, thief \rangle\}$. A meaning of the constituent is selected as the thematic part of **u** on the basis of the *predicate relation* that holds between $\{\langle 3, has \rangle, \langle 4, died \rangle\}$ and **f** as a whole (semantically, the predicate relation provides 'compatibility conditions' for meanings of *the thief* and the rhema of **u** as already established). Suppose the meaning of *the thief* that is characterized by (12a) has been selected.

The *content* of **u** as formulated in (12b) ("if (12a) is true, then, whomever ... ") is now obtained directly from the thematic part and the rhema.

The *directive part* of **u** as formulated in (12b) ("V_1 wants any addressee of V to assume, at least provisionally, that") is determined on the basis of the *declarative relation*, a syntactic relation of a new type. This relation holds between syntactic constituents f_1 and 'constituent categories' K: 'f_1 is a *declarative K* (relative to *f, s,* and *S*)', where f_1 is a constituent of *f*, and K a constituent category of S such as VGr(-, S) ('verb group of S') or NGr(-, S) ('noun group of S'). In particular, **f** = *the thief has died* is a declarative verb group ('sentence') of **S** relative to **f**, the previously assumed structure **s**, and **S**.

This very rough sketch of meaning composition would have to be made more precise in a number of ways (for a possible line of attack, cf. Lieb 1976, Sections 4.3f, which, however, has to be modified with respect to detail). In the present paper, I shall not pursue the problem of meaning composition any further.

Sentence meanings are meant to be as exemplified by **u**. For characterizing my conception of syntactic meanings in a more precise way, I will reconstruct **u** within my framework for syntactic meanings (Section 3). I begin by a clarification of underlying concepts (Section 2), in particular, the concepts of reference, reference basis, and propositional attitude.

2 CLARIFICATION OF UNDERLYING CONCEPTS

2.1 Reference

In characterizing **u** in (12) we had to make use of the concept of reference both for the thematic and the rhematic parts of **u**. The term "refer" was used as a relational one. We formally introduce a family of n relational constants as follows:

(14)   "V_1 is (n-)referring by f_1 in V to $z_1 \ldots z_n$", abbreviated as "$\mathrm{Ref}^n V_1 f_1 V z_1 \ldots z_n$".

The variables "V", "V_1", and "f_1" are to be understood as in (8) and (3b), respectively. The variables z_i range over whatever will be allowed as 'objects of reference'; in the simplest case,

(15)   "z", "z_1", etc. for any perceivable entity or any property of relation that is 'ultimately reducible' to perceivable entities.

(By (15), these variables are ambiguous with respect to logical type.)

No attempt will be made to define the constants in (14). Some properties of the reference relation or relations will be assumed informally as follows. Referring in the intended sense is to imply or presuppose that V_1 produces a part of V that 'corresponds' to f_1; furthermore, referring is to imply that in doing so, V_1 has the intention of 'singling out' $\langle z_1, \ldots, z_n \rangle$ for any or some addressee of V, in the sense of directing the addressee's attention to $\langle z_1, \ldots, z_n \rangle$. Referring is *not* to imply that the speaker's intention is successfully implemented; and referring is *not* to imply or presuppose 'predication' in any sense of the term. On this account, referring is essentially characterized by a hearer-oriented intentional attitude of the speaker that is directed towards an n-tupel of entities $z_1, \ldots, z_n$ $(n > 0)$.

The following example will serve to bring out an aspect of referring that has just been passed over rather hastily: in referring the speaker has the intention to single something out *from* something; what are the objects that form the 'basis' for the reference?

(16)   a. f = *the thief has died*
        b. f_1 = df *the thief*
        c. f_2 = df $\{\langle 2, thief \rangle\}$
        d.   S: the English idiolect system assumed in (11a).
        e.   s: the syntactic structure assumed in (11b).
        f.   V: a certain physical event.
        g. V_1: a certain person.
        h.   z: a certain person different from V_1.
        i.   V is a normal utterance of f and s in S.
        j. V_1 is referring$_1$ by f_1 in V to z.

Because of (16j), V_1 intends to single z out for any or some addressee of V, and V_1 has this intention at precisely the point when he starts producing the f_1-part of V, the part of V that corresponds to f_1. Obviously, V_1 does not try to single the person z out from the set of entities that anybody might ever wish to refer to but from a much more restricted set. On our conception, this is the set of all z such that at the point of producing the f_2-part of V, V_1 is willing to apply to z a certain 'concept' that is 'associated' with f_2, in the sense that V_1 is willing either to assume that z can be 'subsumed' under the concept or to assume that z cannot be subsumed under it. It is from this set that V_1 intends to single out the person z; i.e. V_1 intends to direct the addressee's attention to z as different from any other element of this set. We shall call this set the *reference basis* for f_2 relative to V, V_1, and the concept. Put in a nutshell, then, *referring is trying to single out from a reference basis*.

For a more precise account we have to explain what we understand by a concept and how we construe lexical meanings (for details, cf. Lieb forthcoming, 1977a).

2.2 Concepts and lexical meanings

We adopt a notion of concept that relates concepts to individual perceptions and conceptions. These are mental events or states resulting from physiological and psychological processes. Thus, a perception of person z by speaker V_1 (cf. (16)) would be a mental event resulting from a process of perceiving in the course of which V_1 consciously or subconsciously attributes certain properties to what he believes is the source initiating the process. The set of these properties, most of which may be highly situation specific, is the *content* of the perception. Instead of a content that consists of properties, a perception may also have a content that consists of relations-in-intension. Conceptions are construed in an analogous way.

The contents of different perceptions or conceptions may be partly identical (may contain the same properties or relations). In this case, the perceptions or conceptions themselves have a common property: the property of being a conception or perception such that specific properties (or relations) occur in its content. For a more precise formulation, we first introduce the following variables, and a convention for constants:

(17) a. "b", "b_1", etc. for arbitrary properties of perceptions or conceptions.

  b. *Convention*. English words between raised dots — $\cdot thief \cdot$ — are names of specific properties b.

Concepts are identified with certain properties b by the following assumption:

(18) For any concept b, there are properties or relations such that b = the property of being a perception or conception whose content contains these properties or relations.

The properties (similarly, the relations) assumed in (18) are properties of entities z understood, in the simplest case, as in (15); they might be properties of perceivable entities.

With any concept we can associate a 'comprehension' and an 'extension'. Concepts are 'n-place' depending on the elements of their comprehensions:

(19) For any concept b,
  a. *the comprehension of b* ($^c b$) = df the set of properties or relations satisfying (18) ("*the* [set]" can be justified);
  b. *the extension of b* ($^e b$) = df the set of all z such that for each property or relation in $^c b$, z has the property, or the relation holds between the components of (the n-tupel) z;
  c. b is *n-place* iff n = 1 and $^c b$ consists of properties, or n > 1 and $^c b$ consists of n-place relations (-in-intension). (In the second case, b is *relational*.)

There are many problems that would have to be discussed (vagueness, family resemblance, and others). The present rough sketch is, however, sufficient for our immediate purposes.

A concept may be 'associated' with an 'elementary' syntactic constituent like $f_2 = \{\langle 2, \textit{thief} \rangle\}$. This idea is made precise in Lieb 1976: (64b). In the present paper, I will only partly clarify the way in which a concept is 'associated' with a constituent (choosing a somewhat different approach from Lieb 1976): such concepts are 'lexical meanings' of the constituent, in agreement with the following assumption and definition:

(20) a. Each meaning in S of a word paradigm or stem paradigm of S is a concept.

      b. Let f be a syntactic unit of S, and s a syntactic structure of f in S. Then b is a *lexical meaning* of f_1 relative to f, s and S iff there is a word paradigm of S such that:

          α. f_1 is a constituent of f relative to s and is an 'occurrence' of some form of the paradigm.

          β. b is a meaning in S of the paradigm.

(The terms "word paradigm", "stem paradigm", "meaning in . . . of . . . ", "occurrence", and "form" would have to be explicated. Word paradigms are to include idiom paradigms, and 'words' like conjunctions that do not seem to form paradigms are reconstructed as 'improper' paradigms.)

'Association' of a concept with a syntactic constituent is to satisfy the following condition:

(21) [f, s, and S as in (20b).] If b is associated with f_1 in f, s, and S, then b is a lexical meaning of f_1 relative to f, s, and S.

Thus, a certain concept $\dot{t}hief_1\dot{}$ might be associated with $\{\langle 2, \textit{thief} \rangle\}$ in f, s, and S (cf. (16)):

(22) (The one-place concept) $\dot{t}hief_1\dot{}$ is associated with $\{\langle 2, \textit{thief} \rangle\}$ in f, s, and S.

The notion of reference basis may now be clarified.

2.3 The notion of reference basis

In discussing (16), we informally characterized a reference basis, using the notion of 'applying' a concept to certain objects. Given our conception of concepts, "apply" may be defined as follows:

(23) For any n-place concept b, V_1 (n-) *applies* b to $z_1, \ldots, z_n$ iff either V_1 assumes that, for each property or relation in $^c b$, $z_1, \ldots, z_n$ has the property or the relation holds between $z_1, \ldots, z_n$ (in this order), or V_1 assumes that there is a property or

relation in ^cb such that $z_1, \ldots, z_n$ does not have the property or the relation does not hold between $z_1, \ldots, z_n$.

"Applies" is now used to define "reference basis":

(24)   For any n-place concept b, the (n-place) *reference basis* for f_1 relative to V, V_1, and b [$\text{reb}^n (f_1, V, V_1, b)$] = the set of $\langle z_1, \ldots, z_n \rangle$ such that
a. V_1 produces V.
b.   There is exactly one V_2 such that:
  α. V_2 is a part of V.
  β. V_2 corresponds to f_1.
  γ. V_1 is willing at V_2 to n-apply b to $\langle z_1, \ldots, z_n \rangle$.

(Definition (24) differs from (30) in Lieb forthcoming in using "apply" instead of "predicate" in (bγ). The change was introduced to avoid certain problems pointed out to me by Östen Dahl.) "Corresponds" in (bβ) and "is willing at . . . to . . . " in (bγ) have to be explicated. As to the second term, willingness should be understood as a disposition, possibly unconscious ('preparedness'), that exists at the point when V_1 starts producing V_2 as a part of V and lasts at least through the production of V_2 ("at V_2").

As an example, consider once more (16): $\mathbf{f}$ = *the thief has died*, and s and S are as in (16). Assuming (22), the concept ˙thief$_1$˙ is associated with $\mathbf{f}_2 = \{\langle 2, thief \rangle\}$ as one of the lexical meanings of $\mathbf{f}_2$. The (one-place) reference basis of $\mathbf{f}_2$ relative to $\mathbf{V}$, $\mathbf{V}_1$ and ˙thief$_1$˙ ($\mathbf{V}$ and $\mathbf{V}_1$ as in (16)) is now identified with the following set: the set of (perceivable entities) z such that: $\mathbf{V}_1$ produces $\mathbf{V}$ (implied by (16j) anyway) and there is exactly one part of $\mathbf{V}$ that corresponds to $\mathbf{f}_2$ such that $\mathbf{V}_1$ is willing, in producing this part, to apply ˙thief$_1$˙ to z, i.e. $\mathbf{V}_1$ is willing to assume that z has all the properties in the comprehension of ˙thief$_1$˙ or to assume that some property in the comprehension of ˙thief$_1$˙ is not a property of z.

The notion of reference basis as defined in (22) has a number of important properties that are brought out by the following comments.

Comment 1. The concept of referring was not used in the definition of "reference basis", either directly or indirectly; thus, "reference basis" could be used in a definition of "refer".

Comment 2. The decisive factor for delimiting a reference basis is a cognitive speaker disposition, willingness to apply a certain concept. In defining "reference basis" it was entirely left open what determines (causes) the speaker's disposition. Certain typical factors immediately come to mind.

Thus, in (16) the speech event **V** may have been preceded by speech events produced either by V_1 or by some addressee of **V**, and a number of objects may have been referred to in them; the speaker's disposition to apply ˙thief$_1$˙ may now be restricted to previously referred-to objects. Some of them (say, a book and a tree) may have so few properties in common with the objects in the extension of ˙thief$_1$˙ that the speaker is not even willing to assume, in realizing $\{\langle 2, \textit{thief}\rangle\}$, that some property in the comprehension of ˙thief$_1$˙ is *not* a property of these objects: they are simply dismissed from consideration. Even though there may be factors that typically determine the speaker's disposition, it is the disposition — whatever causes it — that determines the reference basis; this is an essential feature of our conception.

Comment 3. A reference basis provides the 'basis for making references'. But this is only a special aspect of a more general function. The reference basis of a syntactic constituent relative to a speaker, speech event, and concept contains not only the entities of which the speaker is (at the given moment) willing to assume that they are in the extension of the concept; it also contains the entities of which he is willing to assume that they are *not* in the extension of the concept. Thus, in the case of quantifying sentences such as

(25)   *each thief has died*

— it is the reference basis for $\{\langle 2, \textit{thief}\rangle\}$ relative to the speaker, the speech event, and the concept (say, ˙thief$_1$˙) with respect to which $\{\langle 1, \textit{each}\rangle\}$ has to be interpreted: the reference basis functions as a 'universe of discourse'. Moreover, the reference basis is determined by a disposition of the speaker at the point of realizing $\{\langle 2, \textit{thief}\rangle\}$ in the speech event. If the same syntactic unit, say, $\{\langle 1, \textit{thief}\rangle\}$, occurs at different places in a sentence, the reference bases for the corresponding constituents may be different even with respect to a single speaker, speech event, and utterance: the reference bases function as *momentary universes of discourse.*

Comment 4. A reference basis can and must be assigned to any constituent that has a concept associated with it. Such a constituent may not be involved in any acts of referring when the sentence is uttered by a speaker. This is typically true of verbal predicate constituents. Thus, for

(1)   **f** = *the thief has died*

we may assume that the following two-place relational concept,

(26)   ˙die$_1$˙ = the property of a perception or conception that consists

in having a content which contains the following relations between processes and organisms: . . . ,

is associated with $\{\langle 4, \textit{died} \rangle\}$ in **f**, **s**, and **S**. (Note that the process appears as an independently specified entity: the comprehension of $\dot{\text{die}}_1\dot{}$ is not a set of properties of organisms but of relations between processes and organisms. This exemplifies an essential feature of our conception of verb meanings.) Assuming **V** and $\textbf{V}_1$ as in (16), we have the following reference basis for $\{\langle 4, \textit{died} \rangle\}$ relative to **V**, $\textbf{V}_1$ and $\dot{\text{die}}_1\dot{}$:

(27) $\text{reb}^2(\{\langle 4, \textit{died} \rangle\}, \textbf{V}, \textbf{V}_1, \dot{\text{die}}_1\dot{}) =$ the set of $\langle z_1, z_2 \rangle$ such that $\textbf{V}_1$ produces **V** and there is exactly one part V_2 of **V** that corresponds to $\{\langle 4, \textit{died} \rangle\}$ such that $\textbf{V}_1$ is willing at V_2 to apply $\dot{\text{die}}_1\dot{}$ to $\langle z_1, z_2 \rangle$,

where z_1 is a process, z_2 an organism, and $\textbf{V}_1$ is willing at V_2 either to assume that, for each relation in the comprehension of $\dot{\text{die}}_1\dot{}$, the relation holds between z_1 and z_2, or to assume that this is not true for some relation in the comprehension. (Note that the organism z_2 may be in any stage of z_1, including the terminal one, if the relations in $^{\text{C}}\cdot\text{die}_1\cdot$ hold between z_1 and z_2.)

So far we have been discussing the notion of reference and related notions. For reconstructing syntactic meanings like **u** we must also consider, at least briefly, concepts such as presupposition, wanting, or believing (cf. (12)), which are usually discussed as 'propositional attitudes'.

2.4 Propositional attitudes

The following cursory remarks are not meant to substitute for an in-depth analysis of notions like presupposition. They are mainly to indicate how 'propositional attitudes' will be formally construed.

Consider presupposition. In (12), the following preliminary formulation was used:

(28) V_1 presupposes that whomever he is referring to in realizing *the thief* in V is a thief.

Remembering that *the thief* = $\textbf{f}_1$ by (16) and that $\dot{\text{thief}}_1\dot{}$ is associated with $\{\langle 2, \textit{thief} \rangle\}$ in **f**, **s**, and **S** by (22), we reformulate (28) by means of "refer" and "extension" (Sections 2. 1f):

(29) V_1 presupposes that, for all z, if V_1 is referring by $\textbf{f}_1$ (= *the thief*) in V to z [Ref$^1 V_1 \textbf{f}_1 Vz$], then z is in the extension of $\dot{\text{thief}}_1\dot{}$ [$^{\text{e}}\cdot\text{thief}_1\cdot z$].

Consider the part "whomever . . . " of (28). This is an open sentential formula with "V" and "V_1" as its only free variables. Consider the relation-in-intension u_1 between arbitrary V_2 and V_3 that consists in V_2 and V_3 satisfying the condition "whomever . . . " in (28) (formally, we use a λ-operator, "$\lambda V_2 V_3$", for "the relation-in-intension between arbitrary V_2 and V_3 such that"):

(30)   a. u_1 = df the relation-in-intension between arbitrary V_2 and V_3 such that: for all z, if V_3 is referring by f_1 in V_2 to z, then z is in the extension of ˙thief$_1$˙.

        b. u_1 = df $\lambda V_2 V_3$ $((z)$ $(\text{Ref}^1 V_3 f_1 V_2 z \rightarrow^e \cdot\text{thief}_1 \cdot z))$.

Given the relation u_1 as defined in (30), we reformulate (29) and (28) as follows:

(31) V_1 presupposes u_1 of V and V_1, i.e. V_1 presupposes of V and V_1 the relation-in-intension between arbitrary V_2 and V_3 such that: [cf. (30)].

In (29) the logical status of the *that*-clause, hence, of "presupposes" itself, remained to be clarified. On the analogy of "necessary that" and similar phrases, "presupposes" might have been rendered by a sentential operator in a language of logic. In (31) there is no *that*-clause, and the logical status of "presupposes" is that of a four-place relational constant denoting a relation (-in-extension) among arbitrary entities V_{11}, V_{12}, V_{13}, and u (u will be taken as the fourth not the second member because it may have to be denoted by a complex name that best appears last). On this account, it is the relation-in-intension u that plays the rôle traditionally assigned to 'propositions' in the treatment of 'propositional attitudes'. (This way of dealing with 'propositional attitudes' is essentially due to Quine 1956.) Using "Pres" for "presupposes", we formally restate (31), (29), and (28) as

(32)   Pres$V_1 VV_1 u_1$.

It may be argued that the time of the presupposing should be taken into account by a separate variable; the speech event V is, however, a spatio-temporal entity and may suffice for temporal location.

Despite recent criticism it should be possible to define the constant "Pres" in terms of doxastic attitudes of both the speaker and the hearer; I will not, however, discuss this question any further.

Presupposition is the only 'propositional attitude' directly involved in the thematic part of u (cf. (12a)); referring as construed in Section 2.1 is not a propositional attitude although.its analysis will have to rely on speaker intentions.

There are two 'propositional attitudes' involved in the rhematic part of **u** as defined in (12b), a volitional attitude of the speaker (wanting) and a doxastic attitude of the (any) addressee (assuming). Both attitudes are treated in analogy to presupposing; i.e. we introduce two constants "Want" and "Ass" (for "assume, at least provisionally") for relations-in-extension among arbitrary entities V_{11}, V_{12}, V_{13}, and u:

(33)   a.   Want $V_{11} V_{12} V_{13} u$.
       b.   Ass $V_{11} V_{12} V_{13} u$.

This concludes the outline of the theoretical notions that will now be used for formally restating (12), the informal characterization of the meaning **u** of **f**.

3 FORMAL EXAMPLE OF A SENTENCE MEANING

3.1 The thematic part of **u**

The thematic part of **u** was informally characterized as,

(12a) V_1 is referring to exactly one person in realizing *the thief* in V and presupposes that whomever he is referring to is a thief.

Not only is this a preliminary formulation, (12a) also represents an incomplete analysis: the 'reference conditions' are not exhausted by the singularity of the reference object, we must also assume that the reference object is 'selected from' the reference basis for a concept associated with $\{\langle 2, thief \rangle\}$ (Section 2). Moreover, the reference object can be further characterized in one of two ways: either the speaker is 'indicating' or 'pointing out' the object (by a pointing gesture) in realizing $\{\langle 2, thief \rangle\}$ in the speech event, or he believes that the hearer 'knows of' the object. Choosing the first possibility and selecting ˙thief$_1$˙ as the concept associated with $\{\langle 2, thief \rangle\}$, we obtain the following reformulation of (12a):

(34) V_1 is referring to exactly one person in realizing *the thief* in V; and whomever V_1 is referring to in realizing *the thief* in V is in the reference basis for $\{\langle 2, thief \rangle\}$ relative to V, V_1, and ˙thief$_1$˙ and is being pointed out by V_1 at $\{\langle 2, thief \rangle\}$ in V; and V_1 presupposes that whomever he is referring to is a thief.

Using the framework of Section 2, (34) is reformulated as in (35), first in a verbalized form and then in customary symbolic notation (as before, $f_1 = $ *the thief* and $f_2 = \{\langle 2,\ thief \rangle\}$; u_1 as defined in (30)):

(35)   a.   There is exactly one z such that V_1 is referring by f_1 in V to z [$Ref^1 V_1 f_1 Vz$]; and for all z, if V_1 is referring by f_1 in V to z, then z is in the reference basis for f_2 relative to V, V_1, and ˙thief$_1$˙ [$reb^1(f_2,\ V,\ V_1,\ ˙thief_1˙)z$], and V_1 is pointing z out at f_2 in V [$Point V_1 z f_2 V$]; and V_1 presupposes u_1 of V and V_1 [$Pres V_1 V V_1 u_1$].

       b. $(\exists !z)Ref^1 V_1 f_1 Vz$ & (z) $(Ref^1 V_1 f_1 Vz \rightarrow reb^1(f_2,\ V,\ V_1,$ ˙thief$_1$˙$)z$ & $Point V_1 z f_2 V)$ & $Pres V_1 V V_1 u_1$.

(12a), hence, (35), is to characterize a complete syntactic meaning of $f_1 = $ *the thief* in f, s, and S (cf. Section 1.3). Following (8a) the meanings of *the thief* must be construed as relations-in-intension between (speech events) V and (speakers) V_1. We obtain a name of such a relation directly from (35), in analogy to the transition from (29) to (30) (as before, the variables "V" and "V_1" in (35) are replaced by the variables "V_2" and "V_3", respectively, in (36), to avoid using the same variables "V" and "V_1" as free variables in (35) and bound variables in (36)):

(36)   a. $u_2 = {}_{df}$ the relation-in-intension between arbitrary V_2 and V_3 such that: there is exactly one z such that V_3 is referring by f_1 in V_2 to z; and for all z, if V_3 is referring by f_1 in V_2 to z, then z is in the reference basis for f_2 relative to V_2, V_3, and ˙thief$_1$˙ and V_1 is pointing z out at f_2 in V_2; and V_3 presupposes u_1 of V_2 and V_3;

       b. $u_2 = {}_{df} \lambda V_2 V_3 ((\exists !z)\ Ref^1 V_3 f_1 V_2 z$ & $(z)\ (Ref^1 V_3 f_1 V_2 z \rightarrow reb^1(f_2,\ V_2,\ V_3,$ ˙thief$_1$˙$)z$ & $Point V_3 z f_2 V_2)$ & $Pres V_3 V_2 V_3 u_1)$.

($f_1 = $ *the thief*, $f_2 = \{\langle 2,\ thief \rangle\}$, u_1 as in (30)). u_2 is our first example of a complete syntactic meaning; we formally assume that

(37) u_2 is a complete syntactic meaning of f_1 relative to f, s, and S,

where f_1, f, s, and S are as in (16): $f = $ *the thief has died*, $f_1 = $ *the thief*, S a certain English idiolect system, s a syntactic structure of f in S that includes a 'statement intonation' structure.

u_2 is only one of the meanings of *the thief* (for others, cf. Lieb forthcoming, Section 3.3). These meanings jointly represent a necessary condition for normal non-reportive utterances of **f** and **s** in **S**; i.e. speech event V and speaker V_1 are related by at least one of the relations; cf. (9b).

The thematic part of the meaning **u** of *the thief has died* consists simply of u_2:

(38)   The thematic part of $u = \{u_2\}$.

(The choice not of u_2 but of the unit set of u_2 cannot here be explained, cf. Section 4.1, below.)

Given u_2, (12a) is most briefly restated as,

(39)   a. u_2 holds between V and V_1.
        b. $u_2 V V_1$.

We next consider the rhematic part of **u**.

3.2 The rhematic part of **u**

3.2.1 Introduction. The rhematic part of **u** was specified as follows:

(12b) V_1 wants any addressee of V to assume, at least provisionally, that, if (12a) is true, then, whomever V_1 is referring to in realizing *the thief* in V died before V_1's realizing of $\{\langle 3, has \rangle, \langle 4, died \rangle\}$ in V.

The directive part of **u** is characterized by "V_1 wants ... that", and the content of **u** by the rest of (12b). We first reformulate the characterization of the content, beginning with the *rhema*, more specifically, with

(40)   died before V_1's realizing of $\{\langle 3, has \rangle, \langle 4, died \rangle\}$ in V.

As a first step we define a relation that can be taken as a *syntactic meaning of* $\{\langle 3, has \rangle, \langle 4, died \rangle\}$.

3.2.2 Meaning of the predicate constituent. The content of **u** establishes a relation between whomever V_1 is referring to by *the thief* and a pair $\langle z_1, z_2 \rangle$ in the extension of $\dot{d}ie_1$ (if this is the concept associated with $\{\langle 4, died \rangle\}$, cf. (26)), where z_1 is a process and z_2 somebody involved in it. Moreover, only pairs $\langle z_1, z_2 \rangle$ may be considered that are 'relevant' to the speaker at the given time, i.e. pairs that are in the reference basis for $\{\langle 4, died \rangle\}$ relative to V, V_1, and $\dot{d}ie_1$. Furthermore, the process z_1 must be 'entirely before' that part of V that corresponds to $\{\langle 3, has \rangle, \langle 4, died \rangle\}$; more briefly, z_1 must be entirely before $\{\langle 3, has \rangle, \langle 4, died \rangle\}$ in V. There are other conditions, such as z_2 being different from the speaker V_1, which will here be left unspecified.

The meaning we wish to assign to $\{\langle 3, has \rangle, \langle 4, died \rangle\}$ should account for all these conditions and at the same time allow for an appropriate relation between whomever V_1 is referring to by *the thief* and a pair $\langle z_1, z_2 \rangle$ in the extension of $\dot{}die_1\dot{}$. The following relation **d** (defined in (41c)) qualifies as a meaning:

(41)   a. $f_3 =_{df} \{\langle 4, died \rangle\}$.
        b. $f_4 =_{df} \{\langle 3, has \rangle, \langle 4, died \rangle\}$.
        c.   **d** $=_{df}$ the relation-in-intension between arbitrary z_3, z_4, V_2, and V_3 such that: $\langle z_3, z_4 \rangle$ is in the reference basis for f_3 relative to V_2, V_3, and $\dot{}die_1\dot{}$, and is in the extension of $\dot{}die_1\dot{}$; z_3 is entirely before f_4 in V_2 [Before$z_3 f_4 V_2$] ; ...
        d.   **d** $=_{df}\lambda z_3 z_4 V_2 V_3$ (reb^2(f_3, V_2, V_3, $\dot{}die_1\dot{}$)$z_3 z_4$ &
        e. $\dot{}die_1\dot{}z_3 z_4$ & Before$z_3 f_4 V_2$ & ...).

The relation **d** is an example of a non-complete syntactic meaning, more specifically, an *intermediate syntactic meaning (ism)*, as specified by the following assumption:

(42)   **d** is an intermediate syntactic meaning (ism) of f_4 relative to **f**, **s**, and **S**.

Obviously, intermediate meanings such as **d** are of a type different from complete meanings like u_2 (36), which are relations between entities V and V_1. There is a third kind of syntactic meanings, *basic syntactic meanings*, of a still different type; they are obtained directly from lexical meanings of syntactic constituents (cf. (20b)). Basic meanings will not be discussed. **d** is obtained as an intermediate meaning of $\{\langle 3, has \rangle, \langle 4, died \rangle\}$ from a basic meaning of $\{\langle 4, died \rangle\}$ 'on the basis of' a syntactic 'determination' relation (not mentioned in Section 1.4, Comment 5) that holds between $\{\langle 3, has \rangle\}$ and $\{\langle 4, died \rangle\}$.

Given **d**, (40) is reformulated as the following open formula:

(43)   a.   **d** holds among z_1, z_2, V, and V_1.
        b.   **d**$z_1 z_2 V V_1$.

3.2.3 The rhema of **u**. Our next task is the reformulation of the entire rhema part of (12b):

(44)   whomever V_1 is referring to in realizing *the thief* in V died before V_1's realizing of $\{\langle 3, has \rangle, \langle 4, died \rangle\}$ in V.

The reformulation has to bring out the relation between whomever the speaker is referring to and the process-patient pair $\langle z_1, z_2 \rangle$. Obviously, (44) should be understood in the sense of: *for all z_2 that V_1 is referring to, there is a z_1* such that **d** (as defined in (41)) holds among z_1, z_2, V, and V_1; equivalently:

(45)   a.   For all z_2 there is a z_1 such that if V_1 is referring by $\mathbf{f}_1$ (= *the thief*) to z_2 in V, then **d** holds among z_1, z_2, V, and V_1.

        b. $(z_2)(\exists z_1)(\text{Ref}^1 V_1 \mathbf{f}_1 V z_2 \rightarrow \mathbf{d} z_1 z_2 V V_1)$.

The rhema of **u** can be identified with the following relation $\mathbf{u}_3$:

(46)   a. $\mathbf{u}_3 =_{df}$ the relation-in-intension between arbitrary V_2 and V_3 such that: for all z_2 there is a z_1 such that, if V_3 is referring by $\mathbf{f}_1$ to z_2 in V_2, then **d** holds among z_1, z_2, V_2, and V_3.

        b. $\mathbf{u}_3 =_{df} \lambda V_2 V_3 ((z_2)(\exists z_1)(\text{Ref}^1 V_3 \mathbf{f}_1 V_2 z_2 \rightarrow \mathbf{d} z_1 z_2 V_2 V_3))$.

We formally assume that

(47) $\mathbf{u}_3 =$ the rhema of **u**.

The briefest restatement of (44), the rhema part of (12b), is

(48)   a. $\mathbf{u}_3$ holds between V and V_1.

        b. $\mathbf{u}_3 V V_1$.

3.2.4 The content of **u**. The content part of (12b), "if (12a) is true, then ... ", is restated by combining (39), the briefest restatement of (12a), and (48):

(49)   a.   If $\mathbf{u}_2$ holds between V and V_1, then $\mathbf{u}_3$ holds between V and V_1.

        b. $\mathbf{u}_2 V V_1 \rightarrow \mathbf{u}_3 V V_1$.

The content of **u** itself is identified with the following relation $\mathbf{u}_4$:

(50)   a. $\mathbf{u}_4 =_{df}$ the relation-in-intension between arbitrary V_2 and V_3 such that: if $\mathbf{u}_2$ holds between V_2 and V_3, then $\mathbf{u}_3$ holds between V_2 and V_3.

        b. $\mathbf{u}_4 =_{df} \lambda V_2 V_3 (\mathbf{u}_2 V_2 V_3 \rightarrow \mathbf{u}_3 V_2 V_3)$.

(51) $\mathbf{u}_4 =$ the content of **u**.

At this point it should be appropriate to give at least a partial reexpansion of definition (50) of the content of **u**, based on the definitions of $\mathbf{u}_2$ (36) and $\mathbf{u}_3$ (46):

(52) u_4 [= the content of **u**] = the relation-in-intension between arbitrary V_2 and V_3 such that:

if

a.   there is exactly one z such that V_3 is referring by f_1 (= *the thief*) in V_2 to z;

b.   for all z, if V_3 is referring by f_1 in V_2 to z, then z is in the reference basis for f_2 relative to V_2, V_3, and $thief_1$ and V_3 is pointing z out at f_2 (= $\{\langle 2, thief\rangle\}$) in V_2;

c. V_3 presupposes u_1 (cf. (30)) of V_2 and V_3,

then

d.   for all z_2 there is a z_1 such that, if V_3 is referring by f_1 to z_2 in V_2, then **d** (cf. (41c)) holds among z_1, z_2, V_2, and V_3.

The content of **u** may now be conjoined with the directive part of **u**.

3.2.5 The directive part of **u**. In (12b) the directive part of **u** was characterized by the following formulation:

(53) V_1 wants any addressee of V to assume, at least provisionally, that . . .

Here we have a speaker attitude (wanting) aiming at a hearer attitude (assuming) that is directed towards a 'proposition' (the relation u_4). We first introduce a name, "is communicating", for this relationship. The following definition assumes the conception of propositional attitudes proposed in Section 2.4, in particular (33):

(54)   a.   *V_1 is communicating u by V* iff V_1 wants of V and V_1 the relation-in-intension between arbitrary V_2 and V_3 such that, for all V_4, if V_3 addresses V_2 to V_4, then V_4 assumes, at least provisionally, u of V_2 and V_3.

b.   Comm$V_1 V u \leftrightarrow_{df}$ Want $(V_1, V, V_1, \lambda V_2 V_3 ((V_4)$ (Addr $V_3 V_2 V_4 \rightarrow$ Ass$V_4 V_2 V_3 u)))$.

It is this relation Comm that we identify with the directive part:

(55)   Comm = the directive part of **u**.

3.2.6 The complete rhematic part of **u**. In the case of (12b) it is the 'proposition' u_4 that is being communicated. Using (50) and (54), we reformulate (12b) as

(56)   a. V_1 is communicating u_4 by V.

          b. $\text{Comm} V_1 V u_4$.

This, then, is the briefest formal restatement of the rhematic part of **u** identified as follows:

(57) $\langle u_4, \text{Comm} \rangle$ = the rhematic part of **u**.

In the next section, we shall give a condensed restatement of (12) in its entirety, which will then be expanded into an equivalent longer version.

3.3 The meaning **u**

Combining (39) and (56), the briefest restatements of (12a) and (12b), we obtain a complete reformulation of (12):

(58)   a.   **u** = $_\text{df}$ the relation-in-intension between arbitrary V and V_1 such that:

             α. u_2 holds between V and V_1.

             β. V_1 is communicating u_4 by V.

          b.   **u** = $_\text{df} \lambda V V_1 (u_2 V V_1 \ \& \ \text{Comm} V_1 V u_4)$.

("u_2", "u_4", and "Comm" as defined in (36), (50), and (54), respectively.) The internal structure of **u** is brought out more clearly if "u_4" is replaced by its definiens in (50) and "u_3" in the latter eliminated on the basis of (46):

(59)   a.   **u** = the relation-in-intension between arbitrary V and V_1 such that:

             α. u_2 holds between V and V_1.

             β. V_1 is communicating u_4 by V: the relation-in-intension between arbitrary V_2 and V_3 such that: if u_2 holds between V_2 and V_3, then for all z_2 there is a z_1 such that, if V_3 is referring by f_1 (= *the thief*) to z_2 in V_2, then **d** holds among z_1, z_2, V_2, V_3.

          b.   **u** = $\lambda V V_1 (u_2 V V_1 \ \& \ \text{Comm} V_1 V \lambda V_2 V_3 (u_2 V_2 V_3 \ \to \ (z_2)$ $(\exists z_1) (\text{Ref}^1 V_3 f_1 V_2 z_2 \to d z_1 z_2 V_2 V_3)))$.

This reformulation explicitly shows the relationship between the thematic and the rhematic parts of **u**: the thematic part 'recurs' as the antecedent of the content of **u**.

We formally assume that

(60)   **u** is a complete syntactic meaning of **f** relative to **f, s,** and **S**.

(**f, s,** and **S** as in (16): **f** = *the thief has died*; **S** a certain English idiolect system; **s** a syntactic structure of **f** in **S** that includes a 'statement intonation' structure.) **u** is a meaning of the sentence **f**, obtained as a limiting case of a constituent meaning (**f** is a constituent of **f**). There are obviously other meanings of **f**, if for no other reason but for the fact that u_2 is only one of the meanings of *the thief*. All meanings of **f** relative to **f**, **s**, and **S** jointly represent a necessary condition for normal utterances of **f** and **s** in **S** in the sense that at least one of the meanings (i.e. a certain relation) must hold between speech event and speaker in any normal non-reportive utterance of **f** and **s** in **S**.

Before discussing definition (38) any further, I shall give an equivalent expanded formulation in which the defined constants "u_2", "u_4", and "Comm", and most defined constants used in their definitions, are replaced (cf. (36) for "u_2"; (50) for "u_4"; (54) for "Comm"; (46) for "u_3"; (30) for "u_1"; (41) for "**d**"; (41b) for "f_4"; (41a) for "f_3"; (16c) for "f_2"; (16b) for "f_1"; cf. also (19b) for "the extension of b" and (24) for "reference basis", two defined terms that will not be replaced):

(61)   **u** = the relation-in-intension between arbitrary V and V_1 such that:

a.   the relation u_2 defined in (36) holds between V and V_1; i.e.

α. there is exactly one z such that V_1 is referring by *the thief* in V to z;

β. for every z, if V_1 is referring by *the thief* in V to z, then z is in the reference basis for $\{\langle 2, \mathit{thief}\rangle\}$ relative to V, V_1 and ˙thief_1˙, and V_1 is pointing z out at $\{\langle 2, \mathit{thief}\rangle\}$ in V;

γ. V_1 presupposes of V and V_1 the relation u_1 defined in (30); i.e. V_1 presupposes that, for all z, if V_1 is referring by *the thief* in V to z, then z is the extension of ˙thief_1˙.

b. V_1 is communicating by V the relation u_4 defined in (50); equivalently, V_1 wants any addressee of V to assume, at least provisionally, u_4 of V and V_1; equivalently, V_1 wants any addressee of V to assume, at least provisionally, that, if u_2 as defined in (36) holds between V and V_1, then u_3 as defined in (46) holds between V and V_1, that is: for every z_2 there is a z_1 such that, if V_1 is referring by *the thief* in V to z_2, then **d** as defined in (41) holds among z_1, z_2, V, and V_1, which is to say:

α. $\langle z_1, z_2 \rangle$ is in the reference basis for $\{\langle 4, died \rangle\}$ relative to V, V_1, and $\dot{d}ie_1$;

β. $\langle z_1, z_2 \rangle$ is in the extension of $\dot{d}ie_1$;

γ. z_1 is entirely before $\{\langle 3, has \rangle, \langle 4, died \rangle\}$ in V;

.

.

.

.

This concludes our formal characterization of a selected sentence meaning. In the next section the general conception of sentence meanings will be presented, and some of its consequences discussed.

4 A GENERAL CONCEPTION OF SENTENCE MEANINGS

4.1 Sentence meanings

The sentence selected — $\mathbf{f}$ = *the thief has died* — is syntactically very simple. The meaning $\mathbf{u}$ of $\mathbf{f}$ may seem rather complex and one may wonder whether more complicated sentences would lead to even more complex meanings. Actually, $\mathbf{u}$ already exemplifies all essential features of sentence meanings that are meanings of non-compound sentences of German or English idiolect systems. (A *non-compound sentence* is one that does not involve coordination, be it by conjunctions or by 'asyndetic' juxtaposition.) In particular, adnominal modifiers and all sorts of adverbials are accounted for by sentence meanings such as $\mathbf{u}$. There is just one generalization that is necessary. In $\mathbf{f}$, there is only one 'referring' constituent, viz. $\mathbf{f}_1$ = *the thief*. Obviously, this restriction has to be lifted. Already in a subject-predicate-object sentence there would be other 'referring' expressions (e.g. $\{\langle 5, the \rangle, \langle 6, landlord \rangle\}$ in *the thief has deceived the landlord*). Hence, the thematic part of a sentence meaning must not be identified with a single relation like $\mathbf{u}_2$ but with a set of relations, which may contain a single element as a limiting case (cf. (38)). For sets of this kind we use the following variable:

(62)   "U" for sets of relations u.

Although the conception exemplified by $\mathbf{u}$ is based on a study of sentence meanings in English and German, the following assumption is tentatively generalized to arbitrary languages (note the nature of this assumption as an empirical hypothesis):

(63)   *Assumption on sentence meanings.* Let S be a system of any

idiolect. Let f be a syntactic unit of S, and s a syntactic structure of f in S such that f is 'characterized as a non-compound sentence of S in s'. Then, for every complete syntactic meaning u of f relative to f, s, and S, there is exactly one U, u_1, and R such that

a. U is non-empty;

b. for each $u_2 \epsilon U$ there is an f_1 such that

   α. u_2 is a complete syntactic meaning of f_1 relative to f, s, and S;

   β. u_2 is a relation between arbitrary V and V_1 'that consists in V_1 making certain references by f_1 in V and, possibly, making certain presuppositions in making these references';

c. u = the relation-in-intension between arbitrary V and V_1 such that,

   α. each $u_2 \epsilon U$ holds between V and V_1;

   β. R holds between V_1, V, and the relation-in-intension between arbitrary V_2 and V_3 such that, if each $u_2 \epsilon U$ holds between V_2 and V_3, then u_1 holds between V_2 and V_3.

("R" is an ad hoc variable for relations like Comm, "is communicating".) The phrase "characterized as a non-compound sentence of S in s" would have to be explicated beyond "non-compound", which was explained above; in particular, we must answer such questions as whether simple imperatives ("go!") are covered or not (it seems that they may be covered without invalidating (63)).

The key feature of (63) is assumption of *exactly one U, u_1, and R*; it is only this feature that justifies the following definitions, by which our key concepts, thematic part, rhema etc., are formally introduced:

(64) Let f, s, S, and u be as in (63).

a. *The component sequence of u relative to f, s, and S* (comp(u, f, s, S) = df the triple $\langle U, u_1, R \rangle$ such that U, u_1, and R satisfy (63a, b, c) relative to f, s, and S.

b. *The thematic part of u relative to f, s, and S* = df the set U such that, for some u_1 and R: $\langle U, u_1, R \rangle$ = comp(u, f, s, S).

c. *The rhema of u relative to f, s, and S* = df the u_1 such that, for some U and R: $\langle U, u_1, R \rangle$ = comp(u, f, s, S).

d. *The content of u relative to f, s, and S* = df the u_2 such that, for some U, u_1, R: $\langle U, u_1, R \rangle$ = comp(u, f, s, S) and u_2 = the relation-in-intension between arbitrary V and V_1 such that, if each $u_3 \in U$ holds between V and V_1, then u_1 holds between V and V_1.

e. *The directive part of u relative to f, s, and S =* df the R such that, for some U and u_1: $\langle U, u_1, R \rangle =$ comp(u, f, s, S).

f. *The rhematic part of u relative to f, s, and S =* df the $\langle u_2, R \rangle$ such that $u_2 =$ the content of u relative to f, s, and S, and $R =$ the directive part of u relative to f, s, and S.

Relativization not only to u but also to f, s, and S is due to the assumption (cf. (63bα)) that the elements of U should be complete syntactic meanings of 'referring' constituents of f. Our previous assumptions on the components of sentence meaning **u** ((38), (47), (51), (55), (57)) have to be reformulated accordingly. Definitions (64) are then exemplified as follows:

(65)   Let **f**, **s**, and **S** be as in (16), and **u** as in (58), (60), and (61). Then

a. the component sequence of **u** relative to **f**, **s**, and **S** = $\langle \{u_2\}$, u_4, Comm$\rangle$, where u_2 is as defined in (36), u_4 as defined in (50), and Comm as defined in (54);

b. the thematic part of **u** relative to **f**, **s**, and **S** = $\{u_2\}$;

c. the rhema of **u** relative to **f**, **s**, and **S** = u_3 (see (46));

d. the content of **u** relative to **f**, **s**, and **S** = u_4 as defined in (50);

e. the directive part of **u** relative to **f**, **s**, and **S** = Comm;

f. the rhematic part of **u** relaive to **f**, **s**, and **S** = $\langle u_4$, Comm$\rangle$.

We conclude this paper by a number of comments that emphasize consequences of the proposed conception of sentence meanings.

4.2 Comments

Comment 1. In evaluating the conception put forward in Section 4.1, the following points should be remembered.

The concepts defined in (64) depend on assumption (63). Hence, they apply with respect to arbitrary languages only if assumption (63), which is based on empirical research into only two languages, is correct.

Assumption (63) and therefore all concepts (64) are restricted to the meanings of 'non-compound' sentences. For lifting this restriction it might be necessary to replace u_1 and R in (63) and (64) by *sets* of relations.

(63) does not imply any assumption about the syntactic basis for the composition of meanings. In Section 1.4, Comment 5, we suggested specific

syntactic relations as the basis on which meanings of sentence f could be constructed. On our conception, the mechanism for meaning composition is provided, in arbitrary idiolect systems, by syntactic relations (or rather, syntactic functions: cf. Lieb 1976: Section 5.1). However, the relations that are relevant in particular idiolect systems may differ from one language to the next.

Comment 2. The content and the rhema of a meaning have been construed in a way that allows dealing with so-called 'scope-ambiguities of quantifiers', as in the following standard example.

Consider

(66)   *every man loves a woman*

as a sentence of an English idiolect system, together with an appropriate syntactic structure of the sentence. (66) has at least two meanings, as indicated by the following paraphrases:

(67)   a.   'every man loves some woman'.
        b.   'every man loves the same woman'.

For both sentence meanings we start from the same meaning for $f_1 = {}_{df}$ *every man*:

(68) $u_1 = {}_{df}$ the relation-in-intension between arbitrary V_2 and V_3 such that, for all z, V_3 is referring by f_1 in V_2 to z iff z is in the reference basis for $\{\langle 2, man \rangle\}$ relative to V_2, V_3, and ˙man_1˙ and is in the extension of ˙man_1˙, and V_3 presupposes that . . . ;

where ˙man_1˙ is a concept associated with $\{\langle 2, man \rangle\}$. We also assume a single intermediate meaning d for $\{\langle 3, loves \rangle\}$ of the type: $dz_1 z_2 z_3 V_2 V_3$, where z_1 is a state ('being in love') of z_2 that is caused by z_3 (cf. also d in (41)).

For $f_2 = {}_{df} \{\langle 4, a \rangle, \langle 5, woman \rangle\}$ we posit two complete meanings:

(69)   a. $u_2 = {}_{df}$ [as in (68), with "f_2" for "f_1"; "$\{\langle 5, woman \rangle\}$" for "$\{\langle 2, man \rangle\}$"; and "˙$woman_1$˙" for "˙$man_1$˙"; without the final clause].
        b. $u_3 = {}_{df}$ the relation-in-intension between arbitrary V_2 and V_3 such that: there is exactly one z such that V_3 is referring by f_2 in V_2 to z; for all z, if V_3 is referring by f_2 in V_2 to z, then z is in the reference basis for $\{\langle 5, woman \rangle\}$ relative to V_2, V_3, and ˙$woman_1$˙ and V_3 is pointing z out at $\{\langle 5, woman \rangle\}$ in V_2; and . . . ;

where 'woman$_1$' is a concept associated with $\{\langle 5, woman \rangle\}$ and the dots indicate conditions that partly differ from the presupposition condition for the corresponding meaning of *the woman* (cf. u_2 in (37)).

The contents of the two sentence meanings (67) are now assumed as follows:

(70) a. The content of (67a) = $\lambda V_2 V_3 (u_1 V_2 V_3 \ \& \ u_2 V_2 V_3 \rightarrow (z_2)(\exists z_3)(\exists z_1)(\text{Ref}^1 V_3 f_1 V_2 z_2 \rightarrow \text{Ref} V_3 f_2 V_2 z_3 \ \& \ dz_1 z_2 z_3 V_2 V_3))$.

      b. The content of (67b) = $\lambda V_2 V_3 (u_1 V_2 V_3 \ \& \ u_3 V_2 V_3 \rightarrow (z_2)(z_3)(\exists z_1)(\text{Ref}^1 V_3 f_1 V_2 z_2 \ \& \ \text{Ref}^1 V_3 f_2 V_2 z_3 \rightarrow dz_1 z_2 z_3 V_2 V_3))$.

(70a) says, very roughly, that assuming the speaker refers to arbitrary men and women (in the reference bases), then for any reference object of *every man* there is a reference object of $\{\langle 4, a \rangle, \langle 5, woman \rangle\}$ and a state of being-in-love-with such that the first reference object is in the state with respect to the second. (70b) says that assuming the speaker refers to arbitrary men and exactly one woman (in the reference bases), then for any reference object of *every man* and any of $\{\langle 4, a \rangle, \langle 5, woman \rangle\}$ there is a state of being-in-love-with such that the first reference object is in the state with respect to the second.

Comment 3. Sentence meanings have frequently been construed as 'propositions'. On our construal of sentence meanings it is the content of a sentence meaning that functions as a 'proposition': it is the content on which the directive part of the meaning 'operates'. The content is a relation-in-intension between speech events and speakers. We might say that a sentence *expresses* any relation that is the content of one of its meanings, and call any relation so expressed a *proposition* of the sentence.

To the extent that 'propositional attitudes' are involved in syntactic meanings, the rôle of traditional 'propositions' is taken over by relations-in-intension between speech events and speakers. The same is true for 'propositions' as 'expressed' by a speech act. Thus, to the extent that we need them, propositions have a well-defined status. (We still need a logic that makes sense of relations-in-intension but only for interpreting our grammatical metalanguage *not* for interpreting the expressions of the idiolect systems.)

Comment 4. The content of a sentence meaning determines the type of (direct) speech act that can be performed by a normal non-reportive utterance of the sentence (see above, Section 1.4, Comment 4). It is not, however, possible to fully differentiate the various speech acts in terms of syntactic meanings. This agrees with a widely held position in speech act theory but is more relevant here for two reasons: (i) differently from traditional speech act theory we adopt a meaning-as-use conception for sentence meanings; (ii) we are in a position to precisely indicate why syntactic meanings are not sufficient.

In Lieb 1976: (93), the speech act of asserting as outlined by Searle 1969: 66 is reconstructed as a function "ass" of the following kind:

(71) $\text{ass}(f, v, s, S) V_1 u V V_2$: "$V_1$ asserts (sincerely and non-defectively) u by V towards V_2 and relative to f, v, s, and S",

where $\langle v, s \rangle$ is a 'morphosyntactic' structure of f in S, to be assumed in a fuller account instead of syntactic structures. The definiens for (71) includes the conditions that V is a normal utterance of f, v, and s in S and that V_1 addresses V to V_2. On our account of syntactic meanings, it is explicit recognition of the addressee, if nothing else, that makes it impossible to reconstruct the notion of asserting completely in terms of syntactic meanings.

Comment 5. Taking our lead from the previous Comment, we may finally indicate a criterion for distinguishing 'nonsemantic' conditions on normal utterances from 'semantic' ones. Stated informally,

(72)   a.   A condition on normal utterances of a sentence and a (mor-pho)syntactic structure of the sentence in an idiolect system is a semantic one only if
                a. it is a condition on actions, intentions, or assumptions of the speaker or the addressee relative to the speaker, the speech event, or entities the speaker is referring to in the speech event;
                b. it involves the addressee only through intentions or assumptions of the speaker.

This informal criterion specifies a property that all semantic conditions on normal utterances *must* have. It thus opens up an entire field for non-semantic ones, among them, pragmatic ones.

Freie Universität Berlin

REFERENCES

Lieb, H.: 1970, *Sprachstadium und Sprachsystem: Umrisse einer Sprachtheorie*, Stuttgart etc.: Kohlhammer.

Lieb, H.: 1976, 'Grammars as theories: the case for axiomatic grammar (Part II)', *Theoretical Linguistics* 3, 1–98.

Lieb, H.: 1977a, 'Bedeutungen als Begriffe', *Zeitschrift für Literaturwissenschaft und Linguistik* 27/28, 29–45.

Lieb, H.: 1977b, *Outline of integrational linguistics: preliminary version*, Berlin (West): Freie Universität, Fachbereich 16 (= Linguistische Arbeiten und Berichte Berlin (West) 9).

Lieb, H.: forthcoming, 'Principles of semantics', in F. Heny and H. Schnelle (eds.), *Selections from the Third Groningen Round Table*, New York etc.: Academic Press (= Syntax and Semantics 10).

Quine, W. V. O.: 1956, 'Quantifiers and propositional attitudes', *Journal of Philosophy* 53, 177–187.

Searle, J. R.: 1969, *Speech acts: an essay in the philosophy of language*, Cambridge etc.: Cambridge University Press.

SITUATIONAL CONTEXT AND ILLOCUTIONARY FORCE

1. THE PROBLEM

In the last few years questions concerning the relations between social inter-action and language have come to the fore in linguistic research. Language is more and more considered to be an instrument of interaction, after a long period of favouring the investigation of linguistic expressions used to describe facts in reality. Since language mainly was studied from the viewpoint of its descriptive function, the connection between language structure and condi-tions of communication has not been focussed on. Consequently, the nature of language has been viewed rather narrowly. In his criticism of Chomsky's approach to linguistic theory Searle (1972) focussed attention on just this point.

The new field of empirical and theoretical interest in linguistics includes the study of speech acts, which has been brought to the attention of linguists by philosophers. For the time being we can hardly maintain that this field of research has already led to a sufficient degree of clarity. Neither the empirical facts nor the theoretical basis needed to describe and explain facts are at an advanced level of explication. For example, we are rather left in the air as to the separation of linguistic aspects in the investigation of interaction from aspects of other branches of science like sociology, social psychology, psy-chology, philosophy. Very frequently we find that facts and concepts which we hope to obtain from other sciences are still undetected or rather vague, respectively, in these sciences. For linguistic research, problems of great im-portance arise from this situation:

(1)   Is there a specific linguistic approach to the study of actions performed by means of language?

(2)   To what extend does a linguistic analysis depend on a more general theory of social action?

The framework developed by Searle, following Austin, has been widely ac-cepted by linguists as a proposal for a linguistic approach to the study of language actions. The theoretical basis of this approach comprehends at least the following assumptions:

155

J. R. Searle, F. Kiefer, and M. Bierwisch (eds.), Speech Act Theory and Pragmatics,
155–168.

(i)   An utterance performed in a certain situation is an action of a certain type.

(ii)   The type of utterance can be investigated by analysing the use of linguistic devices indicating illocutionary force. In principle, information about the type of action performed by uttering an expression of a language can be given explicitly by means of language. Therefore, the fundamental structure of a sentence is assumed to have the form: $F(p)$, where p is a 'proposition' and F a symbol for linguistic description of information about the type of action performed when uttering a sentence which includes p.

(iii)   For each language a (finite?) set of types of speech acts is available. A theory of speech acts has to provide a theoretically established system of these types. It has to explain which class of propositions may possibly cooccur with a certain type of speech act. A theory of speech acts not only provides an explanation of illocutionary forces, it moreover offers a basis for explaining so-called indirect speech acts (Searle, 1975 b).

Although (ii) does not necessarily entail that a description of the meaning of illocutionary force indicating devices (IFIDs) is identical with a description of speech acts, the whole framework presupposes a close interrelation between linguistic analysis and analysis of conditions of interaction. Despite the heuristic value of this approach — which needs no further comment — it seems mandatory to develop a theoretical frame which allows a more exact investigation of the dependence between language and social interaction. Problems along this line have been discussed by Wunderlich (1976), Ehlich and Rehbein (1972) and others. It has been pointed out by these authors that:

(1)   The framework for the study of speech acts has to be sufficiently complex and extended in order to cover all facts relevant for the description of illocutionary forces. In particular, it is considered to be insufficient to study illocutions under highly isolated conditions. On the contrary, it is required to study the interactional function of an expression in concrete situations in which the language action takes place.

(2)   The social nature of speech acts can only be grasped if at least a sketch of a theory of human social activity is available.

This view falls into line with some fundamental ideas of Marxist philosophy: The exchange of ideas by means of language is part of what Marx calls 'the

real process of social life'. Being a component of social activity, communication by language can only be understood if we study its embedding in the
totality of social activities forming concrete, historically developing social
systems. The core of this complex totality determining other kinds of activity
is the economic process of reproduction of social life. Since the conditions of
life are different for social groups and classes communication cannot simply
be investigated from the viewpoint of an ideal community. Every method-
ologically legitimate abstraction of this complex background has to be aware
of the restriction of viewpoints and of the preliminary character of the scientific results.

Wunderlich and some other linguists have tried to sketch a framework for
a global theory of interaction closely connected with a general theory of
social intercourse. A similar proposal has been put forward by A. A. Leont'ev
(1971). All proposals offered so far are only vague orientations. Yet it seems
to me inevitable to proceed further on this way on account of the following
reflections:

The meaning of an utterance u of language L in a situational context SC −
symbolised by $SM(u)$, situational meaning of u − is constituted by at least
two kinds of information:[1]

(i)   Language meaning of the utterance provided by the grammar A
        of language L;
(ii)   Information on properties of the situational context, relevant to
        the interpretation of u in SC; symbolised by $I(SC(u))$.

It is the task of a *theory of symbolic interaction* (a) to provide a general basis
for the description of possible $I(SC(u))$, i.e., of knowledge relevant to the
interpretation of utterances in a concrete situational context,[2] and (b) to
specify how the situational meaning of an utterance $SM(u)$ is constituted by
language meaning $LM(u)$ and context information $I(SC(u))$.

Since $I(SC(u))$, at least in part, can be expressed by linguistic devices of
the utterance in question $LM(u)$ partially includes information on $I(SC(u))$.
The study of devices of a language serving to indicate aspects of the interactional context in which a proposition is expressed can be called linguistic
pragmatics. Linguistic pragmatics is, for example, concerned with the means
a language has for indicating illocutions, propositional attitudes, valuations,
topicalization. Apparently, linguistic pragmatics is included in a theory of
symbolic interaction.

To study language means which serve to describe or indicate properties of
situational contexts is impossible on purely linguistic grounds. The investi-

gation of IFIDs has shown that performative formulas used to indicate illocutionary forces cannot be considered as grammaticalized forms. Performative
formulas are different, in an unsystematic way, as to grammatical structure;
and other kinds of devices such as modal verbs, particles, intonation have
more than one function. It seems to be a wildgoose chase trying to define
types of illocutions on purely linguistic grounds.

Evidently, Searle's proposal for a classification of illocutionary acts
(Searle, 1975a) is not the result of a purely linguistic analysis of meaning of
IFIDs. His conditions for successful performance of a certain type of speech
act are properties of situational contexts. Searle, however, did not succeed
in elucidating the internal organisation of those properties. His approach
only provides some empirical hints to facts which can be explained by a
theory of symbolic interaction. Questions like 'Which types of condition
should be considered relevant?' and 'How are these conditions organized?'
go beyond the scope of a linguistic analysis of meaning. Therefore, a theory
of speech acts cannot be the result of inductive generalization drawn from
the analysis of appropriate devices of a language. It seems to be necessary,
starting from empirical facts — in part obtained by a rather intuitive analysis
of speech acts — to build up a tentative theoretical frame for a specification of $I(SC(u))$. In this paper I want to give a short sketch of an approach
to the specification of the information on the situational context which
is part of the situational meaning of an utterance performed in a certain
situation.

2. REPRESENTATION OF INFORMATION CONCERNING THE SITUATIONAL CONTEXT

A theory of symbolic interaction has, among others, to specify the aspects
and properties of the situational context the speaker has to take into consideration when he draws up a plan for an utterance. More precisely, it has to
provide a representation of the mental state of a speaker reflecting the situational context. A situation becomes a communicative situation due to the
intention of a person to influence the mind(s) of an audience by means of an
utterance. He plans a language action in order to transmit his intention to the
mind(s) of the audience. It may be supposed that the hearer uses the same
kind of knowledge, following, however, another mechanism. The speaker
anticipates the role of the hearer and makes assumptions about the ability
of the hearer to specify the situation. In an ideal case he only supplies the
information in his utterance which the hearer is assumed to be unable to gain

from the situation.[3] In many cases, though not in all, this will be information about his intention and his attitudes.

In our sketch, a rather restricted class of situations is considered. Two persons speak about actions to be performed by one of them. The concept 'action' is used in a rather informal way. We suppose the ideal condition to be that the speaker analyses his own mental state without any error and that he anticipates the hearer's attitudes correctly as well. Both are acting in a rational manner, i.e., they act conforming to certain postulates and do not accept inconsistent mental states. Furthermore, we assume some 'general conditions', in the sense of Searle (1969), to be satisfied.

The mental state of the speaker reflecting a situational context is structured. The elements of a structure representing a mental state of that kind are called *attitudes*.[4] The whole structure is called a *configuration of attitudes*. There are several kinds of attitude to be distinguished:

Motivational attitudes characterize the desirability of an action (in our case). A more elaborate approach would have to distinguish between desirability of an action and desirability of the state resulting from that action. In fact a whole scale of degrees of desirability could be drawn up. Furthermore we have to keep in mind that the motivation for a specific desirability may be very different.

It seems plausible to distinguish two scales. One ranging from a high degree of desirability of an action to a neutral position, the other from a high degree of desirability of the omission of an action to a neutral position. These scales may overlap in the neutral position. Omitting degrees of desirability the scales can be represented in the following way:

(i) P_i DESIRE A P_i −DESIRE A;
(ii) P_i DESIRE −A P_i −DESIRE −A.

In our sketch only two cases are considered:

P_i DESIRE A and P_i DESIRE −A.

Comment: 'P_i' = a certain person; 'A' = performance of an action by an actor; '−A' = omission of an action. 'A' includes the actor and can be represented by: A = a (P_x). 'a' = a predicate describing the action with unspecified actor, 'P' = a variable for actor, with different quantifications. Thus 'P_i DESIRE A' has more than one reading. In this paper the different readings are not systematically distinguished.

Epistemic and doxastic attitudes are mental entities of which those characterizing anticipated mental states of the hearer are of direct concern in this paper. Again a scale indicating degrees of certainty can be assumed. We select KNOW and ASSUME. Other predicates representing attitudes of these kinds are, for example, CONJECTURE, GUESS, BELIEVE, BE CONVINCED, DOUBT.

The anticipation of motivational attitudes of the hearer is represented by the following formula:

$$P_1 \text{ ASSUME } (P_2 \text{ DESIRE A})$$

Read: Speaker P_1 assumes that hearer P_2 desires action A.

Intentional attitudes. To intend an action means that someone has decided to perform an action. To desire an action does not mean to intend that action. However, there is a relation between intention and desirability which is expressed in formula (F 1)

(F 1) P_i INTEND A $\rightarrow P_i$ DESIRE A $\vee P_i$ ASSUME (P_j DESIRE A),

(F 1) excludes the possibility that a person intends an action which is neither desired by him nor by his partner. An action is only intended by a person, if he follows up his own interest or some other person's interests. Analogously (F 1'):

(F 1') P_i INTEND $-$A $\rightarrow P_i$ DESIRE $-$A $\vee P_i$ ASSUME (P_j DESIRE $-$A).

To intend the omission of an action is certainly the result of a mental activity, more complicated than the intention of an action. (F 1'), therefore, is perhaps only valid under specific conditions.

We furthermore assume the following relations between attitudes:

(F 2) P_i INTEND A $\rightarrow P_i$ ASSUME (P_i ABLE TO A).
(F 3) P_i ABLE TO A $\rightarrow$ POSS(A).

Formula (F 2) states that a person who intends an action assumes that he is able to perform the action in question. (F 3) asserts that being able to perform an action presupposes the possibility of that action.

Normative attitudes. To intend an action is connected with a checking of social norms relevant in the situation in which the action is planned. If the speaker wants to perform an action he takes into account the norms the hearer expects to be observed by him. If the hearer is the actor, the speaker postulates norms to be observed.

We assume that speaker and hearer rely on norms, maxims, conventions etc. valid in certain social contexts or in general. With this background they may be in a position to demand, prohibit or permit an action. A more detailed analysis would have to account for the social basis of normative attitudes.

We distinguish four normative attitudes in accordance with deontic logic. However, in our approach the elementary situation where one person postulates normative attitudes to be observed by a second person is envisaged. The four attitudes are:

(i) P_i DEMAND a (P_j).
(ii) P_i DEMAND $-a$ (P_j).
(iii) P_i $-$DEMAND a (P_j).
(iv) P_i $-$DEMAND $-a$ (P_j).

We leave it undecided whether (iii) and (iv) should be interpreted as variants in special contexts or as different types of permissions.

We assume that the following relations hold between normative and motivational attitudes:

(F 4) P_i DEMAND a (P_j) $\rightarrow P_i$ DESIRE A.
(F 5) P_i DEMAND $-a$ (P_j) $\rightarrow$ P_i DESIRE $-$A.

Again these are postulates which we believe to be valid for normal, rational action. Of course, being postulates they can be violated.

3. ATTITUDE CONFIGURATIONS. SOME EXAMPLES

3.1. Future actions of the hearer

The apparatus developed so far can be used to represent attitude configurations characterizing situations in which the speaker wants to get the hearer to perform an action or to refrain from performing an action. We distinguish two cases:

P_1 DESIRE (P_2 INTEND A).
P_1 DESIRE (P_2 INTEND $-$A).

I.e., the speaker wants the hearer to intend an action or to intend the omission of an action. A corresponding intention of a speech action can be represented as follows:

P_1 INTEND SA$_i$, where S(SA$_i$) =

(a) P_2 INTEND A;

(b) P_2 INTEND $-$A.

Comment: SA$_i$ = speech action proper, S(SA$_i$) = states resulting from the execution of a speech action of type SA$_i$.

Since application of (F 2), in a modification proper, resp. (F 3) is possible, we obtain:

P_1 ASSUME (P_2 ABLE TO A) $\wedge$ POSS(A).

It seems to be plausible to presuppose the following relations:

(F 6) P_1 DESIRE (P_2 INTEND A)$\rightarrow P_1$ DESIRE A.

(F 7) P_1 DESIRE (P_2 INTEND $-$A) $\rightarrow$ P_1 DESIRE $-$A.

I.e., a person who wants a second person to plan an action under normal circumstances wishes the action to be performed. On the other hand, if someone wants somebody to refrain from an action he does not desire the action in question.

In the next step, all combinations with intentions (a) and (b) above, motivational and normative attitudes allowed by the formulas are constructed.

I. (1)   (i) P_1 DESIRE (P_2 INTEND A);

         (ii) P_1 INTEND SA$_i$, where S(SA$_i$) = P_2 INTEND A;

         (iii) P_1 ASSUME (P_2 ABLE TO A) $\wedge$ POSS(A);

         (iv) P_1 DEMAND a (P_2);

         (v) P_1 DESIRE A;

         (vi) P_1 ASSUME (P_2 DESIRE A).

    (2)   (i)–(v) = (1) (i)–(v).

         (vi) P_1 ASSUME (P_2 DESIRE $-$A).

Conforming to (F 6) only configurations with P_1 DESIRE A are allowed. Since case (b) by definition presupposes that the speaker intends to cause, by a speech act proper, that P_2 INTEND $-$A, line (iv) in the configuration, however, presupposes that the hearer must do A, the configuration is ruled out. It is not allowed by the general postulate not to permit contradictory elements in a configuration of attitudes.

I (1): Characterizes a situation in which the speaker will use a polite form of asking. He probably will not stress the command because he assumes that the hearer is not in conflict with him as to the desirability of the action in question. A more detailed analysis would have to account for specific social contexts which determine the linguistic form of utterances; e.g., in military and administrative institutions special conditions should be observed. This is valid for the following illustrations too.

I (2): In this case the speaker assumes a conflict of motivational attitudes. He has to get the hearer to intend the action in question against his negative motivation. It is likely that the speaker will use an utterance which explicitly expresses the command. Perhaps he gives some hints to norms which oblige the hearer to perform A or he will threaten him with some sanctions.

II. (1) (i) P_1 DESIRE (P_2 INTEND $-A$);
  (ii) P_1 DESIRE SA_i, where $S(SA_i) = P_2$ INTEND $-A$)
  (iii) P_1 DEMAND $-a$ (P_2);
  (iv) P_1 DESIRE $-A$;
  (v) P_1 ASSUME (P_2 DESIRE $-A$).
(2) (i)–(iv) = (1) (i)–(iv).
  (v) P_1 ASSUME (P_2 DESIRE $-A$).

In case of prohibition only (b) is possible. According to (F 5) configurations containing P_1 DESIRE A are not allowed.

II (1): The speaker prohibits action A. He assumes the hearer is also un-interested in A. In this situation a speech action is likely only under special circumstances, e.g., when the speaker is not sure whether the hearer knows that he forbids A. The speaker has to keep in mind that to utter a prohibition which is fully accepted by the hearer because of his knowledge of norms can be taken for an insult by the hearer.

II (2): In this situation an explicit prohibition is necessary, because the hearer, having a positive motivation concerning A, does not agree with the norms or interpretations of norms which the speaker postulates to be relevant.

III. (1) (i) P_1 DESIRE (P_2 INTEND A);
  (ii) P_1 INTEND SA_i, where $S(SA_i) = P_2$ INTEND A;
  (iii) P_1 $-$DEMAND a (P_2) v P_1 $-$DEMAND $-a$ (P_2);
  (iv) P_1 DESIRE A;
  (v) P_1 ASSUME (P_2 DESIRE A).
(2) (i)–(iv) = (1) (i)–(iv).
  (v) P_1 ASSUME (P_2 DESIRE $-A$).
(3) (i) P_1 DESIRE (P_2 INTEND $-A$);
  (ii) P_1 INTEND SA_i, where $S(SA_i) = P_2$ INTEND $-A$;
  (iii) P_1 $-$DEMAND a (P_2) v P_1 $-$DEMAND $-a$ (P_2);
  (iv) P_1 DESIRE $-A$;
  (v) P_1 ASSUME (P_2 DESIRE $-A$).

(4) (i)–(iv) = (3) (i)–(iv).
     (v) P_1 ASSUME (P_2 DESIRE A).

III (1): The speaker wants the hearer to perform A. He assumes that the hearer wants A as well. The speaker cannot command A. In this case he will request the hearer to do A.

III (2): In this case the speaker will request the hearer in more impressive terms, stressing the importance of A for the speaker.

III (3): The speaker wants the hearer to refrain from A. He cannot command it, i.e., he cannot forbid A. The hearer does not desire A. The situation is similar to II (1).

III (4): In this case, since the hearer has a positive motivation for A, the speaker has to request him to refrain from A. He has to convince him to refrain from A.

3.2. Future actions of the speaker

As a second example we consider the case in which the speaker intends an action and he wants the hearer to know that he plans that action. This attitude can be represented by

$$P_1 \text{ DESIRE } (P_2 \text{ KNOW } (P_1 \text{ INTEND A})).$$

Again we have to distinguish between three fundamental normative situations (IV through VI):

IV. (1) (i) P_1 DESIRE (P_2 KNOW (P_1 INTEND A));
         (ii) P_1 INTEND SA_i, where $S(SA_i)$ = P_2 KNOW (P_1 INTEND A);
         (iii) P_1 ASSUME (P_2 DEMAND a (P_1));
         (iv) P_1 DESIRE A;
         (v) P_1 ASSUME (P_2 DESIRE A).
    (2) (i)–(iii), (v) = (1) (i)–(iii), (v).
         (vi) P_1 DESIRE $-$A.
    (3) (i) P_1 DESIRE (P_2 KNOW (P_1 INTEND $-$A);
         (ii) P_1 INTEND SA_i, where $S(SA_i)$ = P_2 KNOW (P_1 INTEND $-$A);
         (iii) P_1 ASSUME (P_2 DEMAND a (P_1));
         (iv) P_1 DESIRE $-$A;
         (v) P_1 ASSUME (P_2 DESIRE A).

IV (1): The speaker intends A which is commanded by the hearer. He has a positive motivation for A. In this situation the speaker will inform the hearer that he accepts the commitments commanded in that situation or that he agrees to accomplish what the hearer expects.

IV (2): The speaker intends A against his motivational attitude concerning A. He accepts that the hearer has reason to command A. The speaker will express his agreement perhaps with reservation. An explicit promise is possible if the speaker wants to stress his agreement to take on a commitment.

IV (3): The speaker does not agree to the command of the hearer. He has to express his disagreement. It is likely that he doubts the normative basis of the hearer or at least the interpretation of norms.

According to (F 4) only configurations containing P_2 DESIRE A are allowed.

V. (1)   (i) P_1 DESIRE (P_2 KNOW (P_1 INTEND A));
        (ii) P_1 INTEND SA$_i$, where S(SA$_i$) = P_2 KNOW (P_1 INTEND A);
      (iii) P_1 ASSUME (P_2 DEMAND $-a$ (P_1));
     (iv) P_1 DESIRE A;
      (v) P_1 ASSUME (P_2 DESIRE $-A$).

   (2)   (i) P_1 DESIRE (P_2 KNOW (P_1 INTEND $-A$));
        (ii) P_1 INTEND SA$_i$, where S(SA$_i$) = P_2 KNOW (P_1 INTEND $-A$);
      (iii) P_1 ASSUME (P_2 DEMAND $-a$ (P_1));
     (iv) P_1 DESIRE $-A$;
      (v) P_1 ASSUME (P_2 DESIRE $-A$).

   (3)   (i)–(iii), (v) = (2) (i)–(iii), (v).
      (iv) P_1 DESIRE A.

V (1): The speaker intends an action which is forbidden by the hearer. He has to express his intention arguing the hearer out of his command to refrain from A.

V (2): The speaker agrees with the prohibition of A. He will express his agreement.

V (3): The speaker agrees with the prohibition of A against his positive motivation.

VI. (1)   (i) P_1 DESIRE (P_2 KNOW (P_1 INTEND A)):
        (ii) P_1 INTEND SA$_i$, where S(SA$_i$) = P_2 KNOW (P_1 INTEND A);
      (iii) P_1 ASSUME (P_2 $-$DEMAND a (P_1) v P_2 $-$DEMAND $-a$ (P_1));
     (iv) P_1 DESIRE A;
      (v) P_1 ASSUME (P_2 DESIRE A).

(2) (i)–(iv) = (1) (i)–(iv).
     (v) P_1 ASSUME (P_2 DESIRE –A).
(3) (i) P_1 DESIRE (P_2 KNOW (P_1 INTEND –A));
     (ii) P_1 INTEND SA$_i$, where S(SA$_i$) = P_2 KNOW (P_1 INTEND –A);
     (iii) P_1 ASSUME (P_2 –DEMAND a (P_1) $\vee$ P_2 –DEMAND $-a$ (P_1);
     (iv) P_1 DESIRE –A;
     (v) P_1 ASSUME (P_2 DESIRE –A).
(4) (i)–(iv) = (3) (i)–(iv).
     (v) P_1 ASSUME (P_2 DESIRE A).

VI (1): The speaker intends action A which is desired by himself and the hearer. He is not obliged to do A. It is up to him to take on a commitment by an explicit promise or merely to predict his intention to do A. Even in the latter case, however, he takes on an obligation.

VI (2): The speaker intends an action which he assumes to be undesired by the hearer. A promise is impossible in this situation. Probably the speaker will announce his intention connected with his comments about the motivational conflict.

VI (3): The speaker intends to refrain from A which is neither commanded nor forbidden. He as well as the hearer have a negative attitude as to A. A speech action is only likely in specific situations.

VI (4): In this case the motivational attitudes of speaker and hearer conflict. The speaker will probably give some reasons for his decission to refrain from A.

4. SITUATIONAL CONTEXT AND APPROPRIATE UTTERANCE

Linguistic aspects of especial interest are the relations between attitude configurations and the grammatical structure of utterances. Among these are questions like: Which part of the whole information a configuration provides has to or can be included in the semantic information of the respective utterance?[5] Which grammatical forms and devices does a language possess serving to indicate information on attitude configurations? Which lexical elements have properties of situational contexts as their denotative domain? The latter question is connected with a further question of great importance, namely: Is there a difference between a proper semantic analysis of lexical elements — say performative verbs, adverbs denoting attitudes, etc. — and an analysis based on a theory of symbolic interaction? I assume that there is no difference because semantic information of lexical elements denoting properties of situational contexts is probably of the same type as information on situational context provided by a theory of symbolic interaction.

In this paper we cannot treat these problems systematically. We merely wanted to give some comments concerning the relations between attitude configurations I–VI and appropriate utterances.

5. SOME CONCLUSIONS

In our example we have investigated situations determining the use of IFIDs of the directive or commissive types, respectively (Searle, 1975a). With appropriate extensions the same apparatus can be used to characterize situations in which an action already performed supplies the occasion for a speech action. Two fundamental cases can be distinguished: either the speaker or the hearer has performed the action. In the former case the speaker comments on his own actions; in the latter case the speaker evaluates the hearer's actions. A great number of types can be distinguished; e.g., self-justification, self-criticism, apology, self-praise, big talk, on the one hand, and praise, appreciation, congratulation, gratitude, homage, reproof, reproach, accusation, offense, insult, on the other. The examples mentioned belong to Searle's class of expressives. In a similar way so-called representatives are describable. Only declaratives demand special treatment.

The apparatus sketched in this paper is merely a tentative theoretical basis for an analysis of empirical material. The logical structure of this apparatus as well as its empirical justification remain desiderata for further research. It seems, however, possible to discuss some problems raised in the framework of 'speech act theory' on a new basis.

Academy of Sciences of GDR, Berlin

NOTES

[1] For a more detailed analysis see M. Bierwisch (in this volume pp. 000–000).

[2] A theory of symbolic interactions has as its subject matter not only actions performed by means of linguistic utterances but any kind of symbolic action. Thus $I(SC(u))$ includes, among others, information on paralinguistic actions which accompany linguistic utterances.

[3] The term 'situation' comprehends mental states of the speaker and hearer, reflecting

intentions, evaluations, analysis of physical and social environment, knowledge about the interactional context, etc.

[4] The term is used in a narrower sense in social psychology. In our terminology we follow Wunderlich (1976, pp. 73 ff.).

[5] These questions offer a way to study optimal utterances, i.e., utterances which provide neither too much (redundant) nor too little information.

BIBLIOGRAPHY

Bierwisch, Manfred: 1980, in this volume, pp. 1–35.

Ehlich, Konrad: 1972, Jochen Rehbein, 'Zur Konstitution pragmatischer Einheiten in einer Institution: Das Speiserestaurant,' in D. Wunderlich (ed.), *Linguistische Pragmatik*, Frankfurt A. M.

Leont'ev, A. A.: 1971, 'Sprache, Sprechen, Sprechtätigkeit,' translated and edited by C. Heeschen and W. Stölting, Stuttgart, Berlin, Köln, Main.

Searle, John R.: 1969, *Speech Acts*, London.

Searle, John R.: 1972, 'Chomsky's Revolution in Linguistics,' New York Review of Books, June 29.

Searle, John R.: 1975a, 'A Classification of Illocutionary Acts,' in Gunderson and Maxwell (eds.), Minnesota Studies in Philosophy of Science, Vol. 6. Minneapolis.

Searle, John R.: 1975b, 'Indirect Speech Acts,' in Cole and Morgan (eds.), *Syntax and Semantics*, Vol. 3 *Speech Acts*, New York, San Francisco, London.

Wunderlich, Dieter: 1976, *Studien zur Sprechakttheorie*, Frankfurt A. M.

ROLAND POSNER

SEMANTICS AND PRAGMATICS OF
SENTENCE CONNECTIVES IN NATURAL LANGUAGE*

> When a diplomat says "yes",
> he means 'perhaps';
> when he says "perhaps",
> he means 'no';
> and when he says "no",
> he is no diplomat.
>
> When a lady says "no",
> she means 'perhaps';
> when she says "perhaps",
> she means 'yes';
> and when she says "yes",
> she is no lady.
>
> Voltaire

One need be neither a diplomat nor a lady to use the word *perhaps* to mean 'yes' one time and 'no' another. But what is the meaning of a word like *perhaps* if everyone can make it mean either 'yes' or 'no' as he pleases? Can one in any sense talk about a fixed word meaning here? But if not, what is it Voltaire is telling us when he maintains that the diplomat's uttering "yes" as well as the lady's uttering "no" *means* 'perhaps'?

What is *said* and what is *meant*, coded information and its use in communication, do not seem to coincide in all cases. But, when they don't, which content elements of an utterance should be traced back to *word meanings* and which to the specific *use of the words* in the situation in question?

In semiotic terms, I am going to deal with the delimitation of semantics and pragmatics in the description of verbal communication. In treating this problem, I shall discuss the following points:

1. Two strategies for the description of verbal communication
2. The monism of meaning
3. The monism of use
4. The identification of meaning and use
5. The use of meanings
6. Meaning versus suggestion
7. Sentence connectives: maximization of meaning

169

J. R. Searle, F. Kiefer, and M. Bierwisch (eds.), Speech Act Theory and Pragmatics,
169–203.

8. Sentence connectives: minimization of meaning
9. The duality of semantic and pragmatic interpretation.

1. TWO STRATEGIES FOR THE DESCRIPTION OF VERBAL COMMUNICATION

In uttering verbal expressions to achieve communicative goals, we must be able to use these expressions appropriately. But how do we proceed? Does every word have a fixed meaning that language users reproduce in their utterances? Or are there no fixed meanings but only rules of use that guide the language users in their formulations?

These questions delineate two competing strategies for the description of verbal communication. For linguists pursuing the first strategy, verbal communication can be exhaustively described by reference to word meaning, sentence meaning, and the meaning relations holding among verbal expressions. Linguists pursuing the second strategy seek to avoid assuming the existence of meanings; they try to describe the same phenomena in terms of language use. Both approaches have come to develop highly elaborated and finely articulated systems of terminology:

— While proponents of the first strategy speak of meaning, semantic features and the realization of semantic features, proponents of the second talk about use, rules of use and the application of rules of use;

— while one side speaks of semantic categories, of literal versus transposed meaning, of uniqueness of meaning versus ambiguity, the other is concerned with modes of use, literal versus transposed use, consistent versus inconsistent use;

— while one side speaks of hierarchies of semantic features, involving union, intersection, and opposition of features, the other discusses hierarchies of semantic rules, involving union, intersection and opposition of rules;

— while one side speaks of presuppositions, the other talks about conditions of use; constraints on the realization of semantic features appear as constraints on the application of semantic rules; feature change appears as rule change; modifications in the meaning of a word appear as modifications in the use of that word.

These two strategies I will call *the monism of meaning* and *the monism of use*.

Comparing the two strategies in such an abstract manner might lead one to regard them as merely terminological variants of the same theory, equally applicable and equally efficient in the description of verbal communication, were it not for the fact that they involve different empirical hypotheses and apply different methods of investigation: Monists of meaning usually assume that we have direct empirical access to word meanings and that rules of word use, if such things exist, are easily derivable from word meanings. Monists of use tend to believe that only the use of a word is empirically accessible, and that the meanings of that word, if such things exist, must be derived from its use. Common to each monism, however, is the assumption that its respective approach can give a complete linguistic explanation of how language functions.

In what follows I will show that both positions fail to satisfy some rather simple theoretical and methodological requirements for the description of language. Focusing on sentence connectives, I am going to argue against monistic approaches and in favor of a theory that assigns complementary roles to the meaning and to the use of words in verbal communication.

Since the discovery of truth-tables in the logic of the late 19th century, many logicians have offered an explication for the so-called logical particles of natural language. Nevertheless, doubts about the adequacy of such explications have never stilled. Recently, this century-long discussion has been given a new turn by the American philosopher of language Herbert Paul Grice, whose 'Logic of Conversation' indicates a new and promising direction to take in the description of sentence connectives in natural language.[2] Grice's approach has not been received without controversy, however, and the essential arguments against it must be taken into account as well. In order to show the proper role Grice's approach can play in empirical semantics, I shall begin by sketching the history of the monisms of meaning and of use, including some of their psycholinguistic ramifications.

2. THE MONISM OF MEANING

At the end of the 19th century the conceptual semantics inherited from the Age of Enlightenment came under the influence of a newly developed empirical discipline, psychology. This interaction resulted in a linguistic conception that can be characterized as follows. To communicate is to transmit concepts and in order to transmit concepts one must utter words whose meanings are concepts. According to Wilhelm Wundt, "every independent conceptual word [. . .] elicits a certain conceptual idea that is vivid to the degree to which the meaning of the word is concrete."[3] Edward Titchener taught, "The word *dog* has a meaning for us because the perception of this word elicits the idea of a dog in us."[4] While not every word is an independent conceptual word and, as such, able to transmit an idea, every word has (at least) one constant meaning which, when combined with the meanings of other words, contributes to the meaning of the expression as a whole. Thus, a speaker transmits the intended concepts by uttering the appropriate words, with which the addressee associates appropriate conceptual ideas of his own. Associations can be interpreted and tested according to the mechanism of stimulus and response. In order to find out which ideas are associated, addressees are subjected to standard tests such as drawing the associated objects or picking out their putative qualities from a list.

Unfortunately, the association experiments did not, when carried out on a large scale, confirm this theory in the expected way. The ideas elicited by a particular word differed greatly according to the context. Thus, it gradually became a commonplace of meaning-monist word semantics to claim, "The boundaries of word meaning are vague, blurred, fluid."[5] Even linguists like Karl Otto Erdmann, who took such statements as the starting-point for the introduction of new distinctions in his 'Essays from the Borders of Psycholinguistics and Logic', were not able to neutralize their force.

3. THE MONISM OF USE

The consequences of this failure were drawn by behaviorist psychology. If the association test does not provide reliable access to word meaning, it is useless as a linguistic method. And, if we are forced to assume that word meanings are fluid, then the concept of meaning loses its theoretical value for the description of verbal communication as well. John Watson formulated this insight most emphatically, "From the position of a behaviorist the problem of meaning is a mere abstraction."[6] And Burrhus F. Skinner laconically concurred, "The speaker does not utter any ideas or images but only words."[7]

Even Charles W. Morris prided himself on being able to do away with meanings altogether. Indeed, he thought he had renewed the connection with experimental psychology by taking dispositions into account in his semiotic program.[8] Whereas association psychologists had put word and meaning on the same level with stimulus and response and had regarded word meaning as a directly observable variable, Morris took word use to be a disposition that mediates between stimulus and response in the communication situation. Being dispositions, the rules of use cannot be directly observed but must be inferred from manifest behavior in the form of intervening variables. Thus, in the case of word use the hypothesis of direct empirical accessability was abandoned just as it had been in the case of word meaning.[9] Not even the difficulty encountered by Erdmann disappeared for monists of use; it merely became more clearly formulated. How one and the same word can play a role in fundamentally different behavioral dispositions is a question still looking for an answer.

4. THE IDENTIFICATION OF MEANING AND USE

These empirical problems and methodological difficulties deprived the two monist positions of their initial theoretical attractiveness. To be sure, it was not only for methodological reasons that Ludwig Wittgenstein advised, "Don't ask for the meaning, ask for the use".[10] He believed that he could also give this maxim theoretical underpinnings, claiming, "For a large number of uses of the word 'meaning' — even if not for all its uses — this word can be explained thus: The meaning of a word is its use in the language".[11] But Wittgenstein failed to develop satisfactory methods for systematically collecting and describing word uses and restricted himself to analyzing examples. For this reason, he prepared the way for an elaboration of the use-monist terminology rather than for the introduction of explicit criteria justifying its application. What survived was the slogan in its truncated version: "The meaning of a word is its use". Because of the lack of guiding criteria it was no surprise that this identification of meaning to use was soon made to apply in the opposite direction. This has led to today's uncritical contamination of the terminology of meaning with the terminology of use.

Of course, even such contamination can be justified, if only in the form of an analogy: are not meaning and use just two aspects of one and the same phenomenon, like temperature and particle velocity in thermodynamics or like wave and corpuscle in quantum physics? Yet, whoever holds this view, must take into account that physics has confirmed each of the two aspects experimentally so that the coexistence of the two terminologies is justified empirically.

But, can this be said of the two aspects of language?

The lack of direct experimental evidence for the existence of meanings and of rules of use has already been pointed out. Nevertheless, it must be conceded that there are phenomena in language that are more easily describable in terms of meaning and that there are other phenomena for which a description in terms of use is more convincing. For example, consider the German color words *gelb* and *blond*. If we take these words to denote those parts of the color spectrum that are reflected by yellow and blond objects, respectively, then *gelb* and *blond* have approximately the same meaning. They are, however, used in different ways; indeed, their uses in German are mutually exclusive: *blond* generally refers to human hair; everything else reflecting the color waves in question is called *gelb* or *gelblich*. It is true, there are certain marginal uses as in: *Herr Ober, bitte ein kühles Blondes!* ('Waiter, please bring me a light ale'). But even here there is no mutual substitutivity, since no one would say, *Herr Ober, bitte ein kühles Gelbes!* The words *gelb* and *blond* can therefore be said to have the same meaning but to be in *complementary distribution*.

The following example is equally instructive. When we hear little Peter say at the hairdresser's: "Mommy, look, Annie is being mowed," we smile, but we understand what he wants to say. *Mow* means the same as *cut*, but its use is restricted in such a way that human (and animal) hair is excluded.[12] What we must take into account here are the *conditions of use* that restrict the occurrence of a word beyond what its meaning would allow. In the lexicon such conditions of use normally appear as parenthetical supplements to the specification of meaning, e.g., "*blond*: 'yellow (of human hair)' " and "*mow*: 'cut (of grasslike vegetation)' ".

In recent years it has become commonplace to regard conditions of use as presupposed semantic features of a word and thus to integrate them into the meaning of the word. Correspondingly, *blond* would mean something like 'having yellow human hair' and *mow* something like 'cut grasslike vegetation'. But such a solution can be maintained only with great difficulty.[13] Once again color words demonstrate quite clearly how indispensable the specification of conditions of use can be. If the color of a cotton coat that Germans call *rot* ('red') occurs on a plastic wall, they tend to call it *braun* ('brown'). Thus, the color word is changed when the area of application changes, even though the color waves have remained the same. Monists of meaning might try to cope with this situation in the same way as they did in the cases of *gelb* and *blond*; they might say: The meaning of *rot* includes the presupposed semantic feature of 'having a rough surface', and the meaning of *braun* includes the presupposed semantic feature of 'having a smooth surface'. But this is plainly wrong, for it would also be perfectly acceptable to call a rough surface *braun* and a smooth surface *rot*. In contrast to the cases of *gelb* and *blond*, the transfer from one area of application to another does not affect the acceptability of use of the words *rot* and *braun*, but their meaning. If applied to smooth surfaces, *rot* denotes a different section in the color spectrum than if applied to rough surfaces. The same is true for *braun*. There seems to be a mutual dependency here between the meaning and the context of use and that makes sense only if meaning and use are independently characterizable.

These brief examples may suffice to call into question the identification of meaning and use and to show that the two kinds of terminology are not interchangeable in all areas of lexical semantics.

5. THE USE OF MEANINGS

The difference between semantic features and conditions of use has been elaborated most clearly by Grice. In his William James Lectures, held at Harvard in 1968, he succeeds in liberating himself from the simplistic opposition of "meaning versus use".[14] In contrast to Watson and Skinner, Grice is prepared to claim that in communication we deal not only with words or concatenations of words but also with word meanings and sentence meanings. What is involved here is the use of meanings. Grice strives to discover the rules according to which we use meanings in order to achieve our communicative goals.

Let us compare the following five sentences:

(1)   Please take the garbage out.
(2)   (a) I want you to take the garbage out.
        (b) Can you take the garbage out?
        (c) Will you take the garbage out?
        (d) Have you taken the garbage out?

In everyday family communication each of these five sentences evidently can be uttered for the same purpose, that is, to express a request for someone to take out the garbage. Nevertheless, when we isolate each of these sentences from its context and describe it as such, we rightly say: (1) is an imperative sentence, (2a) is a declarative sentence, and (2b) through (2d) are interrogative sentences. But how can one, in uttering an assertion or question get someone to fulfill a request? How can we explain that the son who hears his mother ask, "Have you taken the garbage out?", understands this as a request for him to take the garbage out? This is the sort of problem that concerns Grice.[15] In order to solve it, we must take into account the context of utterance and apply certain principles from the theory of rational behavior. Let us begin with the situation in which mother and son are standing in the kitchen in front of the full garbage can. Both can see with their own eyes that the garbage can is full and can infer that it has not yet been taken out and emptied. Nevertheless, the mother asks her son, "Have you taken the garbage out?" If he takes this sentence in its literal meaning, its utterance can only be a question for information. But as such it would lack any communicative function. The son knows that the question would have to be answered in the negative and he knows that his mother knows that, too. In this situation that question seems to be absurd and its utterance by the mother irrational. Rational behavior would conform to the following maxim:

(M1)   Make your contribution such as is required, at the stage at which it occurs, by the accepted purpose of the action in which you and your partners are engaged.

This maxim is called "cooperation principle" by Grice; by appropriate specification it can also be applied to communication, understood as verbal cooperation:

(M2)   Make your utterance such as is required, at the stage at which it occurs, by the accepted purpose of the talk-exchange in which you and your partners are engaged.

What purpose might the mother be pursuing when standing with her son in the kitchen in front of the full garbage can? From the rest of his mother's behavior the son knows, "Mother likes everything to be clean and neat and wants me to be so, too." But does the mother's question serve this purpose? "If taken literally, no." Does it serve another purpose? "If taken literally, no." Did the mother want to say something pointless? "No, this is something she normally does not do." In order to avoid such a conclusion, the son prefers to reinterpret the sentence and to give the utterance a new meaning by relating it to the accepted purpose of the talk-exchange: "Mother likes everything to be clean and neat and wants me to be so, too. I would be neat if I took the garbage can out and emptied it. Mother's question evidently is supposed to draw my attention to a fact which she and I already know but from which I have not yet drawn the desired consequence. Evidently, it is desired that I should now take out the garbage can and empty it. Since I would like to continue communicating with my mother and to achieve my own communicative purposes, too, I will take the present purpose of communication seriously and behave as if mother had requested me to take out the garbage can and empty it." These considerations lead the son to the result that he has to treat the question as a request. Reasoning of this kind is normally performed automatically and remains below the threshold of consciousness. But it has to be taken into account if the behavior of the addressee is to be adequately explained.

Of course, the utterer regularly anticipates such reasoning. In fact, the mother only formulated her utterance as a question because she could assume that her communication partner was in a position to reconstruct the intended request from it. She used the literal meaning of (2d) in order to convey the literal meaning of (1). In doing so, she did not only combine words with lexical meanings according to grammatical rules to produce the literal meaning of a sentence, she also used the sentence meaning according to pragmatic rules to convey a message normally conveyed with different words and different grammatical rules. She used an assertion or a question in order to suggest a request.

But in what kind of situation does one prefer to rely upon the reasoning of the addressee instead of saying literally what one wants to convey? The answer becomes obvious if we consider how an obstinate son could respond to the utterances (1) and (2) if he took them literally:

(1')   No, I won't.
(2')   (a') You can do it.
          (b') I can, but I don't want to.
          (c') I will, but right now I'm doing something more important.
          (d') No, because I have more important things to do.

As these examples demonstrate, the utterances under (2) leave open to the addressee the possibility of understanding them not as requests but as assertions or questions and to respond to their literal meanings. Interpreted in this way, they can provide an opportunity for a discussion whether the conditions for a sensible request are satisfied at all. In using such a formulation the utterer makes it possible for his addressee to argue against making a request before such a request has in fact been uttered; he spares him an open conflict and avoids losing face himself. In short, the use of meanings like those of (2a) through (2d) to suggest a request is more polite than the use of the literal meaning of (1).

If this explanation of the function of suggestions proves right, it gives us a strong argument for the existence of meanings; for, the entire explanation would collapse if meaning were reducible to use.

6. MEANING VERSUS SUGGESTION

The construction of suggestions originates in the effort of the addressee to interpret the verbal behavior of his communication partner as rational behavior. If the speaker utters a sentence whose meaning, taken literally, does not contribute to the recognized purpose of communication, then the addressee asks himself if the speaker means something different from what he has said literally. He evaluates the verbal and non-verbal context of the talk-exchange, looking for supplementary information that, applied to the literal meaning, will let him infer a message conforming to the recognized purpose of communication.[16] This reasoning is a heuristic operation; it follows certain rules, but its results are not strictly deducible since it often remains unclear what the purpose of communication is and which circumstances of the context are relevant to it.

In order to get such a reasoning process going, it is important to discover which maxim of rational behavior the utterance would have violated if it had been taken literally. Therefore, Grice has tried to supplement his principle of cooperation with a series of special maxims which are valid in particular for the exchange of information during a conversation.[17] Grice sets up these conversational maxims by facetiously employing Kant's table of categories:

(M3)   I   Maxims of Quantity
           1. Make your contribution as informative as is required . . .
           2. Do not make your contribution more informative than is required . . .
       II Maxims of Quality
           1. Do not assert what you believe to be false.
           2. Do not assert that for which you lack adequate evidence.
       III Maxim of Relation
           Say only things which are relevant . . .
       IV Maxims of Manner
           1. Avoid obscurity of expression . . .
           2. Avoid ambiguity . . .
           3. Be brief (avoid unnecessary prolixity) . . .
           4. Be orderly . . .

The dots following these formulations indicate that the maxims of quantity, relation and manner can only be understood with respect to the purpose of communication accepted for a particular stage of a conversation.

This list of maxims is neither complete nor systematically organized in a satisfying way, and the individual maxims are neither of equal importance nor completely independent from one another (e.g., compare the relationship between I/2 and III). However, these flaws do not rule out the possibility that the maxims mentioned are actually applied in the production and interpretation of conversational suggestions. Therefore one must also take them into account when describing these processes.

How this is done may be illustrated with an example that has given logicians many headaches: A First Mate does not get along well with his Captain. The Captain is a prohibitionist and the Mate is often drunk. Therefore the Captain is looking for a pretext to have the Mate fined when the ship comes to port. One day, as the Captain has the watch, the Mate starts bellowing out a sea chantey again. The Captain can stand the Mate's excesses no longer and writes in the log:

(3)   (a) Today, March 23rd, the Mate was drunk.

A few days later, when the Mate himself has the watch, he discovers the Captain's entry in the log and wonders what he can do about it without compromising himself any further. Finally, he also makes an entry in the log, which reads:

(3)   (b) Today, March 26th, the Captain was not drunk.

This is not an ordinary conversation, but Grice's conversational maxims are nevertheless applicable, since the institution of the log serves an accepted purpose of communication that can be realized by following the maxims. Both entries are true statements; however, there is an important pragmatic difference between them, which is revealed by the reader's reaction. Whereas the Captain's entry is interpreted and understood without hesitation, any reader who comes across the Mate's entry cannot help asking, "Why is that written in here? What relevance can the statement have in a log that the Captain was not drunk on a certain day?" Once the reader has established that this entry would, if taken literally, violate the maxim of relation, the next steps of his reasoning are easy. "If the writer wanted to establish communicative cooperation with the reader of the log at all, he must have considered this entry relevant himself. A log serves to register exceptional occurrences on a voyage. Evidently the writer wanted to indicate that the Captain's sobriety on March 26th was exceptional. Sobriety is, of course, exceptional if one is usually drunk. Under these circumstances the writer wanted to suggest with his entry that the Captain was usually drunk during the voyage." Thus the reasoning prompted by the Mate's entry has, on the basis of assumptions about the purpose and context of communication, turned a trivially true statement into a false statement of a rather defamatory nature. This example shows how one can lie with true statements when the utterance of those statements violates one of Grice's conversational maxims. In our case it is the maxim of relation (III) that is involved. There are similar examples for the violation of other maxims.

What is peculiar in this defamatory suggestion is the fact that it is hardly possible to take legal action against it. When confronted with the alternative of calling the Mate to account for false statements or for disorderly conduct, any court would choose the latter.

The two examples from household and sea demonstrate that the discrepancy between what an utterer formulates and what he intends to convey can be explicated on the basis of the distinction between literal meaning (which is determined grammatically) and suggested content (which is determined pragmatically). Furthermore, our analyses of these examples have shown how the utterer proceeds to produce conversational suggestions on the basis of literal meanings and how the addressee proceeds in his efforts to reconstruct these suggestions from the literal meanings. If these analyses are not misguided, they force the linguist to postulate *duality* in the description of verbal communication. He must not only determine the literal meaning of the verbal expression uttered but must also examine how the utterer uses this meaning.

Illuminating as this conception may seem, it leads to theoretical and methodological questions that are hard to answer. How can a linguist determine which content elements of a given message must be considered as the literal meaning of the words or sentences uttered? Can we rightly claim that the sentence *Have you taken the garbage out*? is an interrogative sentence, if it can obviously be used as a request? If the negation of the word *drunk* can be used to indicate that the person in question was the opposite of sober, why do we continue connecting its affirmative with the opposite of sobriety?

One thing is certain: an undifferentiated treatment of all the uses we can find will not bring us any nearer to the literal meaning of a word or sentence. Rather it is necessary to select from among the many uses of a word or sentence those uses in which the literal meaning does not appear to be subjected to any modifications required by specific features of the verbal or non-verbal context.

However, by being asked in this way the question is in danger of becoming circular. We are saying: (a) the meaning of a verbal expression will not be submitted to a context-dependent reinterpretation if its utterance does not violate any conversational maxims; (b) the utterance of a verbal expression does not violate a conversational maxim if it is unnecessary to reinterpret its literal meaning in a context-dependent manner. In this perspective, the literal meaning appears to be like Wittgenstein's beetle in a box: even if we assume that the beetle exists, we cannot tell how big it is.[18]

There seems to be only one way out of this dilemma, and that is the attempt to reconstruct the process of comprehension itself.

1. According to our initial assumption, the addressee proceeds from the literal meaning of an expression and, on this basis, establishes certain conversational suggestions corresponding to the particular features of the verbal and non-verbal context. A comparative analysis of the comprehension processes for all essential uses of an expression could thus furnish us with those content elements which are always involved, as against those elements that play a role only in certain classes of context. We may assume that the content elements involved in the comprehension of all the uses of an expression belong to the literal meaning of that expression; as to the other content elements, we may conclude that they are dependent on special circumstances of communication and are produced only in the process of special interpretive reasoning. This is the *postulate of variability* for suggestions.

2. Since conversational suggestions change as the situation of conversation changes, we can cancel them through the choice of certain contexts. Even simple verbal additions will do the job, and by claiming the contrary we can annul an alleged suggestion without giving rise to a contradiction. This is the Gricean *postulate of cancellability* for suggestions.[19] If, after asking one of the questions (2b) through (2d), the mother in the kitchen had added, "But I'm not requesting you to do it now," no request would have been suggested. Likewise, the Mate could have avoided a defamatory use of his entry without contradicting himself, if he had supplemented (3b) by the sentence, "The Captain is never drunk." Such additions cannot, however, prevent other suggestions from arising, in case the complete utterance, understood literally, still violates *some* conversational maxim.

3. Finally, one cannot avoid a conversational suggestion by simply choosing another formulation with the same literal meaning. Suggestions of the relevant sort do not result from the use of special words but rather from the specific use of meanings. Therefore a suggestion generated by a particular utterance in a given situation is detachable from the words, but not from the literal meaning of that utterance. This is the Gricean *postulate of non-detachability* for suggestions.[20] In our examples, the mother's suggestion would not have been changed if she had said, "Has the garbage been taken out?" and the Mate's suggestion would not have been changed if he had written, "Today, March 26th, the captain was sober."

Variability, cancellability and non-detachability are useful indications, but, unfortunately, they are not sufficient as criteria in determining which content elements have to be excluded from the literal meaning of an expression.[21]

Nevertheless, we have to work with them, as long as there are no better analytical instruments. The imperfections of this procedure only confirm once more what meaning-monists and use-monists had to discover by experience, namely that neither the meaning of a word nor the rules for the use of a word are directly accessible to the empirical linguist, but must be inferred from manifest verbal behavior.

Now if it is theoretically certain that all verbal behavior is based upon literal meanings as well as upon rules for the use of meanings it becomes necessary in the course of linguistic analysis to estimate how much of the content of a given utterance may be traceable to its literal meaning and how much is to be construed as suggestion. This is a procedural problem that gains importance in view of the fact that there is hardly any word of a natural language whose uses have been exhaustively analyzed. As long as we are in the position of creating hypotheses, we can again choose between two strategies that take up the positions of the old monists in a weakened form. *Meaning-maximalists* attempt to deduce as much as possible from the literal meanings of verbal expressions and tend to assume richness and ambiguity in the meanings of words. On the other hand, *meaning-minimalists* attribute more importance to the pragmatic rules of reinterpretation as opposed to literal meanings and tend to accept only minimal meanings and unambiguous words.[22] Let us now consider the consequences of these strategies for the analysis of sentence connectives in natural language, particularly, of the word *and* in English.

7. SENTENCE CONNECTIVES: MAXIMIZATION OF MEANING

When the logical particle *et* (written as "&", "∧", "." according to the various notational conventions) occurs between two propositions, it turns them into one complex proposition that is true if and only if both constituent propositions are true. This statement, which defines the connective *et* of propositional logic, also seems to apply to the word *and* as found between declarative sentences of English. What would then be easier than to assume that this definition also characterizes the meaning of this sentence connective?

However, the truth-functional definition of *and* has consequences that run counter to many uses of the word *and* in natural language. For example, it allows sentences to be connected to one another without regard to their meaning. But any speaker of English would consider the following expressions absurd and unacceptable:

(4)   (a) 2 × 2 = 4 and it is impossible to analyze further the concept
            of *intention*.
       (b) Müller just scored a goal and eels spawn in the Sargasso Sea.

Moreover, the truth-functional definition of *and* places exactly the same
condition on the two connected declarative sentences; so they should be
interchangeable. But any speaker of English will interpret (5a) differently
from (5b):

(5)   (a) Peter married Annie and Annie had a baby.
       (b) Annie had a baby and Peter married Annie.

Of course, these observations are not contested by anybody. What is contro-
versial is how they should be explained.

The meaning-maximalist draws the following conclusions: The meaning
of the word *and* is richer than the meaning of the logical connective *et*; it
includes not only the truth-functional feature of *conjunctivity*, but also the
feature of *connexity* and the feature of *successivity*. On the basis of connexity, the *and*-sentence conveys that the facts described in the second constituent sentence are part of the same situation as the facts described in the
first. On the basis of successivity, it conveys that the facts described in the
second constituent sentence appear at a later time than the facts described in
the first.

Such an analysis of meaning, however, is liable to quite a number of objections.

1. What about the three postulates of variability, cancellability and non-
detachability? It is by no means true that every use of the sentence connective *and* implies a temporal sequence between the facts described:

(6)   (a) 2 × 2 = 4 and $\sqrt{4} = 2$.
       (b) The moon revolves around the earth and the earth revolves
            around the sun.

This shows that successivity is variable and not fixed to the word *and*. The
assumption of successivity can also easily be cancelled by an additional utterance of the right kind. Continuing with:

(7)   But I don't know in which sequence that happened.

after having said (5a), rules out the basis for the conclusion that the baby
came *after* the wedding. On the other hand, one cannot get around the
successivity assumption by merely reformulating the constituent sentences

in such a way as to preserve their meaning. The successivity assumption is non-detachable.

These observations indicate that successivity should be regarded not as a semantic feature of the word *and*, but as a conversational suggestion. Whenever we use coordinate sentences to describe events in time, we relate the sequence of the sentences uttered to the sequence of the events they describe, even without the help of the word *and*. The utterer would violate the conversational maxim "Be orderly ..." (IV/4), if he were not to keep the temporal sequence parallel on both levels.

However, such an objection will not deter a meaning-maximalist, since, according to him, the absence of assumptions about the sequence of the facts described in (6) should be explained in a different way. Even when we speak of *chocolate hearts, paper tigers,* or *roses of glass,* we do not imply that the hearts beat or that the tigers and roses are alive. Evidently, quite simple syntactic procedures like the addition of an attribute to a noun can lead to the deletion of semantic features of this noun.[23] This deletion occurs during the amalgamation of the semantic features, in order to satisfy a requirement to avoid contradiction. Let us apply this explanation to our example (6): If one had to assume both that the facts described in (6) are time-independent and that they occur one after another, a contradiction would arise. So the addressee, preferring a non-contradictory interpretation, will delete the feature of successivity in his interpretation according to the meaning-maximalists.

With this procedure we now have two proposals for grasping variable content elements. These approaches impute converse operations to the process of comprehension. According to one approach, the addressee proceeds from a literal meaning with few semantic features and reaches the required interpretation with the help of conversational maxims relying on additional information specific to the verbal and non-verbal context of utterance. According to the other approach, the addressee proceeds from a rich literal meaning and deletes, according to certain preference rules, those semantic features which would come into conflict with the verbal or non-verbal context.

What is remarkable here is that both approaches are based on a similar theoretical apparatus. As shown by the requirement to avoid contradiction, even the meaning-maximalists need additional pragmatic maxims of interpretation besides grammar and the lexicon. And if even meaning-maximalists cannot manage without pragmatic rules, then we are justified in asking why they trust this instrument so little, why they apply it only to restrict meaning and not to produce new content. One might suppose that they have become victims of hypostatizing their own concept of meaning.

2. In order to support the meaning-maximalist analysis of the word *and*, one often compares it with the word *but*.[24] *But* seems to share with *and* the semantic features of conjunctivity and connexity. Instead of successivity it has *adversativity* as its third semantic feature. Someone who says *but* implies that the facts described in the following sentence are unexpected or contrary to the present context.[25]

However, this parallelism is misleading. In contrast to the successivity of *and* the adversativity of *but* is not cancellable. Someone who says:

(8)   (a) Annie is Martha's daughter, but she is married to Peter.

and then goes on to say:

(9)   However, I don't mean to say that there is an opposition between the two facts.

will not be taken seriously, since there is then no way to explain his saying *but* in (8a). Finally, non-detachability does not hold for adversativity. In many cases the assumption of adversativity will vanish if the *but*-sentence is reformulated in such a way that the rest of its content is preserved. Let us compare (8a) with (8b):

(8)   (b) Annie is Martha's daughter and she is married to Peter.

In (8b) there is no longer any trace of unexpectedness or opposition.

Besides, whereas an *and*-sentence may or may not convey successivity, depending on the context and on the facts described in the constituent sentences, *but* without adversativity is unthinkable. In contrast to *paper tigers* and *chocolate hearts*, this semantic feature never disappears, even in the face of a possible contradiction:

(10)   (?) $2 \times 2 = 4$, but $2 \times 2 = 4$.

We will tend to simply reject an utterance like (10) as unacceptable instead of asserting that the meaning of *but* is reduced to the features of conjunctivity and connexity here.[26]

This and other observations will also make us wonder about the meaning-maximalist explication of *and*. It seems that the model of feature amalgamation in attributes and nouns is inappropriate as a model for the interpretation of sentence connectives.

3. There are, however, stronger objections to the meaning-maximalist description of utterances with *and*. Let us compare the sentences (11a) through (11g) with the versions under (11'), in which the word *and* has been replaced

with a lengthier formulation and at least one possible interpretation of the respective initial sentence is preserved.

(11)   (a) Annie is in the kitchen   (11′) (a′) . . . and there . . .
and she is making
doughnuts.

    (b) Annie fell into a deep   (b′) . . . and during this
sleep and her facial   time . . .
color returned.

    (c) The window was open   (c′) . . . and coming
and there was a draft.   from it . . .

    (d) Peter married Annie   (d′) . . . and after
and she had a baby.   that . . .

    (e) Paul pounded on the   (e′) . . . and thereby . . .
stone and he shattered it.

    (f) Give me your picture   (f′) If you give me your
and I'll give you mine.   picture, I'll give your
                                    mine.

    (g) The number 5 is a   (g′) . . . and therefore . . .
prime number and it is
divisible only by 1 and
itself.

The reformulations show right away that successivity need not play a role at all in *and*-sentences, even for events bound in time. The strategy of deletion of semantic features in the examples under (11) will not help either since *other* relations besides conjunctivity and connexity are expressed between the facts described by the constituent sentences. And those relations can in no way be acquired on the basis of successivity.

The sentences under (11) leave the meaning-maximalist no other choice but to assume that the word *and* is ambiguous. He will say: There is not only a successive *and* (as in (d)), but also a simultaneous *and* (as in (b)), a local *and* (as in (a)), a directional *and* (as in (c)), and an instrumental *and* (as in (e)), a conditional *and* (as in (f)), and an explanatory *and* (as in (g)). He will be inclined to assume that all these different *and*s share the semantic features of conjunctivity and connexity and differ only with regard to the third semantic feature.

However, even this position seems plausible only as long as no further questions are asked. To begin with, one must observe that the word *and* also occurs in the reformulations under (11′), which are supposed to make the content of the original sentences more explicit. If the word *and* on the left means the same as one of the expressions listed on the right, i.e., *and there, and during this time, and after that*, etc., then what does the word *and* mean *in these expressions*? It is obvious that none of the seven meanings already mentioned can be considered. Now what about obtaining the meaning of this *and* by deleting the third semantic feature of one of the complete *and*s on the left? This proposal could be pursued. But from which of our seven *and*s should we proceed? From the successive or the simultaneous, the instrumental or the conditional *and*? As long as such a question cannot be answered, it would seem to be easier to postulate an eighth meaning. This one, though, would already closely approximate the truth-functional meaning of the connective of propositional logic, *et*.

4. An even stronger objection to the meaning-maximalist position can be found in the observation that the *and* in the sentences under (11) can also be omitted without involving a change of content.[27] Let us replace the *and* with a semicolon, as in the sentences under (12), or with some other punctuation mark:

(12)   (a) Annie is in the kitchen; she is making doughnuts.
          (b) Annie fell into a deep sleep; her facial color returned.
          (c) The window was open; there was a draft.
          (d) Peter married Annie; she had a baby.
          (e) Paul pounded on the stone; he shattered it.
          (f) Give me your picture; I'll give you mine.
          (g) The number 5 is a prime number; it is divisible only by 1 and by itself.

We can communicate practically the same information with (12) as with (11) or (11'). This may make us ask how the content elements explicated by the formulations of (11') are conveyed in (12). Should we say that the semicolon itself has a meaning — or rather seven different meanings? Or should we say that the meaning is somewhere in the air and that it must be read "between the lines?" If one proceeds, like a meaning-maximalist, from seven different meanings and projects them, in (11), all on the word *and*, then, to be consistent, one would have to say the same about the semicolon (and about the articulatory pause between the utterances of the constituent sentences) in (12).

The only possibility left for someone who rejects this solution is to talk about contextual determination of content elements. But he must then be ready to answer the question as to whether such a solution would not be just as appropriate for the *and*-sentences unter (11).[28]

5. The conclusive argument against the meaning-maximalist analysis of the sentence connectives, however, is based on the fact that the list of sentences under (11) could be extended at will and thus give rise to a virtually infinite number of new meanings of *and*. Depending upon what the communication partners take to be the actual relationship between the facts described in the constituent sentences, one could speak about an adversative *and*, a consecutive *and*, a diagnostic *and*, etc., as in the sentences under (13):

(13)   (a) Peter is a reactionary   (13′)   (a′) . . . and
            and he is crazy about   nevertheless
            Mao.   . . .
        (b) The locks were opened   (b′) . . . so that . . .
            and the ship was able to
            move on.
        (c) The control lamp went   (c′) . . . which showed
            on and the oil pump was   that . . .
            broken.

        .   .   .
        .   .   .
        .   .   .

In the case of ambiguous words we can usually count the number of individual meanings on the fingers of one hand. Words with three meanings are not unusual and one could even accept a word with twenty-seven meanings, but a word with an infinite number of meanings would be a contradiction in itself. Besides the practical difficulty that the lexicon cannot allow infinitely long entries, such a word would also raise theoretical difficulties: how could a language user learn to cope with a word of infinitely many meanings? The only solution here would be to assume a generative system of rules for the production of such an infinite number of meanings. Such a rule system cannot, by definition, be part of the lexicon, but would have to be assigned either to a prelexical linguistic component or to a postgrammatical component. However, after all that has been said, it is superfluous to assume that we are dealing with an infinity of word meanings.

8. SENTENCE CONNECTIVES: MINIMIZATION OF MEANINGS

The collapse of the meaning-maximalist position now brings us back to the beginning of the last section. So let us restrict ourselves to the content elements common to all previously mentioned uses of the word *and*: to *conjunctivity*, which requires that two sentences connected by *and* are true if and only if the entire complex sentence is true; and to *connexity*, which requires the facts described by the constituent sentences to be part of the same situation. And let us attempt to reconstruct all the supposed additional content elements on the basis of conversational maxims.

A meaning-minimalist would most probably go one step further; he would ask if conjunctivity and connexity could not be explained away in the same manner as successivity. It is easy to see how this would work in the case of connexity. The examples under (4), whose absurdity had led us to postulate such a semantic feature for *and*, do not lose any of their characteristics when one omits the *and*:

(14)   (a) 2 X 2 = 4, it is impossible to analyze further the concept of *intention*.

        (b) Müller just scored a goal, eels spawn in the Sargasso Sea.

Even when formulated asyndetically, these sentences are odd, as long as the utterer cannot rely on additional information specific to the situation of utterance that would allow the addressee to establish a connection between the facts described. This shows that the construction of a relation between the facts described by coordinate sentences is not at all specific to the use of the word *and*. It must always be possible if the addressee does not want to assume that the utterer has violated a conversational maxim. The maxims concerned here are particularly those of manner (IV, especially IV/1 "Avoid obscurity of expression . . . ," and IV/4 "Be orderly . . . "). Reasoning involving these maxims is available at any time; nothing prevents the addressee from also applying it in the event that the coordinate sentences are connected by *and*. Therefore it really is unnecessary to consider connexity to be a special semantic feature of the word *and*.

However, these considerations should not mislead us into trying to eliminate conjunctivity from the meaning of *and*. Of course, it is true that conjunctivity survives in many cases in which one omits the sentence connective *and*; that is especially so for coordinate sentences (cf. the examples under (12)). But what is interesting here is the cooccurrence of *and* with other sentence connectives in complex sentence structures. Let us consider the following conversations:

(15)   A: Annie has married, she has had a baby.

        B: ⎧ That's not so. ⎫
             ⎨ That's nice.   ⎬
             ⎩ That's too bad. ⎭

A: { What's not so? }
{ What's nice? }
{ What's too bad? }

B: { It's not so }
{ It's nice }   that Annie has married and that
{ It's too bad }   she has had a baby

In B's last utterance it is not possible simply to omit the word *and* or to replace it with a semicolon. The *raison d'être* of this word lies in its combinatory function (not in its connecting function). In using his last utterance to elucidate the meaning of his comment "That's not so," B makes it clear that he thinks one of the constituent sentences of A's initial utterance is false, but that he does not want to specify which. It is the semantic feature of conjunctivity that enables B to do this, as can easily be seen from the following truth-table:

(M4)

p	q	$p \wedge q$	$\neg (p \wedge q)$
T	T	T	F
T	F	F	T
F	T	F	T
F	F	F	T

(The lower case letters "p" and "q" stand for the constituent propositions, "$\neg$" stands for *it's not so that* . . ., and the capital letters "T" and "F" stand for the truth-values 'true' and 'false'. For the operators *It's nice that* . . . and *It's too bad that* . . . we arrive at analogous results.) If one claims that the formula in the right hand box of the truth-table is true, one actually leaves three possibilities for the distribution of truth-values among the constituent propositions p and q (cf. the truth-values of p and q as noted in the corresponding lines of the left hand boxes). This example shows that in certain cases we cannot do without the word *and* if we want to communicate conjunctivity: when *and* is removed, conjunctivity is also lost. This, then, is a case where conjunctivity is detachable from the meaning of the rest of the sentence.

Conjunctivity also violates the other two criteria for the occurrence of a conversational suggestion: it is neither variable nor cancellable.[29] To assert:

(16)   Peter married Annie and Annie had a baby; the complete sentence
         is true, but one of its constituent sentences is false.

is to contradict oneself.

Now that we have demonstrated that conjunctivity is a semantic feature of
the literal meaning of *and*, we must show how it is possible to construe as
conversational suggestions at least the seven other content elements discussed
earlier.

re (11a): If someone explicitly states that Annie is in the kitchen and then
adds *without specifying another place* that she is making doughnuts, then he
is guilty of *suppressing relevant information* if he thereby wants to convey
that the doughnuts are being made outside of the kitchen. This would be a
violation of maxim I/1. In order to avoid assuming such a violation, the
addressee interprets the formulation of (11a) as a *suggestion of identity of
place* (. . . *and there* . . .).

re (11b): If someone explicitly states that Annie fell into a deep sleep but
then adds *without specifying another time* that her facial color returned, then
he is guilty of *suppressing relevant information* if he thereby wants to convey
that the two events took place at a completely different time. This would
again be a violation of maxim I/1. In order to avoid assuming such a violation,
the addressee interprets the formulation of (11b) as a *suggestion of simul-
taneity* (. . . *and during this time* . . .).

re (11c): If someone explicitly states that a window is open and then adds
without specifying another source that there is a draft, then he is guilty of
communicating irrelevant information if he does not want to convey that the
draft is coming from that window. This would be a violation of maxim III.
In order to avoid assuming such a violation, the addressee interprets the
formulation of (11c) as a *suggestion of the source* of the draft (. . . *and
coming from it* . . .).

re (11d): If someone begins by reporting that a woman got married and
then immediately adds *without specifying another time* that she had a baby,
then he is guilty of *distortive reporting* if he thereby wants to convey that the
wedding took place after the baby was born. This would be a violation of
maxim IV/4. In order to avoid assuming such a violation, the addressee
interprets the formulation of (11d) as a *suggestion of a temporal parallelism*
between the reporting utterances and the reported events (. . . *and after that*
. . .).

re (11e): If someone explicitly reports someone's action upon a certain
object and then, *without specifying another action*, reports a result of that

person's acting upon that object, then he is guilty of *communicating irrelevant information*, if he does not want to convey that this result was brought about by the action mentioned. This would be a violation of maxim III. In order to avoid assuming such a violation, the addressee interprets the formulation of (11e) as a *suggestion of an instrumental relation* between the action and its result (. . . *and thereby* . . .).

re (11f): If someone asks a favor and, in the same sentence, predicts an action of his own that can be considered as compensation for that favor, then he is guilty of *communicating irrelevant information* or of *obscure procedures of negotiation* if he does not want to make a conditional promise dependent on the accomplishment of the favor. This would be a violation of maxims III or IV, respectively. In order to avoid assuming such a violation, the addressee interprets the formulation of (11f) as a *suggestion of a conditional relation* between the two actions mentioned (*if* . . . , *then* . . .).

re (11g): If someone uses one and the same sentence to make two statements about a number each of which implies the other, he is guilty of *prolixity* if he does not use one statement to justify or explain the other. This would be a violation of maxim IV/3. In order to avoid assuming such a violation, the addressee interprets the formulation of (11g) as a *suggestion of an explanatory relation* between the two statements (. . . *and therefore* . . .).

These paradigms of the sources of conversational suggestions would not be complete without the following comments:

1. Conversational suggestions are dependent on the context of utterance. Any addition of a verbal utterance or of a detail of situation can direct the reasoning of the addressee in another direction. The seven paradigms should be read *with this reservation*.

2. Each reasoning process takes reference to the formulation of the sentence in question. Instead of doing this in an *ad hoc* way one could systematically compare the suggestion-producing qualities of sentences. On this basis, it should be possible to arrive at generalizations about the production of conversational suggestions and to approach explanatory adequacy. This can be an important methodological starting-point for progress in *descriptive stylistics*.

3. Conversational suggestions arise for the most part from specific qualities of the literal meanings conveyed. If a sentence manifests several such qualities at the same time, then several suggestions can arise. Thus
 – (11a) is interpretable not only as local, but also as simultaneous;
 – (11b) is interpretable not only as simultaneous, but also as explanatory and local;

— (11c) is interpretable not only as directional, but also as simultaneous and explanatory;

— (11d) is interpretable not only as successive, but also as explanatory;

— (11e) is interpretable not only as instrumental, but also as simultaneous, explanatory, and local;

— (11f) is interpretable not only as conditional, but also as successive.

The fact that we obtain *multiple suggestions* is a further confirmation of the meaning-minimalist approach, since it explains the vague and expressive character of the suggestive use of language. Which of the possible suggestions dominates in each case depends amongst other things on how the corresponding semantic dimensions are realized in the sentence in question. Thus, time plays a less significant role in (11a) than in (11b) through (11e), since (11a) is formulated in the present and not in the past tense. Place plays a more important role in (11a) than in (11b) or (11d), since (11a), in contrast to the other sentences, contains an explicit specification of place (*in the kitchen*). Abstract conceptual relationships play an exclusive role in (11g), since the facts described in both its constituent sentences are valid at any time and place.

4. From the structure and results of the reasoning processes sketched above we can conclude that the given suggestions are not to be added to the conjunctivity of *and* as semantic features of the same sort; rather, they are made possible only through the combinatory function of this word. Nor do those suggestions have the same status as connexity, since they embody rather special kinds of connection between the facts described, a connection whose existence is suggested by the contiguity of the utterances of the constituent sentences. Therefore, I propose to call them *connexity-suggestions*. With his "thesis of the dual control of linguistic structure" Charles W. Morris drew attention to this phenomenon as early as 1938, when he wrote: "From the interconnectedness of events on the one hand, and the interconnectedness of [communicative] actions on the other, signs become interconnected [...]."[30]

The paradigms of suggestion-producing reasoning have shown the usefulness of Grice's maxims and have made it plausible that the other possible suggestions a speaker of English may intend in uttering *and*-sentences are also reconstructed pragmatically by the addressee. The truth-function defined in propositional logic has revealed itself to be the only semantic feature of the sentence connective *and* in English. And the hypothesis that other sentence connectives of natural languages also have a purely truth-functional meaning has gained in plausibility. A fresh start should be made in considering in detail whether it is possible to identify at least the literal meanings of the sentence connectives *and, or, if,* and *not* with the meanings of the connectives of propositional logic *et, vel, si,* and *non*, even if their use occasionally appears to be radically different.

At this point the meaning-minimalist position seems to have won the argument. However, this judgement may still be somewhat premature since here again things are not quite so easy. Therefore, I do not want to end this discussion without at least touching upon those difficulties.

9. THE DUALITY OF SEMANTIC AND PRAGMATIC INTERPRETATION

Problems arise in the use of *and* in complex sentence structures. Let us consider the utterance of a conditional sentence that contains the word *and* in the first clause and suggests successivity:

(18)   If Annie has married and has had a baby, grandfather will be happy.

Let us assume that (18) is true. The truth-functional analysis of the word *if* indicates that, if the antecedent clause is true, the consequent clause must also be true. The truth-functional analysis of the word *and* indicates that the entire sentence is true if and only if both constituent sentences are true. Under these conditions the grandfather would have to be happy if it is true that Annie has married and if it is true that she has had a baby. But sentence (18) is not normally so interpreted. Even if (18) is true, it can also happen that the grandfather will not be happy at all, if he hears that the child came before the wedding. So the truth of the consequent clause is dependent here upon the realization not only of the literal meaning of the antecedent clause, but also of its successivity-suggestion.[31]

Thus conversational suggestions arising from constituent sentences can be crucial in the evaluation of the truth of the entire sentence. In these cases one can no longer speak of a purely truth-functional use of the sentence connectives. The choice of explanations available creates a dilemma:

— whoever wants to save the truth-functionality of *and* by asserting that the subordinate clause of (18) is true because each of its constituent clauses is true, sacrifices the truth-functionality of *if*, since he must admit that the consequent clause can still be false.

— whoever wants to save the truth-functionality of *if* by asserting that the consequent clause in (18) is only false if the antecedent clause is false, sacrifices the truth-functionality of *and*, since he must admit that the antecedent clause can be false even if each of its constituent sentences is true.

In view of this dilemma we are on the verge of losing our motivation for a truth-functional treatment of the sentence connectives: it would only be of theoretical importance if it could be extended to all relevant sentence connectives.

A homogeneous treatment of the sentence connectives concerned seems possible only if we weaken the thesis that in natural language the truth-value of the entire sentence is a function of the truth-value of the constituent sentences. This thesis cannot be held in the sense that in complex sentence structures the truth-value of the entire sentence is directly deducible from the truth-values of the smallest constituent sentences. Rather, after each step in the truth-functional deduction, it must be considered whether the resulting conversational suggestions alter the derived truth-value. Each deduction in the value distribution of the complex sentence on the basis of the value distributions of two constituent sentences must be open to reinterpretation according to the context in which the sentence has been uttered.[32]

This is certainly not a very elegant solution. It complicates the process of interpretation to such an extent that we might have doubts about the presuppositions of this analysis, in particular, the division of the content elements into word meaning and word use.

However, another solution is hard to find, considering the arguments against the meaning-maximalists given above. Moreover, there is a series of additional arguments that make this solution more plausible than any imaginable alternative:

1. Let us compare the following versions of sentence (18) with one another:

(18)   (a) If Annie has married and has had a baby, grandfather will be happy.
        (b) If Annie has married and she has had a baby, grandfather will be happy.
        (c) If Annie has married and if she has had a baby, grandfather will be happy.
        (d) If Annie has married and if Annie has had a baby, grandfather will be happy.

Only the subordinate clause differs each time. The number of syntactic transformations performed on the subordinate clause is greatest in (a) and is reduced progressively until (d).[33] What is significant is that in (18) the strength of the successivity-suggestion also varies. It is strongest in (a) and diminishes progressively down to (d). Obviously, the intensity of the communication of a connexity-suggestion depends on the *degree of syntactic connectedness* of the constituent sentences concerned. What we have here is a typical iconic relationship between content and syntactic form. The effect of this relationship is also noticeable, although to a lesser degree, where *and* is the only sentence connective involved:[34]

(17)   (a) Annie has married and has had a child.
        (b) Annie has married and she has had a child.
        (c) Annie has married and Annie has had a child.
        (d) Annie has married. And Annie has had a child.

2. The difference between the sentences under (17) and the sentences under (18) can be generalized in the following way: the strength of a connexity-suggestion depends on the *degree of embedding* of the clause concerned in the entire sentence. Compare (19) with (18), (20) with (19), as well as (20), (19), and (18) with (17):

(19)   If grandfather finds out that Annie has married
$$\left.\begin{array}{l} \text{and} \\ \text{and she} \\ \text{and that she} \\ \text{and that Annie} \end{array}\right\} \text{has had a baby,}$$
        he will be happy.

(20)   If grandmother finds out that Fritz has told grandfather that Annie has married
$$\left.\begin{array}{l} \text{and} \\ \text{and she} \\ \text{and that she} \\ \text{and that Annie} \end{array}\right\} \text{has had a baby,}$$
        she will be happy.

This generalization also proves valid when we reverse the sequence of sentences connected by *and* and formulate:

(17′)   Annie has had a baby
$$\left.\begin{array}{l} \text{and} \\ \text{and she} \\ \text{and Annie} \\ \text{.And Annie} \end{array}\right\} \text{has married.}$$

(18′) If Annie has had a baby

$$\left.\begin{matrix} \text{and} \\ \text{and she} \\ \text{and if she} \\ \text{and if Annie} \end{matrix}\right\} \text{has married, grandfather will be happy.}$$

(19′) If grandfather finds out that Annie has had a baby

$$\left.\begin{matrix} \text{and} \\ \text{and she} \\ \text{and that she} \\ \text{and that Annie} \end{matrix}\right\} \text{has married, he will be happy.}$$

(20′) If grandmother finds out that Fritz has told grandfather that Annie has had a baby

$$\left.\begin{matrix} \text{and} \\ \text{and she} \\ \text{and that she} \\ \text{and that Annie} \end{matrix}\right\} \text{has married, she will be happy.}$$

In all these sentences the strength of the successivity-suggestion diminishes according to the degree of embedding, and the content of the sentence connectives *if* and *and* comes progressively closer to their truth-functional meaning. In the most expanded version of the sentences under (20), it surely is irrelevant to the grandmother's joy whether the events occurred in one sequence or another.[35]

3. The force of embedded connexity-suggestions correlates with still other factors. Let me only mention as a last case the *meaning of the higher verb*:

(21) If Fritz

$$\left\{\begin{matrix} \text{reports to} \\ \text{relates to} \\ \text{communicates to} \\ \text{tells} \\ \text{informs} \end{matrix}\right\} \text{grandfather}$$

that Annie has had a baby and has married, grandfather will be happy.

In a "report", the sequence of the events conveyed is essential. Here, the person reporting tends to make his utterances follow the events. If he should happen to deviate from the natural sequence he would make sure that his addressees realize that. Thus, if Fritz reports something to the grandfather and the grandfather is happy about it, the sequence of the events must undoubtedly be considered among the reasons for his being happy. In a simple transmission of information, however, the sequence of the utterances can depend on any kind of accident and does not allow any conclusion about the sequence of events. Here, then, the sequence of events will not be among the reasons for the grandfather's joy. In this way, the strength of a connexity-suggestion can be controlled by the choice of the higher verb.

These last three observations make it clear that connexity-suggestions are characterized not only by considerable variability, but also by change of intensity — a property never found in literal meanings. No grammar describes cases in which the syntactic qualities of the surrounding sentence exert an influence on the semantic value of a word such that one of its semantic features is either foregrounded or suggested with varying strength or even eliminated entirely.

All this indicates then that connexity-suggestions are not lexical phenomena but have to be accounted for by pragmatics. And since that is so, there seems no way to avoid the dual procedure previously discussed for the interpretation of complex sentences. It is not without irony that pragmatic rules should play an essential role in the interpretation of expressions the analysis of which has for decades been considered the core of semantics.[36]

After this general conclusion it may be appropriate to summarize the individual results to which we were led by our discussion of the sentence connectives:

1. The delimitation of *semantics* and *pragmatics* in language description must follow the difference between *meaning* and *use* of words in verbal communication.

2. The meaning and the use of a word are not just two sides of the same thing, but have to be distinguished systematically. Speakers of a natural language master not only fixed word-meanings, but also fixed rules for the use of words. Both are *empirically testable*, even if there is *no direct experimental access to them*.

3. The criteria of *variability, cancellability* and *non-detachability* can help to answer the question of which content elements of a given utterance come into play through the literal meaning and which through the use of words in verbal communication.

4. On the basis of these criteria, the meaning of sentence connectives such as *and, or, if,* and *not* in natural language may be equated with the defining properties of the connectives of propositional logic *et, vel, si,* and *non*. Corresponding to the special purpose and circumstances of communication further content elements can be acquired by a sentence connective on the basis of the formulations, the meanings and the facts described in the connected

sentences. These content elements occur as *conversational suggestions*, more specifically, as *connexity-suggestions*.

5. The differentiation of semantics and pragmatics in language description, and the differentiation of meaning and use in verbal communication are *theoretical* distinctions; it would be false to assume that in the actual process of comprehension one begins by applying all and only the semantic rules and then continues with the pragmatic rules. Examples with a sentence connective occurring in the scope of another sentence connective show that the meaning of a complex sentence depends not only upon the meanings of its parts, but also upon their conversational suggestions, and thus, upon their use.

6. To summarize this summary:

a. The use of a verbal expression is partially determined by the meaning of this expression.

b. The meaning of a complex verbal expression is determined not only by the meanings of its constituents, but also by their specific use.

In short, in verbal communication we not only make use of meanings but this use even makes sense.

Technical University Berlin (West)

NOTES

* For helpful comments on earlier versions of this paper I am grateful to Jerry Edmondson, Donald Freeman, Frans Plank, and David Schwarz. I also want to express my gratitude for stimulating discussions of the material involved to students of linguistics, semiotics, and philosophy of the universities of Hamburg, Montreal, Chicago, Los Angeles, Berkeley, and Stanford. The usual disclaimers apply, of course.
[1] The two *façoncs de parler* can be found in any historic-systematic presentation of linguistics, cf. Lyons (1968) and Ebneter (1973). A book exclusively applying the terminology of meaning is Schmidt (1967); presentations applying the terminology of use are Leisi (1953) and Brown (1974).
[2] Cf. Grice (1968) and Grice (1975).
[3] Cf. Wundt (1900, p. 596).
[4] Cf. Titchener (1912, pp. 367 ff.). See also Hörmann (1970, pp. 166 ff.).
[5] Cf. Erdmann (1900; 4th edition 1925, p. 5).
[6] Cf. Watson (1919; 2nd edition 1924, p. 354).
[7] Cf. Skinner (1937). See also Hörmann (1970, p. 165).
[8] Cf. Morris (1938, pp. 43–48).
[9] Cf. Kutschera (1971, 2nd edition 1975, pp. 87 f.).
[10] Cf. Alston (1963, p. 84).
[11] Cf. Wittgenstein (1953, I, 43).
[12] Cf. Leisi (1953; 4th edition 1971, pp. 73f.).

[13] Cf. Kempson (1975) and Wilson (1976).

[14] Cf. Grice (1968).

[15] For this example cf. Gordon and Lakoff (1971).

[16] Cf. Dascal (1976, p. 23).

[17] Cf. Grice (1968), 2nd lecture.

[18] Cf. Wittgenstein (1953, I, 293).

[19] Cf. Grice (1968), 2nd lecture.

[20] Cf. Grice (1968), 2nd lecture.

[21] For the methodological value of the three criteria cf. Walker (1975, pp. 169 ff.).

[22] Cohen (1971), who makes a similar distinction, talks about "semanticists" on the one hand and "conversationalists" on the other. However, he does not distinguish between the literal meaning (of a word or a sentence) and the lexical meaning (of a word).

[23] Cf. Cohen (1971, p. 56).

[24] Cf. Cohen (1971, p. 57).

[25] Cf. Wilson (1976, pp. 118 ff.). See also Abraham (1975).

[26] Cf. Lang (1977, pp. 230 ff.).

[27] However, sentences (12d) and (12g) are ambiguous for many speakers of English. The fact described in the second sentence in (12d) need not be taken to occur later than that described in the first sentence, it can also be taken to have been a reason for the first to occur. The fact described in the second sentence in (12g) need not be taken to be explained by the fact described in the first sentence, it can also be given as a reason for it.

[28] Naess (1961) has conducted a series of tests which show that even the decision whether the sentence connective *or* must be interpreted as an exclusive or inclusive disjunction depends on the facts described by the disjuncts involved. See also Seuren (1977, pp. 371 ff.).

[29] Of course, we are dealing here only with the *and* that occurs between sentences or their transformational variants, not with the phrasal *and*, as occurring in *Peter and Annie went to Saarbrücken*. The proposed treatment can easily be applied to all cases where *and* is used to connect the propositional content of two sentences, even if these sentences are uttered with non-declarative illocutionary force. The treatment of the *and* that connects speech acts of different illocutionary force must, however, be postponed to another occasion.

[30] Cf. Morris (1938, pp. 12 f.).

[31] Cf. Cohen (1971, pp. 58 f.). There are a number of other interpretations possible for (18). Even if the order of wedding and birth is as it should be, it is possible that the grandfather is not happy because Annie's husband was not the baby's father. On the other hand, it is conceivable that the truth of all constituent sentences still does not entail the truth of the entire sentence in its intended sense because the grandfather could be happy about something else that he has learned simultaneously. These interpretations are eliminated if we formulate (18) in a more explicit way: *If Annie has married and has had a baby, this is a reason for grandfather to be happy.*

[32] Of course, the criteria of variability, cancellability, and non-detachability also apply to embedded sentences. E.g., a cancellation of an embedded conversational suggestion is achieved by the following context: *If Annie has married and has had a baby, grandfather will be happy. But the sequence of these events will not leave him unaffected.*

[33] The first and second versions are generated by conjunction reduction, and the second and third by pronominalization; in the underlying structures of the first three versions *if* dominates *and*, in the last *if* is dominated by *and*.

[34] Cf. Freeman (1978), as opposed to Boettcher and Sitta (1972), who consider sentences like those under (17) to be different forms of realization of the same (semantic) category and the same (pragmatic) structure. Such a characterization would make it impossible to account for the semantic and pragmatic differences of these sentennces.

[35] Of course, these analyses should not make us blind to the fact that the sequence of the formulations can also express other aspects than the sequence of the events described. Compare *Annie now is a young mother. The fact that she has had a baby and that she has married has made grandfather very happy.* Here the sequence of the embedded clauses is rather used to foreground Annie's new role of a young mother.

[36] Compare the procedures of formal logicians, who admit only a truth-functional relation between the complex sentence and its constituents and exclude all pragmatic aspects.

BIBLIOGRAPHY

Abraham, Werner: 1975, 'Some Semantic Properties of Some Conjunctions,' in S. P. Corder and E. Roulet (eds.), *Some Implications of Linguistic Theory for Applied Linguistics*, Brussels and Paris: Aimav and Didier, 1975, pp. 7–31.

Alston, William P.: 1963, 'The Quest for Meanings,' in *Mind* 72 (1963), pp. 79–87.

Boettcher, Wolfgang and Sitta, Horst: 1972, *Zusammengesetzter Satz und äquivalente Strukturen* (= Deutsche Grammatik III). Frankfurt a. M.: Athenäum, 1972.

Brown, Cecil H.: 1974, *Wittgensteinian Linguistics*, The Hague and Paris: Mouton, 1974.

Chao, Yuen Ren: 1968, *Language and Symbolic Systems*, Cambridge: University Press, 1968.

Cohen, Jonathan L.: 1971, 'Some Remarks on Grice's Views about the Logical Particles of Natural Language,' in Y. Bar Hillel (ed.), *Pragmatics of Natural Languages*, Dordrecht: Reidel, 1971, pp. 50–68.

Creelman, Marjorie B.: 1966, *The Experimental Investigation of Meaning – A Review of Literature*, New York: Springer, 1966.

Dascal, Marcelo: 1976, 'Conversational Relevance,' Working paper, Colloquium on 'Meaning and Use', Jerusalem, 1976.

Douglas, Mary (ed.): 1973, *Rules and Meanings – The Anthropology of Everyday Knowledge*, Harmondsworth/England: Penguin, 1973.

Ebneter, Theodor: 1973, *Strukturalismus und Transformationalismus – Einführung in Schulen und Methoden*, München: List, 1973.

Erdmann, Karl Otto: 1900, *Die Bedeutung des Wortes – Aufsätze aus dem Grenzgebiet der Sprachpsychologie und Logik*, Leipzig: Avenarius, 1900. Reprint of the 4th edition of 1925, Darmstadt: Wissenschaftliche Buchgesellschaft, 1966.

Freeman, Donald: 1973, 'Keats's "To Autumn": Poetry as Pattern and Process,' in *Language and Style* XI (1978).

Gazdar, Gerald: 1978, *Formal Pragmatics for Natural Language*, London and New York: Academic Press, 1978.

Gloy, Klaus: 1975, *Sprachnormen I. – Linguistische und soziologische Analysen*, Stuttgart and Bad Cannstatt: Frommann-Holzboog, 1975.

Gloy, Klaus and Presch, Gunter, (eds.): 1976, *Sprachnormen III. Kommunikations-orientierte Linguistik — Sprachdidaktik*, Stuttgart and Bad Cannstatt: Frommann-Holzboog, 1976.

Gordon, David and Lakoff, George: 1971, 'Conversational Postulates,' in *Papers from the Seventh Regional Meeting of the Chicago Linguistic Society*, Chicago: Chicago Linguistic Society, 1971.

Grice, Herbert P.: 1968, 'The Logic of Conversation,' Working paper. Berkeley: University of California, 1968.

Grice, Herbert P.: 1975, 'Logic and Conversation,' in P. Cole and J. L. Morgan (eds.), *Syntax and Semantics. Vol. 3: Speech Acts*, New York: Academic Press, 1975.

Grimm, Hannelore and Wintermantel, Margret: 1975, *Zur Entwicklung von Bedeutungen — Forschungsberichte zur Sprachentwicklung II*, Weinheim and Basel: Beltz, 1975.

Heringer, Hans Jürgen (ed.): 1974, *Der Regelbegriff in der praktischen Semantik*, Frankfurt a. M.: Suhrkamp, 1974.

Hörmann, Hans: 1967, *Psychologie der Sprache*. Berlin, Heidelberg and New York: Springer 1967. Translated into English by H. H. Stern: *Psycholinguistics — An Introduction to Research and Theory*. Berlin, Heidelberg and New York: Springer, 1970.

Isenberg, Horst: 1971, Überlegungen zur Texttheorie,' in J. Ihwe (ed.), *Literaturwissenschaft und Linguistik*, Vol. 1, Frankfurt a. M.: Athenäum, 1971.

Kasher, Asa: 1974, 'Mood Implicatures: A Logical Way of Doing Generative Pragmatics,' in *Theoretical Linguistics* 1 (1974), pp. 6–38.

Kempson, Ruth M.: 1975, *Presupposition and the Delimitation of Semantics*, Cambridge: University Press, 1975.

Kutschera, Franz von: 1971, *Sprachphilosophie*, München: Fink, 1971, 2nd edition, 1975.

Kutschera, Franz von: 1975, 'Conventions of Language and Intensional Semantics,' in *Theoretical Linguistics* 2 (1975), pp. 255–283.

Lang, Ewald: 1977, *Semantik der koordinativen Verknüpfung* (= studia grammatica XIV), Berlin (GDR): Akademie-Verlag, 1977.

Lehrer, Adrienne and Lehrer, Keith, (eds.): 1970, *Theory of Meaning*, Englewood Cliffs/N. J.: Prentice Hall, 1970.

Leisi, Ernst: 1953, *Der Wortinhalt — Seine Struktur im Deutschen und Englischen*, Heidelberg: Quelle and Meyer, 1953, 4th edition 1971.

Lewis, David: 1969, *Convention — A Philosophical Study*, Cambridge: Harvard University Press, 1969. Translated into German by R. Posner and D. Wenzel: *Konventionen — Eine sprachphilosophische Abhandlung*, Berlin and New York: de Gruyter, 1975.

Lorenzer, Alfred: 1970, *Sprachzerstörung und Rekonstrukton — Vorarbeiten zu einer Metatheorie der Psychoanalyse*, Frankfurt a. M.: Suhrkamp, 1970.

Lyons, John: 1968, *Introduction to Theoretical Linguistics*, Cambridge: University Press, 1968.

Mooij, Jan J. A.: 1976, *A Study of Metaphor — On the Nature of Metaphorical Expressions, with Special Reference to Their Reference*, Amsterdam, New York and Oxford: North-Holland, 1976.

Morris, Charles W.: 1938, *Foundations of the Theory of Signs*, Chicago: University Press, 1938. Translated into German by R. Posner and J. Rehbein: *Grundlagen der Zeichentheorie*, München: Hanser, 1972, 2nd edition, 1975.

Naess, Arne: 1961, 'A Study of "or",' in *Synthese* 13 (1961), 49–60.

Posner, Roland: 1972 a, *Theorie des Kommentierens – Eine Grundlagenstudie zur Semantik und Pragmatik*, Frankfurt a. M.: Athenäum, 1972.

Posner, Roland: 1972 b, 'Commenting – A Diagnostic Procedure for Semantico-Pragmatic Sentence Representations,' in *Poetics* 5 (1972), pp. 67–88.

Posner, Roland: 1972c, 'Zur systematischen Mehrdeutigkeit deutscher Lexeme,' in *Linguistik und Didaktik* 12 (1972), pp. 268–276.

Presch, Gunter and Gloy, Klaus, (eds.): 1976, *Sprachnormen II. Theoretische Begründungen – ausserschulische Sprachnormenpraxis*, Stuttgart and Bad Cannstatt: Frommann-Holzboog, 1976.

Raz, Joseph: 1975, *Practical Reason and Norms*, London: Hutchinson, 1975.

Richards, David A. J.: 1971, *A Theory of Reasons for Action*, Oxford: Clarendon, 1971.

Rollin, Bernard E.: 1976, *Natural and Conventional Meaning – An Examination of the Distinction*, The Hague and Paris: Mouton, 1976.

Sadock, Jerrold M.: 1974, *Toward a Linguistic Theory of Speech Acts*, New York: Seminar Press, 1974.

Schmerling, Susan F.: 1975, 'Asymmetric Conjunction and Rules of Conversation,' in P. Cole and J. L. Morgan (eds.), *Syntax and Semantics. Vol. 3: Speech Acts*, New York: Academic Press, 1975.

Schmidt, Wilhelm: 1967, *Lexikalische und aktuelle Bedeutung – Ein Beitrag zur Theorie der Wortbedeutung*, Berlin (GDR): Akademie-Verlag, 1967.

Searle, John R.: 1969, *Speech Acts – An Essay in the Philosophy of Language*, Cambridge: Univ. Press, 1969.

Seuren, Pieter A. M.: 1977, *Zwischen Sprache und Denken – Ein Beitrag zur empirischen Begründung der Semantik*. Wiesbaden: Athenaion, 1977.

Skinner, Burrhus F.: 1937, 'The Distribution of Associated Words,' in *Psychol. Rec.* 1 (1937), pp. 71–76.

Slobin, Dan I.: 1971, *Psycholinguistics*, Glenview/Ill. and London: Scott, Foresman and Comp., 1971.

Titchener, Edward B.: 1912, *Lehrbuch der Psychologie*, Part 2, Leipzig: Barth, 1912.

Travis, Charles: 1975, *Saying and Understanding – A Generative Theory of Illocutions*, Oxford: Basil Blackwell, 1975.

Ulmann, Gisela: 1975, *Sprache und Wahrnehmung – Verfestigen und Aufbrechen von Anschauungen durch Wörter*, Frankfurt a. M. and New York: Campus Verlag, 1975.

Walker, Ralph C. S.: 1975, 'Conversational Implicatures,' in Simon Blackburn (ed.): *Meaning, Reference and Necessity*, Cambridge: University Press, 1975.

Watson, John: 1919, *Psychology from the Standpoint of a Behaviorist*, Philadelphia and London: Lippincott 1919, 2nd edition, 1924.

Wilson, Deirdre: 1976, *Presuppositions and Non-truth-conditional Semantics*, London, New York and San Francisco: Academic Press, 1976.

Wittgenstein, Ludwig: 1953, *Philosophical Investigations*, ed. by G. E. M. Anscombe and R. Rhees, Oxford: Basil Blackwell, 1953.

FRANÇOIS RÉCANATI

SOME REMARKS ON EXPLICIT PERFORMATIVES, INDIRECT SPEECH ACTS, LOCUTIONARY MEANING AND TRUTH-VALUE

I

Performatives are declarative sentences, and declarative sentences are sentences the typical use of which is to make assertions, or at least to *say that* something is the the case. Furthermore, performatives do not constitute an exception to the principle that to utter seriously a declarative sentence is to say that something is the case: as Warnock (1973) has pointed out, someone who says 'I promise' says that he promises. But if this is so, why not construe performative utterances as straightforward assertions? Many philosophers have argued along this line,[1] and ascribed to performatives the sole peculiarity of being verified by their use. The serious utterance of a performative sentence (i) results in a statement and (ii) makes it true. From that a consequence follows, which has not been so far emphasized by philosophers. The consequence is that, by (or in) the serious utterance of a performative sentence as such — i.e., as performative — two different speech acts are performed. To utter 'I order you to go' performatively is both to say that I order you to go and to order you to do. Making that point, some linguists[2] have underlined the connection between performative utterances and 'indirect speech acts':

As an analogy, consider the sentence *Can you reach the salt?* (. . .) An utterance of this sentence is typically construed as a request for the salt, even though, taken strictly, it expresses a question about the hearer's reaching ability. (. . .) Asking the question is thus an indirect way of requesting the salt; it CONVEYS the request without actually EXPRESSING it. In the same fashion, the utterance of *I assert that John loves Mary* may be only an indirect way of asserting that John loves Mary. It may convey this assertion to the hearer even though, strictly speaking, it does not express it. (What it actually expresses is only the assertion that it is being asserted that John loves Mary.)[3]

Two problems are raised by such a view of performatives as sentences used to perform indirect speech acts.

First, we must explain how the 'indirect' illocutionary force is conveyed. To arrive at such an explanation we may, following Cornulier (1975 and forthcoming), use a principle which he calls Meaning Detachment: to say that *p* and then to say that what has just been said (or the saying of it) means that

205

J. R. Searle, F. Kiefer, and M. Bierwisch (eds.), Speech Act Theory and Pragmatics,
205–220.

q amounts to saying that q. Owing to this principle, to say 'p, I mean that q' amounts to saying that q. The usefulness of Meaning Detachment in explaining how performatives work depends on its being extended so as to cover two special cases. (a) Someone says that p and then says that he meant it as, for instance, an order: this amounts, as Extended Meaning Detachment must predict, to issuing an order. (b) Someone says that what he is saying (or the saying of it) means that q: this must amount to saying that q. Performative utterances have something in common with each of these two special cases: to say 'I order you to go' is to say that this very utterance is meant as an order that you should go. Extended Meaning Detachment helps us to understand why this utterance is actually meant as an order that you should go, and why it is, therefore, somehow equivalent to the less sophisticated order 'Go!'.

Next, the following objection has to be faced. When someone seriously utters a performative sentence, he doesn't seem to perform two different illocutionary acts. It is much more likely that only the indirect illocutionary act is performed: as Austin puts it, in saying 'I order you to go' I order you to go but I don't *assert* that I do so. With this I whole-heartedly agree. But, one might object, I have stated earlier as obvious that in uttering 'I order you to go' I say that I order you to go. There is, I would reply, no inconsistency here. Although it is true that, when someone says 'I promise' performatively, his utterance can be described or reported in two ways: (a) he says he promises, and (b) he promises, nevertheless two different illocutionary acts haven't been performed, because the (a) sentence does not (*in this use*) describe or report any illocutionary act. In saying 'I promise' performatively, one obviously says that he promises, but in so doing he does not perform an illocutionary act of assertion or whatever: what he performs besides the illocutionary act of promising I shall call, following Austin, a *locutionary act* — the locutionary act of 'saying that'.

II

As many philosophers have rightly noted,[4] the Austinian notion of locutionary act or meaning is very unclear. Austin calls 'locutionary meaning', as distinct from illocutionary force, two quite different things:

(1)   the meaning of an utterance as dependent upon
          (a) the linguistic meaning of the sentence uttered (*phatic* meaning)

and (b) the context of utterance and the intentions of the speaker, which disambiguate the sentence uttered if it is ambiguous and fix the reference of its referring parts.

(2) the proposition expressed by the sentence as uttered in that context.

In the first sense, 'Ouch!' and 'Damn!' have a locutionary meaning (for they are meaningful English sentences seriously uttered in a determinate context), but in the second sense they haven't (for they don't express any proposition); in the second sense locutionary meaning is force-neutral ('John will go' and 'Will John go?' express the same proposition[5]), while in the first sense it is not, because the contribution word-order and mood make to the linguistic meaning of the sentence consists in a rough indication of illocutionary force. For clarity's sake let's follow John Searle and talk of 'proposition' instead of 'locutionary meaning' in the second sense. The problem is, how are we now to construe locutionary meaning in the first sense?

Our first move must be to distinguish between illocutionary force as roughly expressed by the sentence uttered in virtue of its linguistic meaning alone, and illocutionary force as expressed by uttering that sentence in such and such a context. To utter seriously the sentence 'It is raining' in any context whatsoever is to *say that* it is raining, while to utter it in such and such a context is, more precisely, to *warn* someone that it is raining, or to *guess* at the weather, or to make an *assertion*. This distinction is relevant to our problem, because Austin calls 'locutionary act' (in the first sense) the act of uttering seriously a sentence with a certain meaning, and this meaning appears from his examples to include not the full illocutionary force of the utterance (as dependent partly upon the context) but the generic illocutionary force associated with such meaningful components of the sentence as word-order and mood. According to Austin, to say 'It is raining' is to perform the locutionary act of saying that it is raining, to say 'Get out' is to perform the locutionary act of telling the addressee to get out, to say 'Is it in Oxford or Cambridge?' is to perform the locutionary act of asking whether it is in Oxford or Cambridge. It seems pretty clear, then, that Austin's locutionary act is identical with the (generic) illocutionary act corresponding to the illocutionary force roughly expressed by the sentence in virtue of its linguistic meaning, as opposed to the (specific) illocutionary act corresponding to the illocutionary force expressed by uttering that sentence in such and such a context. Accordingly, there is no real difference between the 'locutionary' act (saying that) and the illocutionary act (warning, guessing or asserting): they are the same act, described more or less precisely; the description, in one case, is based on the linguistic meaning of the sentence and relies solely on the evidence provided by whatever illocutionary force indicating devices there may be in the sentence, while in the second case it takes into account the context of utterance and is therefore more specific.

Some philosophers[6] have argued that the locutionary/illocutionary distinction so construed is "only a special case of the distinction between literal meaning and intended meaning, between what the sentence means and what the speaker means in its utterance, and (. . .) has no special relevance to the general theory of illocutionary forces, because intended illocutionary force is only one of the aspects (sense and reference are others) in which intended speaker-meaning may go beyond literal sentence-meaning" (Searle 1968 p. 149). What is wrong with such a view is that Austin explicitly took up the opposite position and equated locutionary (or rhetic) meaning with utterance-meaning, as opposed to literal sentence-meaning, or phatic meaning. As Forguson puts it, "where the pheme [= the sentence] has meaning in the determinable sense, the rheme has meaning in the determinate sense. To specify what the utterance means in the determinate sense involves (. . .) a specification of the speaker's intentions with respect to sense and reference, which intentions function within the limits set by the conventions of the language. The rhetic act, therefore, *disambiguates* the meaning of the pheme" (Forguson 1973 p. 164). But if the rhetic, locutionary meaning of the utterance is more than the phatic, linguistic meaning of the sentence, nevertheless it does not include the full illocutionary force as determined partly by the linguistic meaning of the sentence and partly by the context of its utterance, but only the rough illocutionary force expressed by the sentence in virtue of its linguistic meaning alone. There are three levels in Austin's analysis, and not only two. These are: (1) the linguistic meaning of the sentence (phatic level); (2) the rhetic meaning of the utterance, i.e., the linguistic meaning contextually specified with respect to sense and reference, but not with respect to force (locutionary level); (3) the complete meaning of the utterance, including full illocutionary force (illocutionary level). The problem now becomes, why has Austin felt the need to distinguish the second and third levels? Why should we not accept the less complicated two-levelled analysis which Cohen and Searle have set forth?

III

My reason for favouring Austin's three-levelled analysis is that it allows us to take into account the ambiguity of the sentence meaning/utterance meaning distinction. Searle says that intended speaker-meaning, or utterance-meaning, may go beyond literal sentence-meaning. For example, the sentence 'I will go' means *I will go*, and the speaker uttering that sentence means more, viz. that he, John, will go to London in October. Now there is another distinction, which Searle also labels the sentence-meaning/utterance-meaning distinction:

> In hints, insinuations, irony, and metaphor — to mention a few examples — the speaker's utterance meaning and the sentence meaning come apart in various ways. One important class of such cases is that in which the speaker utters a sentence, means what he says, but also means something more. For example, a speaker may utter the sentence *I want you to do it* by way of requesting the hearer to do something. The utterance is incidentally meant as a statement, but it is also meant primarily as a request, a request made by way of making a statement. In such cases a sentence that contains the illocutionary force indicators for one kind of illocutionary act can be uttered to perform, IN ADDITION, another type of illocutionary act. There are also cases in which the speaker may utter a sentence and mean what he says and also mean another illocution with a different propositional content. For example, a speaker may utter the sentence *Can you reach the salt?* and mean it not merely as a question but as a request to pass the salt.[7]

Clearly, 'sentence-meaning' is not here the same thing as before. It is not linguistic meaning *simpliciter*, but linguistic meaning contextually specified with respect to sense and reference, that is, what Searle in his 1968 paper called 'utterance meaning'. Sentence-meaning is now what the speaker says when uttering a sentence in such and such a context: for example, what I say when I utter 'I want you to do it' is that I, John, want you, George, to surrender. In addition to this 'sentence meaning', there is what Searle now calls 'utterance meaning' in a new sense, viz. what is conversationally implicated by the utterance, what is meant without being said. So we have two different sentence meaning/utterance meaning distinctions, sentence-meaning in the second distinction (= sentence-meaning$_2$) being identical with utterance-meaning in the first distinction (= utterance-meaning$_1$). We are consequently left with three levels of analysis:

A	B	C	
Sentence-meaning$_1$	utterance-meaning$_1$ = sentence-meaning$_2$	utterance-meaning$_2$	Searle 1968 Searle 1975

I wish to argue that these three levels are the three levels of Austin's analysis: level A is the phatic level, level B is the rhetic, locutionary level and level C is the illocutionary level.

A prima facie objection would run as follows. It may well be that we need to distinguish the B-level of what is said and the C-level of what is meant without being said, and it may well be that some illocutionary acts are performed at the C-level, being performed non literally by means of a sentence which contains no illocutionary force indicator for that act. It remains true, nevertheless, that what is performed at the B-level is an illocutionary act, not another kind of act, locutionary so-called. If, at the C-level, a request is made by uttering 'Can you pass the salt?', there is also an illocutionary act performed at the B-level in uttering this sentence, viz. the illocutionary act of asking whether you can pass the salt; therefore, to distinguish between the B and C levels is to distinguish between two kinds of illocutionary acts; it is *not* to distinguish between 'locutionary' and illocutionary acts. So here again the locutionary/illocutionary distinction seems to collapse.

But is it true that when someone says 'Can you pass the salt?', he puts a question to his addressee? I am not sure it is. It seems to me that he asks for something, namely the salt, but he doesn't ask for an answer, and I cannot imagine anyone putting a question without asking for an answer.[8] There is clearly a distinction here to be drawn, between the illocutionary act linguistically indicated and the illocutionary act actually performed, and this is, I maintain, Austin's locutionary/illocutionary distinction. Let's take for granted what an illocutionary act is. The *locutionary act performed* in uttering a sentence is the *illocutionary act indicated* by this sentence, whether it is actually performed or not; and it is to be distinguished from the *illocutionary act performed* in uttering this sentence, whether it is linguistically indicated or not.[9] In uttering the interrogative sentence 'Can you pass the salt?', the speaker performs the locutionary act of 'asking whether' the hearer can pass the salt, and he performs the illocutionary act of requesting him to do so. It is therefore true, as Cohen and Searle have emphasized and as is obvious from Austin's examples of locutionary acts (to ask whether, to say that, to tell to), that locutionary and illocutionary acts are of the same nature; but it is not true that the locutionary/illocutionary distinction, on that ground, is useless and empty, because we need to distinguish between the illocutionary act as actually performed, and the illocutionary act as linguistically indicated.

IV

We need such a distinction not only because sometimes the illocutionary act performed happens not to be the illocutionary act linguistically indicated, but also because, very often, the illocutionary act performed *could not even have been* linguistically indicated. By this I don't mean that only rough illocution-ary types of genera (to say that, to tell to, to ask whether) can be indicated, while specific illocutionary acts (to assert, to order) cannot. My point is that most specific illocutionary acts are not even species of these rough illocutionary genera. Advising is not a species of 'saying that' any more than it is of 'telling to', and one can advise as well in saying that *p* (= in uttering a declarative sentence) as in telling someone to act in such and such a way (= in uttering an imperative sentence). Moreover, although one promises generally in saying that *p*, we have no reason to construe promising as a species of 'saying that'. It is simply not true that for every illocutionary act x, x either can be linguistically indicated or is a species of an illocutionary act which can be so indicated.

An objector might reply that the illocutionary act of promising *can* be linguistically indicated, by using the adverbial phrase 'without fail'; and this example allegedly shows that mood, word-order and intonation contour are not the only illocutionary force indicating devices. But this is, in my opinion, to conflate two different kinds of illocutionary force indicators, which I shall call primary and secondary indicators. The meaning of a primary indicator consists entirely in its indicating, when uttered as part of a sentence, which illocutionary act is performed in this utterance. Its indicating function is its meaning, whereas the meaning of a secondary indicator cannot be reduced to its indicating function. It has a certain meaning which is a function of the meaning of its component parts, and which explains how it can act as an illocutionary indicator, even if it has become conventionalized as such. Now when I say that a sentence S linguistically indicates an illocutionary act A, I mean that S includes a *primary* indicator associated with A; and 'without fail' is, according to my criteria, only a *secondary* indicator.

Clearly, the meaning of 'without fail' (like the meaning of 'probably') cannot be reduced to its indicating function, but explains it. It contributes to the literal meaning of the sentence in which it occurs, and this literal meaning does not include any commissive illocutionary force. The promise performed in saying 'I shall without fail' is on a par with the request performed in saying 'Can you pass the salt?': in both cases, the illocutionary act performed is not literally or linguistically indicated by means of what I call a primary indicator; rather, the actual illocutionary force of these utterances is conveyed by impli-cation. In saying 'I shall without fail', I imply that, if I don't act in such and such a way, I shall fail in my duty.[10] Which duty? The duty imposed on me by the very utterance of 'I shall without fail'. This duty is brought into being by my alluding to it, as is your ownership when I give you something by saying to you 'It's yours'. In saying 'It's yours' when actually (we both know or believe that) it's mine, I conversationally implicate that I give it to you. Likewise, in saying 'I shall without fail' when I am under no obligation to act in the way I say I am bound to act, I implicate that my utterance puts me under this obligation. The commissive illocutionary force of 'I shall without fail', therefore, is implied, as is the directive illocutionary force of 'Can you pass the salt?'.

Of course, 'without fail' has become conventionalized as an illocutionary indicator of promise; but in 'Can you pass the salt?' also the directive illocutionary force is conventionally indicated: that is why there is so big a difference between this sentence and the (quasi-)synonymous 'Are you able to pass the salt?', which may be used to request the salt, but is not conventionally or idiomatically so used.[11] The fact remains that the directive illocutionary force of 'Can you pass the salt?', though conventionally indicated, is not indicated in the same way as it is when the sentence 'Pass the salt' is used, because in 'Can you pass the salt?' the indicator, whatever it is, has a meaning which is distinct from its indicating function and which contributes to the literal, non directive meaning of the interrogative sentence, while the imperative mood has no meaning besides its pragmatic function. As Searle (1975) once said, and as Morgan (1978) has ably maintained, there are conventions of use which are not meaning conventions. Meaning conventions attach to some linguistic forms, like the imperative mood, a meaning which consists, partly or wholly, in their pragmatic, indicating function, whereas conventions of use attach to some linguistic forms which already have a meaning an indicating function which makes them secondary pragmatic indicators.[12] The illocutionary force associated with a primary indicator belongs to the literal meaning of the sentence where this indicator occurs, but the illocutionary force associated with a secondary indicator does *not* belong to the literal meaning of the sentence.

The difference between 'Can you pass the salt?' and 'I shall without fail', then, is simply this: the illocutionary act of issuing a directive is performed *indirectly* by means of the sentence 'Can you pass the salt?', because it could have been performed more directly by means of the alternative sentence 'Pass the salt', where there is a primary indicator of directive illocutionary force; but there is no primary indicator of promise, and that's why this illocutionary act is not performed *indirectly* by means of 'I shall without fail'; indeed, it could not have been performed more directly.[13]

V

To determine which illocutionary force is linguistically indicated, that is, expressed at the *locutionary* level, only the primary indicators count: so when I utter the declarative sentence 'I shall without fail', I perform the locutionary act of *saying that* I shall without fail; and in saying so I (often) perform the illocutionary act of *promising* that I shall: the secondary indicator comes into play at this second, illocutionary level, and contributes to the actual force of the utterance, not to its illocutionary act potential linguistically expressed at the locutionary level. Using '⊢' as an assertion-sign and 'PR' as a promise-sign, and leaving aside all the problems connected with time and tense, we could symbolise our analysis of 'I shall without fail' as follows:

(1) $\dfrac{\text{PR (my doing it)}}{\vdash \text{(my doing it without fail)}}$ illocutionary level
locutionary level

By the same token, 'Can you pass the salt?' is thus analyzed:

(2) $\dfrac{!\ \text{(your passing the salt)}}{?\ \text{(your being able to pass the salt)}}$ illocutionary level
locutionary level

This analysis clearly shows that the act of requesting is performed indirectly, whereas in 'Pass the salt' it is performed directly or (Gardiner[14] would say) congruently:

(3) $\dfrac{!\ \text{(your passing the salt)}}{!\ \text{(your passing the salt)}}$ illocutionary level
locutionary level

Now there is the same kind of difference between 'I ask you to pass the salt' and 'Pass the salt' as between the latter and 'Can you pass the salt?'. To utter the explicit performative 'I ask you to pass the salt' is to perform the locutionary act of *saying that* I ask you to pass the salt, and the illocutionary act of *asking you to* pass the salt. In Searle's notation for illocutionary acts, 'explicit' and 'primary' performatives cannot be distinguished, so that 'Pass the salt' and 'I ask you to pass the salt' are both analyzed as

!   (your passing the salt)

A notation which takes into account the difference between linguistically indicated and actually performed illocutionary acts is better, because it enables us to contrast 'Pass the salt' with 'I ask you to pass the salt', i.e. (3) with (4):

(4) $\dfrac{!\ \text{(your passing the salt)}}{\vdash \text{(my asking you to pass the salt)}}$ illocutionary level

locutionary level

(In setting forth this way of construing explicit performatives I take for granted that, an explicit performative being a declarative sentence, the only primary indicators that occur in it are of an assertive kind. The performative prefix as a whole is, at best, a secondary indicator.)

To conclude, I shall now argue that my analysis of explicit performatives, based upon the locutionary/illocutionary distinction as I understand it, helps us to solve, or rather dissolve, the famous problem of their truth-valuation.

VI

To solve this problem, we have first to raise the question, where are the bearers of truth and falsity to be found? Some ascribe truth and falsity to the propositional content of any illocutionary act belonging to the assertive genus (i.e. to the content of such acts as asserting, warning, admitting, etc.) while others would say that the propositional content of any illocutionary act whatever bears a truth-value. According to the former view, (the proposition expressed by) 'John is eighteen years old' is true if John is eighteen years old and false otherwise, but (the proposition expressed by) 'Shut the door!' is neither; according to the latter view, (the proposition expressed by) 'Shut the door!' is true if the hearer subsequently shuts the door, and false otherwise. This is of course a very unnatural use of 'true' and 'false', and one might prefer to say that 'Shut the door!' is *obeyed* when the hearer subsequently shuts the door; but everyone is free to use these words the way he likes, provided he is explicit enough. — There is also a third view, according to which truth and falsity are to be ascribed to the proposition expressed by a declarative sentence as uttered in a determinate context, even if that proposition is not expressed with any illocutionary force whatsoever. For example, in 'If George read the paper yesterday, he must have seen John's article', the embedded sentence 'George read the paper yesterday', though devoid of what Hare (1970) calls a 'neustic', is true (or expresses a true proposition) if George read the paper yesterday, and is false (or expresses a false proposition) otherwise.

If we choose the first solution, we shall say that the explicit performative 'I state that the earth is flat' has a truth-value, namely the value false, because to utter this sentence is to express the proposition that the earth is flat with the illocutionary force of an assertion; but 'I order you to shut the door' has no truth-value, because the proposition that you'll shut the door is thereby expressed with a directive, non assertive illocutionary force. Shifting now to the third solution we should say, instead, that both 'I state that the earth is flat' and 'I order you to shut the door' have a truth-value, because these declarative sentences respectively express the proposition that I state that the earth is flat and the proposition that I order you to shut the door, which propositions are true because, in uttering these sentences, I actually state that the earth is flat and order you to shut the door. So we see that, according to the first view, 'I state that the earth is flat' is false, while according to the third view it is true; by the same token, 'I order you to shut the door' is, according to the second view, false if you don't subsequently shut the door, while according to the third view it would remain true under such circumstances.

These views do not, I think, conflict as is often supposed; they are quite compatible, granted that philosophers are free to elect one or the other entity to be the bearer of truth-value. Most philosophers believe that there *is* an inconsistency between these different approaches to the truth-valuation of explicit performatives only because they suppose that e.g. 'I state that the earth is flat' expresses *either* the proposition that the earth is flat *or* the proposition that I state it to be so. But this is not true: the performative utterance 'I state that the earth is flat' expresses *both* the proposition that I state that the earth is flat *and* the proposition that the earth is flat, as is obvious from my way of analyzing this utterance;

(5) $\dfrac{\vdash \text{ (the earth being flat)}}{\vdash \text{ (my stating that the earth is flat)}}$ illocutionary level \
                                             locutionary level

As a matter of fact, the locutionary act performed in uttering a sentence being the illocutionary act indicated by this sentence, we have to distinguish not only between the potential illocutionary force expressed at the locutionary level and the actual illocutionary force of the utterance, but also between the propositional content of the locutionary act (the proposition expressed at the locutionary level) and the propositional content of the illocutionary act proper. For instance, the propositional content of the locutionary act performed in saying 'Can you pass the salt?' is ⟨your being able to pass the salt⟩, whereas the propositional content of the illocutionary act as actually performed is ⟨your passing me the salt⟩. Likewise, the 'locutionary' proposition expressed by 'I think he has children' is ⟨my thinking that he has children⟩, and the 'illocutionary' proposition is ⟨his having children⟩. The same applies to explicit performatives: the proposition locutionarily expressed by 'I state that the earth is round' is ⟨my stating that the earth is round⟩, and the proposition illocutionarily expressed is ⟨the earth being round⟩.

We are now in a position to state that there are four main possibilities of construing the truth-valuation of utterances. We can choose to ascribe truth-value either (A) to the propositional content of a declarative locutionary act (i.e., to the proposition expressed by a declarative sentence, to what is said when such a sentence is uttered), or (B) to the propositional content of any locutionary act, or (C) to the propositional content of any illocutionary act belonging to the assertive genus, or (D) to the propositional content of any illocutionary act. Being a non declarative locutionary act and a non assertive illocutionary act, 'Shut the door!' has a truth-value only under (B) and (D), and this truth-value is the same in both cases, because the propositions expressed at the locutionary and illocutionary levels are identical, which is obvious when we read 'Shut the door!' as

$$
(6) \quad
\begin{array}{ll}
\text{! (your shutting the door)} & \text{illocutionary level} \\
\hline
\text{! (your shutting the door)} & \text{locutionary level}
\end{array}
$$

Likewise, when 'The earth is flat' is seriously asserted, it has a truth-value under (A), (B), (C) and (D) because both a declarative locutionary act and an assertive illocutionary act are performed, and this truth-value also happens to be the same in all cases, owing to the identity of the propositions expressed at the locutionary and illocutionary levels:

$$
(7) \quad
\begin{array}{ll}
\vdash \text{(the earth being flat)} & \text{illocutionary level} \\
\hline
\vdash \text{(the earth being flat)} & \text{locutionary level}
\end{array}
$$

But in explicit performatives, the propositions expressed at the locutionary and illocutionary levels are different. 'I state that the earth is flat' has a truth-value under (A), (B), (C) and (D): it is true under (A) and (B), and false under (C) and (D), because what I (locutionarily) *say* in uttering this sentence, viz. that I state that the earth is flat, is true, whereas what I (illocutionarily) *assert*, viz. that the earth is flat, is false. 'I order you to shut the door', being a declarative locutionary act and a non assertive illocutionary act, has a truth-value under (A), (B) and (D); if the hearer does not subsequently shut the door, it is true under (A) and (B), and false under (D).

It is worth noticing that there are also illocutionary acts which lack a propositional content. For example, if I say 'Hello!', I salute you without expressing any proposition. Such an illocutionary act I symbolize thus ("S" represents the illocutionary force of a salute):

$$S(\emptyset)$$

Now if I say 'I salute you' I perform the same illocutionary act, but a different locutionary act. Using my notation, we can analyze 'Hello!' as (8) and 'I salute you' as (9):

(8) $\dfrac{S(\emptyset)}{S(\emptyset)}$ illocutionary level
locutionary level

(9) $\dfrac{S(\emptyset)}{\vdash \text{(my saluting you)}}$ illocutionary level
locutionary level

In (8), both the locutionary and the illocutionary act are devoid of a propositional content; but in (9) the locutionary act *has* a content. It follows that 'Hello!' has no truth-value under (A), (B), (C) and (D), while 'I salute you', like many other explicit performatives of the behabitive kind, has a truth-value (namely the value true) under (A) and (B), but no truth-value under (C) or (D).

There is also a special problem connected with WH-questions, which do not, according to Searle (1969 p. 31), express a complete proposition, but rather a propositional function. Leaving aside this problem, we can summarize the four different (and somehow compatible) ways of ascribing truth-value to performatives as follows:

	'I state that the earth is flat'	'I order you to shut the door' (but the hearer does not obey)	'I salute you'
illocutionary level locutionary level	⊢(the earth being flat) ⊢(my stating that the earth is flat)	! (your shutting the door) ⊢(my ordering you to shut the door)	$S(\emptyset)$ ⊢(my saluting you)
A	True	True	True
B	True	True	True
C	False	No truth-value	No truth-value
D	False	False	No truth-value

VII

It will be, I hope, obvious from what I have said so far of explicit performatives that a position which Strawson (1973 p. 61) mentions as having "gained popularity with philosophers recently" is indefensible. According to that position, Strawson says,

one who (seriously) utters an explicit performative of the form 'I x . . .' issues the proposition that he xs . . . with the force of an x-ing: e.g., (. . .) someone who says 'I apologize' issues the proposition that he apologizes with the force of an apology; or (. . .) someone who says 'I warn you all that judgement is at hand' issues the proposition that he warns us that judgement is at hand with the force of a warning.

There is a big confusion here. In my opinion, to say that a proposition P is expressed with the force of an assertion simply amounts to saying that *P is asserted*. But when I say 'I assert that John is bald' performatively, *what I assert* is that John is bald, not that I assert that he is. Likewise, when I say 'I warn you that judgement is at hand', what I warn you of is judgement being at hand, not my warning you that judgement is at hand. Confusion arises when we mix the locutionary and illocutionary levels, by coupling the proposition expressed at one level with the illocutionary force expressed at the other. To assert that in saying 'I warn you that he will come' I express the proposition that I warn you that he will come with the force of a warning is like asserting that in saying 'Can you pass the salt?' I express the proposition that you are able to pass the salt with the force of a request; and this amounts to saying that I thereby ask you to be able to pass the salt. Of course, those who defend that position do not intend to maintain such an absurdity. But I don't see how one could make the refusal of this absurdity consistent with the general position from which it arises, because once we have maintained that in saying 'Can you pass the salt?' the speaker expresses the proposition that the hearer can pass the salt with the force of a request we are unable to distinguish between 'Can you pass the salt?' and 'Please be able to pass the salt'. Or shall we deny that in saying 'Please be able to pass the salt' the speaker expresses the proposition that the hearer can pass the salt with the force of a request?

National Center for Scientific Research (CNRS), Paris

ACKNOWLEDGEMENTS

I should like to thank Jonathan Cohen, Benoît de Cornulier, Oswald Ducrot, Julie Jack, John Mackie, Galen Strawson and Geoffrey Warnock for their valuable criticisms. I am especially grateful to Benoît de Cornulier for his help and support.

NOTES

[1] See for instance Lemmon (1962) and Hedenius (1963) or, more recently, Lewis (1970), Wiggins (1971a) and Åqvist (1972).

[2] Cornulier (1975), Anscombre (1977) and Fodor (1977). Among philosophers, Hedenius alone, to my knowledge, has made a similar point. He says that sentences of the form 'I command you to . . .' "do not *directly* express commands but give the information that a command is now being given . . . The utterance of them is intended to bring a command into existence by informing the receiver of the existence of this command" (Hedenius, 1963, p. 123).

[3] Fodor (1977) p. 57.

[4] See e.g., Stawson (1973).

[5] I follow John Searle, who says that a yes-no question expresses the same proposition as the corresponding declarative; it would also be possible to say, as John Mackie has pointed out to me, that a yes-no question expresses two propositions, that e.g., 'Will John go?' expresses both the proposition that John will go and the proposition that he won't.

[6] Mainly Cohen (1964) and Searle (1968).

[7] Searle (1975) p. 60. By the way, I don't see the difference between the two sorts of cases Searle mentions here.

[8] So-called 'rhetorical' questions are not (genuine) questions at all. A rhetorical question, as Gardiner puts it, is question-like in form, but not in function.

[9] In other terms, the answer to the question, Which locutionary act is performed, is the same as the answer to the question, Which illocutionary act is indicated; and it can be given independently of the answer to the question, Which illocutionary act is performed. In the 'Can you pass the salt?' case, I know which locutionary act (viz. 'asking whether') is performed if and only if I know which illocutionary act is linguistically indicated by this sentence, even if I don't know which illocutionary act the speaker actually performs, e.g., that of posing a question or that of politely requesting the hearer to pass the salt.

[10] I am sometimes told that the English word 'fail', as opposed to the French word 'faute', does not convey an idea of duty or obligation, but rather a more general idea of expectation. Be that as it may, with *expectation* instead of *obligation* my point could still be made along the same lines.

[11] See Sadock (1974), p. 78, Brown and Levinson (1978), p. 144, Récanati (1978), pp. 164–165, and a number of papers in Cole and Morgan (1975).

[12] The fact that there are these two sets of conventions explains what Stalnaker (1970, § IV) calls the 'pragmatic ambiguity' of sentences beginning with a parenthetical verb. See Récanati (1978) § § VI.9 and VII.10.

[13] Likewise, the gift is not performed *indirectly* by means of 'it's yours' because, as Wiggins (1971b) has pointed out, there is nothing like a 'donatory mood'. – There is, however, an objection to the restriction I wish to place on the use of 'indirectly'. This objection I owe to John Mackie. "Is there any general reason, he asks, why there should not be promisory or donatory moods? Is it just an accident that our languages do not have them? If it is such an accident, I don't see why we shouldn't say that in 'I shall without fail' the illocutionary act is performed indirectly although (because of this accident) it can't be performed any more directly. An air journey from London to Minneapolis, with a stop and change of planes at New York, is still indirect even if there

is no non-stop service from London to Minneapolis". If John Mackie is right, as he probably is, then it would be better to say, of the promise performed by means of 'I shall without fail', that it is indirect only in a weak sense, in contradistinction to the request performed by uttering 'Can you pass the salt?', which could be dubbed 'strongly indirect'.
[14] See Gardiner (1932) § 61.

BIBLIOGRAPHY

Anscombre, J. C.: 1977, 'La problématique de l'illocutoire dérivé', *Langage et Société* 2, 17–41.
Åqvist, L.: 1972, *Performatives and Verifiability by the Use of Language*, Uppsala: Philosophical Studies.
Berlin, I., et al.: 1973, *Essays on J. L. Austin*, Oxford: Clarendon Press.
Brown, P., and S. Levinson: 1978, 'Universals in language usage: Politeness phenomena', in E. N. Goody (ed.), *Questions and Politeness*, Cambridge: Cambridge University Press.
Cohen, L. J.: 1964, 'Do illocutionary forces exist?', *Philosophical Quarterly* 14, 118–37.
Cole, P., and J. L. Morgan (eds.): 1975, *Syntax and Semantics, vol. III: Speech Acts*, New York: Academic Press.
de Cornulier, B.: 1975, 'La notion d'auto-interprétation', *Etudes de Linguistique appliquée* 19, 52–82.
de Cornulier, B.: (forthcoming), *Meaning Detachment*, Amsterdam: J. Benjamins B.V.
Fodor, J. D.: 1977, *Semantics*, New York: Crowell.
Forguson, L. W.: 1973, 'Locutionary and Illocutionary Acts', in Berlin et al.
Gardiner, A. H.: 1932, *The Theory of Speech and Language*, Oxford: Clarendon Press.
Hare, R. M.: 1970, 'Meaning and Speech Acts', *Philosophical Review* 79, 3–24.
Hedenius, I.: 1963, 'Performatives', *Theoria* 29, 115–36.
Lemmon, E. J.: 1962, 'On sentences verifiable by their use', *Analysis* 22, 86–9.
Lewis, D. K.: 1970, 'General Semantics', *Synthese* 22, 18–67.
Morgan, J. L.: 1978, 'Two Types of Convention in Indirect Speech Acts', in Cole (ed.), *Syntax and Semantics vol. IX: Pragmatics*, New York: Academic Press.
Récanati, F.: 1978, *Les performatifs explicites: contribution à la pragmatique*, unpublished thesis, University of Paris I-Sorbonne.
Sadock, J. M.: 1974, *Toward a Linguistic Theory of Speech Acts*, New York: Academic Press.
Searle, J. R.: 1968, 'Austin on Locutionary and Illocutionary Acts', in Berlin et al.
Searle, J. R.: 1969, *Speech Acts*, Cambridge: Cambridge University Press.
Searle, J. R.: 1975, 'Indirect Speech Acts', in Cole and Morgan (eds.)
Stalnaker, R. C.: 1970, 'Pragmatics', *Synthese* 22, 272–89.
Strawson, P. F.: 1973, 'Austin and "Locutionary Meaning" ', in Berlin et. al.
Warnock, G. J.: 1973, 'Some Types of Performative Utterance', in Berlin et al.
Wiggins, D.: 1971a, 'On sentence-sense, word-sense and difference of word-sense', in Steinberg and Jakobovits (eds.), *Semantics*, Cambridge: Cambridge University Press.
Wiggins, D.: 1971b, 'A reply to Mr. Alston', as above.

JOHN R. SEARLE

THE BACKGROUND OF MEANING

This article is a continuation of a line of investigation I began in 'Literal Meaning'.[1] Its aim is to explore some of the relations between the meaning of words and sentences and the context of their utterance. The view I shall be challenging is sometimes put by saying that the meaning of a sentence is the meaning that it has independently of any context whatever — the meaning it has in the so-called "null context". The view I shall be espousing is that in general the meaning of a sentence only has application (it only, for example, determines a set of truth conditions) against a background of assumptions and practices that are not representable as a part of the meaning.

I

Consider the following sequence of rather ordinary English sentences, all containing the word "cut".

1.   Bill cut the grass.
2.   The barber cut Tom's hair.
3.   Sally cut the cake.
4.   I just cut my skin.
5.   The tailor cut the cloth.
        - - - - - - - - - - - - - - - - - -
6.   Sam cut two classes last week.
7.   The President cut the salaries of the employees.
8.   The Raiders cut the roster to 45.

9.   Bob can't cut the mustard.
10.   Cut the cackle!
11.   Cut it out!

It seems to me the following is more or less intuitively obvious about this list. First of all the occurrence of the word "cut" in the utterances of 1–5 is literal. There is nothing metaphorical or figurative in our understanding of any of these sentences. In understanding sentences 6–8, on the other hand, we do not assign the literal interpretation to "cut" that occurs in 1–5; one might

221

J. R. Searle, F. Kiefer, and M. Bierwisch (eds.), Speech Act Theory and Pragmatics,
221–232.
Copyright © 1980 by D. Reidel Publishing Company.

hesitate to say straight out that utterances of 6—8 contain a metaphorical occurrence of "cut", because the metaphors are dead or frozen, but still in some fairly obvious way the sense or senses in which "cut" would be used in utterances of 6—8 is a figurative extension of the literal meaning in 1—5. A person who doesn't understand 6—8, but still understands 1—5, understands the literal meaning of the word "cut"; whereas a person who did not understand 1—5 does not understand that literal meaning; and we are inclined to say he couldn't fully understand the meaning of "cut" in 6—8 if he didn't understand the meaning in 1—5. I think the distinction between the first group and the second is obvious, but if someone wanted to deny it, a strong argument would be that certain sorts of conjunction reductions will work for 1—5 that will not work for the next group. For example,

12.   General Electric has just announced the development of a new cutting machine that can cut grass, hair, cakes, skin, and cloth.

But if I add to this, after the word "cloth", the expression, from 6—8, "classes, salaries, and rosters", the sentence becomes at best a bad joke and at worst a category mistake. Of course one could with some ingenuity give a literal interpretation to the occurrences of "cut" in utterances of 6—8. For example, if the President cuts each employee's salary with his pair of scissors as he hands over the salaries in cash, then we would have a situation correctly describable with the literal utterance of "cut", and on this interpretation 7 would have to be moved above the line. Even in 1—5 not all conjunction reductions will work equally well. It would sound at least a little fishy to say

13.   Bill cut the grass, the barber Tom's hair, and the tailor the cloth,

though even this would not be as outrageous as if one tried to add the corresponding pairs from 6—8, as in e.g.

14.   Bill cut the grass, and Sam two classes.

When we come to 9—11, the occurrences of the word "cut" are clearly in idioms as the usual tests for idioms will show. We have in short, three kinds of occurrences of the word "cut" in utterances of the members of this list: literal, figurative, and as part of larger idioms. Notice that, in general, 1—5 translate easily into other languages; 6—11 do not.

The feature of this list which interests me for present purposes, and which I will try to explain is this. Though the occurrence of the word "cut" is literal in utterances of 1—5, and though the word is not ambiguous, it determines different sets of truth conditions for the different sentences. The sort of thing that constitutes cutting the grass is quite different from, e.g., the sort of thing that constitutes cutting a cake. One way to see this is to imagine what constitutes obeying the order to cut something. If someone tells me to cut the grass and I rush out and stab it with a knife, or if I am ordered to cut the cake and I run over it with a lawnmower, in each case I will have failed to obey the order. That is not what the speaker meant by his literal and serious utterance of the sentence.

If we reflect on these, and some other equally simple examples, we will see that they present a problem for traditional semantic theory. According to the tradition since Frege, the literal meaning of a sentence is entirely determined by the meanings of its parts and their syntactical combination in the sentence. This axiom has the consequence that the notion of the literal meaning of a sentence is a context free notion, and various recent authors have expressed the idea that the literal meaning of a sentence is the meaning that it has in the "null context", or the "zero context"; that is, the literal meaning is the meaning a sentence has apart from any context whatever. A second axiom in this dominant tradition has been that the meaning of a sentence determines the truth conditions of that sentence, and, according to some authors, a theory of the truth conditions of the sentences of a language is a theory of meaning for that language. But it is hard to see how we can hold both of these axioms and still account for the facts in 1–5, because in those sentences one and the same semantic content, expressed by the word "cut", occurs in each sentence; and yet it seems to make a different contribution to the truth condition of the sentence in each case. Nor does there seem to be any obvious way we can avoid this inconsistency by appealing to the various distinctions that occur in contemporary semantic and pragmatic theory. We do not, for example, appear to be dealing with a difference between literal sentence meaning and speaker's utterance meaning such as we have in irony, metaphor, and indirect speech acts; nor, apparently, are we dealing with ambiguity, vagueness or different presuppositions, as these are traditionally conceived.

Something seems to have gone wrong with our axioms and it is important to try to say exactly what it is: if the contribution that the meaning of an unambiguous word makes to the meaning of a sentence in which that word has a literal occurrence is a contribution to the truth conditions of that sentence, and if "cut" has a literal occurrence in 1–5, then it ought to make exactly the same contribution to the truth conditions of these sentences. But it seems that in 1–5 "cut" does not make the same contribution; what constitutes satisfying the truth condition of "cut" is different in each case.

Something has to give. Defenders of the traditional theory will be reluctant to give up either axiom, so let us imagine what they might say.

First, they might say, "cut" is ambiguous. Just as "bank" has different meanings and thus makes different contributions to the truth conditions of sentences, so "cut" is equally ambiguous in its various occurrences 1–5. After all, don't big dictionaries list different senses of "cut" and wouldn't we say that "cut" was used in different senses in each case? This answer won't do. In the way that "bank" can mean either finance house or side of a river, and is thus ambiguous, "cut" is not ambiguous in 1–5, indeed in each of its occurrences it involves a common semantic content roughly involving the notion of a physical separation by means of the pressure of some more or less sharp instrument. We will see later that stating the semantic content in this form is very misleading, but at this point in the argument it is at least correct to say that this semantic content is common to 1–5. The fact that we get conjunction reductions like 12 or the fact that we can form some comparatives such as, "Bill cut more off the grass than the barber did off Tom's hair", is further evidence that we are not dealing with ambiguity as it is traditionally conceived. Part of the difference between 1–5 and 6–8 is that "cut" is used with the same literal meaning in utterances of the former; and it differs from the meaning or meanings it has or is used with in utterances of the latter.

Second, an ingenious rejoinder has been proposed by Ed Keenan: the concept "cut" is like a variable function in mathematics. Just as, for example, some mathematical functions take different interpretations depending on whether they take an even or an odd number as argument, so the word "cut" has different interpretations in 1–5 but these different interpretations are determined by the different arguments – grass, hair, cake, skin and cloth. In a sense then "cut" is ambiguous, but it is a very special kind of systematic ambiguity since none of the sentences is ambiguous, and that is because by determining in each case only one interpretation of "cut", the argument expression renders the sentence univocal. On this account it is the word "cut", together with the literal meaning of "grass", that determines that in "cut the grass" "cut" has a different interpretation from the literal meaning of "cut" in "cut the cake".

But this reply won't do either, for it is easy to imagine circumstances in which "cut" in "cut the grass" would have the same interpretation it has in "cut the cake", even though none of the semantic contents of the words has changed. Suppose you and I run a sod farm where we sell strips of grass turf to people who want a lawn in a hurry. (Such farms are quite common in certain parts of the country, by the way). Suppose I say to you, "Cut half an acre of grass for this customer"; I might mean not that you should *mow* it, but that you should *slice* it into strips as you could cut a cake or a loaf of bread. But this meaning involves no change in any of the literal meanings of the components of the sentence. Or, analogously, suppose we run a bakery where due to our super yeast strain our cakes grow upwards uncontrollably. "Keep cutting those cakes!", I shout to the foreman, meaning not that he should slice them up but that he should keep trimming the tops off. In these last two examples we have the same literal meaning and yet a different set of truth conditions relative to different contexts of utterance, even though the phenomena are not those of vagueness, metaphor, irony, or indirect speech acts.

A third reply might be that "cut" is vague, and that the contexts of the rest of the sentence in 1—5 enable the hearer to infer what the speaker means even though speaker meaning was not precisely expressed by the literal meaning of the sentence uttered, and further evidence for this is that in many of the cases there are more precise verbs that would have more exactly expressed what the speaker meant, e.g., "mow", "stab", "slice", "trim". On this account the literal sentence meaning of, e.g., 1 would be expressed by

13.   Bill made a separation of the grass using a more or less sharp instrument.

and the speaker meaning would be expressed by

14.   Bill mowed the grass.

According to this account the examples are standard cases of the difference between less precise literal sentence meanings and more precise speaker's utterance meanings. This explanation has a great deal of plausibility, and even some truth, but I am not completely satisfied with it for several reasons.

First, this account would predict that just as we understand the meaning of 1—5, so we should be able to understand

15.   Sam cut the coffee.
16.   Mary cut the sand.
17.   Max cut the sun.
18.   Bill cut the mountain.

But the difficulty with these sentences is that though I understand each of the words, I don't understand the sentences. I do not know what truth conditions are supposed to be determined by these examples. Even if there is plenty of sand present, if somebody instructs me to cut the sand, I do not know what I am supposed to do. For each case, I can imagine a context in which I would be able to determine a set of truth conditions; but by themselves, without the addition of a context, the sentences do not do that. And it would be no help at all to imagine that I might have a set of axioms from which I can deduce, e.g., "Mary cut the sand" is true iff Mary cut the sand, because I do not yet know what it is to cut the sand.

Another difficulty with this account is that if it were true then all kinds of crazy misunderstandings would be literally correct interpretations of the sentence. For example, if I have a contract with you to cut your grass weekly and on successive weeks I stab it with a butcher knife, gouge a hole in it with a buzz saw, and make incisions with my finger nail, have I literally complied with the letter of the contract? I am inclined to say no.

A third difficulty with this account is that it seems most implausible to suppose that in understanding 1—5 we go from a common literal meaning of "cut" by a process of unconscious inference to different speaker meanings, on analogy with the processes by which we understand, e.g. ironical utterances or indirect speech acts. Which is more plausible: that we understand 1 as meaning 13 apart from any context whatever, and then by a series of steps in an inference involving assumptions about the context derive 14, or rather that in a normal context we simply understand 1 as meaning 14? Notice that we certainly don't learn the meaning of "cut" in 1—5 by learning its paraphrase in 13, rather we just learn the meaning of "cut" in sentences like 1—5 with their *common* meaning determining *different* truth conditions. And actually for someone who did not know that 13 was supposed to be a paraphrase of 1, it is hard to see how he could get a definite set of truth conditions out of it at all. If someone told me seriously that Bill made a separation of the grass using a more or less sharp instrument, I would wonder what he was talking about. I have no such problems with "Bill cut the grass".

II

I believe the phenomena we have cited have a simple and obvious explanation — an explanation which is an extension of the one just considered, but which has different implications. The reason that the same semantic content, "cut", determines different sets of truth conditions in these different sentences 1—5 derives not from any ambiguity of a semantic kind, but rather from the fact that as members of our culture we bring to bear on the literal utterance and understanding of a sentence a whole background of information about how nature works and how our culture works. A background of practices, institutions, facts of nature, regularities, and ways of doing things are assumed by speakers and hearers when one of these sentences is uttered or understood. I understand the sentence "He cut the grass" differently from the way I understand "He cut the cake", not because of the different *semantic* content of "cake" and "grass", nor because of any vagueness in the original, but because I know a lot of things about grass, e.g. what people have grass lawns for, what they do to their lawns, etc.; and I also know a lot of things about cakes, e.g. what they are for and what people do with cakes, etc.; and my knowledge that cutting grass is a different sort of business from cutting cakes is part of this larger system of knowledge. This phenomenon seems to me quite general: for a large number of cases (perhaps not all) the literal meaning of a sentence or expression only determines a set of truth conditions given a set of background assumptions and practices. Given one set of these a sentence or expression may determine one set of truth conditions and given another set of assumptions and practices the same sentence or expression with the same meaning can determine a different set of truth conditions even though the semantic content is not indexical or ambiguous and there is no question of vagueness, indirect speech acts, or figurative uses of language, as these notions are standardly understood. Furthermore, these assumptions that determine the interpretation of a sentence are not part of the semantic content of the sentence.

The axiom, in short, that we need to abandon is the one that says that the literal meaning of a sentence determines a set of truth conditions. What we want to say is, rather: the literal meaning of a sentence only determines a set of truth conditions given a set of background practices and assumptions. Relative to one set of practices and assumptions, a sentence may determine one set of truth conditions; relative to another set of practices and assumptions, another set; and if some sets of assumptions and practices are given, the literal meaning of a sentence may not determine a definite set of truth conditions at all. Furthermore, these assumptions and practices are not part of the semantic content of the sentence, and this variability is not a matter of indexicality, ambiguity, indirect speech acts, vagueness or presupposition as these notions are traditionally conceived in the philosophical and linguistic literature. I propose to call the set of assumptions and practices that make interpretation possible "the background".

But, someone might object, if what you say is really true then we ought to get all of these background assumptions and practices out into the open. We ought to make the background fully explicit as part of the semantic content of the sentence or at least as a set of stage directions for using the sentence. If we are to be told that one and the same sentence, such as the imperative "cut the grass!", can have a completely different set of obedience conditions relative to different background assumptions, even though the sentence is not ambiguous and is uttered literally, then in some sense those background assumptions ought to be included as part of the semantics, either as implicit parts of the semantic content, or as presuppositions of the semantic content, or as stage directions for the utterance of the words, or some such.

But this suggestion is unfulfillable, for three reasons. First we would never know when to stop in spelling out the background. Even if, for example, we described the practices of our culture, those practices themselves depend on certain very general facts about what nature is like and what human beings are like, e.g., that grass grows, that it doesn't eat human beings, that grass is softer than steel, that grass growing and cutting goes on at the surface of the earth − and so on indefinitely (though not infinitely). And secondly, for each of our attempts to spell out the "assumptions" we will have to use words in sentences, and those words in sentences determine their own truth conditions only relative to yet other sets of assumptions, which in turn we would have to spell out. And third, it is not at all clear that "assumptions" is even the right word to describe what it is that makes meaning and understanding possible at all, since the expression implies that these assumptions all have propositional content, that they are all representations. But, from the fact that any element of the background can be formulated as a representation, it does not follow that prior to that formulation it existed and functioned as a representation. Have we, for example, always *believed* unconsciously that grass does not eat humans? Well, if I ever saw a stand of grass eating somebody I would certainly be astonished, and that is at least evidence that one of my intentional states is unsatisfied; but it is at best misleading to assimilate that case to the case where, for example, I expect that it is going to keep on raining and find myself surprised to see the sun come out. The conditions which make representation possible need not themselves all be representations, even though each of them is representable or formulatable as a representation.

However, someone might say, all of this relies on a few trick examples with the word "cut", but a few odd examples do not threaten the foundations of traditional semantic theory: all that the examples show is that there is a kind of hidden indexicality even in such apparently non-indexical concepts as "cut", but this is in no way a general feature of language, since there are still plenty of sentences that determine their truth conditions apart from any context whatever, their meaning is the meaning they have in the null context. Consider, for example, an arithmetical sentence such as

$$4 + 5 = 9;$$

or a general sentence about nature such as

Snow is white.

In reply to this objection I want to say that even these sentences only determine a set of truth conditions against a background of human practices and various background assumptions, and these practices and assumptions are so pervasive that we seldom notice them. Thus, consider an example derived from Wittgenstein.[2]

Suppose there was a tribe that always did addition this way:

Case 1.

A   B   A = 4   B = 5   A + B = 9

Case 2.

A B   A = 4   B = 5   A + B = 7

That is, according to their way of doing arithmetic, the correct answer to the addition in case 1 is 9; in case 2 it is 7. We might in describing their practice of arithmetic say that they appear to operate on the principle:

> treat the sum of 4 and 5 as the number of objects that fall under the concept '$fx \lor gx$' if $\exists_4 x(fx)$ & $\exists_5 x(gx)$.

But if so, it would still be a mistake to think that their practice must somehow derive from or be founded on this principle. To see this, imagine that someone objects to their practice as follows: since they have overlapping sets in case 2 they have simply misunderstood the meaning of the concept of addition — the literal meaning of the "+" sign — if they proceed as we describe them. In order to understand addition correctly they would have to proceed at least according to the principle:

> treat the sum of 4 and 5 as the number of objects that fall under the concept '$fx \lor gx$' if $\exists_4 x(fx)$ & $\exists_5 x(gx)$ & $\sim \exists x(fx$ & $gx)$.

Case 1 is really addition, case 2 is cardinality of set union, and cardinality of set union should not be confused with addition.

But this objection fails, for there is nothing in the principle as we originally formulated it that forbids them to proceed in this way.

Case 3.   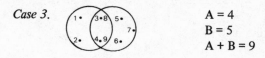   A = 4
                                          B = 5
                                          A + B = 9

Expressions like "cardinality of set union", or the principles we tried to formalize, are themselves grounded in our practices.

It is a fact about human practices that we count certain moves as good arithmetic and certain other moves as bad arithmetic, but there is nothing in the content of the representations that, so to speak, forces us to accept only one set of moves to the exclusion of all others. The representations are not self guaranteeing, and we do not eliminate this dependency by grounding representations in principles, for the principles are further representations which will have different applications relative to different practices and assumptions. Any set of such principles is grounded in practices which are themselves ungrounded.

Similar remarks apply to that citadel of traditional semantic theory, the sentence:

Snow is white.

Even it only determines a definite set of truth conditions against a background of assumptions about how the world works. Different assumptions may give different truth conditions; and against some set of assumptions the sentence may not determine a definite set of truth conditions at all. Suppose that by some fantastic change in the course of nature the earth is hit by an astronomical shower of radiation that affects all existing and future water molecules in such a way that in their crystalline form they reflect a different wave length when in sunlight from what they did prior to the radiation shower. Suppose also that the same shower affects the human visual apparatus and its genetic basis so that snow crystals look exactly as they did before. Physicists after the shower assure us that if we could see snow the way we did before, it would look chartreuse but because of the change in our retinas, which affects our observation of snow and nothing else, snow looks the same color as ever and will continue to do so to ensuing generations. The sale of ski goggles, for example, is unaffected. Would we say that snow was still white? That is, would the truth conditions of "Snow is white" be satisfied relative to this set of assumptions? I suggest that the semantic content of the sentence does not determine a definite set of truth conditions relative to this changed environment — we should have to make a *decision* whether or not to say that snow was still white, but that decision is not forced on us by the existing combination of the semantic content of the sentence and the facts as described.

These and countless other examples support the following hypothesis: the literal meaning of a sentence only determines a set of truth conditions (or other sorts of conditions of satisfaction), against a background of assumptions and practices. The background is not fixed, but it is by no means in flux either. Some elements of the background, e.g. that bodies are gravitationally attracted to the earth, are much more central than others, e.g. that people use lawnmowers to cut lawns. Given different backgrounds, one and the same sentence with one and the same literal meaning may determine different conditions of satisfaction, and given some backgrounds a sentence or concept may not determine a definite set of conditions of satisfaction at all.

III

If this hypothesis is true we naturally want to ask the question: why? Why should semantic content function like that? Assuming that the contextual dependence of the applicability of semantic content is as widespread as I claim, why not simply get rid of it; why not for example invent a language that would not in this way have contextually dependent semantic contents? The answer is that the features we have cited are features not just of semantic contents but of representations generally, in particular they are features of intentional states, and since meaning is always a derived form of intentionality, contextual dependency is ineliminable.

All of the argument for the contextual dependency of the sentences "Bill cut the grass", "4 + 5 = 9" and "Snow is white" are also arguments for the context dependency of the *beliefs* that Bill cut the grass, that 4 + 5 = 9 and that snow is white. The content of those beliefs determines the conditions of satisfaction that they do determine only against a background. "Well", we might imagine our objector saying, "if so that is because those beliefs would naturally come to us in words. But how about wordless intentional states, and how about the primary form of intentionality, perception?" If anything the contextual dependency of perceptual contents is even or more striking than the perceptual dependency of semantic contents. Suppose I am standing in front of a house looking at it; in so doing I will have certain visual experience with a certain intentional content, i.e. certain conditions of satisfaction; but suppose now as part of the background assumptions I assume I am on a Hollywood movie set and all of the buildings are just papier mâché façades. This assumption would not only give us different conditions of satisfaction; it would even alter the way the façade of the house looks to us, in the same way that the sentence "Cut the grass!" would be interpreted differently if we thought that the background was such that we were supposed to slice the grass rather than mow it. Or suppose that as part of the background of having this visual experience I assume I am seeing the house while standing on my head. Then the conditions of satisfaction would alter dramatically, e.g. the house is not resting on what appear to be its foundations — rather it is suspended upside down from them: I wonder how they keep it from falling downward, i.e. toward what would otherwise look like the sky. And again, the whole situation would *look* differently to me, even though the retinal stimulation was exactly the same if I had these different background assumptions. Furthermore the house looks the way it does to me because I have a mastery of the facts about houses which are part of our culture — that opening looks like a door to me, that a window, etc. The phenomena that we uncovered in the case of sentence meaning appear to be general features of intentionality, including the intentionality of perception.

NOTES

[1] *Erkenntnis* 13 (1978), pp. 207–224, reprinted in J. R. Searle, *Expression and Meaning*, Cambridge University Press, 1979.
[2] *Philosophical Grammar*, Blackwell, Oxford, 1974, p. 338.

PETR SGALL

TOWARDS A PRAGMATICALLY BASED THEORY OF MEANING

In the context of our conference, my contribution will probably seem to be a little bit old fashioned, since it is not directly based on an analysis of speech acts. I am afraid, however, that the relationships between speech act theory and semantics are still to be studied from the viewpoint of 'classical' semantics also.

If Searle (1969), elaborating Austin's (1962) bipartition of illocution and perlocution, insists that the distinctions of illocutionary form belong to the system of language rather than to its functioning, then it should be noticed that the attempts to establish operational criteria distinguishing meaning as a language-dependent structuring from factual knowledge are as useful for speech act theory as for any other domain of linguistics. The distinction between illocution (concerning language meaning) and perlocution (including also factual knowledge) can hardly be drawn and checked without such an analysis of the boundary between meaning and knowledge.

I am convinced that there is a core of semantics, which was formulated by Tarski and Carnap, based on truth conditions. Several important extensions and modifications of semantics have been formulated since their time, but there are still various open questions concerning this old core of semantics which may also be puzzling for the more recent extensions. Allow me then to stay with one or two such points in the theory of meaning as opposed to the theory of reference.

I use the term 'meaning' as a linguistic term, and I am not going to discuss *meaning* as the gerund of the English surface verb *to mean*. This verb has several meanings itself, and its counterparts in other languages often do not share all its properties and uses. Therefore I do not take such a sentence as *A means B by uttering C* as a starting point of an investigation of semantics. Rather I use the term 'meaning' in a sense near to that of 'literal meaning', or of the German *Bedeutung* as against *Bezeichnung*.

My paper is intended, first of all, to bring arguments forward to support a claim according to which a theory of meaning in this linguistic sense should be based on certain pragmatic aspects; I don't have in mind here those aspects of pragmatics that are directly investigated by the speech act theory, such as the speaker's purposes and their fulfilment. In these questions it goes without

233

J. R. Searle, F. Kiefer, and M. Bierwisch (eds.), Speech Act Theory and Pragmatics,
233–246.
Copyright © 1980 *by D. Reidel Publishing Company.*

saying that linguistic phenomena are analyzed as partly determined by pragmatical items. I want to argue that even the truth conditions of sentences in natural language are partly determined by pragmatical factors.

1.1. I would like to recall first that I do not consider pragmatics as a separate level of the language system. The level of linguistic meaning (or tectogrammatics, underlying structure) comprizes in my view pragmatic as well as semantic issues (in the terms of Morris' and Carnap's tripartition). I have pointed out elsewhere (Sgall, 1977) that this tripartition is complicated among other things by the fact that the sets of objects and of speakers are not disjunct, so that the boundary between semantics and pragmatics is not nearly so clearcut as that between semantics and syntax; if the meanings of such expressions as *today, tomorrow* are to be described in a coherent way, this must be done at a level including their pragmatic (indexical) as well as semantic (-= *day*) components.

1.2. Another assumption accepted as a starting point for this contribution consists in the conviction that a dividing line between linguistic meaning and factual knowledge (cognitive content) can be drawn, at least for grammatical phenomena (we are not directly concerned here with the meanings of lexical items), on the basis of Tarski's and Carnap's truth-functional semantics, if certain conditions are met. Two of these conditions were discussed by Sgall, Hajičová and Procházka (1977); one of which concerned the necessity to distinguish, in the analysis of natural language semantics, not only extensional and intensional contexts, but also metalinguistic ones, to be able to analyze adequately also such examples as (1), where the fact that (a) is analytical while (b) is not would otherwise be in contradiction to *stay* and *sojourn* being considered (at least for the sake of our discussion here) true synonyms, 'intensionally isomorphic' with Carnap (1947).

(1)   (a) The concept 'stay' is identical with the concept 'stay'.
        (b) The concept 'stay' is identical with the concept 'sojourn'.

The other condition analyzed by Sgall, Hajičová and Procházka (1977) concerns the necessity to formulate a linguistic counterpart of Carnap's 'intensional structure' (the identity of which is necessary for strict synonymy, or for exchangeability in intensional contexts) as an empirical issue, based on the distinction between (i) two surface shapes of a single underlying structure — as e.g. in (2) — and (ii) two different underlying structures (which are not strictly synonymous), as in (3).

(2) (a) The teacher allowed smoking here.
     (b) The teacher allowed to smoke here.
(3) (a) Charles was selling a car to Paul.
     (b) Paul was buying a car from Charles.

1.3. We concluded in the paper cited that the underlying (tectogrammatical) representation of a sentence, which includes free variables for the indexical elements (see Montague, 1970) can be considered an explicit representation of the meaning of the sentence. It must be noted, however, that our formulation concerning belief sentences (p. 49 of the paper cited) was not correct: beliefs are not about meanings of sentences, since a belief does not directly concern a tectogrammatical representation of a sentence, which includes free variables for indexical elements; rather, a belief concerns a representation in which specific values have been assigned to these variables, i.e., the representation of an utterance in a specific context. Such a sentence as *Harry believes that I was late yesterday* may certainly have different truth values with different speakers (reporters) and different time points of the utterance. Speaking more technically, we may say that the content of a belief is a pair (a,b), where a is a meaning (tectogrammatical representation) of a sentence, and b is a specific context. Or, in other words, if sense is characterized as differing from meaning by the included indexical variables having been assigned specific values, the content of a belief is a sense of a sentence.

I would like to recall that even a representation inside which reference is determined differs substantially from that of cognitive content. Rohrer (1971) has pointed out that a representation of content should be so conceived as to correspond directly to the truth conditions of the given sentence. In Montaguian semantics this correspondence is accounted for by means of a formal language of intensional logic. We have attempted elsewhere (Sgall, 1974; Sgall, Hajičová, and Benešová, 1973, §7.6) to establish a starting point for a procedure connecting (via translation) a formal language of logic (representing cognitive content) with the tectogrammatical level (representing linguistic meaning); it should be pointed out that the relationship between meaning and content cannot be classed as a relationship between two levels of linguistic representations, since only meaning has the status of a linguistic level, while content is described, as for its logical aspects, by the formal language (its other aspects belonging to psychology, etc.).

2.1. Still another condition appears as necessary for truth-functional semantics to be able to serve as an adequate basis for the theory of linguistic meaning.

This third condition was mentioned only briefly at the end of the paper by Sgall, Hajičová and Procházka (1977), and it will be discussed as the main point of the present contribution. We would like to substantiate here a view according to which the semantics of natural language is determined by pragmatic factors to such an extent that even the truth conditions of sentences may depend on pragmatic issues in the general case. Not only the truth *value* of individual utterances (uses, tokens, occurrences) of sentences containing pragmatical indices, but often also the truth *conditions* of a sentence are determined by the context (i.e. consituation, not only the verbal context).

The 'emancipation' of semantics from pragmatics in logical studies has been conditioned, among others, by an assumption that the notion of 'actual world' can be taken as one of the basic issues of semantics. It has been noted, however, that it is not possible to assume that we know which particular world is the actual one (cf. esp. Tichý, 1975, p. 91). If such notions as 'actual world' and 'universe of discourse' are to be used not only for an analysis of formal languages of logic, but also for that of natural language, it must be admitted that the universe of discourse, and thus also the actual world (of the speaker, of the hearer, or the intersection of these two) and the whole model changes during the discourse itself.[1]

There are different factors causing different kinds of such changes:

(i) new objects, relations etc. are added to repertoire by the content of what has just been said;

(ii) the universe of discourse may be restricted in that some subset of phenomena of a given kind is specified as relevant for further discourse, the other elements of that kind being left out of consideration (as for an illustration, see the discussion of (14) followed by (8) (a) below);

(iii) reference can be determined and shifted by various means, such as (a) deictic elements, (b) a specification of the type (ii), if narrowed down to a single item, (c) a definite description, (d) shift by means of *another, further, former − latter*, etc.;

(iv) the repertoire itself remains unchanged, but a certain relationship between its elements, namely their relative activation (in the sense of 'being given' immediately; of being well accessible in the memory − probably in the short term memory).

We will be interested here in (iv), i.e., in the change of the hierarchy of activation (foregrounding) of the elements of the stock of knowledge the speaker has and assumes to be shared by the hearer (this notion of the 'stock of shared knowledge' includes not just 'knowledge' in the literal sense, but a wide range of psychological phenomena).[2]

We may state quite briefly that the activated items may function as contextually bound and thus constitute the topic of a sentence, while the non-activated ones are always contextually non-bound, and thus apt to occur inside the focus of a sentence. If I say *Beavers build DAMS* (with the intonation centre denoted by capital letters), the sentence is three ways ambiguous: (a) either the agentive noun refers to the species we have just been speaking about (it is contextually bound and constitutes the topic), while the rest belongs to the focus of the sentence, or (b) the verb has also been activated in the given time point (so that I say only that it is dams beavers build, with Kuno's, 1972, exhaustive listing), or else (c) the sentence represents a 'general statement', without any topic. It seems that with *Dams are built by BEAVERS* the passivization is conditioned (triggered) by the objective being contextually bound, so that (c) is excluded here, which underlies the distinction between the two sentences noted by Chomsky (1974).

A detailed analysis of hundreds of sentences of Czech, as well as of English and other languages, made it possible to formulate a generative framework enumerating the tectogrammatical structures, which include also the bi-partition into topic and focus and the scale of communicative dynamism (represented by the left-to-right order of lexical formatives and determining what in a formal language of logic would appear as the scope of quantifiers). This mechanism, described and discussed in the writings quoted in Note 2, allows for a unified description of the semantic differences of pairs of sentences differing (as to their linguistic structure) only in their topic/focus patterns (and, in the surface, in the means expressing these patterns, i.e. first of all in word order and the placement of intonation centre), be it sentences with overt quantification, such as (4) to (7), or with some kind of covered quantification, e.g. (8) to (10). Also the fact that the elements of such sentence pairs as (4') to (6') express the same factual content (have identical truth conditions) is described by the given framework; this last group is that of sentence pairs sharing the difference in structure with (4) to (6) but containing those types of quantification that neutralize the differences of intensional structure of the corresponding formulas (e.g. iota and epsilon operators).[3]

(4)   (a) Many men read few BOOKS.
            (b) Few books are read by many MEN.
(5)   (a) Everyone in this room knows at least two LANGUAGES.
            (b) At least two languages are known to everyone in this ROOM.

(6)   (a) John talked to few girls about many PROBLEMS.
           (b) John talked about many problems to few GIRLS.
(7)   (a) Londoners are mostly in BRIGHTON.
           (b) In Brighton there are mostly LONDONERS.
(8)   (a) English is spoken in NEW ZEALAND.
           (b) ENGLISH is spoken in New Zealand.
(9)   (a) One smokes in the CORRIDOR.
           (b) In the corridor one SMOKES.
(10)   (a) Smoking is DANGEROUS.
           (b) It's dangerous to SMOKE (or: SMOKING is dangerous.)

(4')   (a) John reads one of those BOOKS.
           (b) One of those books is read by JOHN.
(5')   (a) Tom knows a foreign LANGUAGE.
           (b) A foreign language is known to TOM.
(6')   (a) John talked to those girls about a PROBLEM.
           (b) John talked about a problem to those GIRLS.

The activated items (i.e. the items activated more than a certain threshold
the nature of which is to be investigated) can be referred to by the elements
of the topic of a sentence (where, under certain conditions specific for the
given language they can be deleted, or expressed by enclitical forms, by
morphemes having reduced stress, etc.). There are different kinds of tests to
check this in an operative way (using questions, negative commentaries or
contrastive responses, etc., to distinguish topic and focus). An activated item
may be referred to also by a contextually non-bound element of the sentence
(a part of its focus), and in this case it may have the form of a stressed pronoun. Thus (11) can be followed either by (12) — with the focus consisting
in the verb only, the two persons being 'given' (their counterparts in the stock
of shared knowledge having been activated by (11) and chosen as 'what is
spoken about' for the next utterance by the speaker) — or by (13), where the
speaker does not change the topic (continuing to speak about his experience)
and brings *him* into focus, though it refers to an activated element.

(11)   I saw two young PEOPLE there.
(12)   He KISSED her.
(13)   I've recognized only HIM.

An item that has not been activated, in the given time point of the discourse, can occur only as contextually non-bound. It is an urgent task,
however, to study mechanisms concerning just how close to the given object

(or to its counterpart in the speakers' memory) those other objects are that are activated by a mentioning of the given object: from 'two young people' it is not far to 'he and she', and probably 'his hair' or 'her shoes' could also be included in the topic of the next utterance. Similarly 'to be called a virgin' may activate also 'insult', as in Lakoff's well known example, etc.

By being mentioned in the focus of an utterance (as contextually non-bound), the object becomes activated and can be most naturally chosen as (part of) the topic of the next utterance in the discourse; as we have already seen with (13) above, the speaker is, of course, free to continue without changing the topic,[4] and he certainly has other options, too.

This shows that the hierarchy of activation could be characterized, perhaps, as a relation of partial ordering on the items of the stock of shared knowledge (but certainly not as a linear ordering).

If the newly activated item has not been mentioned in the next utterance, its activation will fade away step by step; it is not likely to be chosen as the topic of some of the further utterances (if not of that opening the next paragraph). The hierarchy of activation is affected by other factors too, that are not easy to describe without a thorough analysis of a large corpus of text (e.g. some topics — first of all those appearing in the titles of chapters — rank higher than others, i.e. their activation does not fade away so quickly as that of the others).

2.2. According to the discussion in 2.1, it is necessary for the description of the meaning of natural language sentences to substitute the concept of a given, steady 'possible world', free from any pragmatic relationships to the participants of the discourse, due to a concept of a stock of knowledge shared by the speaker and (according to his conviction) also by his audience, which changes during the discourse in different ways. To give a quite preliminary formulation of the aspect of its change we are concerned with, let us use some rather primitive means, which might just serve as a starting point for further investigation:

The stock of shared knowledge, denoted K, may be characterized in the terms of Montague's Universal Grammar (see Montague and Schnelle, 1972, esp. pp. 43 f.) as a subset of the set of senses of expressions, i.e. of the set $D_{\langle s, \tau \rangle}, E, I$ (where τ stands for e, t), conceived as a set of functions from the set of possible worlds into the set of designates. Furthermore, the set K should be relativized to the time points of utterances.

Let us assume then that K_t is a given set of senses in the time point t; A is a binary relation on this set, defining a partial ordering of its elements (the hierarchy of activation: A $(a,\ b)$ can be read: b is more activated than a).

The following rules may now be formulated (as empirical hypotheses to be checked; the author may only express his hope that an empirical investigation will soon allow for more elaborated versions):[5]

(i) for any j, k in K_t, if k has been referred to at t by a contextually non-bound element (a part of the focus) of utterance S that included an element referring to j in its topic, then $A(j,\ k)$ holds at $t+1$;

(ii) if an element k of K_t is referred to by (a part of) the topic of an utterance S at t, then $A(p,\ k)$ holds in K_t, p being a fixed element of K (interpreted as the threshold of activation);

(iii) if k (in K_t) was referred to by the focus of S at t, and the utterance S' at $t+1$ does not contain an element referring to k, then there is such a j in K_t that $A(j,\ k)$ holds in K_t while $A(k,\ j)$ holds in K_{t+1}.

It is necessary to investigate what factors are relevant for a change in the hierarchy of activation; rule (i) concerns only a pair of elements one of which was included in the topic and the other in the focus of a single sentence; it is probable, however, that also differences of the degrees of communicative dynamism play a role here (a more dynamic element is more activated than a less dynamic one in the same sentence). Besides this syntagmatic conditioning of change of activation there might be also a paradigmatic factor with a similar effect: if one element out of a linguistically characterized set (e.g. a sister out of the set of relatives) was spoken about in the preceding part of text while the given utterance contains another element of that set (say brother), then this new element will be more activated than its previously mentioned counterpart (even if the new item is included in the topic of the given utterance only). The paradigmatic relationship (between objects referred to by lexical elements of a certain semantic group) has also another effect: if brother is referred to (in a focus) while sister previously was not, then not only brother, but to a certain degree also sister (and similarly mother, father, etc.) becomes activated.

It should be then incorporated into the procedure of interpretation that, if a definite NP is used in an utterance (with the delimiting feature Def, not in a generic sense), its reference is determined — if it is not unique, as with proper names, and not given by means of referential indices, i.e. of deixis — by means of the relation A: if the utterance has been formulated in an adequate way, then there must exist such an element k of K_t that for every other element j in K_t corresponding to the same name $A(j,\ k)$ holds. (With a suitable metrics connected with A one may even postulate that the distance between k and the nextmost activated element of K_t be greater than some determined standard.)

2.3. To illustrate our claim that the change of the stock of shared knowledge (or of the model, if this term should be transferred from logical investigations on semantics into linguistics, being redefined) of the speaker and the hearer affects truth conditions, let us recall that e.g. for such a pair as (8) it is not enough to state that (b) is true with regard to the actual world, while (a) is not. Following e.g. (14), (8)(a) is actually true.

(14)   Is English spoken in New Caledonia or in New Zealand?

Is such a point of the discourse it not only holds that *English* and *speak* are used in the answer as referring to activated items (so that Kuno's, 1972, 'exhaustive listing' is expected, see Sgall, Hajičová and Benešová, 1973, § 4.42) but also that the set of countries relevant to the discourse has been reduced, for the given time point, to New Caledonia and New Zealand, so that only these are the 'universe' of the exhaustive listing. This is a quite specific situation, of course, and without such a context (8)(a) is false.

We can thus speak about at lest two important thresholds of activation inside the stock of shared knowledge: only elements activated above the first (upper) threshold may be used in the topic of the next utterance, and only elements activated above the second (lower) threshold will be taken into consideration for the aims of 'exhaustive listing' (and probably also what regards some other aspects: in attributing a certain property to − or predicating something else about − the boys the speaker most often does not mean the set of all the boys there are − or were, will be, can be − but just a certain subset that has been specified in some such way as (ii) in § 2.1 above).

It is not adequate to say that such differences as those between (a) and (b) in (8) to (10) belong to pragmatics and do not affect their truth conditions, since it is not possible, in many contexts, to exchange the two variants without changing the truth conditions. In these cases, without such specific contexts as (14), one of the two variants is true, while the other is false.

In other cases one of the topic/focus variants just does not meet its presuppositions, while the other meets them and is (in the usual context, in which the 'actual world' is not reshaped) false, as e.g. in (15).

(15)   (a) The king of France visited PRAGUE in September 1977.
         (b) Prague was visited by the king of FRANCE in September 1977.

In (15)(b) one speaks about Prague and tells that at a certain time it was visited by a person referred to by the NP *king of France*; it can be checked (at least in principle) that nobody belonging to the class of living beings denoted by this NP visited Prague at that day, without even asking whether this class is empty or not. Thus the negative sentence corresponding to (15)(b) is true, Prague was not visited by the king of France in September 1977, and (15)(b) expresses a false statement (for the given state of the stock of shared knowledge).

It would be erroneous to assume that the negation of a false sentence must be true. It is well known in linguistics that there are many sentences that meet such a natural response as *Oh no, not only that*, or *Don't exaggerate*, or *Oh no, it is also* . . . [6] :

(16)   This building consists of glass.
(17)   The Pacific is full of coral islands.
(18)   The flag of France is blue and red.

In many contexts (as for (17) and (18), the 'actual world' without specific restrictions may be considered) the negative counterparts of such sentences would also be rejected as not (fully) true.

In this situation it need not be regarded as specifically puzzling that with (8)(b) the situation is similar: neither the sentence itself, nor its negation are true with regard to the 'actual world'. This fact is not a specific characteristics of sentence pairs differing in topic/focus structure and cannot serve as an argument in favour of the view that in (8) to (10) the truth conditions of (a) and (b) be identical. It can be checked easily (by means of testing such sentences in short contexts as for natural responses of informants) that in all such cases the truth conditions differ, and their difference must be connected with the single difference that exists in the linguistic structure of the (a) and (b) variants, viz. with their topic/focus structure. This structure being conditioned by pragmatic factors (i.e. by the hierarchy of more and less activated items in the stock of knowledge shared by the speaker and the hearer), one has to admit that pragmatic issues are relevant for truth conditions of sentences.

It is even possible to say that this pragmatic conditioning of semantic features of natural language semantics has always been admitted. Not only by Carnap (1947), who just considered linguistic semantics to belong to (the non-semantic layer of) pragmatics, but also by all those who, analyzing the semantics (or the logical structure) of sentences, do not go beyond such formulations as e.g. that the truth of *The town has ten thousand inhabitants* depends on what town is referred to in the given occurrence of the sentence (the use of an iota operator in a representation of such a sentence is, of course, also connected with the assumption that "there is exactly one town in the universe of discourse"). It is possible to disregard the question how such formulations should be made more precise, but if the meaning of sentences is to be fully described, it is useful to ask and answer questions of this kind. This is even more necessary if one once starts to investigate also sequences of speech acts from the veiwpoints of illocution and perlocution.

It is then possible to argue that a theory of meaning of natural language would have to include an unlimited number of objects, states of affairs or states of mind, which cannot be accounted for by finite means. If an approach using the notion of a threshold of activation of the elements in the stock of shared knowledge can be elaborated and checked, however, then at least one of the aspects concerning the change of the 'model' during the discourse would be described by a small number of general rules. After the Montaguian inclusion of indexical elements this could be regarded as another step towards an inclusion of relevant pragmatic issues into the theory of meaning (and it would then be of little relevance whether the traditional term 'semantics' will be applied to this theory, contrary to Morris' tripartition, or not).

3. The structure of language came into existence and has developed towards its contemporary state in conditions determined by the functioning of language in human communication, and thus it may be understood that the structure of language has been influenced by this functioning, by certain conditions or requirements of communication.

One of the intrinsic features of human communication consists in the fact that the hearer must find the items referred to during a discourse in his memory, which is a vaste domain. If the speaker wants to be well understood, he naturally attempts to indicate in every utterance some points highly accessible (activated) in the hearer's memory and to point out how these points should be modified, connected with some other points, which are perhaps less accessible, etc. It is possible that this difference in accessibility is connected with that of short term and long term memory, but this is a question concerning psychology.

For linguistics it is important to note that these conditions of human communication, in which natural languages have developed for hundreds of millenia, have left some traces in the structure of language. The division of the elements of the stock of shared knowledge into activated and non-activated has been reflected inside the semantic structure of the sentence, in the form of the topic/focus articulation.

This is only one example of how the communicative function has influenced the structure of language. Another such example is the often quoted anthro-pomorphism of natural language (which is well equipped – in the lexicon as well as in grammar – to serve to human beings when speaking about themselves or others of their species as well as about their actions, properties etc.[7]). Chomsky (1975) denies the possibility of such an influence, claiming that innate ideas or biological factors are the only source underlying linguistic structure, but it may be assumed without any contradiction that linguistic structure is determined by innate properties in some aspects, others being conditioned functionally. If the known features of the human species are considered, it should be noted that Man belongs to those animals the com-petence of which is largely determined by other than innate factors.

Prague

NOTES

[1] This change manifests itself in the influence of context on the meaning of sentences, which was stated and illustrated from several viewpoints by Isard (1975), Kratzer and Stechow (1976), Klein (1976), Rossipal (1976) and others; also Lieb's (this volume) concept of referential base is of high importance in this respect.

[2] An informal discussion of this notion, and also a detailed characterization of our approach to the phenomena of topic (theme) and focus (rheme, comment) can be found in Sgall, Hajičová and Benešová (1973); now cf. also Sgall and Hajičová (1977), and most recently (with a completed formulation of the generative procedure for Czech and a contrastive study of focus in Czech and in English) Sgall, Hajičová and Buráňová (in press).

[3] Capital letters denote the intonation centre. It should be noted that most of the quoted sentences are ambiguous, i.e. correspond to more than one tectogrammatical representation (e.g. the verb may but need not belong to the focus), and our formulat-ions concern only one of these representations for each sentence.

[4] These are the two main types of 'thematic progressions' according to Daneš (1974); it is worth noting that this bipartition of speech act sequences has been recognized and named by Henri Weil, the French founder of topic and focus investigations, as early as in 1844 (cf. his 'marche parallèle' and 'progression', pp. 44 f. of his book).

[5] With an obvious simplification we consider the time of speech as being discrete, since only the time points of the subsequent utterances of a discourse are being considered here; thus $t+1$ denotes the time point of the utterance immediately following the utter-ance made at t. The further elaboration should also take into account that the set of units on which the relation A is defined should probably be specified in terms of linguistic meaning (tectogrammatics) rather than in those of Montague's framework.

[6] Cf. Lakoff (1972); but the methods of fuzzy set theory do not appear to meet all the conditions required for adequacy here: would the weight, or the surface area, or the surface as seen from outside (from the front of the building only?), or from the inside be

decisive for the assignment of numerical values to the 'degree' of truth of (16)? It is advisable to formulate a framework in which the 'degrees' of truth would depend on the means the given language has to denote them (*fully, partly, almost, to a high degree* have their meanings, and these clearly are related to the 'degrees' in a more intrinsic way than numbers can be).

[7] As for the anthropocentric character of syntax, see e.g. Skalička (1962); phenomena of a similar type from other domains of language are pointed out by Kuryłowicz (1976).

REFERENCES

Austin, J. L.: 1962, *How to Do Things with Words*, Oxford, The University Press.
Carnap, R.: 1947, *Meaning and Necessity*, Chicago, Phoenix Books (quoted from the third impression, 1960, of the enlarged edition from 1956).
Chomsky, N. A.: 1974, 'Questions of Form and Interpretation', in *Recherches linguistiques à Montréal* 8, 1–42.
Chomsky, N. A.: 1975, *Reflections on Language*, New York, Pantheon Books.
Daneš, F.: 1974, 'Functional Sentence Perspective and the Organization of the Text', in *Papers on Functional Sentence Perspective*, ed. by F. Daneš, Prague, Academia, pp. 106–128.
Isard, S.: 1975, 'Chnging the Context', in *Formal Semantics of Natural Language*, ed. by E. L. Keenan. Cambridge University Press, pp. 287–296.
Klein, W.: 1976, 'Einige wesentliche Eigenschaften natürlicher Sprachen und ihre Bedeutung für die linguistische Theorie', *Zeitschrift für Literaturwissenschaft und Linguistik (LiLi)* 6, 11–31.
Kratzer, A. and Arnim von Stechow: 1976, 'Äusserungssituation und Bedeutung,' *Zeitschrift für Literaturwissenschaft und Linguistik (LiLi)* 6, 98–130.
Kuno, S.: 1972, 'Functional Sentence Perspective', *Linguistic Inquiry* 3, 269–320.
Kuryłowicz, J.: 1976, 'Some Relations between Expression and Content', *Bulletin de la Société polonaise de linguistique* 34, 56–61.
Lakoff, G.: 1972, 'Hedges: A Study in Meaning Criteria and the Logic of Fuzzy Concepts', in *Papers from the 8th Regional Meeting* (ed. by P. M. Peranteau et al.), Chicago, pp. 183–228.
Montague, R.: 1970, 'Universal Grammar', *Theoria* 36, 373–398.
Montague, R. and H. Schnelle: 1972, *Universale Grammatik*, Braunschweig, Vieweg.
Rohrer, C.: 1971, *Funktionelle Sprachwissenschaft und transformationelle Grammatik*, München, W. Fink Verlag.
Rossipal, H.: 1976, 'Postulatsprache(n) und Kodesprache(n),' in Appendix to Papers from the Third Scandinavian Conference on Linguistics (ed. by F. Karlsson), Turku.
Searle, J. R.: 1969, *Speech Acts*, Cambridge University Press.
Sgall, P.: 1974, 'Focus and Contextual Boundness,' in *Topic and Comment, Contexual Boundness and Focus*, ed. by Ö. Dahl, Hamburg, H. Buske Verlag.
Sgall, P.: 1977, 'Sign Meaning, Cognitive Content and Pragmatics,' *Journal of Pragmatics* 1, 269–282.
Sgall, P. and E. Hajičová: 1977, 'Focus on Focus,' *Prague Bulletin of Mathematical Linguistics* 28, 5–54; 29 (1978), 23–41.
Sgall, P., E. Hajičová, and E. Benešová: 1973, *Topic, Focus and Generative Semantics*, Kronberg/Taunus, Scriptor Verlag.

246   PETR SGALL

Sgall, P., E. Hajičová, and E. Buráňová: in press, *Aktuální členění věty v češtině* (*Topic and Focus* in Czech), Prague, Academia.
Sgall, P., E. Hajičová, and O. Procházka: 1977, 'On the Role of Linguistic Semantics', *Theoretical Linguistics* 4, 32–59.
Skalička, V.: 1962, 'Das Wesen der Morphologie und der Syntax,' *Acta Universitatis Carolinae, Slavica Pragensia* 4, 123–127.
Tichý, P.: 1975, 'What Do We Talk About?' *Philosophy of Science* 42, 80–93.
Weil, H.: 1844, *De l'ordre des mots dans les langues anciennes comparées aux langues modernes*, Paris, Joubert.

DANIEL VANDERVEKEN

ILLOCUTIONARY LOGIC AND SELF-DEFEATING
SPEECH ACTS

Illocutionary logic is the branch of philosophical logic that is concerned with the study of the illocutionary acts (assertions, questions, requests, promises, orders, declarations . . .) that are performed by the utterance of sentences of natural or formal languages. The analytic philosophers (especially J. L. Austin and J. R. Searle) have shown the philosophical importance of a logical analysis of the forms of such speech acts. Illocutionary force is indeed one essential and irreducible component of the sense of a sentence of a natural language. One cannot understand the sense of a sentence without understanding that its literal utterance in a given context of use constitutes the performance of illocutionary acts of such and such forms. Thus for example, in order to understand the sense of the English sentence (1) "Are you going to the theater tonight?" one must not only understand that in a context of use where this sentence is uttered literally, the speaker expresses a proposition that is true in the world of utterance iff the hearer in that world goes to a theater the evening of the day of the utterance. One must also understand that this utterance in that context of use constitutes the asking of a question.

There are many different kinds of illocutionary force indicating devices in natural languages. By *an illocutionary force indicating device* I mean here any expression whose sense determines that a literal utterance of a sentence containing a certain occurrence of that expression has a given illocutionary force. The analytic philosophers have been mainly concerned until now with the illocutionary force indicating devices called performatives.

A performative is any verb X of a natural language which, when applied to a first person singular pronoun and a clause A of a certain form composes a sentence (hereafter called a performative sentence), whose utterance in an appropriate context of use constitutes the performance of an illocutionary act of the force named by that verb X, and whose propositional content is the proposition expressed by A in that context. Some examples of performative sentences are: (2) "I swear that he is the murderer", (3) "I promise that I shall come tomorrow", (4) "I order you to stay here", (5) "I apologize for what I have done". Mood, word-order, punctuation signs are other examples of illocutionary force indicating devices in the following sentences: (6) "Is he

247

J. R. Searle, F. Kiefer, and M. Bierwisch (eds.), Speech Act Theory and Pragmatics,
247–272.

coming?", (8) "Close the door!", (9) "It is raining". Certain expressions of natural languages generate complex performative sentences from simpler ones. I shall call hereafter such expressions *illocutionary connectives*. The illocutionary negator (Searle, 1969) is an illocutionary connective. It is a non-truthfunctional negator that, when applied to a performative sentence A, composes a new performative sentence whose literal utterance in a context of use constitutes the performance of an act such as declining to perform the illocutionary act expressed by A. Such acts are called *acts of illocutionary denegation*. Here are a few examples of performative sentences that are forms of expression for acts of illocutionary denegation: (10) "I do not assert that he is the murderer", (11) "I do not promise that I shall come tomorrow", (12) "I do not apologize for what I have done", (13) "I do not urge you to do this". The logical connective of conjunction is another illocutionary connective. The utterance of a sentence which is the conjunction of two performative sentences constitutes usually the simultaneous performance of the two illocutionary acts expressed by these performative sentences. Thus for example, a speaker who utters the sentence (14) "I apologize for what I have done and I promise you not to do it again" usually performs both an apology and a promise. The indicative conditional is a third case of illocutionary connective. When applied successively to a sentence A and a performative sentence B, it composes a complex performative sentence whose utterance in an appropriate context of use constitutes the performance of the illocutionary act expressed by B on the condition that A is true. Such speech acts are called *conditional illocutionary acts*. Some performative sentences that are forms of expressions for conditional illocutionary acts are: (15) "If it is raining, I bet that he will not come", (16) "If he comes, I promise to stay with you" (The conditional that is mentioned here is neither a conditional for material or strict implication nor a counterfactual conditional). The performative sentences composed by the application of illocutionary connectives are forms of expression for complex illocutionary acts that are function of the illocutionary acts expressed by the performative sentences that are taken as arguments. Some illocutionary connectives can compose forms of expression for complex illocutionary acts from other kinds of sentences than performative sentences. Thus for example, the non performative sentence (17) "If you do not want to take off your hat, leave this house!", expresses a conditional order.

The main tasks of illocutionary logic are:

(1) The definition of the notion of illocutionary force and the characterization of the necessary and sufficient conditions for the successful performance of an illocutionary act;

(2) the formalization of the different kinds of relationships that exist between illocutionary acts in the world of discourse and

(3) the construction of a formal classification of illocutionary forces.

The fundamental questions that should be asked in order to achieve these tasks are respectively:

(1) What are the primitive notions that are needed for a theory of illocutionary acts and which definitions and postulates govern these notions?

(2) What is the nature of the relation of illocutionary commitment? The successful performance of an illocutionary act usually commits the speaker to other illocutionary acts. For example, a speaker who denies that it is raining is committed to asserting that it is not raining. A speaker who orders a hearer to stay and to do something is committed to granting him permission to stay. Hence the question: Given that a speaker in a certain context of use of a natural language performs successfully certain illocutionary acts of such and such forms, what other illocutions does the performance of these acts commit him to?

(3) What are the criteria of classification of illocutionary forces and how can these criteria be represented formally? Is the set of all illocutionary forces definable recursively from a few primitive illocutionary forces and if yes how?

Certain illocutionary acts have contradictory conditions of success. Such acts are called hereafter *self-defeating illocutionary acts*. Thus, for example, an assertion of the form (18) "I assert that I do not make any assertion", a promise of the form (19) "I promist not to keep this promise" and a complex order of the form (20) "I order and prohibit your doing this" are self-defeating illocutionary acts. It is not possible to perform them with success in a context of use. One can say in a certain sense that the machine of language slips out of gear when such acts are performed. Certain (but not all) self-defeating illocutionary acts are paradoxical. Thus, for example, the self-defeating assertion (21) "I assert that all assertions are false", as well as the self-defeating order: (22) "I order you to disobey all orders" are paradoxical illocutionary acts. Performative sentences that are forms of expression for self-defeating illocutionary acts will be called hereafter *illocutionary inconsistent performative sentences*. Here are a few other examples of illocutionary inconsistent performatives sentences: (23) "I assert that it is raining and that I do not believe that it is raining" (This is the Moore paradox.); (24) "I assert that this assertion is false" (This is the liar's paradox.); (25) "I promise you to do this and I inform you that I am absolutely unable to do it"; (26) "I both complain and thank you for coming here."

Any adequate theory of speech-acts must give an account of why certain illocutionary acts are self-defeating. We shall attempt in this paper to specify the primitive notions from which the conditions of successful performance of an illocutionary act can be defined and we shall classify with the help of these notions the different kinds of self-defeating illocutionary acts that exist in the world of discourse. At the same time, we shall indicate an answer to some of the questions raised above.

1. BASIC NOTIONS OF ILLOCUTIONARY LOGIC

Most[1] elementary illocutionary acts are of the form F(P) where F is an illocutionary force and P is a proposition. Thus, for example, the speech act performed by a (literal) utterance of a sentence of the form (27) "I assert that snow is white" is an illocutionary act whose illocutionary force is the illocutionary force of assertion and whose propositional content is the proposition that snow is white. The speech act performed by an utterance of a sentence of the form (3) "I promise that I shall come tomorrow" is an illocutionary act whose illocutionary force is the illocutionary force of promise and whose propositional content is the proposition that the speaker will come to a certain place the day after the day of the utterance. Illocutionary acts of different illocutionary forces may have in common the same propositional content. Thus for example a question of the form (28) "Is the continuum hypothesis independent?" and its answer (29) "Yes, it is independent" are two illocutionary acts of different illocutionary forces with the same propositional content. On the other hand, illocutionary acts of the same illocutionary force may have different propositional contents. An assertion of Gödel's theorem and an assertion of Fermat's theorem are two illocutionary acts of the same assertive illocutionary force with different propositional contents. The nature of an illocutionary act of form F(P) is entirely determined once the nature of both its illocutionary force F and its propositional content P has been determined. In an elementary performative sentence, the main performative is the illocutionary force indicating device and the clause that it takes as argument expresses the propositional content of the illocutionary act. One consequence of this definition of the nature of elementary illocutionary acts is that we shall have to define adequately in illocutionary logic a set Φ representing the set of all illocutionary forces of illocutionary acts that can be performed in the world of discourse of a natural language and a set Prop representing the set of all propositions. Each illocutionary force indicating device X names an illocutionary force F belonging to Φ that will be written from now on ||X||. Illocutionary acts are speech acts performed by utterances of expressions of a language in a context of use of that language. In this context of use, a speaker speaks to a hearer at a certain time and place of a certain world that we shall call the *world of the utterance*. The act by which the speaker emits the graphic or phonetic signs of the uttered expression is called the *utterance act*. The act by which he expresses the proposition that is the propositional content of the performed illocutionary act is called the *propositional act*. (Searle, 1969) Thus for example, when a speaker promises to come by uttering the sentence (30) "I shall come", the utterance act is the act by which he produces the phonems of (30) and the propositional act is the act by which he expresses the proposition that he will come somewhere after the time of the utterance. Different illocutionary acts may be performed by the utterance of the same sentence in different contexts of use. Consider for example two utterances, at different times, of the sentence (31) "I shall come back in five minutes". In one context the utterance it may be an assertion; in another context it may be a promise. Each time, the propositional content of the performed act varies, for the proposition that is expressed is the proposition that the speaker will come back five minutes after the time of the utterance. One consequence of this context-dependent nature of the illocutionary acts that are performed by the utterance of a sentence is that we shall also have to define in illocutionary logic a set I representing the set of all possible contexts of use for a natural language. For each context of use $i \in I$, we shall have to specify who is the speaker a_i, the hearer b_i, what are the moment of time t_i, the place p_i and the world of the utterance w_i constitutive of this context. If the possible context of use $j \in I$ differs at most from i by the fact that $w_j = w \neq w_i$, we shall write $j = i[w/w_i]$. Moreover we shall also need a function ψ from I into $\mathscr{P}(\text{Prop})$ giving as value, for each context of use $i \in I$, the set $\psi(i)$ of all propositions that are expressed by a_i in this context. Thus $\psi(i) = \emptyset$ iff no propositional act is performed in i. The reason why the definition of a possible context of use for a natural language requires a reference to the world of the utterance in addition to a reference to the speaker, hearer, moment of time and place of utterance is the following: In the world of the utterance, the speaker, the hearer and the objects to which they refer have certain properties that are relevant for determining exactly what is the illocutionary force of the utterance. Thus, for example, an utterance by a speaker of the sentence (32) "Please, do this!" may be an indirect order in one world of the utterance (if the speaker is in a position of authority over the hearer in that world and directs the hearer by invoking that position) and in another world of the utterance (where the speaker is not in that position) it may merely be a request.

252   DANIEL VANDERVEKEN

Each proposition P ϵ Prop divides the set W of possible worlds of illocutionary logic into two distinct subsets: the set of possible worlds in which it is true and the set of possible worlds in which it is false. If w ϵ W, we shall write hereafter $P(w)=1$ (=0) as an abbreviation for P is true (is false) in the world w. The set $2=\{1,0\}$ will thus represent in our symbolism the set of truth-values. The set Prop of propositions of illocutionary logic is closed under different operations that generate complex propositions: Thus, if P and Q ϵ Prop, $\sim$P, $\square$P and (P→Q) are new propositions that belong also to Prop. $\sim$P is that function of P such that $\sim P(w)=1$ iff $P(w)=0$; $\square P(w)=1$ iff, for all w' ϵ W, $P(w')=1$; (P→Q) is that function of P and Q such that $P{\rightarrow}Q(w)=1$ iff $P(w)=0$ or $Q(w)=1$. (P$\prec$Q) is often used as an abbreviation for $\square$(P→Q). $\sim$, →, $\square$ and $\prec$ are respectively the operations of truth-functional negation, material implication, universal necessity and strict implication.

A third criterion of material adequacy for illocutionary logic is the necessity of distinguishing clearly between a successful and an unsuccessful performance of an illocutionary act. As any adequate talk of propositions involves the pair of concepts of truth and falsity for characterising truth-values, any adequate talk of speech acts (and of acts in general) involves the pair of concepts of success and failure for characterising the value of the performance. Some illocutionary acts are performed with success in certain contexts of use and with failure in other contexts. A declaration of excommunication for example is successful in a context of use where the speaker has the institutional power of excommunicating by his utterance; it is unsuccessful in all other contexts of use. (The pope can probably succeed in excommunicating me, but I cannot excommunicate him with success.) A self-defeating illocutionary act is a speech act whose performance is always a failure. The successful performances are the paradigmatic illocutionary performances. We shall define hereafter the notion of an illocutionary force and the conditions for a successful performance of an illocutionary act from a series of primitive notions which are the notions of illocutionary point, mode of achievement of an illocutionary point, degree of strength, propositional content conditions, preparatory conditions and sincerity conditions of an illocutionary act. (The ideas formulated hereafter will be developed in a more elaborate way in the forthcoming book *Foundations of Illocutionary Logic* which I am writing with John Searle.)

(a) *The notions of illocutionary point, mode of achievement of an illocutionary point and degree of strength*

The main component of illocutionary force is the illocutionary point. Each illocutionary force has an illocutionary point. The *illocutionary point* (Searle, 1975) of an illocutionary force is what the speaker conventionally intends to do when he performs that illocutionary act of that force. Thus, for example, the illocutionary point of an assertion is to represent a certain state of affairs as actual in the world of the utterance. A speaker who asserts a proposition P in a context of use intends to be committed to the truth of P in the world of the utterance. The illocutionary point of an apology is to express to the hearer a regret or sorrow for a state of affairs. The illocutionary point of a promise is to commit the speaker to carry out a certain future course of action in the world of the utterance. The illocutionary point of an illocutionary force F can be represented in illocutionary logic by defining a relation Π_F between possible contexts of use and propositions. For each context of use $i \in I$ and proposition $P \in Prop$ i is in the relation Π_F with respect to P (symbolically $i\Pi_F P$) iff the speaker a_i succeeds in achieving in the context of use i the illocutionary point of illocutionary force F on propositional content P.

Different illocutionary forces may have in common the same illocutionary point. Thus for example, both requesting, entreating, ordering, begging and urging a hearer to carry out a future course of action have the illocutionary point of being attempts by the speaker to get him to carry out that action. Both swearing, asserting, informing, testifying and conjecturing a proposition P representing a certain state of affairs have the same illocutionary point of representing as actual that state of affairs in the world of the utterance. The illocutionary point is therefore only one component among others of illocutionary force although it is unquestionably the most important one.

Certain illocutionary forces require a special mode of achievement of their illocutionary point. For example a testimony requires that one represents as actual a state of affairs by invoking one's position as a witness. A speaker who simply asserts need not invoke this position. An order is an attempt that a speaker makes to get the hearer to do something by invoking his position of authority or power over him. This is not the case for a request. We shall call the mode with which the illocutionary point of an illocution of force F is to be achieved in case of a successful performance of that illocution *the characteristic mode of achievement of the illocutionary point of F.* The characteristic mode of achievement of the illocutionary point of an illocutionary point of F(P) to some particular ones. It can be represented in illocutionary logic by a function mode (F) from IxProp into truth-values that satisfies the following clause: mode $(F)\langle i,P \rangle = 1$ iff the speaker a_i in the context of use i achieves the illocutionary point of F on P with the characteristic mode of achievement of F. Thus by definition, mode $(F)\langle i,P\rangle=1$ only if $i\Pi_F P$. In case $\{\langle i,P\rangle/\text{mode } (F)\langle i,P\rangle=1\}=\{\langle i,P\rangle/i\Pi_F P\}$, the illocutionary force F is said to have no particular mode of achievment of its illocutionary point.

Certain illocutionary points may be achieved with different degrees of strength, for example a speaker who entreats a hearer to do something makes a stronger attempt than a speaker who simply requests. A speaker who asserts a proposition P commits himself more to the truth of P than a speaker who simply conjectures P. We shall call the degree of strength with which the illocutionary point of an illocutionary act of force F is achieved in case of a successful performance of that act, *the characteristic degree of strength* of F. Illocutionary forces with the same illocutionary point may differ with respect to their degree of strength. The characteristic degree of strength of illocutionary point, degree (F), of an illocutionary force F can be represented by an integer $k \in Z$ or by the empty set $\emptyset$. Thus degree $(F) \in Z \cup \{\emptyset\}$, degree (F) is an integer $k \in Z$ when the illocutionary point Π_F can be achieved with different degrees of strength. Otherwise, degree$(F)=\emptyset$. Certain illocutionary points (for example the illocutionary point of a declaration which is to bring about a state of affairs in the world by the utterance act) cannot be achieved with different degrees of strength. By definition, for two illocutionary forces F_1, $F_2 \in \Phi$ with the same illocutionary point $\Pi_{F_1}=\Pi_{F_2}=\Pi_F$ if degree (F_1) and degree $(F_2) \in Z$, degree $(F_1) <$ degree (F_2) iff the degree of strength with which illocutionary point Π_F is achieved in case of a successful performance of an act of form F(P) is inferior to the degree of strength with which it is achieved in case of a successful performance of an act of form $F_2(P)$. If degree $(F) \in Z$, the set $\Pi_{FP}=\{i \in I/i\Pi_F P\}$ of all possible contexts of use in which the illocutionary point of an illocutionary act F(P) is achieved may be indexed by the set Z. For each integer $k \in Z$, $\Pi_{FP}(k)$ represents the set of all possible contexts of use $i \in I$ where the illocutionary point of F(P) is achieved with degree of strength k. Thus, by definition, $\Pi_{FP}(k) \subset \Pi_{FP}$, and $i\epsilon\Pi_{FP}$ (degree(F)) iff the speaker a_i succeeds in the context of use i in achieving the illocutionary point of F(P) with the characteristic degree of strength of F. The first condition for the successful performance of an illocutionary act of force F may now be defined as follows: a speaker a_i succeeds in performing in a context of use i of a language L an illocution of form F(P) only if he succeeds in achieving in that context the illocutionary point of F(P) with the characteristic mode of achievement and degree of strength of F.

Abbreviation. We shall often write hereafter $i\amalg_F*P$ as an abbreviation for $i\amalg_F P$, mode $(F)\langle i,P\rangle=1$ and $i\in\amalg_F P(\text{degree }(F))$.

(b) *Propositional content conditions*

Certain illocutionary forces F impose conditions on the form of propositions that can be taken as propositional contents of an illocutionary act of force F. For example, the propositional content of a prediction must be a future proposition with respect to the time of the utterance. The propositional content of a promise made in a context of use i must be a proposition that represents a future course of action of the speaker a_i. The illocutionary forces of assertion and of declaration on the other hand have no propositional content conditions. The second condition for the successful performance of an illocutionary act of form $F(P)$ in a context of use i is that the speaker expresses the proposition P that is the propositional content of this act and that this proposition P satisfies the propositional content conditions of F with respect to the context i. The propositional content conditions of an illocutionary force F can be represented formally by a function Prop_F from I into $\mathscr{P}(\text{Prop})$ that gives as value, for each possible context of use $i \in$ I, the set $\text{Prop}_F(i)$ of all propositions that satisfy the propositional content conditions of F with respect to i. Thus, for example, $\text{Prop}_{\|\text{request}\|}(i)=\text{Prop}_{\|\text{order}\|}(i)=\{P \in \text{Prop}/P$ represents a future course of action of b_i with respect to the moment of time $t_i\}$. $\text{Prop}_{\|\text{assert}\|}(i)=\text{Prop}$.

(c) *Preparatory conditions*

Each illocutionary act has preparatory conditions. *A preparatory condition* for the performance of an illocutionary act in a context of use is a state of affairs that the speaker presupposes to be actual in the world of the utterance when he performs this act in that context. Thus, for example, a preparatory condition for a promise is that the speaker is capable of keeping that promise. Any speaker who promises to do something in a context of use presupposes indeed that he is capable of doing it. A preparatory condition of an assertion is that the speaker has reasons for the truth of the propositional content in the world of the utterance. A preparatory condition of a request is that the hearer is capable of satisfying it. The preparatory conditions of an illocutionary act of force F can be represented by defining a relation Σ_F between possible contexts of use and propositions to be interpreted as follows: $i\Sigma_F P$ iff all preparatory conditions for the performance of the illocutionary act $F(P)$ in the context i are actualised at time t_i in the world w_i.[2] The preparatory conditions that the speaker presuppose need not be actualised in the

world of the utterance in order that his illocutionary performance be successful. Thus, for example, a speaker may succeed in promising to do something
that he is not capable of doing. (He promises to speak to someone who just
died two days ago.) A speaker may succeed in asserting a proposition without
having any reasons for the truth of that proposition. (The history of answers
to exam questions is full of such assertions.) Nevertheless, even if this is the
case, the fact that the speaker presupposes that the preparatory conditions
obtain is internal to the performance of the illocutionary act. This is shown
clearly by the fact that it is paradoxical to perform an illocutionary act and
to deny simultaneously one of its preparatory conditions. Consider, for example, a speech act of form (24). A third condition for the successful performance of an illocutionary act is thus that the speaker *presupposes* that all
preparatory conditions of that illocutionary act obtain in the world of the
utterance. A successful illocution whose preparatory conditions do not hold
in the world of the utterance is called a *defective* illocution. Every non-
defective speech act is successful but not every successful speech act is non-
defective. The preparatory conditions of an illocutionary act are expressible
i.e., for each illocutionary act F(P) and possible context of use $i \in I$, there is a
smallest set of propositions $\sigma(FP,i) \subset$ Prop which are simultaneously true in a
world w iff $i[w/w_i]$ Σ_FP. A speaker who performs F(P) in a context of use
$i \in I$ presupposes that each proposition $Q \in \sigma(FP,i)$ is true in the world of
utterance w_i. In order to determine which presuppositions are made in a context of use, there is a function Σup from I into $\mathscr{P}$(Prop) that gives as value
for each context $i \in I$, the set Σup(i) of all propositions that are presupposed
to be true in the context i. There is often a logical relation between the mode
of achievement of the illocutionary point of an illocution and its preparatory
conditions. A speaker who succeeds in achieving the illocutionary point of
an illocutionary act in a particular mode presupposes that he has the position
that he invokes in that mode. For example, someone who testifies P presupposes that he has been a witness of the state of affairs represented by P.

(d) *The sincerity conditions*

By performing an illocutionary act a speaker usually expresses also a certain
psychological state relating to the propositional content.[3] This psychological
state is a function of the nature of the illocutionary force. Thus, for example,
a speaker who promises to do something expresses his intention to do it. A
speaker who orders expresses his desire that the hearer carries out a certain
future action. A speaker who asserts a proposition expresses his belief in the
truth of that proposition. The speaker is *sincere* if he has the psychological

state that he expresses. Although the speaker need not be sincere in order that his illocutionary performance be successful (a lie may be a successful assertion) a condition for the successful performance of an illocutionary act is that the speaker *expresses* the psychological state that corresponds to it. The fact that the expression of the psychological state is internal to the performance of the act explains why it is paradoxal for a speaker who performs an illocutionary act to deny simultaneously that he has the corresponding psychological state. Consider for example the Moore paradox (22). The sincerity conditions of illocutionary acts of force F are represented by a relation Ψ_F between possible contexts of use and propositions. For each context $i \in I$ and each proposition P, $i\Psi_F P$ iff the speaker a_i in context i has the psychological state corresponding to F(P). Thus, for example $i\Psi_{||assert||}P$ iff a_i in i believes that P. As the preparatory conditions, the sincerity conditions are expressible; for each context of use $i \in I$ and for each illocutionary act F(P), there exists a proposition that we shall write hereafter $\psi_{Fa_i}P$ that is true in a world w iff $i[w/w_i]\Psi_F P$. A speaker who performs F(P) in a context of use i expresses the psychological state represented by that proposition. One determines in illocutionary logic which psychological states are expressed in which contexts by defining a function Ψup from I into $\mathscr{P}$(Prop) that gives as value, for each context $i \in I$, the set Ψup(i) of all propositions representing psychological states that the speaker a_i expresses in the context i. The psychological states expressed in the performance of an illocutionary act may be more or less strong depending on the illocutionary force. For example, a speaker who supplicates expresses a stronger desire than a speaker who simply requests. We shall call the degree of strength with which the psychological state is expressed within the performance of an illocutionary act of force F, *the characteristic degree of strength of the psychological state* of F. As the degree of strength of the illocutionary point, the degree of strength of the psychological state $\eta(F)$ of an illocutionary force F can be represented by an integer k or by the empty set. Usually, $\eta(F)$=degree(F) i.e., the characteristic degree of strength with which the psychological state of an illocution of force F is expressed is identical with the degree of strength with which its illocutionary point is achieved. Thus, for example, the degree of strength of the belief expressed within the performance of an assertion is identical with the degree of commitment to truth of that assertion. But there are exceptions to this i.e., there are cases where degree(F) > $\eta(F)$. For example, a speaker who orders achieves the directive illocutionary point with a greater degree of strength than a speaker who simply requests, but he does not express a stronger desire or want. What increases the degree of strength of the illocutionary point here is the mode of achievement of orders. The sets $\Psi\mathrm{up}(i)$ are indexed by Z. For each $k \in Z, \Psi\mathrm{up}(i)\langle k \rangle$ is the set of all propositions that represent psychological states that are expressed with degree of strength k in the context i. The functions $\Sigma\mathrm{up}$ and $\Psi\mathrm{up}$ are not independent. Many psychological states are indeed such that it is not possible for a speaker to express them without presupposing the existence of certain state of affairs. For example, a speaker who expresses dissatisfaction for a state of affairs presupposes that this state of affairs is bad. A speaker who expresses gratitude for a past action presupposes that this action was good for him. Thus, it is often the case that if a certain propositions P belong to $\Psi\mathrm{up}(i)$, other propositions Q belong to $\Sigma\mathrm{up}(i)$.

Just as the performance of an illocutionary act can commit the speaker to an illocutionary act that he does not perform explicitly, so the expression of a psychological state can commit him to having a psychological state that he does not express. The set of all psychological states to which the speaker is committed in each context of use is represented by a function $\Psi\hat{\mathrm{u}}\mathrm{p}$ from I into $\mathscr{P}(\mathrm{Prop})$. For each $i \in \mathrm{I}, \Psi_{\mathrm{F}}a_i\mathrm{P} \in \Psi\hat{\mathrm{u}}\mathrm{p}(i)$ iff a_i is committed in i to having the psychological state expressed in the performance of F(P). By definition, $\Psi\mathrm{up}(i) \subset \Psi\hat{\mathrm{u}}\mathrm{p}(i)$. The speaker is committed to having the psychological states that he expresses. Since one can be committed to having a psychological state with different degrees of strength, the sets $\Psi\hat{\mathrm{u}}\mathrm{p}(i)$ like the sets $\Psi\mathrm{up}(i)$ are indexed by Z. There is a distribution of $\Psi\hat{\mathrm{u}}\mathrm{p}$ with respect to &. P_1 and $\mathrm{P}_2 \in \Psi\hat{\mathrm{u}}\mathrm{p}(i)$ iff $\mathrm{P}_1 \& \mathrm{P}_2 \in \Psi\hat{\mathrm{u}}\mathrm{p}(i)$.

Definition of the notion of an illocutionary force

The six notions of illocutionary point, mode of achievement of an illocutionary point, degree of strength, propositional content conditions, preparatory conditions and sincerity conditions permit us to define the notion of illocutionary force. An illocutionary force $\mathrm{F} \in \Phi$ is indeed entirely defined once one has specified (1) its illocutionary point, Π_{F}; (2) its characteristic mode of achievement of that illocutionary point, mode (F); (3) its characteristic degree of strength of illocutionary point, degree (F); (4) its propositional content conditions $\mathrm{Prop}_{\mathrm{F}}$; (5) its preparatory conditions, Σ_{F}; (6) its sincerity conditions, Ψ_{F} and (7) its characteristic degree of psychological state $\eta(\mathrm{F})$. Two illocutionary forces are identical when their illocutionary points, modes of achievement of that illocutionary point, degrees of strength, propositional content conditions, preparatory conditions and sincerity conditions are respectively identical. Thus each illocutionary force F is a septuple of the from $\langle \Pi_{\mathrm{F}}, \mathrm{mode}(\mathrm{F}), \mathrm{degree}(\mathrm{F}), \mathrm{Prop}_{\mathrm{F}}, \Sigma_{\mathrm{F}}, \Psi_{\mathrm{F}}, \eta(\mathrm{F}) \rangle$, where $\Pi_{\mathrm{F}}, \Sigma_{\mathrm{F}}$ and Ψ_{F} are three relations on IxProp, mode(F) is a function from IxProp into 2,

Prop$_F$ is a function from I into $\mathscr{P}$(Prop) and degree (F) and η(F) belong to ZU$\{\emptyset\}$. As a consequence of this, the set Φ that represents in illocutionary logic the set of all illocutionary forces is a subset of the set (IxProp)x2 (IxProp)xZU$\{\emptyset\}$$x$(I$x$Prop)$x$(I$x$Prop)$x$(ZU$\{\emptyset\}$)) Here are a few examples of illocutionary forces that differ from the illocutionary force of assertion under (at least) one of their six constitutive aspects. The illocutionary force of an act of testifying differs from the illocutionary force of assertion by the fact that the speaker who testifies acts in his status as a witness when he represents a state of affairs as actual. (This is a particular mode of achievement of the assertive illocutionary point.) The illocutionary force of a conjecture differs from the illocutionary force of assertion by the fact that a speaker who conjectures the truth of a proposition P commits himself with a smaller degree of strength of commitment to the truth of that proposition. The illocutionary force of prediction differs at most from assertion by the fact that it has a particular condition on the propositional content namely that it is a future proposition with respect to the time of utterance. The illocutionary force of reminding differs at most from assertion by the fact that it has the additional preparatory condition that the hearer once knew and might have forgotten the truth of the propositional content. Finally the illocutionary force of complaining differs at most from assertion by the fact that it has the additional sincerity condition that the speaker is dissatisfied with the state of affairs represented by the propositional content.[4]

Definition of a successful performance of an illocutionary act

We shall say that *a speaker succeeds in performing an illocutionary act F(P) in a context of use i* of a language [symbolically: F(P) is $\Omega(i)$] iff the different necessary conditions which relate to the illocutionary point, the mode of achievement of the illocutionary point, the degrees of strength, the propositional content conditions, the preparatory conditions and the sincerity conditions of that act are satisfied, i.e., iff:

(1) the speaker a_i succeeds in achieving in the context i the illocutionary point of illocutionary force F on proposition P with the characteristic mode of achievement and degree of strength of F;

(2) he expresses in that context the proposition P and P satisfies the propositional content conditions of an act of force F with respect to i;

(3) he presupposes that the preparatory conditions for the performance of F(P) in i are actualised in the world of utterance w_i and finally

(4) he expresses with the required degree of strength η(F) the psychological state corresponding to the sincerity conditions of F(P).

Thus, F(P) is $\Omega(i)$ iff $i\Pi_F^*P$; $P \in \varphi(i) \cap \text{Prop}_F(i)$; $\sigma(FP,i) \subset \Sigma\text{up}(i)$ and $\psi_{Fa_i}P \in \Psi\text{up}(i) \langle\eta(F)\rangle$. For example, a speaker succeeds in asserting a proposition P representing a certain state of affairs in a context of use iff (1) he represents that state of affairs as actual in the world of the utterance (his degree of strength of commitment to the truth of P being the degree of strength of an assertion); (2) he performs the propositional act which consists in expressing P; (3) he presupposes that he has reasons for the truth of P and (4) he expresses his belief in P with a medium degree of strength. He succeeds in predicting P if in addition to this P is a future proposition with respect to the time of utterance. He succeeds in testifying P if in addition to (1). . . . , (4) he acts in his status as a witness when he represents the state of affairs as actual (his degree of strength of commitment to truth being greater than the degree of strength of assertion).

Definition of a non-defective performance

An illocutionary act F(P) is non-defectively performed in a context of use i[symbolically: F(P) is $\mathfrak{N}(i)$] when it is successful and all its preparatory conditions hold. Thus, F(P) is $\mathfrak{N}(i)$ iff both F(P) is $\Omega(i)$ and $i\Sigma_FP$.

Notation for a complex illocutionary act

A speaker who succeeds in performing simultaneously several illocutionary acts $F_1(P_1)$, . . . , $F_n(P_n)$ performs a complex illocutionary act that we shall represent by the notation: $F_1(P_1)x \ldots xF_n(P_n)$.

Definition of the relation of commitment between illocutionary acts

We shall say that *illocutionary acts* $F_1(P_1)$, . . . , $F_n(P_n)$ *commit the speaker to illocutionary act* F(P) [symbolically $F_1(P_1)$, . . . , $F_n(P_n)$ ▷ F(P)] iff in all possible contexts of use i where a speaker a_i succeeds in performing simultaneously illocutionary acts $F_1(P_1)$, . . . , $F_n(P_n)$, (1) he achieves the illocutionary point of F on proposition P with the characteristic mode of achievement and degree of strength of F, (2) he presupposes that the preparatory conditions of F(P) obtain (3) he commits himself to having with the required degree of strength the psychological state of F(P) and (4) proposition P satisfies the propositional content conditions of F with respect to i. Thus $F_1(P_1)$, . . . , $F_n(P_n)$ ▷ F(P) iff, for all $i \in I$, if $F_1(P_1)$ and . . . and $F_n(P_n)$ are $\Omega(i)$ then $i\Pi_F^*P$, $P \in \text{Prop}_F(i)$, $\sigma(FP,i) \subset \Sigma\text{up}(i)$ and $\psi_{Fa_i}P \in \Psi\hat{u}\text{p}(i) \langle\eta(F)\rangle$.

An important consequence of this definition of the relation of commitment between illocutionary acts is the following: it accounts for the fact that if F is an illocutionary force that differs at most from another illocutionary force F_2 by the fact that it has a more restricted mode of achievement of

SELF-DEFEATING SPEECH ACTS 261

illocutionary point, an additional propositional content conditions, an additional preparatory condition or an additional sincerity condition then all successful performances of an illocutionary act of form $F_1(P)$ commit the speaker to illocutionary act $F_2(P)$.

Thus, for example to testify that P commits the speaker to asserting P for a speaker who testifies P simply achieves the illocutionary point of an assertion that P (commits himself to the truth of the propositional content) while acting in his status as a witness. Similarly, a prediction or a report that P commit the speaker to asserting P for these illocutionary forces have simply more propositional content conditions than assertion. Predictions are assertions about the future, reports are assertions about the present or the past. To remind a hearer that it is true that P commits the speaker to asserting P for the illocutionary force of an act of reminding has simply more preparatory condition than assertion. To remind is to assert while presupposing that the hearer once knew and might have forgotten the truth of the propositional content. Finally, a complaint about P commits the speaker to an assertion that P, for to complain is simply to assert while expressing one's dissatisfaction with the existence of the state of affairs represented by the propositional content.

We shall often write $F_1(P), \ldots, F_n(P_n) \rhd F_1'(P_1'), \ldots, F_k'(P_k')$ as an abbreviation for: for all m such that $1 \leqslant m \leqslant k$, $F_1(P), \ldots, F_n(P) \rhd F_m'(P_m')$. In case it is the case both that $F_1(P_1), \ldots, F_n(P_n) \rhd F_1'(P_1'), \ldots, F_m'(P_m')$, and that $F_1'(P_1'), \ldots, F_m'(P_m'), \rhd F_1(P_1), \ldots, F_n(P_n)$, we shall write: $F_1(P_1), \ldots, F_n(P_n) \simeq F_1'(P_1'), \ldots, F_k'(P_k')$. The relation $\simeq$ is called the relation of *illocutionary congruence* between sequences of illocutionary acts.

Definition of a successful illocutionary commitment

A speaker has *a successful illocutionary commitment to an illocutionary act* $F(P)$ in a context of use i [symbolically: $F(P)$ is $\Omega(i)$] iff he performs with success in this context illocutionary acts which commit him to $F(P)$. Thus, $F(P)$ is $\Omega(i)$ iff for some $n \geqslant 1$, $F_1(P_1)$ and ... and $F_n(P_n)$ are $\Omega(i)$ and $F_1(P_1), \ldots, F_n(P_n) \rhd F(P)$.

A speaker may have a successful illocutionary commitment to an illocutionary act without expressing its propositional content or its psychological state. A speaker who asserts that all philosophers waste their time and that he is a philosopher is certainly committed to asserting that he wastes his time even if he does not express that proposition.

Illocutionary incompatibility and self-defeating illocutionary acts

Two illocutionary acts $F_1(P_1)$, $F_2(P_2)$ are *relatively incompatible* when it is not possible for a speaker to have a successful illocutionary commitment to both in a context of use. Symbolically: $F_1(P_1) \asymp F_2(P_2)$. Thus, by definition, $F_1(P_1) \asymp F_2(P_2)$ iff, for all $i \in I$, if $F_1(P_1)$ is $\underline{\Omega}(i)$ then it is not the case that $F_2(P_2)$ is $\underline{\Omega}(i)$. For example, an illocutionary act F(P) and its illocutionary denegation $\neg$ F(P) are relatively incompatible for the illocutionary points of these acts are relatively inconsistent. The illocutionary point of an act of illocutionary denegation of form $\neg$ F(P) is indeed to put the speaker in a position of explicit non-commitment to F(P).

The preceding definitions lead to the following definition of the nature of a self-defeating illocutionary act.: an illocutionary act is *self-defeating* iff it is relatively incompatible with itself i.e., if it is not possible for a speaker to be successfully committed to it in a context of use. Thus F(P) is self-defeating [symbolically $\rangle F(P)\langle$] when, for no $i \in I$, F(P) is $\underline{\Omega}(i)$. A complex illocutionary act $F_1(P_1)x \ldots xF_n(P_n)$ is self-defeating symbolically: $\rangle F_1(P_1)x \ldots xF_n(P_n)\langle$ when it is not possible for a speaker to have simultaneously a successful illocutionary commitment to all $F_k(P_k)$, $i \leq k \leq n$.

The formulation of the definitions and postulates governing the sets I, Φ and Prop, the relations Π_F, Σ_F, ψ_F, and the functions η, degree, Prop_F, $\Sigma\mathrm{up}$ and $\psi\mathrm{up}$ is the main task of illocutionary logic. The achievement of this task requires a complete characterisation of the formal properties of the relation $\rhd$ of illocutionary commitment between illocutionary acts. We shall now mention a few important clauses (postulates, theorems, definitions) governing this relation. Some of these clauses are necessary for characterising the nature of the self defeating illocutionary acts.

I. *Reflexivity of* $\rhd$

By definition, $F_1(P_1), \ldots, F_n(P_n) > F_k(P_k)$ for any k such that $1 \leq k \leq n$.

II. *Transitivity of* $\rhd$

If $F_1(P_1), \ldots, F_n(P_n) \rhd F_1'(P_1'), \ldots, F_k'(P_k')$ and $F_1'(P_1'), \ldots, F_k'(P_k') \rhd F_1''(P_1''), \ldots, F_m''(P_m'')$ then $F_1(P_1), \ldots, F_n(P_n) \rhd F_1''(P_1''), \ldots, F_m''(P_m'')$.

III. *The law of identity of illocutionary forces*

For all F_1, $F_2 \in \Phi$, $F_1 = F_2$ iff, for all propositions $P \in \mathrm{Prop}$, $F_1(P_1) \simeq F_2(P_2)$.

Two illocutionary forces F_1, F_2 are identical when all pairs of illocutionary acts of form $F_1(P)$, $F_2(P)$ are illocutionary congruent (i.e., involve exactly the same illocutionary commitments).

IV. *Propositional identity*

For all $P_1, P_2 \in Prop, P_1 = P_2$ iff, for all $F \in \Phi, F(P_1) \simeq F(P_2)$.
Two propositions P_1, P_2 are identical when for all illocutionary force F, it is the case that illocutionary acts $F(P_1), F(P_2)$ are illocutionarily congruent. (This postulate states a precise relation between sense and use.) Note that since there are necessarily equivalent propositions P_1, P_2 (propositions such that, for all $w \in W, P_1(w) = P_2(w)$) for which it is the case that for some illocutionary forces F, $F(P_1) \not\triangleright F(P_2)$), identity of truth values across possible worlds is not a criterion of propositional identity in illocutionary logic.

Definition of a strong illocutionary act

We shall say that the successful performance of illocutionary acts $F_1(P_1), \ldots,$ $F_n(P_n)$ in a context of use i constitutes the performance of a *strong speech act* in that context [symbolically: $F_1(P_1)x \ldots x F_n(P_n) \triangleright$] when these illocutionary acts commit the speaker to all illocutionary acts to which he is successfully committed in that context. Thus, $F_1(P_1)x \ldots x F_n(P_n) \triangleright$ iff $F_1(P_1)$ and $F_n(P_n)$ are $\Omega(i)$ and, for all $F \in \Phi$ and $P \in Prop$, if $F(P)$ is $\underline{\Omega}(i)$ then $F_1(P_1), \ldots, F_n(P_n) \triangleright F(P)$.

V. *The axiom of foundation*

If $F(P)$ is $\underline{\Omega}(i)$ then for some positive integer n, $F_1(P_1)x \ldots x F_n(P_n) \triangleright$ and for all k such that $F'_1(P'_1), \ldots, F'_k(P'_k) \triangleright, F_1(P_1), \ldots, F_n(P_n) \simeq F'_1(P'_1), \ldots,$ $F'_k(P'_k)$.
The axiom of foundation asserts the existence of a strong illocutionary act that is unique modulo illocutionary congruence in all contexts of use where a speaker has a successful illocutionary commitment. This axiom implies that the chains of illocutionary commitments of a speaker have a starting point.
By definition, the functions Σup and Ψup obey the following clauses:

VI. *The possible sincerity of the speaker*

If $P \in \Psi\hat{u}p(i)$, then, for at least one possible world $w \in W, P(w) = 1$.
The speaker can only succeed in committing himself to a psychological state that it is possible for him to have.

VII. *Compatibility of strict implication with respect to $\Psi\hat{u}p$*

If $P \prec Q(w_i) = 1$ and $P \in \Psi\hat{u}p(i)$, then $Q \in \Psi\hat{u}p(i)$.
If it is not possible for a speaker to have a psychological state without having another psychological state, and if he commits himself to having the first psychological state, then he is also committed to having the second one.

VIII. *Non deniability of the preparatory or sincerity conditions*

For all $i \in$ I, $\Sigma\text{up}(i) \cup \{P/i \ \Pi_{\|\text{assert}\|}P\} = \Psi\hat{\text{u}}\text{p}(i) \cup \{P/i \ \Pi_{\|\text{assert}\|}P\} = \emptyset$.
The sets $\Sigma\text{up}(i)$ and $\{P/i \ \Pi_{\|\text{assert}\|}P\}$ and the sets $\Psi\text{up}(i)$ and $\{P/i \ \Pi_{\|\text{assert}\|}P\}$
are disjoint. No speaker can succeed in simultaneously presupposing the truth
of a proposition P and asserting $\sim$P. No speaker can succeed in simultaneously
commit himself to having a psychological state and asserting that he does not
have that psychological state.

2. THE NATURE OF THE SELF-DEFEATING ILLOCUTIONARY ACTS

Given the definition of the conditions of success of illocutionary commitment, an illocutionary act F(P) is *self-defeating* iff no speaker can simultaneously:

(1) achieve the illocutionary point of F on P with the characteristic mode
of achievement and degree of strength of F,

(2) presuppose the preparatory conditions of F(P),

(3) be committed to the psychological state of F(P) with the required degree of strength and/or

(4) if the propositional content P of the act cannot satisfy the propositional content conditions of F.

There are thus four main cases of impossibility of success of illocutionary
commitment to an illocutionary act of form F(P). Let us consider now a few
examples of each case.

(1) *The impossibility of achieving the illocutionary point of F on P with the
required mode of achievement and degree of strength*

If, for all $i \in$ I, it is not the case that $i\Pi_{F}^{*}P$, then $\rangle F(P)\langle$. This impossibility
exists in the following sub-cases:

(i) *The illocutionary point of F(P) is empty.*
If, for all $i \in$ I, it is not the case that $i\Pi_{F}P$, then $\rangle F(P)\langle$.
Here are a few examples of sentences that express such self-defeating illocu-
tionary acts:

(18)   "I assert that I do not make any assertion."

Clearly to succeed in committing oneself to the truth of the proposition that
one is not committed to the truth of any proposition is impossible because it
is self-contradictory.

(33)   "Disobey all directives!"

(34)   "I commit myself to never keeping any commitment."

Clearly also to make an attempt to get the hearer not to respond to any attempt or to commit oneself not to keep any commitment are self-contradictory illocutionary points. Self-defeating illocutionary acts (33) and (34) have the same paradoxical form as the paradox of the skepticism (21) "I assert that all assertions are false."

(ii) *The illocutionary point of F(P) is not empty but the characteristic mode of achievement of illocutionary point required by F is impossible.*
If there exists some $i \in I$ such that $i\Pi_F P$ but for, no $i \in I$, it is the case that mode $(F)\langle i, P \rangle = 1$, then $\rangle F(P)\langle$.

Examples:

(35)   "I order you to disobey all orders."
(36)   "I promise you not to keep any promise."

A speaker can certainly succeed in attempting to get a hearer to disobey all directives made to him by invoking a position of authority or of power. But in that case he must not direct himself the hearer by invoking a position of authority or of power. Otherwise his attempt is self-contradictory. Similarly for (36). The mode of achievement of the illocutionary point of a promise puts the hearer in an obligation to do what he commits himself to doing.

(37)   "Obey this command that I do not have the authority to give you."

No speaker can succeed in achieving an illocutionary point by invoking a certain position (in this example a certain authority over the hearer) if the achievement of this illocutionary point implies (explicitly) that he does not have that position.

(2) *The inadequacy of the propositional content*
If for all $i \in I$, $P \notin \text{Prop}_F(i)$, then $\rangle F(P)\langle$.

(38)   "I predict that I was sick two days ago."
(39)   "I thank you for something that has absolutely nothing to do with you!"

Such illocutionary acts are self-defeating because (1) the propositional content of a prediction must be a future proposition and (2) the propositional content of giving thanks must always attribute to the hearer a certain action or property.

(3) *The impossibility of presupposing the preparatory conditions*

If, for all $i \in I$, it is not the case that $\sigma(FP,i) \subset \Sigma up(i)$ then $\rangle PF \langle$.

   (40)   "I assert that I do no exist."

   (41)   "I promise you to do something that I will never be able to do."

No speaker can succeed while making an assertion in presupposing that there are reasons for his non-existence in the world of his utterance for his illocutionary performance by definition implies his existence. No speaker can succeed in presupposing that he is able to do something that he recognizes that he will never be able to do.

(4) *The impossibility of committing oneself to the psychological state*

If, for all $i \in I$, $\psi_{Fa_i}P \notin \Psi up(i)$ then $\rangle F(P) \langle$.

   (42)   "I complain about this past action that you have done and which is good."

   (43)   "I thank you for having done this bad thing."

The reason for the self-defeating nature of (42) is that one cannot successfully commit oneself to having dissatisfaction for an action that one says to be good. Similarly, for (43), one cannot succeed in committing oneself to having gratitude for an action that one says to be bad. By the axiom of possible sincerity, any psychological state that is impossible to be held, is a psychological state to which it is impossible to be committed. From this axiom follows the following theorem:

THEOREM 1. If, for all $w \in W$, and for all $i \in I$, $\psi_{Fa_i}P(w)=0$ then $\rangle F(P) \langle$.

Any illocutionary act $F(P)$ with inconsistent sincerity conditions is a self-defeating illocutionary act.

   (44)   "I assert that $1 = 0$."

Such an assertion is self-defeating for it is impossible for a speaker to believe literally in the truth of this arithmetical proposition. Anyone who understands the proposition that $1 = 0$ understand it is necessarily false and consequently cannot believe in its truth.

Most self-defeating illocutionary acts are acts that are more than just incompatible with themselves. They are self-defeating because they commit the speaker to other illocutionary acts that are themselves relatively incompatible. An important theorem of illocutionary logic about self-defeating illocutionary acts is indeed the following:

267 SELF-DEFEATING SPEECH ACTS

THEOREM 2. If $F_1(P_1), \ldots, F_n(P_n) \rhd F(P)$, $F'(P')$ and $F(P) \times F'(P')$ then $\rangle F_1(P_1)x \ldots x F_n(P_n)\langle$.

By definition, two illocutionary acts are relatively incompatible iff they have relatively inconsistent conditions of success. $F_1(P_1) \times F_2(P_2)$ iff, for all $i \in I$, if $F_1(P_1)$ is $\underline{\Omega}(i)$ then (1) it is not the case that $i\Pi_{F_2}^* P_2$, or (2) $P \notin \text{Prop}_F(i)$ or (3) $\sigma(FP,i) \not\subseteq \Sigma\text{up}(i)$ or (4) $\psi_{Fa_i}P \notin \psi\text{up}(i)\langle \eta(F)\rangle$.

In particular, two illocutionary acts are relatively incompatible if they have (1) relatively inconsistent illocutionary points, (2) relatively inconsistent modes of achievement of their illocutionary point, (3) relatively inconsistent propositional content conditions, (4) preparatory conditions that cannot simultaneously be presupposed, (5) psychological states to which one cannot simultaneously be committed or, (6) if the illocutionary point or mode of achievement of the illocutionary point of one is relatively inconsistent with the act of presupposing the preparatory conditions or with the act of committing oneself to having the psychological state of the other. From this follows the following corollaries about self-defeating illocutionary acts:

COROLLARY 1. If $F_1(P_1), \ldots, F_n(P_n) \rhd F(P)$, $F'(P')$ and, for all $i \in I$, if $i\Pi_F P$ then it is not the case that $i\Pi_{F'}P'$, then $\rangle F_1(P_1)x \ldots x F_n(P_n)\langle$.

Illocutionary acts that commit the speaker to two illocutionary acts with relatively inconsistent illocutionary points are self defeating. Here are a few examples of performative sentences that are forms of expression for such defeating acts:

(45)   "I assert and deny Fermat's theorem."

Illocutionary act (45) clearly commits the speaker to both asserting and denying the same arithmetical proposition. Now the illocutionary point of a denial of a proposition P is to represent the state of affairs corresponding to P as not actual in the world of the utterance. This illocutionary point is relatively inconsistent with the illocutionary point of an assertion that P. Hence the self-defeating character of (45).

(46)   "I promise you to come tomorrow and I tell you that I shall not come."

The illocutionary point of a promise (i.e., to commit oneself to a future course of action) is relatively inconsistent with the illocutionary point of an assertion of the negation of its propositional content (namely to say that one will not keep the promise in question).

(20)   "I order and prohibit your doing this."

To prohibit s.o. from doing something being the same as ordering him not to do it, the illocutionary points of an order and of a prohibition with the same propositional content are relatively inconsistent.

(47)   "I forbid you to do this and I permit you to do it."

To permit is to perform the illocutionary denegation of an act of forbidding. Consequently, the illocutionary points of an act of forbidding and of an act of granting permission to carry out the same course of action are relatively inconsistent.

(24)   "I assert that this assertion is false" (The liar's paradox).

Assertion (24) which is of the form (48) "I assert that, for some proposition P, I assert P and P is false and P is that proposition that I assert" is paradoxical because it commits the speaker to both assertions (49) "I assert that for some proposition P that I assert, P is false" and (50) "I assert that all propositions P that I assert are true" which are relatively incompatible. The propositional content of (50) is indeed the truth functional negation of the propositional content of (49).

(51)   "I request you not to satisfy this request."
(19)   "I promise you not to keep this promise."
(52)   "I order you to disobey this order."

Self-defeating illocutionary acts (51), (19), (52) have the same paradoxical form as the paradox of the liar. They commit the speaker to two illocutionary acts of the same force which are relatively incompatible because the propositional content of one is the truth-functional negation of the other.

COROLLARY 2. If $F_1(P_1)$, ..., $F_n(P_n) \rhd F(P)$, $F'(P')$ and, for all $i \in I$ if mode $(F)\langle i,P\rangle = 1$ then mode $(F')\langle i,P'\rangle = 0$ then $\rangle F_1(P_1)x \ldots xF_n(P_n)\langle$.

An illocutionary act that commits the speaker to two speech-acts with relatively inconsistent modes of achievement of their illocutionary point is self-defeating. Example:

(54)   "I order and supplicate you to do this."

Such an illocutionary act is self-defeating precisely because the mode of achievement of the directive illocutionary point of an order which implies that the speaker invokes a position of authority or of power over the hearer is incompatible with the humble mode of achievement of a supplication which leaves an option of refusal to the hearer.

COROLLARY 3. If $F_1(P_1), \ldots, F_n(P_n) \rhd F(P)$, $F'(P')$ and, for all $i \in I$, $P \in \text{Prop}_F(i)$ iff $P' \notin \text{Prop}_{F'}$ then $\rangle F_1(P_1)x \ldots xF_n(P_n)\langle$.

An illocutionary act which commits the speaker to two speech acts with relatively inconsistent propositional content conditions is self-defeating. Example:

(55)   "I report this past state of affairs and I predict it has not been the case."

Such an illocutionary act is self-defeating because, if a proposition P satisfies the propositional content conditions of a report with respect to a content of use i (i.e., is past or present with respect to the time of utterance t_i), its negation $\sim$P cannot satisfy the propositional content conditions of a prediction with respect to that same context (i.e., be future with respect to t_i).

COROLLARY 4. If $F_1(P_1), \ldots, F_n(P_n) \rhd F(P)$, $F'(P')$ and, for all $i \in I$, if $\sigma(FP,i) \subset \Sigma\text{up}(i)$ then $\sigma(F'P',i) \not\subset \Sigma\text{up}(i)$ then $\rangle F_1(P_1)x \ldots xF_n(P_n)\langle$.

COROLLARY 5. If $F_1(P_1), \ldots, F_n(P_n) \rhd F(P)$, $F'(P')$ and, for all $i \in I$, if $\psi_{Fa_i}P \in \Psi \hat{u}p(i)$ then $\psi_{F'a_i}P' \notin \Psi\hat{u}p(i)$, then $\rangle F_1(P_1)x \ldots xF_n(P_n)\langle$.

Illocutionary acts that commit the speaker to two illocutionary acts whose preparatory conditions cannot be simultaneously presupposed or whose psychological states cannot be simultaneously expressed or held are self-defeating. Such is for example:

(56)   a threat and a promise to carry out the same action.

A preparatory condition of a threat is indeed that the future course of action represented by the propositional content is bad for the hearer. On the other hand the preparatory condition of a promise is that the future course of action represented by the propositional content is good for the hearer. Clearly no speaker can succeed in presupposing that the same action is both good and bad from the same point of view for the hearer.

(26)   "I both complain and thank you for coming here."

No one can commit himself to simultaneously experiencing dissatisfaction and satisfaction from the same point of view for the same state of affairs. Now these two psychological states are the characteristic psychological states of a complaint and of an act of thanking. Moreover no one can succeed in presupposing that one state of affairs is both for and against his interest. These are the respective preparatory conditions of thanking and complaining. Illocutionary act (26) is thus paradoxical for two different reasons.

COROLLARY 6. If $F_1(P_1), \ldots, F_n(P_n) \triangleright F(P), F'(P')$ and, for all $i \in I$, $i\Pi_F P$ or mode $(F)\langle i,P \rangle = 1$ only if $\sigma(F'P',i) \not\subset \Sigma up(i)$ or $\psi_{Fa_i}P' \not\in \Psi \hat{u}p(i)$ then $\rangle F_1(P_1)x \ldots xF_n(P_n)\langle$.

If an illocutionary act commits the speaker to two illocutionary acts such that the illocutionary point or the mode of achievement of the illocutionary point of the first is relatively incompatible with the presupposition of the preparatory conditions or with a commitment to the psychological state of the second, it is a self-defeating illocutionary act.

The main postulate that states the relative inconsistency of an illocutionary point with the presupposition of a preparatory condition or with the commitment to a psychological state is postulate VIII. One consequence of this postulate is that an illocutionary act and the denial of a preparatory condition of that illocutionary act are relatively incompatible illocutionary acts. This explains the self-defeating nature of the illocutionary acts performed by the utterance of the following sentences:

(25) "I promise you to do this and I inform you that I am absolutely unable to do it."

A preparatory condition of a promise is indeed the ability of the speaker to keep that promise.

(57) "I assert that there is gold on Venus and that I have no reason to believe this."

(58) "I command you to report to your officer and I assert that I do not have any kind of authority over you."

Since the particular mode of achievement of the directive illocutionary point of a command is part of the preparatory conditions of that command, a command and an assertion by the speaker that he has no authority over the hearer are relatively incompatible illocutionary acts. A second consequence of postulate VIII is that an illocutionary act and the denial of a sincerity condition of that illocutionary act are relatively incompatible. This explains the self-defeating illocutionary acts that have the paradoxical form of Moore's paradox, such as:

(59) "I apologize for having done this and I assert that I do no feel any regret or sorrow for it."

(60) "I request you to leave and I assert that I have absolutely no desire and do not want you to leave."

NOTES

[1] The other elementary illocutionary acts are of the form $F(u)$ where u is an individual object or some other entity of the universe of discourse. Here are a few sentences that express such acts in English (61) "Long live Quebec", (62) "Hurrah for the Californians".
[2] There are two kinds of preparatory conditions of illocutionary acts. First, there are the preparatory conditions that are specific to the kind of illocutionary force F of the illocution which is performed. For example, if a speaker gives an order, he must presuppose that he is in a position of authority or of power over the hearer. Secondly there are the preparatory conditions that are derived from the propositional content such as for example the presuppositions of existence, uniqueness or truth. The presuppositions of the propositional content P must be true in the world of the utterance in order that P be true in that world. Propositional presuppositions are independent from illocutionary force. Thus for example, an assertion of form (63) "I assert that you will speak to Bob", an order (64) "Speak to Bob!" and a question (65) "Will you see Bob?", are three different illocutionary acts which have in common the same propositional presupposition that Bob exists in the world of the utterance.
[3] The verb "express" in English is ambiguous. People are said both to express propositions which are senses and to express feelings and psychological states. To the first sense corresponds the act that we have called the propositional act. To the second sense corresponds the act of expressing the psychological state specified by the sincerity conditions.
[4] This definition of the notion of an illocutionary force permits us to shed some light on the question: Is the set of all illocutionary forces definable recursively from a few primitive illocutionary forces? Certain illocutionary points determine indeed certain propositional content conditions, preparatory conditions and sincerity conditions. For example, all directive illocutionary forces whose illocutionary point is to get the hearer to do something have in common the same propositional content condition that the propositional content represents a future course of action of the hearer, the same preparatory condition that the hearer is capable of doing that action and the same sincerity condition that the speaker wants or desires this action of the hearer. This is a consequence of the definition of the directive illocutionary point. Propositional content conditions, preparatory conditions and sincerity conditions that are common to all illocutionary forces with an identical illocutionary point are called *general* propositional content conditions, preparatory conditions and sincerity conditions of these illocutionary forces. Propositional content conditions, preparatory conditions and sincerity conditions of an illocutionary force F that are not general are said to he *particular* to F. For example,

the condition that the propositional content represents a future speech act of the hearer is a particular propositional content condition of the illocutionary force of question. The set Φ of all illocutionary forces is definable recursively from a few primitive illocutionary forces if the following hypothesis is true:

The hypothesis of constructibility

(a) There is a small number n ε ω of basic illocutionary points that relate in a primitive way the propositional content to the world of utterance. To each basic illocutionary point corresponds a unique primitive illocutionary force having this basic illocutionary point, no particular mode of achievement of that illocutionary point, a mean degree of strength and only general propositional content conditions, general preparatory conditions and general sincerity conditions.

(b) All other illocutionary forces F ε Φ are obtained from these few primitive illocutionary forces by the application of a finite number of operations on the illocutionary point, the mode of achievement, the degrees of strength, the propositional content conditions, the preparatory conditions or the sincerity conditions. Some of these operations have been mentioned. Thus for example there is the operation which consists in restricting the mode of achievement, the operations which consists in increasing or decreasing the degrees of strength, and the operations which consists in adding particular propositional content conditions, particular preparatory conditions or particular sincerity conditions. These operatons are recursive. Some operations like the operation of illocutionary negation modify simultaneously several components of illocutionary forces. This hypothesis is developed in Searle and Vanderveken (forthcoming).

BIBLIOGRAPHY

Austin, J.-L.: 1962, *How to do Things with Words*, Oxford, The Clarendon Press.
Searle, John: 1969, *Speech Acts*, Cambridge University Press.
Searle, John and Daniel Vanderveken: forthcoming, *Foundations of Illocutionary Logic*.
Searle, John: 1975, 'A Classification of Illocutionary Acts', in *Minnesota Studies in Philosophy of Science*, vol. 6, Minneapolis, Un. of Minnesota Press.

ZENO VENDLER

TELLING THE FACTS

I

In the article 'Other Minds' we find the first allusions to the doctrine of speech-acts in J. L. Austin's published writing.[1] There he clearly recognizes some of the performative features of the verb *to promise*, but only to claim that the same characteristics apply to another verb, of far greater philosophical importance, namely *to know*. In the light of his later and more developed theory it appears, however, that this latter verb is by no means a performative in the technical sense of the word.[2] Nevertheless, since even mistakes are often instructive in philosophy, and Austin's mistakes are likely to be more so than most, it might be interesting to look into the reason for his original erroneous belief. Yet this study is not intended to be a mere piece of exegesis. I am going to show that some of the features of *know* that Austin picks out indeed hold true, but require another explanation, which also casts light on the behavior of many related verbs, including a major group of the real performatives.

But first a few words to show that *know* is not a performative. The formulae Austin later offers to recognize performatives on the intuitive level all fail with this verb. Let us, indeed, compare *know* with the paradigm performative, *promise*, in this respect. First of all the *to say* formula, i.e.:

> To say (in the appropriate circumstances) "I promise to *x*" is to promise to *x*.

This fails with *know*: it is not the case, in any circumstances, that to say "I know that *p*" constitutes knowing that *p*. For one thing, if what the speaker says, namely that he knows that *p*, is true, then it still would be true even if he did not open his mouth at all. On the contrary, if he does not know that *p* without saying anything, then saying so will not make it so by any means. With promising the utterance (verbal or equivalent) is essential: it constitutes the promise, sincere or otherwise, and nothing else.

The second formula, *in saying*, equally fails. Consider

> In saying "I promise to *x*" he promised to *x*.

273

J. R. Searle, F. Kiefer, and M. Bierwisch (eds.), *Speech Act Theory and Pragmatics*, 273–290.

and then compare the parallel for *know*:

>In saying "I know that *p*" he knew that *p*.

The very sentence sounds deviant, and, for the reasons already mentioned, incomprehensible: in saying this or that you can promise, order or apologize, but not know, believe or doubt.

Finally, the *hereby* mark: the sentence

>I hereby promise to *x*

is used to make the promise quite explicit and official.

>I hereby know that *p*

on the other hand once more falls short of the requirements of grammar and good sense.

This difference between *promise* and *know* is not a matter of some accidental feature peculiar to *promise*. All the performatives, by virtue of their very nature as performatives, fit into these formulae, but *know* does not. This should be enough, yet there is a more fundamental reason for disqualifying *know* as a bona fide performative. The function of a performative verb is to mark the illocutionary force of a speech act. Accordingly, all such verbs conform to the achievement schema in their tense-structure.[3] The point is too obvious to belabor again. Just think of the incongruity of saying things like: "Since when does he promise ... ?", "How long did he assert ... ?", "Does he still apologize ... ?" Now with *know*, all these questions make sense; *know*, like *believe*, *doubt*, etc., are state-verbs: one can know something *for* a period of time, *since* a certain date, and so forth.

II

Why is it, then, that Austin had thought that *know* is similar to *promise*? Here is the crucial passage in which the analogy is proposed:

But now, when I say 'I promise', a new plunge is taken: I have not merely announced my intention, but, by using this formula (performing this ritual), I have bound myself to others, and staked my reputation, in a new way. Similarly, saying 'I know' is taking a new plunge. But it is *not* saying 'I have performed a specially striking feat of cognition ... ' ... When I say 'I know', *I give others my word*: *I give others my authority for saying* that 'S is P'.[4]

I draw your attention to the last phrase: "give others my authority for saying". Thus, Austin claims, just as in promising I commit myself to the execution of my announced intention, so in saying "I know" (notice, one cannot put it this way: *in knowing*) I commit myself to the truth of the belief I express.

Such a warranty, moreover, is transferable in both cases:

If someone has promised me to do A, then I am entitled to rely on it, and can myself make promises on the strength of it: and so, where someone has said to me 'I know', I am entitled to say *I* know too, at second hand. The right to say 'I know' is transmissible, in the sort of way that other authority is transmissible.[5]

Thus what Austin sees here is the possibility of a chain of promises and a chain of knowers (or, to be more faithful, a chain of "I know" sayers). And, he implies, the links of the chain are forged, in either case, of transmitted authority.

All chains, of course, must begin somewhere, but where the knowledge chain begins there is one more step to be considered with respect to the first know-sayer:

If you say you *know* something, the most immediate challenge takes the form of asking 'Are you in a position to know?', that is, you must undertake to show, not merely that you are sure of it, but that it is within your cognizance.[6]

And, interesting enough, only things in the present and the past can be within one's cognizance:

. . . The conditions which must be satisfied if I am to show that a thing is within my cognizance . . . are conditions, not about the future, but about *the present and the past*: it is not demanded that I do more than *believe* about the future.[7]

Thus the whole story shapes up as follows. There is the first know-sayer who is entitled to this act by what is "within his cognizance", something present or past. And he uses the verb in transmitting this information to add his personal warranty for its truth. And, in their turn, so do the others in the chain.

Looking at things this way, it indeed appears that the function of *know* is quite like that of *promise*: as this latter verb is used to guarantee the execution of an expressed intention, so the former is used to guarantee the truth of an expressed belief. What a clever sleight-of-hand! "To say 'I promise' is to promise . . . right? And to say 'I know' is to know . . . right? Thus by reminding you of how *I promise* functions, I told you the essentials about promising . . . And by reminding you of how *I know* functions, I told you the essentials about knowing . . . right?"

III

Now what is wrong? Plenty. To know is not to say "I know", and to say "I
know" or "He knows" is not to give a warranty, but to state something which
is either true or false. Granted, it is not to report on "a specially striking feat
of cognition, superior, in the same scale as believing and being sure, even to
being merely quite sure" . . . .[8] Nay, it is to report on something else: on a
causal connection between the person who knows something and the fact
known. And even if that connection involves other people as intermediaries,
the chain they form is not a chain of transmitted authority; it remains a
causal chain.

Compare these two claims:

> Joe has died.
> Joe has been murdered.

Now to say the second is not merely to report on poor Joe's sad demise, but
to attribute it to some outside agency. Similarly, the difference between these
two:

> He "sees" pink rats.
> He sees pink rats.

need not consist in some difference between the qualities of the attributed
experiences; the victim of D. T. may "see" what he "sees" quite vividly. The
point is that only the second claim links his experience to a specific cause, to
wit, pink rats.[9]

Now I would like to say that the case with *know* is similar to these. When I
say "I know (or he knows) that *p*", I attribute my (or his) subjective condition
to a specific cause, immediate or remote, namely the fact that *p*. That fact,
furthermore, is either within the immediate cognizance of the knower, or has
reached him via the intermediacy of other persons who told him what is the
case, who informed him of the facts.

This hypothesis accounts for all the features correctly recognized by
Austin. First, that what we know must have been, at some point at least,
"within somebody's cognizance", i.e., somebody's knowledge that *p* must
have been directly caused by the fact that *p*. Second, whereas the facts of
the present and the past can indeed be regarded as causes, those concerning
the future cannot yet. Hence Austin's modesty about the knowledge of the
future is sustained. Finally, there are indeed knowledge-chains: perhaps most
of what we know is not within our own cognizance; we were told of the facts,

learned them from others in other ways, read them in books, and so forth. And the persons telling these things, and the books and papers reporting them, are indeed links of a chain: a succession of causes, not just authorities. Authorities, as such, merely engender belief; for knowledge something more is required: an unbroken, though often quite long, chain of causation. This alone can assure the objectivity, or factivity, knowledge requires. Belief operates in another sphere: there firmness, good reasons and persuasion hold their sway; but even at their best they never guarantee that one cannot be wrong. Austin was right in claiming that when I say "I know" I guarantee, but he give the wrong reason. *I know* does not *mean* that I guarantee, thus what *know* means cannot be explained in terms of how *I know* is used; yet in saying "I know" (or "He knows" for that matter) I cannot help but guarantee, precisely because of what *know* means.

Notice, moreover, that this account is compatible with the fact that knowing something is a mental state, albeit caused by an appropriate agency, and with the fact that ascriptions of knowledge, whether in the first person or the third, whether in the present tense or the past, are true or false — two facts at odds with Austin's hypothesis.[10]

IV

"How do I know that I know something rather than merely believe it?" This is a question of epistemology, which, directly at least, I shall not discuss in this paper. "When shall I say, when am I entitled to say, that I know something rather than merely believe it?" This looks like a moral problem, or at least one pertaining to the domain of prudence. At any rate, I am not going to address it here either. My query is more basic than these concerns: what do we mean when we say that somebody knows something rather than merely believes it? Thus what I shall do is conceptual analysis, with some implications for descriptive metaphysics.

A few years ago, in an essay by this time somewhat notorious, I came to the conclusion that knowledge and belief cannot have the same object, in other words, that it is impossible to believe and know exactly the same thing.[11] At this point I shall not repeat the arguments I used to establish this result in any detail. Still, it might be useful to mention the main points, since they will play a role in the discussion of some other verbs in a later part of this paper.

The first thing I noticed was a sharp divergence between *believe* and *know* with respect to coocurrences with *wh*-nominals, traditionally, though somewhat misleadingly, called indirect questions.[12] Consider the following contexts:

$$\text{She knows} \left\{ \text{*She believes} \left\{ \begin{array}{l} \text{who stole the money} \\ \text{why he did it} \\ \text{how he did it} \\ \text{what he did with it} \end{array} \right. \right.$$

and so forth. It appears that although *know* and *believe* both can take *that*-clause complements, only *know* can accept their *wh*-transforms.

The plot thickens as we realize that they cannot even share superficially identical *that*-clauses. This can be demonstrated as follows. Taken the sentence:

(1)　　　I believe what you said.

Its derivation is obvious:

I believe that p　　　You said that p
I believe *that*　　　　*which* you said
I believe *what* you said.

Thus *what* in (1) replaces *that p*, i.e., the verb-object shared by *believe* and *say*. In a similar way

I believe what you believe

means that we hold the same belief, in order words, that we share a belief. Now let us try these:

(2)　　　I know what you said
(3)　　　I know what you believe.

Both sentences are perfectly grammatical and unambiguous. But they clearly do not mean that if you said, or believe, that p, then I know that p. Their derivation once more comes through the *wh*-nominal: I know what it is that you said, or that you believe. And this, of course, does not mean at all that my knowledge and your saying or believing have the same object. Suppose you believe that Carter is a great president. Now if I believe what you believe, then I too believe that he is a great president. But even if I know what you believe, this fact does not imply that I know that he is a great president. It seems, therefore, that the *that*-clause complement of *say* or *believe* is unacceptable for *know*. Now let us reverse the order and produce

(4)   *I believe what you know.

The sentence is ungrammatical, because both interpretations of *what* are blocked. *What you know* cannot be a *wh*-nominal, since *believe* does not take such. But, again, why cannot the *what* be regarded as a pronoun replacing a shared *that p*, i.e., one denoting the common object of your knowing and my believing? The answer is simple: because there is no such thing. *That p*, the object of *know*, is not of the kind that could be taken on by *believe*, in the same way as in the previous example the object of *believe* has proved to be indigestible for *know*. There, however, the *wh*-nominal-interpretation rescued (3). For (4) even this detour is barred. The conclusion seems to be unavoidable: in spite of the surface identity of the *that*-clauses following *know* and *believe*, they are different; and only one of them is amenable to the formation of *wh*-nominals.

The same thing follows from the consideration of certain nouns that can replace, and can be predicated of, *that*-clauses. Some of them, such as *opinion, theory, assertion, prediction*, and so forth, are suited for the *that*-clauses compatible with *believe*, but others, such as *fact, cause, result, outcome*, and the like, are appropriate to the *that*-clauses demanded by *know*. For this reason, just as knowing what one believes does not mean that there is a thing believed by one and known by another, knowing, say, one's opinion does not entail knowing the same thing which is the object of someone else's opinion. Nay, in both instances the *what* is not a noun-sharing *what*, it is the *wh*-nominal *what*: one knows what it is that the other believes, and one knows what someone else's opinion is. If your opinion is that *p*, and I know your opinion, then what I know is not that *p*, but that your opinion is that *p*. With *believe*, matters stand differently. There is no difficulty to believing someone else's theory, assertion or prediction, and here the belief and, say, the prediction, have the same object: if your prediction is that *p*, and I believe your prediction, then I too believe that *p*. Interestingly enough, this move fails with *opinion* and, for that matter, with *belief* itself. *I believe your belief* is ungrammatical and *I believe your opinion* is marginal. Why? Simply because beliefs and opinions, unlike assertions and predictions, are objects of internal states, thus they are not directly available for other people's believing. This is an interesting difference between mental state verbs and illocutionary verbs, but it is irrelevant to our consideration of *that*-clauses.

The other group, *fact* etc., are proper objects of *know*, but not of *believe*. One can know facts, causes, results and outcomes. It is pretty peculiar, however, to say that one believes these things. *I believe the cause of the explosion, . . . the outcome of the trial, . . . etc.

There is, of course, another difference between these two groups: the former require owners, but not the latter. Opinions, predictions, etc., are formed or made by people, they are their opinions, etc. Facts, causes, and the like are not owned, not made or formed by anybody. They are things objectively given, which we may or may not discover, or find out. Accordingly, opinions, predictions, and the like may be true or false; facts, causes and results are not. These considerations explain two nomenclatures. I called these two kinds of *that*-clauses and their corresponding verbs and replacer nouns objective and subjective respectively. The Kiparskys, in their well known article, called the appropriate contexts factive and nonfactive.[13] In this paper I shall adopt their terminology: thus I shall call, e.g., *know* a factive verb and *result* a factive noun, but *believe* a nonfactive verb, and *prediction* a nonfactive noun.

V

It seem to me that the most reliable grammatical mark of factivity is the possibility of cooccurrences with *wh*-nominals. Why is this so?

In order to answer this question I once more draw your attention to the group of nonfactive nouns, i.e., *belief, opinion, assertion, prediction*, and so forth. These are obviously nominal products of certain 'propositional" verbs: *believe, opine* (antiquated), *assert* and *predict*. The first two of these verbs denote mental states, and the other two are used in reporting or performing speech acts. Let us focus on this last couple. The nominals *assertion* and *prediction* are semantically ambiguous between the performance of the agent, and the product of his act. E.g.: *His prediction of war proved to be a diplomatic blunder*, versus *His prediction of war turned out to be true*. It is interesting to note that only in the former context can *his prediction* be replaced by *his predicting*, because this latter form never denotes the product.[14] In a similar way, somebody's assertion of something may be a courageous thing in the one sense, and true or false in the other. Again, beliefs and opinons may be described as rash or prejudiced as related to the subject who holds them, or false and improbable as to their content.

The genealogy of assertions and predictions pose no problems; they are produced by speech-acts: they are *made* or *issued*. Beliefs and opinions, on the contrary, are internal objects, per se not voiced. They are *conceived*, however, or *formed, embraced, nurtured, held* and sometimes *abandoned* . . .

as if they were children ("brainchild", we often say). I do not wish to discuss here the details of the ontological status of beliefs, opinions, and the like, on the one hand, and of assertions, predictions and their kin, on the other, whether, that is, they are identical with sentences pronounced or silently entertained, in the public language or in a "system of internal representation", or whether they are something more abstract than these. What I have to maintain is merely this: they must have an intentional, representative reality, which makes it possible for them to be true or false, probable or unlikely, which, in other words, enables them to represent a possibility, and thus fit or fail to fit the actual facts.

Now these facts, themselves, together with their cousins, i.e. causes, results and the like, are cut of different cloth. First of all, they are no human creations in the sense of being the products of speech acts or mental acts. That one has thought or said something may be a fact, but this fact is by no means identical with the belief entertained or the assertion made. One can have beliefs, moreover, *about* this fact or any other fact, as one can make assertions *about* them, but what is then believed or asserted are not the facts themselves, but something that at best fits them or corresponds to them. After all, there are false beliefs and false assertions, inaccurate beliefs and imprecise assertions, but there cannot be false facts and inaccurate causes. Only a representation can be true or false, inaccurate or not quite precise − the thing represented, as such, cannot. Much the same way as a picture can be faithful, wrong or inaccurate, but not the object the picture is supposed to represent.

Beliefs and assertions, therefore, cannot be identified merely in terms of the facts they represent. For one thing, there may be no corresponding fact, if the belief or the assertion is false. For another, the same fact may be represented in many ways owing to the variety of referential and similar factors involved; beliefs and assertions are referentially opaque. Thus two persons, or even the same person, may hold two distinct but true beliefs representing a fact about a certain individual. Think of some of the things poor Oedipus believed about his mother and his wife. Even about the same possibility beliefs may agree without being identical. For this reason in reporting beliefs, assertions, and the like, their constituents have to be spelled out in detail: no gaps are permitted. One has to say: "He believes that A is B"; it is not enough, and therefore it is impossible, to say: "He believes *what A is*".

With factive contexts such gaps are permissible: "He knows *what A* is", "He found out *who* killed her", "*How* he saluted the flag caused the scandal", "*What* he did was the result of a confusion", and so forth. The reason is that in these cases we are talking about the facts themselves, which are "there" as it were, objectively given, thus one can identify them without filling in all the gaps. Think of things like "The I. R. S. knows *who* paid *what* to *whom*". It is like referring to individuals: it can be achieved without full description, or, if Kripke is right, even without any descriptive content. Thus in saying "He knows who killed her" one refers to a fact *in rerum natura*, but in saying "He believes that Joe killed her" one describes somebody's mental state.

Why is it, then, that even knowledge-contexts are referentially opaque, at least when the full *that*-clause is given? For, clearly, the abovementioned Oedipus knew that he married Jocasta, yet did not know that he married his mother. Of course, he knew *whom* he married, as we just said. But why the opaqueness? The reason seems to be that although the objects of knowledge are facts, the knowing subject must have a representation, similar to belief, of that fact, and caused by that fact. Thus it becomes a matter of emphasis: if I say "He knows whom he married" the emphasis is on the fact of that fateful union and the causal chain leading to his representation thereof; but if I say "He knows that he married Jocasta" the emphasis is on the representation which is caused by that fact.

VI

X knows that p seems to mean the following: *X has an accessible mental representation, 'p', caused by the fact that p.* Why *accessible*? Because of the possibility of forgetting and remembering again: in the interval the representation must have remained, only the access was blocked. Otherwise remembering again would be relearning, which it is not.

And belief? *X believes that 'p'* seems to mean the following: *X holds the mental representation 'p' as true.* Therefore belief has nothing to do with forgetting, but has disbelief for a counterpart: when *X* holds that representation as false.

Adopting, and holding, a representation as true is an action for which one should have reasons. Hence the question "Why do you believe . . . ?" If the reasons are no good, one has irrational, unwarranted or foolish beliefs.

Having a representation caused by a fact is not an action. Therefore one does not have reason for what one knows. The appropriate question is "How do you know . . . ?" And the answer is not a justification, but usually a causal story: how did one *learn*, how did one come to know. E.g.:

Tommy is a subject in a series of psychological experiments involving sleep-learning. While asleep he is exposed to a recorded voice reciting the

capitals of the African states over and over again. The next day he is asked:
"What is the capital of Upper Volta?" "Ouagadougou" he says. "And of the
Central African Empire?" "Bangui" he answers. And so on. Does he know
the capitals? Of course. How does he know them? From sleep-learning.
Knowledge has nothing to do with justified true belief. How do I know that
the capital of Burma is Rangoon? I have no idea . . . I must have picked it up
somwhere and still remember it.

VII

"How do you know that p?" "Joe told me so." This is a very natural answer.
It seems to be the case, therefore, that quite often the causal link connecting
the fact and the knowing subject consists, in part at least, in the relation of
X's telling Y that p. The verb *tell*, accordingly, must be able to carry the
factive burden. And indeed it does, as the *wh*-test shows: *He told me who
killed the grocer . . . how he did it*, etc. Shall we conclude, then, that *tell* is
as much a factive verb as *know, realize, find out* or *discover*?

The answer is clearly no. For whereas these verbs do not tolerate falsity
in their fully articulated objects, *tell* does. What I mean is this. I cannot
consistently say that X knows that p, but not p; or that X just found out that
p, but p is not the case; or that X falsely discovered that p; and so forth.
On the other hand, although I may report that X told me that p, nothing
prevents me from adding that p is not the case. In other words, one cannot
know falsehoods, but one can tell falsehoods.

Shall we abandon, then, the *wh*-test as the hallmark of factivity? Not
before taking a second look. For consider the following two situations. Joe
tells me that he lives in San Francisco. Later I visit him, and thus confirm that
he indeed lives there. So I may report either that he told me that he lives in
San Francisco, or, if I am more reticent, I may say that he told me where he
lives. Jim also tells me that he lives in San Francisco. Later on, however, I
find out that he actually lives in Oakland. Now in this case I still might report
that he told me that he lives in San Francisco (and may add, if I so choose,
that he lied). What I cannot do, however, is to report truthfully that he told
me where he lives. For, in fact, he did *not* tell me where he lives. Thus we
have made a surprising discovery: telling *that* can be false, telling *what* cannot.
Tell, therefore, is factive in front of a *wh*-clause, but not necessarily in front
of a *that*-clause. Because, remember, *tell* may carry the factive burden even
in the latter case: "How do you know that p?"; "He told me that p". My
hypothesis is the following: whereas *know, find out*, and the like, are fully

factive verbs, *tell* is ambivalent: it can take factive *that*-clauses or nonfactive *that*-clauses. And *since* it can take factive *that*-clauses, it can also take their *wh*-derivatives. But *since* nonfactive *that*-clauses have no such derivatives, the contexts *tell wh* . . . are always factive. If so, then the objection against the *wh*-clause-factivity-connection has turned into an additional proof on the second look.

Notice, moreover, that *tell* is by no means the only verb displaying such a split personality. Consider, for instance, *predict*. At the last presidential elections many people predicted that Carter would win and many that Ford would win. But, since Carter won, only the former group succeeded in predicting *who* would win. The Ford-predictors, despite the fact that they made a prediction, actually failed to predict who would win. Later on I shall mention some other members of this "half-factive" group.[15]

Can all propositional verbs take *wh*-clauses, i.e., can all of them have factive uses? No, there are many that cannot. *Believe*, as we recall, is one of them. Some other are *think, assume* on the domain of mental states, and *say, assert, claim* and *insist* among the performatives. *Wh*-clauses are incompatible with them, and consistently enough, so are the factive nouns, *fact, result, cause*, etc. One can tell the facts, but not say them, one can know the cause of something but one cannot assert it, one can find out the results but not believe them, and so forth.

The result of our reflections thus far seems to be the following. There is a large, and by this time fairly well known genus of "propositional" verbs, roughly those that normally take *that*-clause complements. This class contains a large set of performatives, called "expositives" by Austin, and "representatives" by Searle.[16] In addition, it contains a sizable group of mental act and mental state verbs, which I called "apprehensives" and "putatives" respectively.[17] Now it turns out that this whole domain is in need of a cross-classification into fully factive (like *know*), half-factive (like *tell*) and non-factive (like *believe*) verbs.

VIII

I cannot do more than take the first steps toward a complete classification. I shall consider a representative selection of performatives belonging to this domain and sort them according to the criteria just discovered. The rest of the domain, consisting of mental act and mental state verbs could also be handled in the same manner, but I shall not go into details there. For the "representative selection" I choose the list of "expositives" given in my *Res Cogitans*, but add two, *say* and *mention*; about thirty verbs altogether.

What are the criteria that can be applied to decide the issue in each case? Three will do:

1. The *wh*-criterion: nonfactives (like *assert*) reject *wh*-nominal complements.

2. The *fact*-criterion: nonfactives equally reject the noun *fact* and its kinship: *cause, result, outcome*, and, oddly enough, *truth*.

3. The adverb-criterion: fully factives cannot cooccur with the set of adverbs consisting of *falsely, wrongly, incorrectly*, or simply with the denial of their *that*-clause complements.

Criteria 1 and 2 operate together. Fully factives pass both but fail 3; nonfactives fail 1 and 2 but pass 3; half-factives pass all three.

To our surprise there are but two fully factive items in the selection: *mention* and *remind*. Let the criteria do their work:

> He mentioned where she lives
> He mentioned the fact that . . .
> *He falsely mentioned that . . .
> He reminded me who lives there
> He reminded me of the results of . . .
> *He reminded me that Jane lives in Paris, which is not so.

The group of half-factives is more numerous: besides *tell* and *predict*, which we already encountered, *state, report, guess, inform, admit* and *warn* seem to belong here. They all pass the adverb test: *falsely state, incorrectly report, wrongly guess*, etc. But also:

> He stated why he did it
> He reported the fact that . . .
> He guessed who would win
> He informed us where the mine was buried
> He warned me when it would go off
> He admitted the truth.

The nonfactives make up the largest group: *say, assert, claim, declare, affirm, contend, maintain* and *insist* clearly belong here. But so do many others, although their more complex semantic structure often interferes with the straight application of our criteria: *agree* and *disagree, confess* and *testify, postulate, argue* and *conclude*. They all pass the adverb test, although sometimes in a roundabout way, e.g.

He agreed with her false assertion
He argued that she was innocent, but she was guilty all right.

They all fail the first two tests. Some examples:

*He asserted where he went
*He claimed the cause of the fire
*He maintained the fact that . . .
*He testified who killed the grocer
*He concluded how she did it.

It will be objected that *say* may take the *wh*'s. One indeed hears things like "He said where she works". I think this is substandard, and only tolerated as a hangover from the correct negative form: "He did not say where she works". Why is this correct? I suspect that the reason is this. The *wh* after a negation masks a *whether . . . or . . .* rather than a *that*: . . . *did not say whether she works at A or at B or . . . .* And this is not a factive clause. But this is a very complex matter which I cannot discuss in detail here.

There are a few verbs left over from the original list about which I am not sure: *suggest, submit, concede, deny* and *assure*. I suspect they are all basically nonfactive, but can be forced into factive frames: one can deny the facts, suggest who stole the money, and so forth. Yet this tolerance is not strong or consistent enough to promote them into the ranks of the half-factives.

There is a common deletion transformation which provides additional proof for our classification. *What*-clauses of the kind *what N is* often contract to *N*, e.g.,

I know what his name (address, occupation, etc.) is

yields

I know his name (address, etc.).

Therefore, if our theory is correct, the product of this transformation should be acceptable to factive and half-factive verbs, but not to nonfactives. And it is indeed so:

He mentioned her occupation
He stated his name
He told us her address

but not

*He asserted her address
*He affirmed her occupation

etc.

It should also be noted that the product nominal of half-factives is always nonfactive. No wonder, since these products are subjective creations, representative (if true) of the facts but not identical with them. So although one can state or report facts, one's statement, or report, is not a fact; at best it is only a statement, or report, of a fact.

The same threefold classification can be carried over to the verbs describing cognitive mental states and mental acts. I submit, leaving the proof to the reader, that *think, believe* and *assume* are nonfactive, *anticipate* is half-factive, and *know, find out, discover, notice, realize,* and *remember* are fully factive.

IX

These three classes (factives, half-factives and nonfactives) may represent a linguistic universal operating beyond the confines of the English language, or even the whole Indo-European group. There is a surprising proof of this assumption take from Hungarian. This language, which is less "lexical" than English, uses the same verb-root *mond* (meaning, roughly, *say* or *tell*) in all three frames. Non-factivity is achieved by putting an emphatic pronoun, *azt*, in front, factivity by adding the perfective prefix *meg-*. In the absence of both, the verb seems to be half-factive. Accordingly, for example,

Azt	mondta,	hogy	Bécsbe	ment
(that	he said	that	to Vienna	he went)

is compatible with a claim of falsity: *de hazudott (but he lied)*. Now this from cannot take the equivalents of the *wh*'s:

*Azt	mondta,	hogy	hova	ment.
(that	he said	that	where	he went)

The factive form, *megmond* takes the *wh*-equivalents, and excludes falsity:

Megmondta,	hogy	hova	ment
(he said	that	where	he went)
*Megmondta,	hogy	Bécsbe	ment
(he said	that	to Vienna	he went
de hazudott.
but he lied)

The bare form appears to be half-factive

> Mondta, hogy Bécsbe ment de hazudott.

but

> *Mondta, hogy hova ment de hazudott.

X

"It was your wife I saw in the motel. Now you know it!" "Of course he knows. I just told him." These and similar contexts tell more about the "logic" of *know* than the reams of analysis produced to justify the theory of justified true belief.

If you say "He told me who she was" you *imply* that both he and you know who she was. You came to know as a result of his telling you what he knew. And how did he come to know? Well, there are two ways: either he has discovered it on his own, say, by seeing and recognizing the lady in question or, in other cases, he himself has been told by others in turn. Thus we are back with Austin's knowledge-chain, but with a mighty difference. When X tells Y what is what, his aim is not to create mere belief on the strength of his "warranty", but to cause Y too to know what is what.[18] "I told him that it was his wife" may report an attempt at persuading (causing belief); "I told him who she was" does not.

But what about "I told him who she was, but he did not (want to) believe me"? What this means is the following: the speaker intended to *inform* the addressee of something he knew, but the latter took him to be merely *asserting* something possibly false; the speaker meant to refer to a fact, the addressee took him to be representing and commending a mere possibility; the former intended to convey knowledge, the latter took him to be soliciting mere belief. And he refused to cooperate.

"I told him who she was, but he still does not know it". This is nonsense. The speaker's words amount to the following: "I know who she was and (since he understood me) I produced an appropriate representation in him, which, through my agency, is causally connected to the fact of who she was. But he still does not know it". And this is inconsistent.

But, you ask, is it then possible that the addressee should know, yet not believe, that that lady was his wife? This question is misleading; it assumes, as it were, God's point of view, who knows everything, including who knows what, and who believes what. In our more modest state, we have these two concepts, together with their respective families of factive and nonfactive notions, to choose from in describing our own, and other people's cognitive states, and our verbal interactions in that respect. But we have to be consistent and not jump from one genre to another in the same breath. Thus our speaker, confident as he is, opts for the factive frame: "I told him who she was". But then it would be inconsistent for him to allow that the addressee might still not know it. The addressee, however, for reasons of his own, refuses to play the factive game: he takes the speaker to be merely asserting something, which he is under no obligation to believe. Thus he might say: "He told me that it was my wife, but I don't believe it." But he would mix genres if he reported "he told me who she was, but I don't believe it". Notice, however, that he might say this: "He told me who she was, but I *did not want to* believe it". In this case he adopts the factive frame, but adds that *initially* he tried to reject it. All these variations are made possible, of course, by the half-factive nature of the verb *tell* and its cognates.

To conclude. Expositives (or representatives) are perhaps the most important kind of speech-act verbs. And within this group those that can carry the factive burden hold the primacy, for knowledge is more important than belief. We got language, above all, to tell the truth.

University of California, San Diego

NOTES

[1] *Philosophical Papers*, Oxford, Clarendon Press, 1961, pp. 44–84.
[2] Although Austin still includes it among the expositives, albeit with a question-mark: *How to Do Things with Words*, Oxford, Clarendon Press, 1962, p. 161.
[3] See my 'Verbs and Times' in *Linguistics in Philosophy*, Ithaca, New York, Cornell University Press, 1967, pp. 97–121.
[4] 'Other Minds', *op. cit.*, p. 67.
[5] *Ibid.*, p. 68.
[6] *Ibid.*, p. 68.
[7] *Ibid.*, p. 69.
[8] *Ibid.*, p. 67.
[9] Here I follow H. P. Grice's 'The Causal Theory of Perception' reprinted in *Perceiving, Sensing and Knowing* (ed. R. Swartz), New York, Dobleday, 1965, pp. 438–472.
[10] Cf. Alvin Goldman, 'A Causal Theory of Knowing', *Journal of Philosophy* 44 (1967), 357–372.
[11] 'On What One Knows' in *Res Cogitans*, Ithaca and London, Cornell University Press, 1972, Chapter V, pp. 89–119.
[12] *Ibid.*, p. 95–96.
[13] Paul Kiparsky and Carol Kiparsky, 'Fact', reprinted in *Semantics* (Danny D. Steinberg

and Leon A. Jakobovits eds.), Cambridge, The University Press, 1971, pp. 344–369. Notice, however, that my views, both as to the criteria and the results, are quite different from theirs.

[14] *His prediction*, and similar phrases, are actually triply ambiguous, i.e., between the action (which takes place at a certain time), the fact (which does not), and the product (which is true or false).

[15] I first reported on the idea of half-factives in 'Escaping from the Cave: a Reply to Dunn and Suter', *Canadian Journal of Philosophy* 8 (1978), 79–87.

[16] John R. Searle, 'A Taxonomy of Illocutionary Acts' in *Language, Mind and Knowledge (Minnesota Studies in the Philosophy of Science*, Vol. VII, ed. Keith Gunderson), Minneapolis, University of Minnesota Press, 1975, pp. 344–369.

[17] *Res Cogitans*, Chapter III.

[18] Which fact necessitates certain revisions in Paul Grice's theory of meaning. Most commonly the aim of an expositive speech act is the sharing of knowledge rather than the mere production of belief. And this is particularly true in the absence of an explicit performative verb. See his 'Meaning', *Philosophical Review* 66 (1957), 377–388.

DIETER WUNDERLICH

METHODOLOGICAL REMARKS ON SPEECH ACT THEORY

1. INTRODUCTION

I regard the notion of 'speech act' as one of the most fruitful notions of contemporary linguistic theorizing. It orients our scientfic endeavours towards the function of language in human communication. In doing so, it allows for a combination of different methods and fields of linguistic, as well as of philosophical, investigation, such as, e.g., the theory of grammar, the theory of meaning and the theory of discourse.

The following remarks summarize some of the principles and topics of speech act theory (§§ 2 and 3). I shall also discuss the distinction of pragmatics and semantics (§ 4). Some problems of speech act theory to be discussed here will be illustrated by inspecting a small telephone conversation (§ 5).

2. GENERAL PROPERTIES OF SPEECH ACTS

The universal part of speech act theory deals with the following topics:

(1)   the general structure of speech acts;
(2)   the general structure of speech act sequences;
(3)   the general institutional impacts on speech acts and speech act sequences;
(4)   the general classification of speech acts on the basis of 1–3;
(5)   the general rules for inferring non-literal from literal meaning.

Re (1): It is widely accepted that each speech act can be characterized by its propositional content and its illocutionary force or point. The propositional content in general should, however, not be identified with a proposition. Rather, the type of propositional content and the type of illocutionary force of a speech act are intrinsically interrelated. My assumption is that the propositional content of a speech act can explicitly be expressed by the complement sentence of a reported form of that very speech act. Therefore the primary methodological strategy for construing the types of propositional content is to inspect pieces of reported speech. (This strategy may, however, fail. Many forms of reported speech are language-specific and sometimes

291

J. R. Searle, F. Kiefer, and M. Bierwisch (eds.), Speech Act Theory and Pragmatics, 291–312.

depend on the peculiar kind of verb used to express the illocutionary force in question).

Some of the relevant types of propositional content may be illustrated by the following table:

general type of speech act	complement sentence of a report	designation of the complement sentence	denotation
representative (assertions)	that Paul came	a proposition	a truth value
directive (requests)	to come	a predicate concept	a property of individuals
erotetic (questions)	whether Paul came	a propositional concept	a property of propositions
	who came	an open time-less proposition	a property of term-denotations
	when Paul came	an open tensed proposition	a property of dates

N.B. This table is not fully identical with the views expressed in Wunderlich (1976a, 69, 134). The changes have been prompted by the paper given by Hausser (1977).

The illocutionary force of a speech act should be characterized both (a) in terms of (pragmatically) presupposed mental states of the participants, and (b) in terms of the state of interactions brought about by performing that speech act. This follows from the assumptions that:

(a) in performing a speech act, every speaker has something in mind, consequently the hearer is entitled to infer that the speaker has a certain belief or expectation;

(b) each speech act brings about a certain effect in that it changes the obtaining state of interaction; consequently speaker and hearer are entitled to assume a certain new state of obligations and commitments, of information and of mutual social relationship.

Most generally an illocutionary force can be construed as a characteristic outcome function (Cf. Wunderlich, 1976a, 1977b). This theoretical strategy also conforms to the daily use of speech act-designating expressions. If some-one has ordered something, then we say that there exists an order which one expects to be satisfied in the future course of actions. Here we change our use of the word "order" from the act-perspective to the result- or outcome-perspective. The very purpose of the speech act of ordering is to bring about an order.

Whereas the central notion in dealing with propositional contents is truth, the corresponding notion in dealing with illocutionary outcomes is satisfac-tion. For example, an order is said to be satisfied if the respective addressee performs the ordered action, i.e., if he behaves in such a way that the property denoted by the respective complement sentence of the reported speech comes true of him. In case the propositional content is identical with a proposition, truth and satisfaction coincide. If, however, they do not coincide, the pro-positional content delivers the relevant point of view under which satisfaction has to be defined. This feature characterizes the intrinsic relationship of propositional content and illocutionary outcome.

Incidentally, there is another variant of the notion of satisfaction concern-ing the mental states connected with speech acts. For instance, a desire can be said to be satisfied. These two variants of the notion of satisfaction are, however, closely interrelated (Cf. Searle 1977).

Re 2: No speech act is performed in isolation. Moreover, no speech acts follow each other in an arbitrary sequence. It is generally true of speech acts that they are organized within a certain variable discourse pattern. This feature is reflected in the particular structure of many speech acts as well. For instance, a question is something that calls for an answer, a proposal some-thing that calls for consideration, an apology something that calls for an acknowledgment.

The most important notions for dealing with speech act sequences are as follows:

> turn, move, speech act pattern, complex speech unit and discourse type.

When a participant speaks or makes a contribution to a conservation it is said 'he takes a turn'. A turn may consist of a minimal utterance which doesn't constitute a full speech act but it may also consist of a whole series of speech acts. Each turn includes places where another speaker may start speaking. Turns can also overlap but there is a tendency to reduce such situations. (For details see Sacks/Schegloff/Jefferson 1974).

The notion of move is used to characterize the function of a speech act for the ongoing of the discourse. One may distinguish between initiating, reacting and continuing moves. Let's look at this piece of dialogue:

1   A: It's cold here.
2   B: Do you think so?
3   A: Yes, indeed, couldn't we move a little?

A's assertion (1) serves to initiate a theme, B's question (2) counts as a reaction to it, whereas A's next turn (3), consisting of a confirmation and a question, serves to continue the theme of 1. Reacting moves can be topic-accepting, or topic-rejecting, or neutral, i.e. leave open the option (Cf. Franck, 1977, in preparation). Besides these there may be further reaction types, considered under the viewpoint of a phenomenological classification (Cf. Allwood 1977).

Some speech acts, in particular questions or requests, have a tendency to function as initiating moves. This is not a coincidence, it is rather part of the very nature of these speech acts. (This does not mean that they couldn't also be used in reactions.) On the other hand, confirmations or answers are typical reacting moves. Whether an assertion is called an answer, or a confirmation, or something else, depends solely on its position in the speech act sequence.

For several reasons, in speech act analyses linguists and philosophers tend to over-emphasize the class of initiating speech acts. (a) If one looks at speech acts in isolation, one is intuitively tempted to conceive merely the beginning of a sequence, and not parts of it. (b) A speech act which starts a sequence must make explicit its propositional content and its illocutionary point or force as much as possible. By contrast, a speech act within a sequence can make use of parts of the propositional contents that have been provided by preceding utterances, and its illocutionary force can partly be defined by its position within the sequence. (c) There are in most, if not all, languages two clear-marked grammatical moods: the interrogative and the imperative, which indicate initiatively functioning speech acts. But clearly-marked grammatical moods which indicate reacting speech acts are rare — obviously because there is no need for them.

With respect to the notion of satisfaction it is not yet clear whether, and in what way, it can be expounded to speech acts which function as reacting moves. This is so because speech acts of this class, or at least some of them, do not have an outcome that has to be satisfied in the future but it is their very outcome that they satisfy something.

A speech act pattern is a conventionalized ordered sequence of speech acts. The positions of this sequence have to be filled in by speech acts of a certain kind, which in general must be performed alternately by the participants of the discourse. If one speaker starts with a speech act belonging to a certain pattern then it is expected that the respective addressee, too, should stick to this pattern, even if he interrupts it by a counter-question or alike. (Certain sequences allow for sub-sequences at certain positions.) Some patterns contain positions where certain alternatives are possible. Sometimes there is a possibility of re-opening a part of a pattern such that a repetitive structure emerges.

Prominent speech act patterns are the adjacency pairs in the sense of Sacks/Schegloff/Jefferson, like question-answer, proposal-accounting for the proposal, opening and closing pairs of a conversation. But very often there are also three-place-patterns. For instance, the minimal procedure of securing understanding consists of the reference utterance, a confirmation, and a re-confirmation.

1   A: The lecture takes place in room 14.
2   B: Ah, in room 14.
3   A: Yes, indeed, in 14.

Thanks-giving expressing gratitude for a favour received, consists of the reference action, the thanks-giving, and an acknowledgment.

1   A   (delivers B a package): Here you are.
2   B: Thank you very much.
3   A: You're welcome.

The first example could be a candidate for a rather universal speech act pattern, whereas the second is certainly restricted to some cultural areas. Universally valid speech act patterns could possibly be predicted by a general theory of interaction. Culturally restricted patterns can only be found by a thorough inquiry into real discourse phenomena; only a cross-cultural study could show us, however, to what extent they are distributed among the various language communities. A possible candidate for a speech act pattern, be it a 2-place, a 3-place or a more than 3-place pattern, must at least meet the methodological condition that each position is deemed necessary for establishing a commonly accepted state of interaction.

A complex speech unit consists of several speech acts delivered by a participant. He performs several stages in sequence; each one, however, can be commented on by the addressee to the effect that this stage be enlarged or reduced. Typical complex speech units are narration, argumentation, and description. They normally have a beginning, a variable middle part, and a coda; none of these parts can be completely left out. The structure of complex speech units is due to their complex tasks. A general theory of interaction has thus to be able to characterize the task of a narration, of an argumentation, and of a description.

Complex speech units bring up the problem of decomposition. Are, for instance, the stating of a hypothesis and its justification two different speech acts or just a single one? The first methodological rule might be to consider each complete sentence to be able to convey an individual speech act, although the notion of complete sentence needs further classification. However, this question is not a problem of the universal part of the theory, being rather language-specific.

The discourse type is the most complex unit of speech activity. It is the unit that can be realized by a whole conversation. Typical examples are getting-and-giving direction, instruction, interview, counseling. Each of them may contain descriptions as well as argumentations, and even narrations, and it will certainly contain stages with characteristic speech act patterns. Again, the structure of a discourse type depends on its communicative task, on the structure of the normal experiences of the participants, and on the structure of the reality concerned.

Re 3: We may distinguish primary or natural speech acts, which are necessary for any kind of human interaction, and secondary or institutional speech acts, which are specific for a certain institution. By an institution I mean an organized system of social life which results from the social division of labor, and which is determined to fulfil the specific needs of society. Examples are school-instruction, courtroom-investigation, political debate, commercial advertising. Some institutions are distributed throughout the world according to a certain cultural standard, and not very specific for a language community, whereas others are more specific.

Institutions can have various impacts on the development of speech activities.

(a) An institution can create new kinds of speech acts, mostly of the declaration or of the satisfactive type, such as baptizing, judging, appointing, opening a session. Some of these are performed by means of using specific performative formulas.

(b) An institution can modify primary speech acts. For example, we have a whole range of institutionally modified kinds of questions and requests, such as examination questions, interrogation questions, test questions, or control questions, admonitions, prescriptions, orders, regulations, directions, summons or citations.

(c) An institution can produce new discourse types, which reveal specific complex speech units and speech act patterns. These are sometimes regulatory devices such as standing orders, but it may also happen that the conventions are only implicitly given by the institutional background.

It belongs to the task of the general theory of interaction to characterize the general aspects of processes leading to institutional speech activities, which, of course, must be based on previous empirical work.

Re 4: There is no clear classification of speech acts. Neither Austin's, nor Searle's, nor anybody else's attempts are really convincing. Searle, for example, distinguishes representatives, directives, commissives, expressives, and declarations (Cf. Searle 1976). But there remain some questions and open problems with this classification. Let me mention just three: (a) Commissives are certainly not a universal speech act type, they may rather be considered as possible reactions to directives. (b) According to Searle questions are a subtype of directives. They are, however, grammatically marked and hence a candidate for a generic type of speech act. Searle's considerations are obviously restricted to a strict information question leaving upon the problem of deliberative questions, rhetorical questions etc. (c) Within Searle's five types, there is no place for speech acts like warnings, advices, proposals, offers, which share some properties of the representative and the directive (or the commissive) type (Cf. Wunderlich 1977a).

Addressing is another speech act type which deserves special mentioning because of its peculiar behavior. It plays a rôle in speech act theory which is similar to that of proper names in logical semantics. Proper names serve to identify persons or objects according to a history of familiarity which, ultimately, goes back to a naming situation. By using a vocative, which may, but need not, include an appropriate proper name, addressing serves to identify an addressee and to attract his attention; it is in some sense the speech act-counterpart of proper names.

On the basis of the topics I have discussed thus far we can envisage four main criteria for speech act-classification. It will then depend on the purpose of our theory to which one we want to give priority.

1. Speech acts can be classified according to the main grammatical markers (and their possible functional equivalents) in a given language. These markers are in languages like English and German at least the following ones: (a) the interrogative mood − speech acts of the erotetic type; (b) the imperative mood − speech acts of the directive type; (c) the declarative mood − speech acts of the representative type; (d) specific performative formulas − speech acts of the declaration type (in a broader sense than Searle's).

2. Speech acts can be classified according to (a) the type of propositional content, and (b) the type of illocutionary outcome or the type of satisfaction condition, respectively. Because of the interrelationship of propositional content and illocutionary outcome, an independent classification according to either (a) or (b) is not possible. The results will partly overlap with the results of the first classification, but they will not coincide.

3. Speech acts can be classified according to their function, i.e. as to whether they represent an initiating or a reacting move, or, to put it differently, according to their position within speech act patterns.

4. Speech acts can be classified according to their origin as either primary (natural) speech acts or secondary (institutional) speech acts.

Re 5: Literal meaning is always language-specific. The meaning of an utterance of a sentence s of language L is said to be literal iff it is only composed of the meanings of the words and phrases in s in accordance with the syntactic conventions in L. It is, however, not always clear what the meaning of the words and phrases in s actually is, because the words may have different meanings, and because their meaning often depends on the context c of the utterance. For example, the meaning of indexical expressions such as *I, here, now* in an utterance, or the meaning of anaphoric expression such as *he, then, that* in an utterance depends on c. Even words such as *enough, but, otherwise, big, can*, and many others, have a context-dependend meaning, i.e. their meaning includes a context variable x.

Let me introduce the notion of a neutral context c_0 of a sentence s. This context is a proper part of the full context c of any proper utterance of s. The neutral context c_0 of s provides all the features which are necessary to determine the values of each context variable x in the meanings of words or phrases in s. This means that a neutral context does not affect the propositional structure of s, and that it contributes nothing to the illocutionary force of the utterance of s.

We can, now, redefine our notion of literal meaning. The meaning of an utterance of a sentence s of language L is literal iff the context used to determine the meaning is neutral with respect to s.

The meaning of an utterance of s is non-literal iff, in order to derive the meaning, a richer context c is used than the neutral context c_0 of s.

Derivations of a non-literal meaning always make use of the literal meaning and of certain contextual premises. These include perceptual knowledge, knowledge of the preceding context and of the respective state of interaction, knowledge of the relevant discourse type, of the speech act pattern and of the institutional background, knowledge about the world and about the experiences and mental states of the participants, about preferences, and about the general principles of cooperation. It is the task of the universal theory of speech acts to specify the general structure of these inference procedures. (Cf. for example Grice's notion of implicature, in Grice 1975, and Wunderlich's generalized notion of a practical inference in Wunderlich, 1976b.)

3. LANGUAGE SPECIFIC PROPERTIES

The language specific part of speech act theory deals with the following topics:

(1)   the language specific devices utilized in speech acts;
(2)   the phenomenology of language specific speech act patterns, complex speech units, and discourse types;
(3)   the phenomenology of language specific institutional speech acts;
(4)   the phenomenology of language specific indirect speech act routines and indirect speech act formulas;
(5)   the language specific classification of speech acts on the basis of 1—4.

In a language like German it is possible to distinguish at least the following classes of linguistic means which all serve to indicate the type of speech act at hand:

(a) grammatical mood, (b) explicit performative formulas, (c) reference to another (speech) act in the sequence, (d) expression of a mental state connected with the speech act, (e) implicit contextual realization.

In German, grammatical mood is mainly characterized by the position of the inflected verb, by the position of the subject phrase, and by final intonation. In addition to the unmarked and most general declarative mood, the interrogative and the imperative mood, one may identify two further moods, the exclamatory mood and the optative mood. They are, however, less frequently used, and morphologically they constitute subordinate elliptic clauses with verb final position. Examples:

Wie blaß du aussiehst! (How pale you are!)
Wäre er doch gekommen! (If only he had come!)

Let me postpone for a moment the discussion of the performative formulas. The other three means (c—e) are utilized to indirectly perform speech acts. Examples:

(c)   Willst du mir sagen, wie alt du bist?
           (Will you tell me, how old you are?)

The speaker thematizes the answer to a question, hence his utterance may count as a question about the addressee's age.

(d)   Ich wüβte gerne, wie alt du bist.
           (I would like to know how old you are.)

The speaker expresses his wish which can be satisfied by providing the information about age. For a discussion of this type, of Searle, 1975.

(e)   Es gibt Kinder, die kennen noch nicht mal ihr Alter!
           (There are kids who do not even know their age!)
           Du gehst ja noch nicht mal zur Schule!
           (literally: You are not yet going to school! – uttered to a 8 year old girl forces her to demur and to reveal her school age.)

There are, of course, many other ways of indirectly expressing speech acts, which have to be accounted for by a more elaborate phenomenology.

Performative verbs, i.e. verbs usable in an explicit performative formula, are a proper subset of speech act designating verbs. A starting point for a language specific classification of speech acts (or aspects, functions, or complex units of speech acts) would be a careful inspection of the whole set of speech act designating verbs. This, however, has not been done for any language so far. There is no doubt whatsoever that speech act theory can profit from a phenomenology of the language-specific speech act phenomena mentioned under 2–4. But it seems to me that an examination of the use of explicit performative formulas would be an inappropriate starting point for speech act theory in general, and even for a language specific study of speech acts, for several reasons:

(a) Most speech acts, particularly those of the non-institutional kind, are more frequently realized by grammatical mood or by indirect or implicit means, than by a performative formula.

(b) There are particular conditions of use connected with performative formulas.

– Some speech acts cannot be performed by the use of a performative formula at all.

– Some formulas can only be used if the uptake of a preceding utterance has become problematic or dissentive.

– Some formulas are only used in executing institutional routines.

— The possible use or non-use of performative formulas is due to historical change and diatopic variations.

(c) Performative formulas have an intricate semantic status which is not yet clear. Normally, a performative formula is used non-assertively, i.e. it expresses as a whole nothing which can be proved to be true or false in the given context. There are at least three different approaches to escape this trap in a reasonable way.

(i) The use of performative formula counts as a declaration in Searle's sense. It brings about something true, provided the speech act was sincerely performed. The formula denotes in every normal use the truth brought about (cf. Heim 1977).

(ii) The performative formula provides a non-assertive comment (or specification) on the rôle which the subordinate propositional content is supposed to play in the interaction stage (cf. Wunderlich 1976a). Such an account seems to be necessary on independent grounds in the case of hedged performatives.

"Unfortunately, I must confess that p."

Here the speaker confesses that p and he makes a comment to the effect that there is some necessity which forces him to confess that p, and that he deplores that such a necessity exists. Along the same lines we could say: the speaker asserts that p, and he qualifies his assertion by saying that it is done in the mode of confessing.

(iii) The speaker uses the performative formula assertively. In language, however, a general detachment rule operates with the following effect: if the speaker asserts a performative formula, then he wants to express its subordinate propositional content (cf. de Cornulier, 1977).
Hence the factual effect of the performative formula is to modify (or to specify) this propositional content.

In a language specific investigation of speech acts, particularly in the empirical study of discourse, one has to overcome some problems to which I shall turn presently. This might be done partly on the basis of a pre-established theory, partly on the basis of more precise empirical insights. Let me summarize these problems under the following labels:

(a) *The demarcation problem*: One has to delimit individual speech acts from the continuous flow of speech. Has every, even minimal, turn the status of a speech act of its own? Or is it the sentence which we need as the minimal syntactic unit for conveying a speech act? If this is so, how can we establish the notion of sentence vis-à-vis spoken language? Do complex sentences convey just one speech act, or perhaps more than one?

(b) *The identification problem*: One has to identify the delimited speech acts as belonging to one or another speech act type. What criteria has an utterance to fulfil in order to be identified as a speech act of type A rather than of type B? Are there any other labels for speech acts than the normal predicates (verbs etc.) that are used in reporting that utterance in the language under consideration?

(c) *The classification problem* (This problem is tightly interrelated with the identification problem): One has to establish a workable classificatory scheme for speech acts which can be found in a certain kind of discourse. How many classes or types of speech acts would we want to distinguish? What are the distinctive criteria, and to which degree are they independent on each other? On which theoretical framework do we want to base our classification?

(d) *The specification problem* (This problem arises only in connection with the identification and the classification problem): For each class of speech acts, one has to deal with a whole range of subtypes that may differ in various respects. What are the criteria for subtypes? Which verbal means serve to specify the conveyed speech act, and in which respect? What is the respective strength of the illocutionary force and of the commitment brought about? And, finally, what is the social bias of the speech act?

(e) *The (de)composition problem*: One has to distinguish between simple and more complex speech acts which may be composed of simple speech acts. What is the relationship between simple speech acts in a complex speech unit? Which types of complex units do we have to distinguish, and what are their characteristic composition structures?

(f) *The projection problem*: One has to relate the verbal means, words and constructions, with the sentence meaning, described in terms of possible speech acts performed by an utterance of that sentence. Which verbal means contribute to the kind of speech act (to its illocutionary force), which ones contribute to the related propositional content, which ones contribute to the placement of the speech act in the discourse, which ones comment on the speech act itself or on the mental states connected with the speech act? What is the interrelationship between these different components of speech?

From the above summary of these problems it becomes quite clear that most of them have hitherto not yet been settled to any degree. The questions I asked may, however, function as a methodological guide for a more precise and a more empirically based study of speech acts.

4. ON THE RELATIONSHIP OF SEMANTICS AND PRAGMATICS IN SPEECH ACT THEORY

The notion of speech act theory, as I understand it, is not on a par with the notion of pragmatics of natural languages. Speech act theory includes both a semantical and a pragmatical part.

Let me shortly discuss two positions about the distinction of semantics and pragmatics put forth on the 12th International Congress of Linguists in the speeches of John Lyons' and Renate Bartsch's. According to Lyons, semantics is concerned with the meaning of sentences described in terms of grammatical form, whereas pragmatics is concerned with the meaning of utterances described in terms of their function. The puzzle with this position is that there is nearly no meaning at all, be it the meaning of words or the meaning of constructions that can be described independently on any context of use. Even the central notion of semantics, the notion of truth, cannot be established without reference to a possible utterance situation.

Indeed, semantics has to deal with grammatical form but it must also deal with its contribution to the function of utterances. Furthermore, pragmatics has indeed to deal with the function of utterances, but it must also consider the complex interrelationship of the grammatical form of sentences uttered with other factors of the utterance situation that contribute to the function.

On the other hand, Bartsch claimed that semantics deals with truth conditions, whereas pragmatics deals with expressions that do not contribute to truth conditions. Now, the puzzle with this position is that there would be a large number of sentences, the meaning of which could not be described within semantics. In the end, Bartsch's position would mean that only propositional content is the subject matter of semantics; whereas none of the other verbal means that do not directly contribute to the propositional content can be the subject matter of semantics. The truth, however, is that in semantics, truthfunctional methods are indeed predominant, but there are phenomena that do not themselves contribute to the propositional content, and hence to the truth conditions of an utterance, but which can nevertheless be described by means of essentially truthfunctionally based methods. In pragmatics other methods are predominant, for example Gricean implicatures or practical reasonings of the speaker and the hearer.

Obviously, Lyons' position is more linguistically oriented in the traditional sense of semantics where semantics is conceived of as the theory of meaning (of sentences); whereas Bartsch's position is more logically oriented in the

Tarskian sense of semantics where semantics is considered to be the theory of truth conditions exclusively. My own position is somewhere in between.

In my view, semantics deals with literal meaning, i.e. with the interpretation of sentences or sentence fragments in a neutral context, which only provides the values of contextual variables occuring in the description of sentence meaning. Hence I am subscribing to Bartsch's view insofar as I think that semantics is always concerned with utterances, but with utterances of sentences in a neutral context. As far as illocutionary force is concerned, I think that satisfaction conditions, though they differ from truth conditions, can be defined in terms of truth conditions. For example, the order brought about by an utterance of the type "do a!" is satisfied iff it is true of the addressee some time after the utterance that he performs the action a.

On the other hand, pragmatics deals with the interpretation of sentences (or utterances) in a richer context, which includes the understanding of the preceding discourse, the beliefs and expectations which speakers and hearers have, their social relationship, their state of obligations, their state of knowledge etc. Hence, pragmatics is concerned with all kinds of non-literal meaning, but also with the perlocutionary effects, i.e. with the conclusions a hearer draws from an utterance and with the consequential reactions of the hearer, independently of whether the speaker intends to induce these conclusions and consequences or not.

As I have demonstrated, there are speech acts that can be marked by grammatical means: questions, requests, assertions, and most speech acts which are performed by the use of an explicit performative formula. In their fundamental characteristics these speech acts can be treated on the semantic level. My proposal now is that the main classes of speech acts should be defined within the semantics of grammatical mood. All possible specifications of a speech act type, or its subclasses, will then be the subject matter of pragmatics, e.g. the specifications of the difference between commands and entreaties within the directive type.

On the other hand, there seem to be speech acts that can only be treated on a pragmatic level, though they are not subtypes of one of the semantically defined types. An example are advices and warnings. In general, unless they are realized by using the words "advice" or "warn", the only difference between them lies in the fact that the advice predicts a subsequent event which is favourable in the light of the addressee's interests, whereas the warning predicts a subsequent event which is against the addressee's preferences. Normally it is thus implicitly imputed that the addressee, like any normal person, would have such and such preferences.

Turn left, and you will get to the police control point.

Is the utterance of this sentence an advice, or a warning? Obviously it depends on whether the addressee would like (or is expected to like) to meet the police control or would rather like to avoid it (cf. Wunderlich 1976a; 1977a).

5. ANALYSIS OF A TELEPHONE CONVERSATION – AN ILLUSTRATION OF SOME PROBLEMS OF SPEECH ACT THEORY

Original transcription adapted from the Freiburg Corpus
(Alltagsgespräche, 1975, 68 f.)

1	E:	Müller
2	⌈R:	Eugen, da bin ich schon wieder
	⌊E:	ja
3	⌈R:	du, Eugen
	⌊E:	ja
4	R:	ich hab mir das überlegt
5		es ist doch vielleicht viel besser, wenn ich zu dir reinkomme
6	E:	((niest))
7	R:	ich sitze da in meinem Auto
8		und mir pfeift der Wind nicht um die Ohren
9	E:	Ach so, nein nein
10		ich ich fahr gern ein bißchen
11	R:	ach so, ja, wenn du gerne fährst
12	E:	naja, eben, ja, doch, doch
13	⌈E:	ich möcht gern ein bißchen fahren
	⌊R:	ach so ja ja
14	R:	ich wollte dir nur sagen
15		sonst wäre ich zu dir gekommen
16	⌈R:	ne?
	⌊E:	och, das ist aber auch sehr nett
17	⌈E:	ne?
	⌊R:	nicht? findest du?
18	E, R:	((lachen))
19	⌈E:	und n bißchen Bewegung Bewegung muß ich haben
	⌊R:	ja, ja ja, ja
20	E:	ich bin jetzt vier Wochen nur gesessen
21		das heißt vier, ja vier Wochen

```
22  ⎡ E:    ja
    ⎣ R:    ja, hm, hm, gut, Eugen, dann bis gleich
23    E:    ja
24  ⎡ E:    bis ein Uhr, nicht?
    ⎣ R:    ne?             ja!
25  ⎡ E:    mit gemahlenem Kaffee
    ⎣ R:    tschüß
26    E:    ((hustet, lacht))
27    R:    ja, ja, ja
28    E:    grüß dich
29    R:    bis dann
```

Approximate translation

```
1     E:    Müller!
2     R:    Eugen, here I am again.
3           Listen, Eugen,
4           I have thought it over:
5           it is perhaps much better, if I come [into town] to your place.
6     E:    ((sneezes))
7     R:    I will be sitting in my car,
8           and the wind won't blow around my ear.
9     E:    Oh, I see; no, no —
10          I want to ride a little bit.
11    R:    Oh, I see; yes, if you want to ride!
12    E:    Well, just that; yes, indeed,
13          I want to ride a little bit.
14    R:    I just wanted to tell you;
15          otherwise I would have come to your place.
16    E:    Oh, that's very kind.
17  ⎡ E:    Isn't it?
    ⎣ R:    Is it? You think so?
18   E, R:      ((laugh))
19    E:    and I need some exercise:
20          I have been doing nothing but sitting down for four weeks.
22    R:    Yes, hm, hm, well, Eugen, see you later!
23    E:    Well,
24          one o'clock, okay?
25  ⎡ E:    With ground coffee!
    ⎣ R:    Ciao.
```

26   E: ((coughs, laughs))
27   R: Okay.
28   E: Take care.
29   R: See you later.

Let me discuss this little piece of telephone conversation at some length. I want to point out some of its properties which may, I hope, well induce a rethinking of our present conception of speech act theory.

This call was preceded by another one, in which E took the initiative. E told R that he had just returned from his Christmas-vacation, and that he would be glad to have a little chat with R. E suggested he would ride on his bike out to R's place, which R accepted. They arranged that E should bring along some coffee powder. Both E and R are male academics.

Utterance 2 of R, "Eugen, da bin ich schon wieder", serves to identify the speaker. The demonstrative "da" ('here') refers to the utterance itself. "schon wieder" ('already again') takes up the presupposition that they spoke to each other some time ago, and R comments on this by saying that the time between this last conversation and the new one is much less than what might have been expected. Hence, the utterance implicitly refers back to the earlier conversation, and in doing so it makes the speaker identifiable. The speech act type of R's utterance cannot be determined easily; we might conceive of it as being of the representative type. However, the utterance *displays* the truth of its propositional content, namely that it is R who is now (back) on line (i.e. the utterance is self-verifying), and it does not *inform* of or *assert* a certain state of affairs. It does, however, inform of the identity of the speaker himself. In any case, Searle's condition that the speaker tries to make the world fit with the words makes no sense here. Nor does the speaker try to establish a correspondence between the world and the words, since it is true from the very beginning that it is he who speaks.

The next part of R's turn, "du, Eugen" (3), is not covered by Searle's classification of speech acts either. This vocative serves to attract the hearer's attention and to signal a certain social recognition.

R's utterance 4 "ich hab mir das überlegt", indicates the purpose of the whole conversation. Literally, R asserts the performance of a certain mental process. The pronoun "das" refers both backwards to the appointments made in the earlier conversation, and forwards to the result of R's considera-tion, which he now wants to present. Hence, the point of the utterance is not so much to describe R's mental efforts, it rather functions as a preparatory formula. That is, it is a means of speech organization and a means of directing the hearer's perception process. It also contributes to an explanation (or justification) of R's conversation initiative, since something that one has thought over might be of common interest.

R's next utterance 5, "es ist doch vielleicht viel besser, wenn ich zu dir reinkomme", presents the result of his consideration. With the particle "doch" the speaker tries to correct some of the hearer's suppositions ("contrary to what you or we might have thought I came to the conclusion . . . , on the basis of premises which, I think, you will share"). The sentential adverb "vielleicht" ('perhaps') makes the strength of the statement dependent on further considerations, in this case — as we shall see — dependent on the hearer's attitude. From the word "besser" we learn that R is comparing two alternatives of action. The first one is the content of the previous appointment,

I: that E rides on his bike over to R's place.

The second one is introduced in the conditional sentence and is made more precise in the connected utterance 7,

II.   that R comes (drives) to E's place.

The utterance evaluates alternative II as being possibly more convenient (or more adequate, or more preferable) than I. But II refers to a future action of R as well. Hence, if it is true that R submits to E something for consideration he places himself under the commitment to perform in due course the action of alternative II. At first sight, the utterance 5 can be classified as an evaluation, maybe even as an evaluative assertion, but this does not seem to meet the ultimate purpose of the utterance. It occurs to me that in some sense the type (and, in addition, the respective strength) of the speech act in question has not been fully determined by utterance 5 itself. The very type of the speech act remains to be clarified by the further interplay between the participants.

In his utterance 7+8 R describes conditions which can be assumed to hold during R's considered motion to E's place. This utterance is clearly related to the preceding one. R makes an argument in terms of convenience which is an argument pro alternative II and contra alternative I ("You will be sitting on your bike, and therefore the wind will blow around your ears"). The utterance serves to transmit to E the proposal that R would be ready to drive in place of E in order to save E from an inconvenience. In the light of this backing argument, utterance 5 turns out to be an offer of a certain kind:

If there are two alternatives of action at hand, and if, under the general point of convenience, alternative II would be better than alternative I, then I am ready to perform alternative II — unless you have a strong inclination towards alternative I.

The pragmatic function of this speech act of offering can be described in 4 points.

(1)   The speech act conventionally initiates a speech act sequence. An offer is expected to be followed either by an acceptance, or a refusal, or a further elaboration of the point or of the conditions of the offer.

(2)   On the basis of 1, the speaker expects the addressee to consider the content of the offer, and to be informed about the results of these considerations. The point of an offer is to induce mental processes in the addressee's mind which lead to a decision, but the decision is left up to the addressee. It is not the point of an offer to get the addressee to accept the content of the offer (whereas, for intance, the point of a request is to get the addressee to accept its content and to take over the desired action, and the point of a promise is to get the addressee to accept its content, and to put the speaker himself under an obligation). From this we can see that the offer is a kind of speech act which cannot be handled within the framework of Searle's classification.

(3)   The speaker commits himself to perform the respective action in case the addressee will accept the content of the offer. This property makes an offer comparable to a promise.

(4)   The speaker signals his acknowledgement of a certain social relationship with the addressee; in this case he indicates his wilingness to save the addressee from an inconvenience.

The reaction of the addressee, E, consists of three steps. In the first step, E asserts his own preference, which is opposed to the assumption of R (9—13). In the second step E reacts to R's renewal of the offer (14—15) by appreciating R's attitude (16—18). The mutual confirmation of this reaction comes about in general laughter. Finally, E reacts in a third step by explaining his preference, and hence his refusal of the offer, with a substantial argument ('I need some exercise since I have been doing nothing but sitting down for four weeks') (19—20).

It is only after this that R really accepts E's refusal, showing this by uttering the pre-closing formula "dann bis gleich" (22). In order to re-establish the social balance, so to speak, E subsequently confirms the other parts of the appointment made in the earlier conversation. We have to take his utterance 24–25 "bis 1 Uhr, mit gemahlenem Kaffee" partly as reminders (which can perhaps be considered a proper subtype of assertions, but which also share some of the properties of a request), partly as confirmations. E seems to wish to express his willingness to carry out the responsibilities stemming from the earlier appointment, inspite of his refusing to accept R's offer.

Let me come back to R's utterances 14–15. "ich wollte dir nur sagen" (14) plays a similar preparatory rôle to "ich hab mir das überlegt" (4). Most important in my view is R's utterance 15: "sonst wäre ich zu dir gekommen" ('otherwise I would have come to your place'). On the one hand R seems to consider his offer to be obsolete, and its content to be counterfactual vis-à-vis E's preferences. On the other hand R seems to regard E's refusal as not yet definitive: R not only explains his initiative once more, he also maintains his offer. R gives E the opportunity to consider his offer again. The propositional content of the offer is firstly made explicit in the context-dependent conjunction "sonst" ('otherwise'), which means here: 'in case you would not have liked to ride'.

As I have outlined in Wunderlich (1977a, p. 32), the offer can be viewed as a speech act belonging to the conditional type. These speech acts interfere with the addressee's planning of actions in that their propositional content, which is a conditional, supplies the addressee with a certain cognitive premise that he can use in his practical inferences. The propositional content of the offer in question may be rendered as follows:

> If you don't want to ride over to my place, then
> I shall go by car to your place.

Obviously this conditional cannot remain without reaction. At least the addressee is expected to express his attitude explicitly to that which is hypothesized in the antecedent. Without such a (contextually or explicitly given) antecedent concerning the attitude of the addressee the utterance would not be an offer.

Let me summarize in what respects speech act theory can profit from this very rough inspection of a real telephone conversation.

1. It requires a large amount of experience to delimit and to adequately identify individual speech acts in a conversation. Obviously there are speech acts that pose serious problems for any classificatory scheme of speech acts hitherto developed in that they are either not covered by the classification, or

that they are sharing properties of more than one of the classes, while other properties required by the analysis are missing. In particular, there are peculiar speech acts which have to do with the interactional ongoing of a conversation and with the continuous establishment of a socially balanced relationship.

2. Occasionally speech acts seem to be performed only tentatively. They may in the sequel be overshadowed or changed in strength and liability. Mutual reactions and confirmations contribute to a clearer elaboration of the intended speech act. The conversation discussed above shows two examples of this kind. The initiator, R, needs three steps to elaborate and to maintain his offer (4–5, 7–8, 14–15), and, likewise, for E it takes a series of three reactions to make his refusal of the offer acceptable (9–10 + 12–13, 16–17, 19–21).

3.   (a) A speech act may convey another speech act.
         (b) Complex speech acts may be composed of more elementary
              speech acts.
         (c) Some speech acts are identifiable only on the basis of their
              position in a sequence.

In our telephone conversation an evaluative statement (5), together with its backing argument (7–8), turns out to convey an offer:

> It is perhaps better, if I come into town to your place
> (because)
> I will be sitting in my car, and the wind won't blow around my
> ears;
> (whereas if you will be sitting on your bike, the wind will blow
> around your ears).
> (Therefore, I am ready to drive into town to your place, unless
> you have an inclination to ride out to my place.)

And likewise, the preferential statement (10, 13), together with a backing argument (19–21), turns out to be a refusal in the context of the preceding offer:

> I want to ride on my bike
> (since)
> I need some exercise
> (since)
> I have been doing nothing but sitting down for four weeks
> (therefore, you need not drive to my place: i.e., I don't accept
> your offer.)

Obviously, a preferential statement by itself neither conveys a refusal nor an acceptance. This can only be done by taking into account the preceding context as well. One might assume that the subsequent refusal is already indicated by E's utterance "nein, nein" (9); this utterance by itself, however, cannot constitute a refusal, since the scope of the negation is not yet clear.

ACKNOWLEDGMENT

I am grateful to Florian Coulmas and Ferenc Kiefer for helpful comments.

Düsseldorf, 1977. This article does not render my present views (Nov. 1979).

BIBLIOGRAPHY

Alltagsgespräche: 1975, Texte gesprochener deutscher Standardsprache III. Munich.

Allwood, J.: 1977, 'Felicity and acceptability', *Symposium on Speech Acts and Pragmatics*, Dobogókö, Hungary.

Bartsch, R.: 1977, 'Basic Problems of Semantics', Plenary Session 1, XIIth International Congress of Linguists, Vienna.

de Cornulier, B.: 1977, 'Shortened expressions and pragmatic indication', *Symposium on Speech Acts and Pragmatics*, Dobogókö, Hungary.

Franck, D.: 1977, *Grammatik und Konversation*, in preparation.

Grice, H. P.: 1975, 'Logic and Conversation', in P. Cole and J. L. Morgan (eds.), *Speech Acts*, New York, pp. 41–58.

Hausser, R.: 1977, 'The semantics of mood', *Symposium on Speech Acts and Pragmatics*, Dobogókö, Hungary.

Heim, J.: 1977, 'Zur Problematik der Darstellung illokutionärer Rollen in der Cresswell-Semantik, mimeo, Constance.

Lyons, J.: 1977, 'Basic Problems of Semantics', Plenary Session 1, XIIth International Congress of Linguists, Vienna.

Sacks, H. Schegloff and Jefferson: 1974, 'A simplest systematics for the organization of turn-taking for conversation,' *Language* 50, 696–735.

Searle, J. R.: 1975, 'Indirect Speech Acts,' in P. Cole and J. L. Morgan (eds.), *Speech Acts*, New York, pp. 59–82.

Searle, J. R.: 1976, 'A classification of illocutionary acts', *Language in Society* 5, 1–23.

Searle, J. R.: 1977, 'Mental states and speech acts', *Symposium on Speech Acts and Pragmatics*, Dobogókö, Hungary.

Wunderlich, D.: 1976a, 'Studien zur Sprechakttheorie,' Frankfurt.

Wunderlich, D.: 1976b, 'Sprechakttheorie und Diskursanalyse', in K. O. Apel (ed.), *Sprachpragmatik und Philosophie*, Frankfurt, pp. 463–488.

Wunderlich, D.: 1977a, 'Assertions, conditional speech acts, and practical inferences,' *Journal of Pragmatics* 1, 13–46.

Wunderlich, D.: 1977b, 'On problems of speech act theory, in R. E. Butts and J. Hintikka (eds.), *Basic Problems in Methodology and Linguistics*, Dordrecht, pp. 243–258.

INDEX OF NAMES

313

INDEX OF SUBJECTS

315

SYNTHESE LANGUAGE LIBRARY

Texts and Studies in Linguistics and Philosophy

Managing Editors:

JAAKKO HINTIKKA (Florida State University)
STANLEY PETERS (The University of Texas at Austin)

Editors:

EMMON BACH (University of Massachusetts at Amherst), JOAN BRESNAN
(Massachusetts Institute of Technology), JOHN LYONS (University of Sussex),
JULIUS M. E. MORAVCSIK (Stanford University), PATRICK SUPPES (Stanford
University), DANA SCOTT (Oxford University).